Long-Term Imprisonment

Long-Term Imprisonment

Policy, Science, and Correctional Practice

Timothy J. Flanagan
Editor

SAGE Publications
International Educational and Professional Publisher
Thousand Oaks   London   New Delhi

Photographs by David Nunnelee, Texas Department of Criminal Justice

For information address:

 SAGE Publications, Inc.
2455 Teller Road
Thousand Oaks, California 91320

SAGE Publications Ltd.
6 Bonhill Street
London EC2A 4PU
United Kingdom

SAGE Publications India Pvt. Ltd.
M-32 Market
Greater Kailash I
New Delhi 110 048 India

Printed in the United States of America

Library of Congress Cataloging-in-Publication Data

Main entry under title:

Long-term imprisonment: policy, science, and correctional practice /
    edited by Timothy J. Flanagan.
        p.   cm.
    Includes bibliographical references.
    ISBN 0-8039-7032-3 (cloth: acid-free paper). — ISBN
0-8039-7033-1 (paper: acid-free paper)
    1. Prison sentences—Government policy—United States. 2. Aged
prisoners—Government policy—United States. 3. Aged prisoners—
Care—United States. 4. Prison administration—United States.
    I. Flanagan, Timothy J.
    HV8708.L65   1995
    364.6′5′0973—dc20   95-1494

This book is printed on acid-free paper.

95 96 97 98 99 10 9 8 7 6 5 4 3 2 1

Sage Project Editor: Susan McElroy

Contents

Afterwords

Foreword

During the past decade, the United States has witnessed a dramatic shift in policy concerning the sanctioning of criminal offenders. In response to the public's perception that crime is out of control and that dramatically tougher sentences are the solution, we are locking up more and more individuals in our nation's prisons and jails. Data compiled by the Bureau of Justice Statistics confirms that we now have in excess of 1 million offenders in state and federal prisons. The numbers have been steadily increasing over the past decade and all indicators point to a continuation of this trend in the future. Although the increase has varied from state to state, no jurisdiction has been immune, including the Federal Prison System, which has experienced a doubling of population in less than 7 years.

Several factors have contributed to the burgeoning numbers of inmates. Recently enacted legislative initiatives, including lengthy minimum-mandatory penalties and "three strikes and you're out" statutes requiring lengthy commitments and even life sentences for repetitive violators, are having a dramatic impact. In addition, the elimination of parole in a number of states and tightened release policies in others have contributed to the growth. These changes will have an even greater impact in the future as the number of offenders committed to custody continues to increase.

One result of these changes can be observed in many correctional systems that are experiencing a significant increase in the numbers of long-term offenders committed under the newly enacted legislation. Though prisons have always housed a relatively small number of inmates serving lengthy sentences, the majority of offenders typically spend several years in confinement prior to release. Correctional administrators understandably focused attention and resources on inmates who would be returning to the community within a relatively brief period of time. Although long-term offenders were not consciously ignored or excluded from programs, little attention was focused on their special problems and needs.

Another manifestation of the changes in sentencing policy is the fact that the average age of the inmate population in many correctional systems has increased and will undoubtedly continue to do so in the future. With the "graying" of the population, correctional administrators are experiencing increased medical and health care costs. Studies have demonstrated that offenders are a relatively unhealthy subset of the general population. Rates of smoking as well as drug and alcohol abuse exceed the national average. The incidence of chronic disease, including tuberculosis, hepatitis, and AIDS, is also higher than in the population at large. These problems have contributed to the rapidly increasing costs of operating prisons and jails.

One fact frequently overlooked is that the vast majority of long-term inmates now in confinement will eventually be released. Many have spent their prime years in prison and will be returning to the community without employable skills, work experiences, or family support. Releasing numbers of offenders back into society at age 50, 60, or even 70 will, without question, further tax existing social and health care systems.

Despite the fact that correctional administrators and other policymakers are aware of the changing inmate population, comparatively little thinking or planning has been done to address the many issues involved. We can anticipate, for example. that larger numbers of long-term offenders will present challenges to existing classification systems as well as institutional programs and operations. Health care services as well as medical costs will be dramatically impacted by the aging population. Buildings and facilities will have to accommodate the disabled.

The chapters contained in this book are particularly relevant at a time when the population of our prisons and jails has reached record highs. Authored by academics, correctional administrators, and inmates themselves, the chapters present a timely discussion of the complex problems involved in managing institutions and programs for long-term offenders. In addition, they frame the debate needed to ensure the development of rational correctional policies.

Norman A. Carlson
University of Minnesota

Preface

This volume originated nearly two decades ago in a graduate seminar titled "Incarceration," in the School of Criminal Justice at the State University of New York at Albany. The late Professor Donald J. Newman wanted students to examine real-world correctional issues of importance to prison administrators. He invited Arthur Leonardo, then director of special housing units in the New York State Department of Correctional Services, to discuss contemporary prison management issues. Leonardo observed that one of the most difficult challenges facing correctional administrators (in 1975) was designing correctional environments and programs for long-term prisoners. He argued that laws, rules, and historical correctional practices tie a long sentence to the need for high security, so options available to prison administrators in managing long-term prisoners were very limited. Moreover, he noted that American prisons don't have much to offer an inmate facing a long sentence anyway, except for a seemingly endless series of short-term training, therapy, and educational programs.

I wish I could report that the situation is different today, because Arthur Leonardo now runs a prison for long-term inmates, and state and federal institutions now house many times more long-termers than they did 20 years ago. But today, as then, when an inmate reaches the sally port with a sentence of 36 months, we prescribe a set of experiences with discrete learning objectives directed toward measurable improvement in skills and knowledge by the time of release. When an inmate arrives who is facing 36 *years*, however, our muddled response reveals that, except for selected work assignments and a few educational programs, we have little insight into planning institutional careers for long-term prisoners.

Newman contended that the wave of interest in determinate sentencing during the mid to late-1970s would have predictable outcomes. The "sentencing reforms" of the period, he argued, would result in more offenders sentenced to prison, longer prison terms, and fewer options and relief valves for prison administrators to deal with the inmate population. The wholesale questioning of the effectiveness of correctional programs, exemplified by the catch phrase "nothing works," together with the ascendancy of incapacitation as the primary goal of American corrections, put research and program development in institutional corrections on virtual hold for more than a decade. As a result, prison administrators today struggle with the fusion of several trends—they have many more prisoners to manage; many more prisoners will spend most of their adult lives in prison; and resources to investigate, design, and deliver meaningful, constructive prison regimes for long-termers are scarce.

For some, this is not an important issue, because many believe that "humane containment" is the best that corrections can offer. In today's political climate, talk of designing "meaningful, constructive" prison careers is unlikely to garner passionate support. Instead, the "principle of least eligibility" is invoked to justify the denial of virtually all positive experiences for the incarcerated. Education programs, television reception, physical fitness equipment, and even work opportunities in prisons are questioned. Withholding these elements of prison life is thought to "send a message" to lawbreakers that society will not coddle those who would victimize us. This cold-storage model ignores the facts that 95% of the incarcerated will eventually return to the community and that involving prisoners in constructive behavior while confined may increase opportunities to lead crime-free lives upon release. Responding to the criticism that such beliefs are soft on crime, Norval Morris wrote two decades ago,

> If we select certain prisoners to bear the brunt of heavier sentences . . . surely we have a moral obligation at least to allow those serving extended terms an opportunity to make some constructive use of the time we have demanded of them. And unless we intend to lock them away forever, our reasons for attempting to rehabilitate these prisoners are not only moral but eminently practical. (1974, pp. 87-88)

The aims of this volume are to strip away some of the conventional wisdom and mythology surrounding long-term imprisonment and to present some of the best social science research on the topic in recent years. The essays included here share common purposes: to further understanding of the impact of long-term imprisonment on prisoners and prison systems and to offer insights and recommendations for better management of these inmates.

This book does not stake out an ideological position on long-term imprisonment. It does not ask whether it is "immoral" to impose long prison sentences on convicted offenders. Such questions are important, but they beg the question in America in the 1990s. The sentencing policy choices being constructed in Washington and state capitals in the mid-1990s are not "should we use long-term imprisonment, or should we rely on shorter sentences as a response to crime?" Instead, long-term imprisonment (especially life without parole) is being considered as a policy alternative to capital punishment. One can rail against the "tough on crime" ideology, but its pervasive influence in America today makes it very unlikely that the movement toward longer prison terms will soon reverse. Accordingly, it is incumbent on all concerned with administering (or paying for) humane and effective prisons to understand the phenomena of long-term confinement. Students who wish to understand the operation and impact of prisons can learn a great deal by focusing on long-term imprisonment. Indeed, if we discover ways to make prisons less destructive and more effective for those who spend decades within them, we will obtain invaluable wisdom about correctional practice and programs for all offenders.

ORGANIZATION OF THE BOOK

Part One, Perspectives on Long-Term Imprisonment, sets the stage for the rest of the book. In the first two chapters, I attempt to outline the primary issues and questions surrounding long-term imprisonment, and I present statistical portraits of the long-term offender population in the United States. The issues to be examined in later chapters include the definition of long-term confinement, the characteristics of long-termers, and modes of adaptation and adjustment to long-term confinement. Finally, the primary correctional policy, practice, and programmatic issues in management of long-term inmates are introduced. The characteristics of long-term inmates in U.S. state correctional facilities from 1974 to 1994 are examined in Chapter 2. Weekes's essay provides a similar overview for the Canadian correctional system.

In Part Two, Long-Term Prisoners on Long-Term Imprisonment, three essays by long-term prisoners frame the issue in highly personal terms. Wikberg and Foster discuss long-term inmates in the Louisiana prison system and ask why some offenders are held so much longer than others. Santos, a federal prisoner serving a long sentence for drug law violations, explores the early phase of long-term confinement in his essay, "Facing Long-Term Imprisonment." Kummerlowe's essay on adaptation strategies is reprinted from a report commissioned by the National Institute of Corrections.

In Part Three, researchers tackle the important controversy surrounding the effects of long-term confinement. As these chapters show, the time-worn notion depicted in movies and fiction of the zombie-like "old con" masks tremendous variation in response to long-term imprisonment. The challenges to physical and mental health that imprisonment imposes are real, but these essays show that their effects are neither ubiquitous nor easily predicted.

Part Four, Adaptation and Survival Among Long-Term Inmates, explores the coping and time management strategies used by long-term prisoners to adjust and cope with the prison experience. Much of this research indicates that the coping problems faced by long-term inmates are perceived to be different from those faced by short-term inmates. The attitudinal and behavioral adaptations utilized by long-term prisoners serve important functions of time bounding, maintenance of relationships, and development of a form of detente with correctional staff members. Zamble examines these strategies in a longitudinal study among Canadian prisoners. Genders and Player, and MacKenzie, Robinson, and Campbell show that coping and adjustment are particularly challenging for women long-term inmates. Fishman's study of wives of prisoners illustrates that inmates do not do time alone; instead, spouses and other family members also face problems of role definition, loneliness, poverty, and stigmatization.

The chapters in Part Five, Correctional Responses and the Management of Long-Term Prisoners, argue that correctional personnel must be aware of and responsive to the stresses and coping problems of long-term prisoners and should be active in developing appropriate responses. Toch's extensive research into person-environment matches in prisons leads him to conclude that contemporary prisons can be very difficult settings in which to serve a long prison term. He suggests that effective classification systems can help to diminish mismatches between personal needs and environmental characteristics. In Chapter 18, leading correctional practitioners describe the management dilemmas posed by long-term inmates and discuss the health care, labor, education, and other institutional systems needed to manage long-termer populations. Mitchell's chapter, "Management of Life Sentence Prisoners in England and Wales," describes a comprehensive systemwide strategy to develop and implement career plans for inmates serving long terms. Mitchell's study shows that prison staff play a crucial role in carrying out the sentence planning model.

Bottoms, Hay, and Sparks consider the issue of prevention of violence and disorder in long-term prisons. They argue that importa-

tion of well-developed community crime prevention techniques into the prison can help to minimize disorder. More important, they argue that treating prisoners as autonomous persons, with fairness and predictability in interactions with staff, also contributes to order maintenance. The pair of chapters by Cowles and Sabath tells the story of a grounded effort to identify the program needs of long-term inmates and to develop and implement programs within the Missouri Department of Corrections that were responsive to long-termers' needs. Their work shows that imaginative thinking and inmate participation can be part of effective correctional program development.

Palmer's description of the *LifeServers* program within a Canadian prison provides a comprehensive overview of a successful, multifaceted program for lifers and long-term prisoners. In the final chapter of this section, I describe the components of comprehensive sentence planning for long-term prisoners. This perspective forces correctional officials to recognize that planning a career in confinement for an inmate who will spend many years inside is very different from program assignments for short-term "tourists."

The final section of the volume, Afterwords, includes two essays on correctional policy and long-term imprisonment. Toch's essay, "The Long-Term Inmate as a Long-Term Problem," discusses the role of staff, environmental attributes, programming, and career planning in developing meaningful institutional careers for long-term prisoners. He reminds us that long-termers are seldom the "squeaky wheels" of the prison, so it is possible to run prisons in which inmates "gradually waste away." In the final chapter, I discuss the components of a correctional policy model for long-term imprisonment. The policy assumes that imprisonment per se is the primary punishment for lawbreakers, so the cardinal objective of correctional practice with long-termers should be to minimize the deleterious "secondary" punishments of prisons. Again, the objective of these chapters is to provoke critical thinking on the part of correctional professionals, students, and interested citizens about ways to organize prisons for long-termers that (a) provide opportunities for growth, maturity, and constructive involvement during confinement and (b) maximize the odds of successful reintegration into society upon release. The alternative "cold-storage" model may seem less expensive, and it may satisfy our desire to use prisons *as* punishment as well as *for* punishment, but it ignores the reality that nearly all long-term prisoners will eventually be released. It is in our interest to reduce offenders' social toxicity during confinement.

REFERENCE

Morris, N. (1974). *The future of imprisonment*. Chicago: University of Chicago Press.

Acknowledgments

Several chapters of this volume were commissioned for a special issue of *The Prison Journal* in 1990 on "Long-Term Incarceration and Long-Term Prisoners." I am grateful to the Pennsylvania Prison Society, publisher of *The Prison Journal,* for asking me to serve as guest editor for the special issue. Janet Leban, former editor of the journal and executive director of the Pennsylvania Prison Society (the nation's oldest citizen-based prison reform group) was especially supportive. I wish to thank all of the contributors to this volume, whose work forms the core of a body of modern research and scholarship on long-term imprisonment. In particular, Hans Toch has been a long-term supporter of my research and a superb colleague; he is a model of the career scholar. I have also learned a great deal about prisons and prisoners from discussions with Ernie Cowles, Mike Sabath, and Mike Quinlan, and I appreciate their contributions to this work. At Sage Publications, Inc., Terry Hendrix enthusiastically encouraged the development of this volume and shared his expertise and vast experience in publishing criminal justice scholarship. Susan McElroy guided the development of the book with great care and good humor. I deeply appreciate her work. Finally, I want to thank Nancy, Erin, and Kevin for their love and support.

PART ONE

■ Perspectives on
Long-Term Imprisonment

1

Long-Term Incarceration

Issues of Science, Policy and Correctional Practice

Timothy J. Flanagan

With growing public concern about victimization and its impact on individuals, families and communities, it is not surprising that politicians, criminal justice officials and a substantial majority of the public in Western nations favour greater use of long prison terms (see Flanagan & Jamieson, 1988; Zimmerman, van Alstyne, & Dunn, 1988). Incarceration has been the primary response to serious crime in North America for nearly two centuries. And while the effectiveness of punitive sanctions in altering criminal behaviour has been questioned for centuries, public policy has focused almost exclusively on manipulating the swiftness, certainty and severity of criminal punishment. Moreover, enhancing the swiftness and certainty of punishment has proven to be difficult, if not elusive, so policy makers have made ready use of the severity component of the equation to demonstrate that they are "tough on crime."

Long-term incarceration is a major factor in the explosion of the American prison population in the last 15 years. The dramatic and unprecedented growth in state and federal prison populations in the United States during that period has been fuelled by increases in both the proportion of convicted offenders who are sentenced to prison terms and the length of such terms (Chapman, 1985). Legislative "reforms" such as mandatory sentence laws, habitual offender statutes and sentence enhancements directed at gun-related and drug-related crimes have driven prisoner populations to historic levels. As a result, appropriations for correctional activities have been the fastest-growing segment of state government spending during most of the 1980s in the U.S. (Gold, 1991).

What has this frenetic legislative activity and public spending wrought? In this article, I examine what we have learned about long-term imprisonment in terms of science, policy and correctional practice. I argue that during the last two decades science has stripped long-term imprisonment of much of its mythical quality. Much of what we believed to be true about the impact of long-term incarceration has not been documented by penological researchers. From the standpoint of policy development, correctional agencies have neither anticipated nor responded to the challenge of increasing long-term inmate populations. Finally, innovations in correctional practice related to the management of long-term prisoners have been isolated, hesitant and piecemeal.

NOTE: Reprinted with permission from *Forum for Corrections Research*, Vol. 4, No. 2, June 1992, pp. 19-24. Copyright 1992 by Correctional Service of Canada.

Despite these shortcomings, however, we have developed a knowledge base on long-term incarceration which is sufficient to serve as the foundation for enlightened policy and innovative correctional practice.

DEFINITIONAL CONCERNS

There is no uniform definition of long-term incarceration. Definitions vary substantially over time and place. The lengthy prison terms being handed out in American courts today would have been appalling in colonial courts and are substantially longer than contemporary prison sentences in other countries. Even within a single country, substantial variation exists in population-based imprisonment rates, in the average length of prison terms and in the composition of institutional populations. In the U.S., for example, some states have responded to the pressure on state prison resources by creating an enormous backlog of convicted felons awaiting transfer to state prisons who remain "backed up" in local jails. In some instances, convicted offenders reach parole eligibility before they are transferred to the state prison system! (Maguire & Flanagan, 1991, p. 600; see also U.S. Department of Justice, Bureau of Justice Statistics, 1988). In other states, relief valves at the other end of the correctional system, such as emergency-release mechanisms, accelerated good-time and parole policies and other practices, have actually reduced the average time served among state prisoners in recent years (Maguire & Flanagan, 1991, p. 664).

Nearly 15 years ago, I felt confident in adopting a criterion of five years of continuous confinement to define long-term imprisonment. Five years was more than twice the average time served in state prisons in the U.S., and only 12% of the state prisoner population in 1974 had actually served five years or more (U.S. Department of Justice, 1986). Ten years later, other investigators defined long-term incarceration as seven years (Correctional Services Group, 1985; see also MacKenzie & Goodstein, 1985). Given that the average prison *sentence* for violent felonies handed out in American state courts in 1988 ranged from 90 to 238 months, one could argue that, today, an expected time served of at least eight to 10 years would qualify a U.S. prisoner as a long-term inmate (Maguire & Flanagan, 1991, p. 518).

COMPOSITIONAL CHANGES

In addition to such growth in size that the *scale* of long-term incarceration is fundamentally different today from a decade ago, some researchers have speculated that changing crime patterns and sentencing laws would alter the *nature* of long-term prisoner populations. Twenty-five years ago, the typical long-term inmate in a U.S. state correctional facility was a white, male offender convicted of homicide, rape or robbery, with little criminal experience, no substantial history of illegal drug use and little propensity for violence in prison. In contrast, the attributes of today's long-term prisoner differ markedly. Some studies have suggested that changes in the composition of the long-term prisoner group have been subtle (Correctional Services Group, 1985; MacKenzie & Goodstein, 1985). However, a recent study of compositional changes in the prisoner population from 1956 to 1989 in New York State revealed that the long-term inmate subgroup had become more homogeneous in offence (higher percentage of homicide offenders), more heterogeneous in terms of race and ethnicity, more violent (in terms of present and previous offences) and more enmeshed in drug abuse (Flanagan, Clark, Aziz, & Szelest, 1990). Several of these characteristics suggest that the "new breed" of long-term prisoner would present heightened security concerns within the prison.

THE SCIENCE OF
ADAPTATION AND ADJUSTMENT

As I mentioned earlier, social-scientific investigations of long-term imprisonment have stripped the topic of much of its mythology. The mythology or conventional wisdom of long-term incarceration, often repeated at professional meetings and among correctional staff, focused on two primary themes. The first theme held that, over time, such prisoners suffered inevitable deterioration of physical and mental health. The second theme of the conventional wisdom was the notion of the long-term prisoner as a model inmate. That is, many correctional workers contended that long-term prisoners were a stabilizing, predictable and largely rule-abiding group within the prison.

The deterioration theme was based on several foundations, including early research on "prison psychoses." The primary contention of this assumption was that after extended exposure to highly regimented, unisexual prison life with limited stimuli, the long-term prisoner would lose the ability to function as an effective, active person. These studies documented symptoms such as flatness of affect (emotion), diminished ability to concentrate, "barrier effects" in time perception and others which suggested that the grinding effects of the prison environment exacted a great toll on the well-being of long-term prisoners (for a review, see Flanagan, 1982b).

With few, isolated exceptions, social scientists have been unable to document these presumed deleterious "effects" of long-term incarceration. A spirited debate has ensued among social scientists about the sensitivity and relevance of measures used in prison research (see Wormith, 1985). However, the consensus of findings of increasingly rigorous research suggests that no systematic or predictable effect of long-term imprisonment exists. As Toch has aptly observed, "paradoxically, some men flourish in this context. Weaklings become substantial and influential, shiftless men strive and produce; pathetic souls sprout unsuspected resources" (Toch, 1975). Perhaps the most rigorous research on this topic has been conducted by Zamble, whose study of Canadian long-term inmates' adjustment over seven years concluded:

> perhaps the most striking general result is in the total *lack* of any evidence for general or widespread deteriorative effects. [Long-term inmates] did not become social isolates in the prison, and neither did they lose contact with the outside world. They did not adapt in ways that would make it more difficult for them to cope on the outside. Most did not sink into despair or rebellion, but rather their emotional states, health and conduct in the institutions all improved over time, and there was some evidence for improved coping abilities as well. (Zamble, 1992)

The "model inmate" view of long-term prisoners is based on the assumption that these offenders are older and more mature than their younger short-term counterparts, accrue substantial experience in the prison environment, develop functional relationships with correctional staff and have a stake in maintaining the status quo within the prison. This view of long-term prisoners has been supported in several studies which reported substantially lower rates of involvement in institutional rule violations among long-term offenders than short-termers (Flanagan, 1980). However, a recent large-scale study by Toch and Adams calls these findings into question: they reported that at least younger long-term inmates in the early stages of their prison sentences had relatively high rates of prison rule violation (Toch & Adams, 1989).

A careful reading of the literature on prison adjustment and adaptation by long-term prisoners leads to the conclusion that generalization is dangerous. On some measures of prisoner adjustment, the research suggests that long-term prisoners, *as a group*, may be better adjusted to the demands of the prison environment than are other prisoners. However, the group average masks substantial differences in *individual responses* to confinement. In fact, the development of our knowledge on adaptation and adjustment among long-term inmates is reminiscent of the debate about the deprivation model and the importation model of prisoner adjustment. After years of research which sought to determine which theoretical model best explained prisoner adjustment, rigorous research revealed that neither model alone was sufficient to explain variation in prisoner behaviour. Instead, elements of both models, and other factors, are important to understanding prisoner adjustment (for a comprehensive review, see Adams, 1991). For correctional policy and practice, the most important implication of this development is that unitary prescriptions for managing long-term prisoner populations are doomed to failure if they fail to account for the variety that exists within this group.

CORRECTIONAL POLICY AND THE LONG-TERM PRISONER

For most of the history of institutional corrections, correctional policy makers put long-term prisoners at the bottom of the list of priorities. There are several reasons for this neglect. First, the heinous crimes and substantial previous records that accompany long-term offenders to prison make them poor candidates for innovative or experimental programs and policies; the general public is believed to be unreceptive to progressive efforts that involve these serious offenders, and the risk and subsequent cost of failure is high. Accordingly, the informal norms and formal policies of many correctional agencies exclude long-term prisoners from participation in programs such as educational release, furloughs and even transfer to specific facilities (Flanagan, Travis, Forstenzer, Connors, & McDermott, 1975).

The second reason for this last-in-line view of long-term inmates relates to the distribution of scarce program resources within correctional agencies. Because long-term prisoners' needs in terms of release are less immediate than those of other prisoners, correctional administrators have traditionally withheld these program opportunities until the possibility of release approaches.

As a result of this "cold-storage model" of resource allocation, the only opportunity within the prison viewed as appropriate for long-term prisoners has been assignment to correctional industry programs. Since long-term inmates are felt to be more responsible and better-behaved prisoners, and many long-termers gravitate to industry positions to earn money and use their time productively, the attractiveness of long-termers as a stable and durable work force to prison officials is apparent. The principal problem with this approach is that opportunities in correctional industry programs have not kept pace with the growth in inmate populations. Today, there are many more inmates than industrial job opportunities in American prisons (Flanagan & Maguire, 1991).

Perhaps the only real correctional-policy debate concerning long-term inmates is the controversy about concentration versus dispersal. Some researchers argue that dispersing long-term prisoners, who are stable, mature and responsible, among the general prisoner population, reduces inmate misconduct and provides positive role models to other inmates for "how to do time" (see, e.g., Mabli, Holley, Patrick, & Walls, 1979). On the other hand, research suggests that the environmental needs of many long-term prisoners, especially older persons, are different from those of young, aggressive, rowdy short-term offenders, and that involuntary mixing of these groups makes it difficult for long-term prisoners to do time (Toch, 1977a). In addition, grouping prisoners by age or sentence length would allow special-

ized programming and services (e.g., health service) to be tailored to the needs of the population.

Most large, state correctional systems in the U.S. have, in reality, pursued a policy of grouping, because inmate-classification systems, designed to assign incoming prisoners to facilities, have always placed a strong emphasis on sentence length which has universally been equated with a presumed need for maximum-security custody. In some states, these classification systems have broken down under the crush of unprecedented rates of new admissions, but it remains the case that most large states have one or more old, walled, fortress-like prisons where long-term prisoners can be found.

I have argued that correctional agencies need to develop explicit, goal-directed, research-based policy statements concerning the management of long-term inmates (Flanagan, 1982a). These statements must recognize that the policy options for this group are constrained but that much can still be accomplished. In my view, the overriding goal of long-term prisoner management must be to minimize the potential secondary effects of confinement. These secondary effects were articulated by Gresham Sykes 35 years ago as the "pains of imprisonment" (Sykes, 1958). To counter the deleterious effects of incarceration, we must focus on objectives such as creating opportunities for institutions and communities to interact for the good of both, creating opportunities within prisons for inmates to contribute to their communities and encouraging long-term prisoners and their families to maintain supportive relationships. Policies directed toward minimizing these secondary effects of confinement are not intended to coddle these serious offenders, nor are they a panacea for the treatment of serious criminals. Instead, they amount to a policy objective of humane containment for such offenders and represent a reasonable, defensible and worthwhile goal for correctional agencies.

PROGRAMS AND PRACTICES

In the U.S., the development of correctional programs oriented to the problems, needs or preferences of long-term prisoners has been minimal. Programs that have been attempted have been insubstantial, limited in scope and poorly documented. Virtually no information has been exchanged across state boundaries, so the few program efforts to date have not been replicated.

The oldest and best-known long-termer programs are the lifers' clubs and similar organizations within prisons. These groups adopt one or more customary orientations. Many are support groups, in which persons with mutual interests come together to pursue common aims, such as legislative reform and the communication of members' needs to organizational hierarchies.

Some long-term prisoner organizations evolve as "prison preventer" groups, with the principal objective of educating youth. Others take on a community-service role and serve the needs of the prison community or the surrounding community. Both the Life Servers program in the Warkworth Institution, in Ontario, and the Long-Termers Program at the Utah state prison in the U.S. have such a community-service orientation (Palmer, 1984). A national assessment of long-term prisoner programming conducted by the National Institute of Corrections in 1985 uncovered a handful of small, narrowly focused programs for long-term prisoners in U.S. prisons (Correctional Services Group, 1985). In each case, the development of the program could be traced to the inmates themselves or to the efforts of a single, supportive staff person within the institution.

After reviewing these and other efforts, I suggested that to garner support for long-term inmate programs within prison systems, these programs should focus on public service and have an external advisory board, supportive staff linkages, limited enrollment and minimal capital costs. In addition, it is important that programs involving long-term prisoners not be competitive with any private-sector interests and that they involve volunteers from outside the institution. Finally, many long-term prisoner programs provide what Toch calls "sanctuary," or respite from the general inmate population in a well-defined place, in which relaxed, natural relationships with staff and inmates can develop (Flanagan, 1985). Cowles and Sabath developed several programs based on these features within the Missouri correctional system. An important feature of their work was that program development flowed from a comprehensive needs assessment conducted with long-term prisoners (Sabath &

Cowles, 1990). Their work indicates that innovative programming for long-term inmates is possible.

Long-term prisoners are perhaps most different from other inmates in that much of their adult, working lives will be spent in the correctional system. As a result, planning constructive use of their time demands a long-range approach. This career-planning concept is very different than the objective-oriented, skills-based approach that is taken with short-term prisoners. Hans Toch introduced the concept of career planning for long-term inmates, and I have suggested that:

> it is incumbent on correctional systems to work with the offender to plan a worthwhile career, one that will be beneficial to both the offender and others, and that will be transferable, and capable of supporting the offender upon his/her eventual release. Moreover, there is no reason why, during their long imprisonment, many long-term inmates cannot make a substantial contribution to society through help provided to other inmates. (Flanagan, 1991)

Mutually beneficial experiences such as these have been described by Toch and Adams (Toch & Adams, 1989). They contend that such experiences build coping abilities among disruptive prisoners.

In my judgment, the most impressive effort to take a comprehensive, organized and coherent approach to long-term inmate programming, to date, is the Revised Strategy adopted by the British Home Office. Barry Mitchell has carefully documented the implementation of the strategy in his book *Murder and Penal Policy* (Mitchell, 1990). The Revised Strategy is a set of policies that incorporates the career-planning model for long-term inmates in a system-wide fashion. Mitchell reported that the Revised Strategy was adopted in response to increases in the number of life-sentence prisoners. It is based on principles which include:

- treating long-term prisoners as a *separate* group with unique needs, but integrating long-termers with other prisoners;
- recognizing the heterogeneity of the long-termer population;

- providing life-sentence prisoners with a sense of purpose and direction;
- career planning, involving goal setting, revision and progression;
- using a variety of physical settings within the prison system; and
- being flexible rather than rigid in security designation.

Mitchell observed that "a crucial factor in the success of the Revised Strategy is the extent to which lifers are motivated to use their sentence constructively." He reported that there were many impediments to effective implementation of the policy, including resentment among long-termers of their compulsory integration with short-term inmates and the need to change staff attitudes toward these offenders. The long-term experience of the Home Office with the Revised Strategy certainly bears watching, since it represents the first comprehensive effort on the part of a major correctional agency to take an integrated approach to long-term prisoner management.

DIRECTIONS AND INFORMATION NEEDS

Fifteen years ago, Hans Toch gave an address, titled "The Long-term Prisoner as a Long-term Problem," at a Canadian conference on long-term incarceration (Toch, 1977b; see Chapter 24 of this volume for his current views on this topic). The challenge of long-term prisoner populations loomed in the 1970s, is upon us in the 1990s and will certainly increase in the years to come. As with the inevitable process of aging, it is futile to deny reality. Common sense requires that we fashion plans to address the inevitable consequences.

Many aspects of long-term inmate management need urgent attention and development. Three of these, intended to be illustrative rather than exhaustive of the implications of long-term incarceration, are: the broad-based effects of an aging prisoner population, the impact of long-term confinement on female inmates and the community reintegration of long-term inmates.

Among correctional administrators, an aging prisoner population is perhaps the most widely recognized consequence of the growing long-term inmate population. The fiscal impact of

an aging prison population on medical services alone is staggering (Dugger, Chapter 17, this volume). In addition, the physical characteristics of prisons present a formidable challenge for aging offenders. Except in the newest facilities, access and mobility for individuals with disabilities is a nightmare in prisons. One correctional administrator remarked that the prospect of managing a correctional institution which contained persons with Alzheimer's Disease was virtually inconceivable. Studies suggest that imprisonment does not systematically damage the physical health of inmates, but inmate populations will not escape the inevitable consequences of aging. As has been the case with the AIDS problem in corrections, states may have to consider early release via "mercy parole" mechanisms or face the mounting costs of treating these patients within the prison.

Female long-term inmates are a special case because few correctional systems are large enough to provide the variety of facility settings and programs to serve the needs of this population. Genders and Player described the "feelings of claustrophobia and despair generated by the miniature scale of the unit and the inevitable restrictions placed upon their freedom of physical movement" among women in the H-Wing at the Durham Prison in England (Genders & Player, Chapter 12, this volume). Responding to the needs of female long-term prisoners in an intelligent and comprehensive manner may require multijurisdictional cooperation and planning.

Finally, despite the well-worn maxim that, eventually, nearly all prisoners will be released to the community, there is virtually no literature on the community reintegration of long-term prisoners. Popular literature is full of compelling images of released long-termers who are confused by modern technology and astounded by social and economic changes in society. Today's prisoners are far less isolated from popular culture and media than in the past, but there is cause for concern. Zamble and Porporino argue that there are few opportunities in the regimented world of the prison for inmates to practise mature, effective coping strategies, and that without these opportunities, the ineffective coping skills which contributed to their incarceration are not likely to improve (Zamble & Porporino, 1988). This conclusion argues not only for a different prison experience but also for a rigorous, planned re-entry program, which should be founded on solid research that examines the important elements of successful community reintegration of long-term prisoners.

In sum, long prison sentences and the problems and needs of long-term inmates present extraordinary challenges for correctional administration. A new framework is required for understanding the role of prisons in a modern, criminal-justice system. Warehousing is not an option, because the human and fiscal costs of warehousing are unacceptably high. Improved management directed by ambitious goals is the preferred option for many reasons, including the fact that lessons learned in pursuit of better management of long-term prisons will advance the state of the art for the correctional system as a whole.

REFERENCES

Adams, K. (1991). *Adjusting to prison: Stress, coping and maladaptation.* Carbondale: Southern Illinois University Press.

Chapman, W. (1985). *Commitments to prison with long minimum terms.* Albany, NY: Department of Correctional Services.

Correctional Services Group. (1985). *The long-term inmate phenomenon: A national perspective.* Kansas City, MO: Author.

Flanagan, T. (1980). Time served and institutional misconduct. *Journal of Criminal Justice, 8,* 357-367.

Flanagan, T. (1982a). Correctional policy and the long-term prisoner. *Crime and Delinquency, 28,* 82-95.

Flanagan, T. (1982b). Lifers and long-termers: Doing big time, In R. Johnson & H. Toch (Eds.), *The pains of imprisonment.* Beverly Hills, CA: Sage.

Flanagan, T. (1985). Sentence planning for long-term inmates. *Federal Probation, 49,* 23-28.

Flanagan, T. (1991). Long-term prisoners: Their adaptation and adjustment. *Federal Prisons Journal, 2,* 44-51.

Flanagan, T., Clark, D., Aziz, D., & Szelest, B. (1990). Compositional changes in a long-term prisoner population, 1956-89. *The Prison Journal, 80,* 15-34.

Flanagan, T., & Jamieson, K. (Eds.). (1988). *Sourcebook of criminal justice statistics 1987.* Washington, DC: Government Printing Office.

Flanagan, T., & Maguire, K. (1991). *A full employment policy for American prisons: Some estimates and implications.* Albany, NY: Hindelang Criminal Justice Research Center.

Flanagan, T., Travis, L., Forstenzer, M., Connors, M., & McDermott, M. (1975). *Long-term prisoner project, task force four: Rules and regulations.* Albany: State University of New York Press.

Gold, S. D. (1991). The story behind state spending trends. *Rockefeller Institute Bulletin,* 4-6. Albany: State University of New York Press.

Mabli, J., Holley, C., Patrick, C., & Walls, J. (1979). Age and prison violence. *Criminal Justice and Behavior, 6,* 175-186.

MacKenzie, D., & Goodstein, L. (1985). Impacts of long-term incarceration and characteristics of long-term offenders: An empirical analysis. *Criminal Justice and Behavior, 12,* 395-415.

Maguire, K., & Flanagan, T. (Eds.). (1991). *Sourcebook of criminal justice statistics 1990.* Washington, DC: Government Printing Office.

Mitchell, B. (1990). *Murder and penal policy.* New York: St. Martin's Press.

Palmer, W. (1984). Programming for long-term inmates: A new perspective. *Canadian Journal of Criminology, 26,* 439-458.

Sabath, M., & Cowles, E. (1990). Using multiple perspectives to develop strategies for managing long-term inmates. (and) Addressing the program needs of long-term inmates. *The Prison Journal, 80,* 58-82.

Sykes, G. (1958). *Society of captives: A study of a maximum security prison.* Princeton, NJ: Princeton University Press.

Toch, H. (1975). *Men in crisis: Human breakdowns in prison.* Chicago: Aldine.

Toch, H. (1977a). *Living in prison: The ecology of survival.* New York: Free Press.

Toch, H. (1977b). The long-term inmate as a long-term problem. In S. Rizkalla, R. Levy, & R. Zauberman (Eds.), *Long-term imprisonment: An international seminar.* Montreal: University of Montreal.

Toch, H., & Adams, K. (1989). *Coping: Maladaptation in prisons.* New Brunswick, NJ: Transaction Books.

U. S. Department of Justice. (1986). *Survey of inmates of state correctional facilities 1984.* Washington, DC: Government Printing Office.

U. S. Department of Justice, Bureau of Justice Statistics. (1988). *Report to the nation on crime and justice* (2nd ed.). Washington, DC: Government Printing Office.

Wormith, J. (1985). The controversy over the effects of long-term incarceration. *Canadian Journal of Criminology, 26,* 423-437.

Zamble, E. (1992). *Coping, behavior and adaptation in long-term prison inmates: Descriptive longitudinal results.* Unpublished paper, Queen's University.

Zamble, E., & Porporino, F. (1988). *Coping, adaptation and behavior in prison inmates.* New York: Springer-Verlag.

Zimmerman, S., van Alstyne, D., & Dunn, C. (1988). The national punishment survey and public policy consequences. *Journal of Research in Crime and Delinquency, 25,* 120-149.

2

An American Portrait of Long-Term Imprisonment

Timothy J. Flanagan

The American correctional system was never designed with long-term prisoners in mind. In his influential social history of prisons, David Rothman observed that one of the primary assumptions of the designers of the American penitentiary system was that most offenders would need only brief exposure to the rigorous environment of these institutions to be rehabilitated. However, as Rothman pointed out,

> These preconceptions proved woefully inadequate. By the outbreak of the Civil War, the . . . penitentiary cells filled up with hardened criminals and even the reformatories received teenagers surprisingly advanced in a life of crime. The intricate designs of the asylum builders did not suit this clientele. Moral treatment had not been planned for the chronic insane, a system of steady labor for the senile, the rules of separation and silence for the ten-to-twenty year convict. Under these conditions, the superintendents were content to administer a custodial program. The public accepted the decision. (Rothman, 1971, pp. 238-239)

This viewpoint dominated thinking about long-term prisoners and long-term imprisonment for most of the history of American corrections. Young first offenders have long been the focus of most correctional efforts. The policies and practices of state correctional sys-

tems emphasize delivering services to young short-term prisoners. For example, vocational training programs offered in prisons are designed for rapid turnover. Most such programs can be completed in 6 to 12 months. Educational programs focus on getting high school dropouts past the General Education Diploma examinations. Life skills training emphasizes the skills needed to find and maintain a job upon release. Even programs developed to maintain and strengthen family ties are often restricted to short-term prisoners or those nearing the end of their terms. With the exception of longer-term education activities such as college degree programs, there are very few activities for long-term inmates besides working and waiting.

In recent years much more attention has focused on long-term incarceration in the context of debates about crime control policy. There has been widespread support for life-without-parole sentences, mandatory minimum terms, and longer sentences for drug offenders and violent criminals. The political fervor with which repeat offender legislation (so called "three strikes and you're out" laws) is promoted exemplifies this trend. This discussion centers on the need to incarcerate more people for longer periods of time but provides little or no guidance to correctional officials about what to *do* with long-term prisoners over the course of a 30-, 40-, or 50-year prison term. Despite the fact that the American corrections system incarcerates at a higher

TABLE 2.1 Incarceration Rates for Selected Nations

1989		*1990/1991*	
Nation	*Rate of Incarceration per 100,000 Population*	*Nation*	*Rate of Incarceration per 100,000 Population*
United States	426	United States	455
South Africa	333	South Africa	311
Soviet Union	268	Venezuela	177
Hungary	196	Hungary	117
Malaysia	126	Canada	111
Northern Ireland	120	China	111
Hong Kong	118	Australia	79
Poland	106	Portugal	77
New Zealand	100	Czechoslovakia	72
United Kingdom	97	Denmark	71
Turkey	96	Albania	55
Portugal	83	Netherlands	46
France	81	Republic of Ireland	44
Austria	77	Sweden	44
Spain	76	Japan	42
Switzerland	73	India	34
Australia	72		
Denmark	68		
Italy	60		
Japan	45		
Netherlands	40		
Philippines	22		

SOURCE: Mauer (1991, 1992)
NOTE: Incarceration rates for 1990/1991 are for either 1990 or 1991, depending on the availability of data for each nation.

rate and for longer terms than other industrialized democracies, we have gained limited insights into how to plan or organize an institutional career for persons who will spend the majority of their adult lives behind bars.

AMERICAN PRISON POLICY AND LONG-TERM INCARCERATION

There is no national sentencing or correctional policy in America, so variation among the states in penal policy, incarceration rates, and the use of long prison sentences is widespread. For example, in 1991 the incarceration rate (per 100,000 residents) in the District of Columbia was more than 26 times higher than the incarceration rate in North Dakota (Maguire, Pastore, & Flanagan, 1993, p. 614). Several key features of American correctional practice serve as relevant background.

First, America uses incarceration as a response to crime at a higher rate than virtually any other nation. Table 2.1 shows national incarceration rates for 16 nations. These data

pertain to 1990-1991 and were compiled by The Sentencing Project (Mauer, 1992). The rate of incarceration is the number of persons incarcerated per 100,000 population. The United States's overall incarceration rate was 46% higher than that of South Africa, the second highest user of incarceration. The U.S. rate was five times higher than the median incarceration rate for the 16 nations listed in 1990-1991. A higher than average incarceration rate does not necessarily mean that a nation is more punitive than others. Much of the difference in incarceration rates across nations can be explained by differences in the crime rate, especially the violent crime rate (Lynch, 1988).

Second, the United States uses long-term incarceration more frequently than other democratic nations. As early as 1968, a study committee of the American Bar Association reported that although a prison term of 5 years was common in the United States, such commitments were rare (and considered excessive) in other countries (American Bar Association, 1968). The international comparative report by The Sentencing Project (Mauer, 1991) observed that America's high rate of incarceration was due to both a high *admission rate* (the percentage of convicted offenders who receive a prison sentence) and longer *length of stay* (resulting from longer sentences).

A recent comparative analysis of sentencing and time served in the United States, Canada, England and Wales, and West Germany sheds light on this issue. When length of sentences imposed for comparable offenses was examined, Lynch reported that "The United States imposes substantially longer sentences for serious crimes than do other industrialized democracies. In some cases, however, these differences are reduced when estimates of *time actually served* are used rather than *imposed sentences*" (Lynch, 1993, p. 655, emphasis added). Lynch found that for serious violent crimes, differences in time served across these five nations were less pronounced than the comparison of sentences imposed indicated. "The large differences in time served between the United States and these other countries are found for property crimes—burglary and larceny" (p. 650). Lynch cautioned, however, that international comparisons were complicated by differing pretrial release practices (time served in jail prior to conviction was not included in his analysis) and by differences in the severity of offenses across countries. For example, it is likely that a higher percentage of burglary and robbery offenses in America involve weapon use than in the other countries. Finally, Lynch's study examined sentencing practices with data from the mid-1980s. The latter half of the 1980s in the United States has been characterized by consistent increases in the proportion of convicted offenders sentenced to prison, sentence lengths, and tightening of parole release criteria. Therefore, the outsized length of prison terms in the United States has undoubtedly increased in the past decade, making this country the world leader in the use of long prison terms.

HOW MANY LONG-TERM PRISONERS IN AMERICA?

The question of how many long-term prisoners are confined in American prisons appears deceptively simple; however, the complicated structure of state and federal sentencing laws makes it a more complicated matter. One cannot rely exclusively on sentence length to identify long-term prisoners because state sentencing provisions vary radically in terms of specifying minimum terms, the rate at which good time credits accrue, and parole eligibility policies.

The state of Texas provides a compelling example of this dilemma. In the late 1980s prison populations soared as a result of rising crime and the tremendous influx of drug offenders into the prison system. Prison capacity did not expand quickly enough to accommodate the rising prisoner population, and the federal courts imposed capacity controls on the prison system as part of a wide-ranging prisoner rights lawsuit. The impact of these population pressures was twofold. First, thousands of convicted felons, who would have otherwise been committed to the state prison system, backed up in the county jails throughout the state. Second, in an effort to regulate the population pressure, parole officials accelerated the flow of offenders by increasing the rate at which inmates were released on parole. The result was that during the period from 1986 to 1991, the number of offenders sentenced to prison increased markedly and sentence lengths imposed on these offenders increased, but the actual time served on the sentence fell 27% and the percentage of the sentence served fell 61% (State of Texas, 1992). As the Texas example illustrates, maximum sentence does not provide a reliable or valid indicator of who will serve long prison terms.

The sentencing provisions of most states require that offenders sentenced to life terms serve a substantial minimum sentence prior to release, although nationwide data on actual time served by lifers is not routinely collected. Nevertheless, data on life sentence prisoners provides a glimpse of one segment of the long-term prisoner population. Table 2.2 lists life sentence prisoners in 47 states in 1992. In these states, 67,804 inmates were serving life sentences. Sixty-six percent of lifers were committed for homicide offenses, 8% for sex offenses, and 7% for drug offenses. Of the life sentence prisoners, 11,200, or 17%, were serving life-without-parole terms.

Perhaps the most conservative method of estimating the number of long-term prisoners in America is to examine time served among released prisoners. Such data are collected under the auspices of the National Corrections Reporting Program of the U.S. Justice Department. Table 2.3 presents information on 201,000 *first releases* from state prisons in 1991. (First releases exclude offenders who were recommitted to prison for a parole violation.) Average time served across all offenses was 22 months. If one adopts a 7-year prison stay as the definition of long-term incarceration, only two categories of homicide offenders, constituting less than 2% of first releases in 1991, served 84 months or more in confinement prior to release. The national data also illustrate the mathematical relationship of maximum sentence length and actual time served. Among all first releases from state prisons in 1991, inmates served an average of 35% of the maximum sentence length (Perkins, 1994, p. 31).

Examining releases from prison undercounts the true number of long-term prisoners in American corrections because it fails to include inmates still confined who have already served lengthy terms. Information on time served among inmates *in custody* is gathered periodically through the series of *Surveys of Inmates of State Correctional Facilities,* conducted by the Census Bureau for the U.S. Department of Justice. These surveys provide snapshots of the American prisoner population at intervals during the past 20 years.

The most recent survey included nearly 14,000 inmates and was conducted in the summer of 1991 (Beck et al., 1993). Table 2.4 shows national estimates of sentence length, time served since admission, and total time expected to be served before release for state prisoners. For offenders convicted of violent crimes (nearly 47% of all inmates) the median sentence imposed by the courts was 15 years, but these violent offenders had served an average of 31 months by the date of the survey. Violent offenders expected to serve an average of 70 months (5.8 years) before release. Prisoners serving time for murder, who constituted nearly 11% of all inmates, expected to serve more than 160 months (13.3 years) before release. Accordingly, a cautious estimate of the percentage of state prisoners confined in 1991 who will serve 7 or more years before release would be 11% to 15% of all state prisoners.

CHARACTERISTICS OF LONG-TERM PRISONERS

The *Surveys of Inmates of State Correctional Facilities* can also be used to examine the characteristics of American prisoners, including long-term prisoners, and to trace changes in these populations over time. Tables 2.5, 2.6, and 2.7 show characteristics of state prisoners from the 1974, 1979, 1986, and 1991 state prisoner surveys. For each survey, inmates have been divided into those who had served less than 5 years (short-term), 5 to 10 years (long-term), and more than 10 years (very long-term) *as of the date of the survey.* The tables present national estimates based on weighted samples and are subject to sampling error.[1]

The first observation one makes about the state prisoner population from these services is that the estimated population rose 280%, from less than 186,000 to more than 705,000 between 1974 and 1991 (see Table 2.5). The percentage of state prisoners who had served 5 or more years in prison varied from 12% to 17% between 1974 and 1991. In 1974, 15% had served 5 or more years as of the survey date, 12% in 1979, 15% in 1986, and 17% in 1991. Very long-term inmates, those who had served more than 10 years as of the survey date, ranged from 2% to 5% of state prisoners during this period. Thus, the population of long-term inmates in American prisons grew proportionately to the growth in the prisoner population generally between 1974 and 1991.

In all three surveys the entire state prisoner population was predominantly male, but females consistently made up a smaller percentage of long-term inmates. In the longest serving group (more than 10 years), women were less than 2% of such state prisoners. The racial composition of the prisoner population underwent a subtle change. The percentage of African American inmates in the short-term inmate group remained constant between 1974 and 1991, at approximately 47% of short-termers. In the long-term group (5 to 10 years), the African American percentage rose in 1979 and 1986 over the 1974 survey but returned to its earlier level in the 1991 survey. Among very long-term prisoners, however, the percentage who were African American increased from 42% in 1974 to 53% in 1991. The racial composition of the very long-term group shifted

(text continued on page 19)

TABLE 2.2 Prison Inmates Serving Life Sentences

By selected characteristics, on Sept. 30, 1992

Jurisdiction	Number Serving Life Sentence Male	Number Serving Life Sentence Female	Offense First Degree Murder	Offense Second Degree Murder	Offense Kidnapping	Offense Drug Charges	Offense Sex Offenses	Offense Other	Have a Specific Sentence of Life Without Parole	Number Sentenced to Life Without Parole Male	Number Sentenced to Life Without Parole Female
Alabama	2,548	58	—	—	—	—	—	—	Yes	685	11
Arizona	739	24	336	94	16	34	87	196	Yes	196	11
Arkansas	467	27	280	2	11	14	126	61	No	X	X
California	11,275	492	6,287	4,206	866	—	—	406	Yes	995	42
Colorado	500	12	386	(a)	(a)	(a)	(a)	(a)	Yes	22	1
Connecticut	149	3	130	8	6	0	2	6	No[b]	X	X
Delaware	397	6	143	77	15	2	141	25	Yes	95	5
District of Columbia	774	10	313	140	21	2	51	257	Yes	10	0
Florida	4,767	145	2,352	608	169	23	970	790	Yes	2,332	44
Georgia	3,236	145	2,100	NA	85	325	475	396	No	X	X
Hawaii	3	0	153	2	3	1	26	22	Yes	28	3
Idaho	189	6	65	32	13	3	64	19	Yes	174	6
Illinois	551	14	472	0	0	1	24	68	Yes	532	14
Iowa	374	17	311	0	65	0	14	1	Yes	374	17
Kansas	488	19	370	0	127[c]	2	0	8[d]	No[f]	X	X
Kentucky	562	24	337	11[e]	27	0	52	159	No[f]	8	X
Louisiana	2,158	72	602	952	33	101	504	38	Yes	2,083	71
Maine	44	0	43	0	1	0	0	—	Yes	11	0
Massachusetts	925	24	399	492	0	0	35	23	Yes	389	10
Michigan	3,086	107	1,721	643	53	149	248	379	Yes	1,729	66
Minnesota	153	7	160	0	0	0	0	0	Yes	1	0
Mississippi	49	0	NA	NA	NA	NA	NA	NA	Yes	151	—
Missouri	1,166	52	572	334	4	6	99	203	Yes	318	24
Montana	27	0	13	0	3	1	2	8	No[g]	8[h]	0
Nebraska	79	5	111	64	7	0	1	1	No	X	X
Nevada	903	31	358	89	53	9	366	59	Yes	214	9
New Hampshire	26	2	28	0	0	0	0	0	Yes	26	2
New Jersey	890	20	728	58	18	22	21	63	No	X	X
New Mexico	156	9	137	12	0	0	11	5	No	X	X

New York	9,033	444	(i)	4,726	100	3,277	97	1,277	No	X	X
North Carolina	2,171	66	646	606	42	2	719	222	No	X	X
North Dakota	12	1	13	0	0	11	0	0	No	X	X
Ohio	2,935	143	1,293	1,089	31	11	254	431	No	X	X
Oklahoma	929	62	657	109	14	17	52	139	Yes	87	8
Oregon	439	23	462	0	0	0	0	0	Yes	17	2
Pennsylvania	2,324	93	1,662	593	0	0	0	162	Yes	—	—
Rhode Island	83	0	58	11	1	0	8	5	Yes	10[j]	0
South Carolina	1,290	67	1,045	0	167	0	1	144	No[k]	X	X
South Dakota	99	3	60	12	8	0	4	18	Yes	99	3
Tennessee	1,246	44	739	87	31	5	132	296	No	X	X
Texas	4,152	85	1,731[l]	X	63	238	660	1,545	No	X	X
Utah	41[m]	X	40	0	1	0	—	—	Yes	NA	NA
Vermont	14	0	7	7	0	0	0	0	Yes	NA	NA
Virginia	1,248	25	688	24	147	1	166	247	No	X	X
Washington	588	20	305	84	2	2	119	96	Yes	125[n]	7
West Virginia	254	6	250	0	10	0	0	0	Yes	124	1
Wisconsin	498	25	519	0	0	0	0	4	No	X	X
Wyoming	108	3	83	13	4	0	10	1	Yes	0	0
Federal Bureau of Prisons	1,177	41	492	NA	139	292	11	284	Yes	(o)	(o)

SOURCE: *Corrections Compendium* (1993, pp. 7-14)
Reprinted from Maguire, Pastore, & Flanagan (1993)

NOTE: This information was collected through a survey of the 50 states, the District of Columbia, and the Federal Bureau of Prisons conducted in the fall of 1992. Alaska, Indiana, and Maryland did not provide information on life-term inmates. The source presents the information as submitted by the responding agencies. No attempt is made by the source to verify the information received.

a. Individuals convicted of these crimes are sentenced to life as habitual offenders. Lifers include 12 offenders with indeterminate sentences (sentenced prior to 1979) and 42 sex offenders sentenced to life but eligible for parole after 1 day.

b. However, certain murder offenses are not parole eligible.

c. Aggravated kidnapping.

d. Out-of-state compact offenders.

e. Manslaughter.

f. Life without parole ended in 1975; however, there are eight remaining inmates serving life-without-parole sentences.

g. Parole ineligibility exists as a separate sentencing enhancement, independent of the crime.

h. For parole ineligibility only.

i. Statute was declared unconstitutional.

j. Includes four in Rhode Island, two from Rhode Island serving out of state, and four from other states serving in Rhode Island.

k. However, a lifer can be ineligible for parole because of the repeat violent offender statute.

l. Includes all homicide offenders with life sentences.

m. Includes both males and females.

n. Includes 11 death sentences.

o. The Sentencing Reform Act of 1984 eliminated parole; therefore any life sentence imposed is, by definition, life without parole. Very few inmates in Bureau of Prisons facilities remain under the old system.

15

TABLE 2.3 First Releases From State Prison, 1991: Sentence Length, Minimum Time to Be Served, and Time Served in Prison, by Offense

First Releases From State Prison

Most Serious Offense	Percentage of Releases	Maximum Sentence Length[b]		Minimum Time to Be Served[c]		Time Served in Prison		Percentage of Maximum Sentence Length[a]	
		Median[d]	*Mean*[e]	*Median*[d]	*Mean*[e]	*Median*	*Mean*	*Estimated Minimum Time to Be Served*	*Actual Time Served*
All offenses	100.0%	48 mos.	71 mos.	20 mos.	28 mos.	18 mos.	25 mos.	39.4%	35.2%
Violent offenses	27.1%	72 mos.	101 mos.	30 mos.	41 mos.	28 mos.	40 mos.	40.6%	39.6%
Homicide	3.0	144	164	59	74	52	68	45.1	41.5
Murder/nonnegligent manslaughter	1.6	240	219	72	99	83	92	45.2	42.0
Murder	1.2	240	227	83	110	88	97	48.5	42.7
Nonnegligent manslaughter	0.4	180	199	66	69	77	77	34.7	38.7
Negligent manslaughter	1.3	84	105	30	42	29	37	40.0	35.2
Unspecified homicide	0.0*	216	189	216	153	59	76	81.0	40.2
Kidnapping	0.4	96	120	36	49	37	49	40.8	40.8
Rape	1.8	96	120	30	45	46	57	37.5	47.5
Other sexual assault	3.3	60	82	24	34	25	32	41.5	39.0
Robbery	12.2	72	106	30	41	30	40	38.7	37.7
Assault	5.7	60	71	24	29	19	26	40.8	36.6
Other violent	0.8	48	59	23	34	19	24	57.6	40.7
Property offenses	33.3%	48 mos.	63 mos.	24 mos.	24 mos.	16 mos.	21 mos.	38.1%	33.3%
Burglary	14.6	54	77	24	29	20	26	37.7	33.8
Larceny/theft	8.5	36	49	16	19	13	17	38.8	34.7
Motor vehicle theft	1.9	36	46	24	27	13	17	58.7	37.0
Arson	0.7	60	88	19	27	20	28	30.7	31.8
Fraud	4.0	36	53	15	20	13	18	37.7	34.0
Stolen property	2.6	36	54	17	17	15	19	31.5	35.2
Other property	1.0	36	49	14	23	11	16	46.9	32.7

First Releases From State Prison

Most Serious Offense	Percentage of Releases	Maximum Sentence Length[b]		Minimum Time to Be Served[c]		Time Served in Prison		Percentage of Maximum Sentence Length[a]	
		Median[d]	Mean[e]	Median[d]	Mean[e]	Median	Mean	Estimated Minimum Time to Be Served	Actual Time Served
Drug offenses	31.2%	48 mos.	60 mos.	18 mos.	22 mos.	15 mos.	18 mos.	36.7%	30.0%
Possession	7.8	48	49	18	20	13	17	40.8	34.7
Trafficking	18.9	48	63	19	24	16	20	38.1	31.7
Other/unspecified drug	4.5	36	62	12	18	13	17	29.0	27.4
Public-order offenses	7.0%	36 mos.	45 mos.	12 mos.	18 mos.	13 mos.	18 mos.	40.0%	40.0%
Weapons	2.4	48	49	20	21	15	21	42.9	42.9
Driving while intoxicated	1.6	36	41	12	13	12	16	31.7	39.0
Other public-order	3.0	36	45	11	18	12	18	40.0	40.0
Other offenses	1.3%	48 mos.	76 mos.	24 mos.	30 mos.	19 mos.	24 mos.	39.5%	31.6%
Number of releases	95,013								

SOURCE: Perkins (1994)

NOTE: Data are based on all first releases with a sentence of more than 1 year for whom the most serious offense, sentence length, minimum time to be served, and time served in prison were reported. All data exclude persons released from prison by escape, death, transfer, appeal, or detainer.

*Less than 0.05%.

a. The percentage of maximum sentence length is calculated by dividing the mean minimum time to be served and the mean time served by the mean maximum sentence length. Detailed percentages may differ because reported means are rounded.

b. Maximum sentence length is the sentence length that an offender may be required to serve for the most serious offense.

c. Minimum time to be served is the jurisdiction's estimate of the shortest time that each admitted prisoner must serve before becoming eligible for release.

d. Includes sentences of life without parole, life plus additional years, life, and death.

e. Excludes sentences of life without parole, life plus additional years, life, and death.

17

TABLE 2.4 Sentence Length, Time Served Since Admission, and Total Time Expected to Serve of State Prisoners, by Type of Offense, United States, 1991 (estimated)

	Sentence Length		Time Served Since Admission		Total Time Expected to Serve	
	Median	Mean	Median	Mean	Median	Mean
Total	108 mos.	150 mos.	17 mos.	32 mos.	37 mos.	66 mos.
Violent offenses	180	216	31	49	70	100
Murder	Life	381	69	81	160	178
Manslaughter	156	185	26	39	66	81
Sexual assault	180	211	27	42	66	95
Robbery	144	200	27	41	58	82
Assault	114	158	18	32	43	68
Property offenses	60 mos.	114 mos.	12 mos.	20 mos.	26 mos.	43 mos.
Burglary	96	140	15	24	32	51
Larceny	48	72	9	15	18	34
Drug offenses	60 mos.	95 mos.	11 mos.	16 mos.	24 mos.	36 mos.
Possession	54	81	9	13	20	28
Trafficking	72	104	12	17	26	40
Public-order offenses	48 mos.	82 mos.	9 mos.	16 mos.	20 mos.	33 mos.

SOURCE: Beck et al. (1993)

TABLE 2.5 Demographic Characteristics of State Prisoners, by Time Served Groups, United States, Selected Years 1974-1991 (estimated percentages)

	1974			1979			1986			1991		
	<5	5-10	>10	<5	5-10	>10	<5	5-10	>10	<5	5-10	>10
Sex												
Male	96	99	100	96	98	99	95	98	99	94	97	98
Female	4	1	*	4	2	1	5	2	1	6	3	2
Race												
White	50	51	57	51	41	44	51	43	41	49	49	45
African American	48	47	42	47	56	54	46	53	54	47	47	53
Asian, Pacific Islander				*	*	*	1	1	2	*	1	1
American Indian				2	2	2	2	2	3	2	2	2
Other	2	2	*	*	0	0	*	*	*	1	*	0
Age at admission												
Less than 21	29	34	31	24	24	25	17	22	24	12	19	23
21 to 25	31	25	24	32	30	37	29	30	29	24	28	34
26 and over	40	40	45	43	45	38	54	48	47	63	53	43
Education												
Less than 8th grade	12	20	32	12	22	26	10	15	21	9	11	14
8th-11th grade	56	56	50	58	53	52	50	52	53	56	57	56
Graduated 12th grade	23	18	11	21	18	16	16	14	13	22	20	18
1 year or more college	9	5	7	8	6	6	24	20	14	13	11	11
Employment												
Full-time	61	66	65	60	62	64	56	61	65	55	54	61
Part-time	7	5	8	10	8	7	12	10	8	12	10	10
No	31	29	27	30	30	29	31	30	27	32	36	29
Total	84	10	5	88	10	2	84	12	3	83	12	5
TOTAL	185,790			274,097			447,642			705,782		

SOURCE: *Surveys of Inmates of State Correctional Facilities*, U.S. Department of Justice. Data made available through the Inter-University Consortium for Political and Social Research, University of Michigan.
*Less than 1%.

TABLE 2.6 Offense and Prior Incarcerations of State Prisoners, by Time Served Groups, United States, Selected Years 1974-1991 (estimated percentages)

	1974			1979			1986			1991		
	<5	5-10	>10	<5	5-10	>10	<5	5-10	>10	<5	5-10	>10
Current offense												
Murder	16	31	37	14	41	51	12	34	61	9	33	55
Sex offenses	6	10	10	6	8	17	9	12	8	9	15	11
Robbery	22	23	21	24	30	19	20	28	20	13	22	18
Assault	5	3	3	7	4	2	7	4	2	7	5	3
Burglary	19	17	10	20	6	2	18	9	4	13	10	3
Larceny	7	5	5	5	2	1	7	2	*	6	2	*
Motor vehicle theft	2	2	3	2	*	*	1	*	*	2	*	0
Drugs	11	3	5	8	3	2	10	2	1	25	5	1
Other	12	6	5	15	6	5	16	8	4	16	8	7
Prior incarcerations												
Priors	63	68	65	57	62	64	56	54	54	55	54	55
No Priors	37	32	35	43	38	36	44	46	46	44	45	44

SOURCE: *Surveys of Inmates of State Correctional Facilities*, U.S. Department of Justice. Data made available through the Inter-University Consortium for Political and Social Research, University of Michigan.
*Less than 1%.

TABLE 2.7 Substance Abuse at Time of Offense for State Prisoners, by Time Served Groups, United States, Selected Years 1974-1991 (estimated percentages)

	1974			1979			1986			1991		
	<5	5-10	>10	<5	5-10	>10	<5	5-10	>10	<5	5-10	>10
Alcohol Use												
Yes	42	48	52	48	45	44	37	38	34	31	35	37
No	57	52	47	34	35	32	46	45	45	49	46	43
Do not know	*	*	*	0	0	*	0	0	0	0	0	0
NA	*	*	*	18	23	24	18	17	21	19	18	20
Drug Use												
Yes	26	19	12	33	24	12	36	37	22	30	32	26
No	67	73	82	44	41	38	44	40	44	22	21	23
Do not know/NA	6	8	6	22	34	49	21	23	35	47	47	51
If yes												
Heroin	13	10	7	11	15	12	7	8	6	6	6	5
Cocaine	*	0	0	4	2	0	9	6	3	9	7	3
Marijuana	7	4	2	19	10	6	20	16	8	8	14	13

SOURCE: *Surveys of Inmates of State Correctional Facilities*, U.S. Department of Justice. Data made available through the Inter-University Consortium for Political and Social Research, University of Michigan.
*Less than 1%.

from a white majority in 1974 to an African American majority since 1979.

The aging of the state prisoner population is reflected in the *Survey of Inmates* data, although it is less pronounced among long-term and very long-term inmates. The percentage of inmates who were 26 or older at admission rose 58% among short-term inmates between 1974 and 1991, and rose 32% among long-termers, but fell 4% among very long-term prisoners. In terms of educational attainment, the surveys show that state prisoners' educational backgrounds improved slightly between 1974 and 1991, but inmates in the long-term categories remained comparatively lower than their colleagues. Pre-prison unemployment rates among the longer-term inmates were slightly lower than among shorter-term prisoners. The surveys show that about one third of state prisoners were unemployed during the month prior to their arrest, and that unemployment rate has been stable across the four surveys.

Table 2.6 shows the distribution of offenses for state prisoners from 1974 to 1991. The data reveal several notable trends. First, the long-term and very long-term inmate groups were increasingly characterized by conviction for murder, sex offenses, and robbery. In 1974, for example, 68% of very long-term prisoners were convicted of these three offense categories; in 1979, 87%; in 1986 the figure was 89%; and in 1991 the figure was 84%. These data suggest a hardening of the long-term inmate population over time. At the same time, the percentage of long-term and very long-term inmates convicted of burglary, larceny, and other property crimes declined across the four surveys. Note also that the percentage of prisoners convicted of drug offenses increased markedly in the short-term prisoner category between 1986 and 1991, illustrating the changing laws and sentencing practices embodied in the national "war on drugs" of the late 1980s (Irwin & Austin, 1994). Given that many drug offenders were sentenced to long prison terms with mandatory minimum sentences as a result of increased drug law enforcement, it is likely that many of these offenders will appear among the ranks of long-term and very long-term inmates.

Table 2.7 shows the self-reported substance abuse records of state prisoners. The data report on whether these prisoners were under the influence of alcohol and/or drugs *at the time of the offense* for which they were serving time. Between one third and two fifths of state prisoners were under the influence of alcohol when they committed the offense that brought them to prison, and between one quarter and one third of these offenders reported being under the influence of one or more drugs at the time of the offense. Across each time served category, alcohol use declined slightly across the four surveys, but drug use increased. Self-reported heroin used declined while cocaine and marijuana use increased. The largest increase in drug use has been among very long-term prisoners (who served more than 10 years).

CONCLUSION

Taken together, the available national data on long-term prisoners and long-term incarceration suggest a growing reliance on imprisonment, and on long prison terms, as a response to crime. As prison populations soar in state and federal correctional systems in the United States, an important component of the increase is that more offenders will serve longer prison terms. A single offender sentenced to a 25-year minimum sentence will occupy a cell for 25 person years. In financial terms, if the cost of incarceration in a jurisdiction is $15,000 per cell per year (a low estimate for maximum security confinement), a single 25-year inmate represents an "investment" of $375,000 for operating costs alone (not including construction costs or debt service to build the prison). A "standard" 2,200 bed prison filled with such offenders will accrue life-cycle costs of $825 million over a 25-year period. Thus long-term confinement represents a major financial and human resource investment in America.

More important than the financial obligation posed by long-term imprisonment, however, is the penological challenge long-term prisoners represent. As noted earlier, the *idea* of the penitentiary never envisioned massive institutions in which thousands of offenders spent decades in penal confinement. There are few if any analogous situations within which human behavior and adaptation have been studied (Cohen & Taylor, 1972). As many of the chapters in this volume indicate, adaptation to long-term imprisonment is a complex issue. For correctional officials, designing prison regimes for such inmates which permit safety, productivity, growth, and humane containment is a formidable task. We must never lose sight of the fact that despite their long prison sentences, more than 95% of all state prisoners confined today will someday be released. I believe that knowledge and insights gained from studying inmates and correctional personnel struggling with long-term confinement will be beneficial for all prisoners, for prison staff, for the taxpayers who support the correctional apparatus, and for the citizens who will share communities with these inmates upon their release.

NOTE

1. For information on sampling methods, estimation procedures, and other matters concerning the *Surveys of Inmates of State Correctional Facilities*, see the documentation provided by the National Archive of Criminal Justice Data. The 1974 survey is ICPSR study number 7811, the 1979 survey is 7856, the 1986 survey is 8711, and the 1991 survey is 6068. Contact the Inter-University Consortium for Political and Social Research, P.O. Box 1248, Ann Arbor, MI 48106 at (800) 999-0960. Information on the various state inmate surveys is also published in annual editions of the *Sourcebook of Criminal Justice Statistics*, published by the U.S. Government Printing Office.

REFERENCES

American Bar Association. (1968). Project on standards for criminal justice. *Sentencing alternatives and procedures.* Approved draft.

Beck, A., Gilliard, D., Greenfeld, L., Harlow, C., Hester, T., Jankowsi, L., Snell, T., Stephan, J., & Morton, D. (1993). *Survey of state prison inmates, 1991* (NCJ-136949). Washington, DC: U.S. Department of Justice, Bureau of Justice Statistics.

Cohen, S., & Taylor, L. (1972). *Psychological survival: The experience of long-term imprisonment.* New York: Vintage.

Corrections compendium. (1993, January). Lincoln, NE: CEGA Publishing.

Irwin, J., & Austin, J. (1994). *It's about time: America's imprisonment binge.* Belmont, CA: Wadsworth.

Lynch, J. (1988). A comparison of prison use in England, Canada, West Germany, and the United States: A limited test of the punitive hypothesis. *Journal of Criminal Law and Criminology, 79*(1), 180-217.

Lynch, J. (1993). A cross-national comparison of the length of custodial sentences for serious crimes. *Justice Quarterly, 10*(4), 639-660.

Maguire, K., Pastore, A., & Flanagan, T. (1993). *Sourcebook of criminal justice statistics—1992.* Washington, DC: Government Printing Office.

Mauer, M. (1991). *Americans behind bars: A comparison of international rates of incarceration.* Washington DC: The Sentencing Project.

Mauer, M. (1992). *Americans behind bars: One year later.* Washington, DC: The Sentencing Project.

Perkins, C. (1994). *National corrections reporting program, 1991* (NCJ-145861). Washington, DC: U.S. Department of Justice, Bureau of Justice Statistics.

Rothman, D. (1971). *The discovery of the asylum: Social order and disorder in the new republic.* Boston: Little-Brown.

State of Texas. (1992, July 20). *An overview of prison sentences and time served in Texas. Special report.* Austin: Criminal Justice Policy Council.

3

Long-Term Offenders in Canada

John R. Weekes

The Task Force on Long-Term Sentences, commissioned by the Correctional Service of Canada, recently tabled its recommendations concerning the management and treatment of inmates serving long prison terms. Highlights of the Task Force's 37 recommendations include:

- the development of a management model for long-term sentences;
- staff training to meet the specific needs of long-term offenders; and
- the development of programming for long-term offenders.

Supporting these recommendations, recent research has underscored the unique nature of this offender group and has argued that innovative methods of service delivery and programming opportunities are necessary to meet the needs of long-term offenders adequately.

This article strives to provide a clearer picture of the characteristics of the long-term offender population, based on an overview of available statistical information. It should be noted that this is a diverse group of offenders. In this article, the term "long-term offenders" refers to offenders serving life sentences, indeterminate sentences and determinate sentences of 10 years or more. A sampling of criminal offences yielding long-term sentences includes:

- life sentences—first-degree/capital murder, second-degree/non-capital murder, manslaughter, attempted murder, etc.;
- indeterminate sentences—dangerous offender, dangerous sexual offender and habitual criminal designations and commitments on a Lieutenant Governor's Warrant; and
- determinate sentences of 10 years or more—aggravated sexual assault, robbery, kidnapping and abduction, etc.

TOTAL FEDERAL-OFFENDER POPULATION

Long-term offenders comprise about one quarter (25.3%) of the total federal-offender population (including incarcerated offenders and those on some form of release). On 31 January 1992, there were 22,121 offenders under the jurisdiction of the Correctional Service of Canada; of these, 5,595 were serving long-term sentences.

AUTHOR'S NOTE: This article was prepared with the assistance of Sue Séguin, Bart Millson and David Robinson of the Research and Statistics Branch, Correctional Service of Canada.
NOTE: Reprinted with permission from *Forum for Corrections Research*, Vol. 4, No. 2, June, 1992, pp. 3-7. Copyright 1992 by Correctional Service of Canada.

Almost three out of five long-term offenders (57.5%) were incarcerated, while the rest were on some form of release.

TYPES OF LONG-TERM SENTENCES

Almost three of every five long-term sentences are either life sentences for first- or second-degree murder, or life or indeterminate sentences for some other offence.

Specific types of long-term sentences, in decreasing order of frequency, are:

- determinate sentence of 10 years or more—41.4% of long-term offenders (10.5% of the total offender population);
- second-degree/non-capital murder—37.9% of long-term offenders (9.6% of the total offender population);
- other life and indeterminate sentences—10.8% of long-term offenders (2.7% of the total offender population); and
- first-degree/capital murder—9.8% of long-term offenders (2.5% of the total offender population).

INCARCERATED POPULATION

Just over one quarter of the incarcerated offender population (27.8%) is serving a long-term sentence (excluding those on day parole). On 31 January 1992, 3,449 inmates were serving long-term sentences under the jurisdiction of the Correctional Service of Canada.

Most long-term inmates (90.7%) are housed in either medium- or maximum-security institutions:

- maximum security—45.9% of all long-term offenders;
- medium security—44.8%;
- minimum security—6.3%; and
- community correctional centres or provincial jails—3%.

CONDITIONAL RELEASE POPULATION

About one of every five offenders on conditional release (22%) is a long-term offender.

On 31 January 1992, there were 2,146 long-term offenders on conditional release. The offence or sentence breakdown of these offenders, in decreasing order of frequency, is:

- determinate sentence of 10 years or more—46.7% of long-term offenders on conditional release (of these, 18.6% are on day parole, 64.4% on full parole and 17% on mandatory supervision);
- second-degree murder—39% (of these, 21.6% are on day parole and 78.4% on full parole);
- other life and indeterminate sentences—10.2% (of these, 14.7% are on day parole, 81.4% on full parole and 3.9% on mandatory supervision); and
- first-degree murder—4.2% (of these, 4.7% are on day parole and 95.3% on full parole).

REGIONAL DISTRIBUTION OF LONG-TERM OFFENDERS

There are marked differences in the distribution of long-term offenders across the regions. Quebec and Ontario have larger proportions of long-term offenders than other regions.

However, when we compare the proportion of long-termers with the proportion of short-termers (i.e., those serving a sentence of less than 10 years) in each region, we see that Quebec and the Pacific region have proportionately more long-term offenders, and the Atlantic and Prairie regions have proportionately fewer long-termers (see Figure 3.1).

The regional distribution of long-term offenders is:

- Atlantic—5.4% of long-term offenders versus 9.7% of all offenders (proportionately fewer long-termers);
- Quebec—34.6% of long-term offenders versus 29.8% of all offenders (proportionately more long-termers);
- Ontario—27.7% of long-term offenders versus 26.6% of all offenders (approximately the same proportion of each);
- Prairies—15.6% of long-term offenders versus 20.9% of all offenders (proportionately fewer long-termers); and

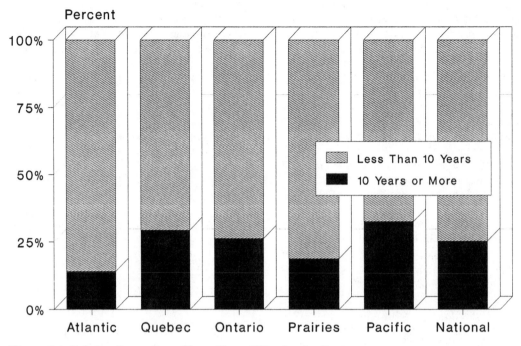

Figure 3.1. Relative Proportion of Long-Term Offenders by Region

- Pacific—16.6% of long-term offenders versus 12.9% of all offenders (proportionately more long-termers).

POPULATION TRENDS

As Figure 3.2 shows, there was a 41.5% increase in the number of long-term offenders under the jurisdiction of the Correctional Service of Canada from 1981 to 1991. During this same period, however, the total incarcerated population grew in a similar manner. On 31 December 1981, there were 2,672 long-term offenders in federal institutions, representing 26.4% of the inmate population. Ten years later, on 31 December 1991, long-termers still represented 26.4% of all inmates; however, the total number of long-termers had grown to 3,782.

ADMISSIONS

From 1981 to 1991, the number of annual admissions of long-term offenders increased from 382 admissions to 453. However, it appears that proportionately fewer long-term of-fenders are being admitted to federal institutions than 10 years ago: in 1981, long-term offenders represented 7.3% of a total 5,248 admissions but by the end of 1991, this percentage had decreased to 6.4% of a total 7,021 admissions.

RELEASES

From 1981 to 1991, the number of annual releases of long-term offenders increased dramatically from 265 to 448. In fact, it appears that we are releasing proportionately more long-term offenders: in 1981, long-term offenders represented 5.6% of a total 4,754 releases, but by 1991, this percentage had increased to 7% of a total 6,392 releases.

PREVIOUS FEDERAL INCARCERATIONS

The number of previous federal incarcerations of long-term offenders and short-term offenders (i.e., those serving sentences of less than 10 years) is strikingly similar. The major-

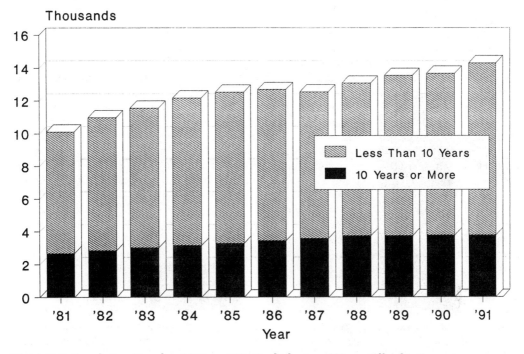

Figure 3.2. Population Trends—1981 to 1991 (Includes Long-Term Offenders)

ity of both groups have no previous federal incarcerations.

On 31 January 1992, the federal incarceration history of our offenders was as follows:

- no previous federal incarcerations—58% of long-termers versus 60.1% of short-termers;
- one previous federal incarceration—18.9% of long-termers versus 16.1% of short-termers; and
- two or more federal incarcerations—23.1% of long-termers versus 23.8% of short-termers.

However, as Figure 3.3 shows, when we divide long-term offenders into those serving life or an indeterminate sentence and those serving a determinate sentence of 10 years or more, we find that those serving a life sentence or an indeterminate sentence are less likely to have two or more previous federal incarcerations.

RECIDIVISM AND RETURN RATES

A group of 294 long-term offenders released in 1986 was followed over a five-year period.

Of every five of these long-term offenders released in 1986:

- three did not have any readmissions or reconvictions (58%);
- one was readmitted for technical violations of parole (19.7%); and
- one was readmitted with new offences (22.8%).

The readmission rate for long-termers serving determinate sentences (i.e., sentences of 10 years or more) was higher than for long-termers serving life or indeterminate sentences (50.8% versus 28. 1%). Of the 75 murderers who were released, only 11 (14.6%) were subsequently reconvicted of a criminal offence. Although some of these offenders were convicted of serious crimes such as aggravated sexual assault and attempted murder, none received subsequent convictions for either murder or manslaughter.

FEMALE LONG-TERM OFFENDERS

On 31 January 1992, there were 491 female offenders under the jurisdiction of the Cor-

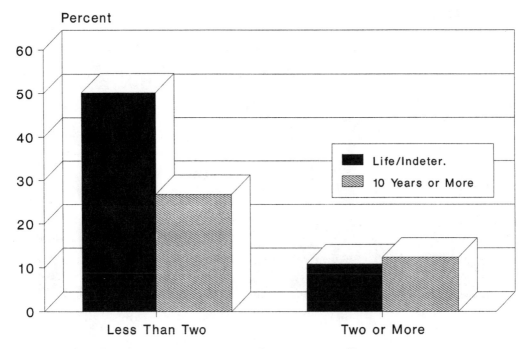

Figure 3.3. Number of Previous Incarcerations by Long-Term Offense Category

rectional Service of Canada, representing 2.2% of the total federal-offender population. Just under one quarter of these women (24%) were serving a long-term sentence.

The proportion of males and females serving long-term sentences is almost identical:

- long-term sentences—24% of female offenders versus 25.3% of male offenders;
- sentences of less than 10 years—76% of female offenders versus 74.7% of male offenders.

However, as Figure 3.4 shows, it seems that female offenders are more likely than males to be serving sentences for murder, whereas males are more likely to be serving other life and indeterminate sentences or determinate sentences of 10 years or more.

AGE

On 31 December 1991, the average long-term offender was almost 38 years old. The oldest long-term offender was 80 years old and the youngest was 17. Interestingly, long-term

offenders as a group appear to be aging: between 31 December 1981 and 31 December 1991, the average age of long-term offenders increased by almost three years, from an average of about 35 years to almost 38 years of age.

As Figure 3.5 illustrates, while the average age of offenders sentenced to other life and indeterminate sentences has remained relatively unchanged, the average age of offenders convicted of first-degree murder, second-degree murder and other determinate sentences has increased. In particular, the average age of offenders convicted of first-degree (capital) murder has increased from about 32 years to 38 years.

In addition, the average age of long-term offenders being admitted into our institutions is also increasing: in 1981, the average age of long-term offenders admitted was about 30 years, whereas in 1991, it was slightly over 34 years.

ETHNICITY

On 31 January 1992, the overwhelming majority of long-term offenders (almost 85%)

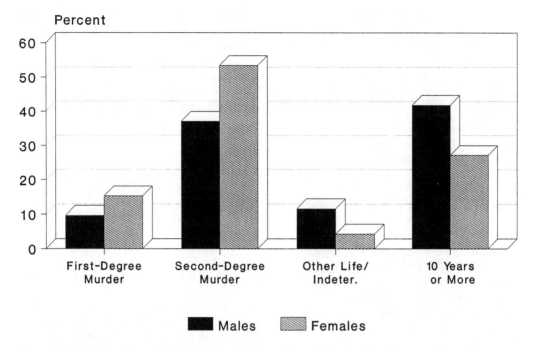

Figure 3.4. Distribution of Male and Female Long-Term Offenders by Sentence Type

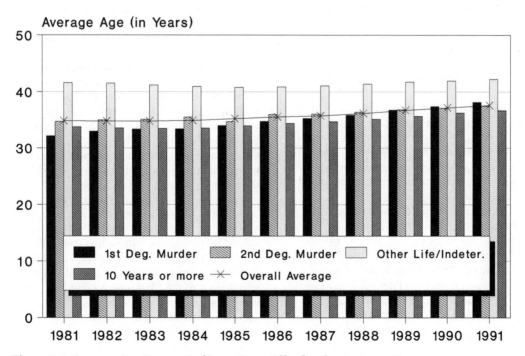

Figure 3.5. Average Age (in years) of Long-Term Offenders by Sentence Type

were Caucasian. The remaining group consisted of inmates from diverse ethnic backgrounds, including native people, Asiatics, blacks and others. The distribution of long-term offenders across ethnic backgrounds is similar to the ethnic distribution for the total offender population, although there was a somewhat higher proportion of Caucasians and a somewhat lower proportion of native people in the long-term offender group.

The ethnic breakdown, in decreasing order of frequency, is:

- Caucasian—84.7% of long-termers versus 80.2% of the total offender population;
- native—6.7% of long-termers versus 9.8% of the total offender population;
- black—2.5% of long-termers versus 3.7% of the total offender population;
- Asiatic—1.4% of long-termers versus 0.9% of the total offender population; and
- other (including not specified)—4.7% of long-termers versus 5.4% of the total offender population.

This distribution suggests that members of diverse ethnic groups (i.e., non-Caucasians) are not overrepresented in the long-term offender population.

MARITAL STATUS

Available data indicate that about half of incarcerated offenders reported their marital status as single. Sentence length appeared to have no bearing on this finding. However, long-term offenders appeared somewhat less likely than other offenders to be involved in common-law relationships.

The breakdown of marital status, in decreasing order of frequency, is:

- single—50.5% of long-term inmates versus 47.5% of short-term inmates;
- common-law—21.5% of long-term inmates versus 28.6% of short-term inmates;

- married—13.5% of long-term inmates versus 11.9% of short-term inmates;
- separated or divorced—11.1 % of long-term inmates versus 10.6% of short-term inmates; and
- other (including not specified)—3.4% of long-term inmates versus 1.4% of short-term inmates.

SUMMARY

About one quarter of the total federal-offender population is serving a long-term sentence (i.e., 10 years or more). This is true of both male and female offender populations. Three out of five long-termers are incarcerated and two out of five are on some form of conditional release.

Quebec and the Pacific region have proportionately more long-term offenders, while the Atlantic and Prairie regions have proportionately fewer. Ontario has a more equitable proportion of long-termers.

During the past 10 years, the number of long-term offenders under federal jurisdiction increased by the same proportion as the number of federal offenders in general. During this same period, federal corrections admitted proportionately fewer long-termers, and released proportionately more long-termers, than offenders in general.

The vast majority of long-termers are Caucasian. About half of all long-term offenders are single, while about one in three is married (includes common-law). During the past 10 years, the average age of long-term offenders has increased by almost three years and is now about 38 years. Offenders serving life sentences for first-degree murder as a group, show the most dramatic increase in age.

Long- and short-term offenders have similar histories of federal incarceration, with the majority of both groups having no previous federal incarceration. After a five-year follow-up, only about one in five long-term offenders had been reconvicted of a criminal offence, while none of the 75 released offenders serving life sentences for murder had been subsequently reconvicted of murder.

PART TWO

■ Long-Term Prisoners on

Long-Term Imprisonment

4

The Long-Termers

Louisiana's Longest Serving Inmates and Why They've Stayed So Long

Ronald Wikberg

Burk Foster

What is a "lifer"? The dictionary definition sounds pretty conclusive: "A person sentenced to imprisonment for life." But as everyone who works in corrections knows (and most members of the public suspect), a life sentence rarely means life. Good-time, parole, and executive clemency are important variables that combine to make a life sentence usually much less lengthy than natural life.

The Bureau of Justice Statistics reports that of those released from a life sentence in 1983, the median time served was 8 years and 7 months; about 20% served 3 years or less (Bureau of Justice Statistics, 1987, p. 47). (On a life sentence? No wonder the public is suspicious.) An earlier report, comparing sentences for several serious crimes in 12 states, found that the average time served for criminal homicide (murder and manslaughter) ranged from a low of 39 months in Oklahoma to a high of 78 months in Ohio (Bureau of Justice Statistics, 1984, p. 3). Not all of these were life

sentences, obviously, but most of them sounded much longer in court than the 3 to 6½ years they turned out to be in prison. We can understand, then, why "lifers" might be smirking when their life sentences are imposed; they know the odds are in their favor.

But aren't prisons filling up with old men? Haven't the experts been warning us that we have to begin preparing for the "graying" of our prison population? It is true that the prison population is aging, from a median age of 26 in 1979 to a median of 28 in 1986. Several circumstances appear to be involved here: increasing crime among those older than 50; the gradual aging of the society from which prisoners come; a trend toward longer sentences for violent offenders, now in the statistical majority in the national prison population; and the accumulation of many older habitual offenders in prison. Most of the inmates older than 50 now in prison are there either for first offenses or for failing to "burn out" on crime

AUTHORS' NOTE: This is a revised version of paper presented to the annual meeting of the Academy of Criminal Justice Sciences, Washington, D.C., March 29, 1989.
NOTE: Reprinted from *The Prison Journal*, Vol. 80, No. 1, Spring/Summer 1990, pp. 9-14. Copyright 1990 by Sage Publications, Inc.

as middle-aged criminals are supposed to do. They are back for their 3rd or 4th or 10th rap (likely a much longer rap than what they started with) instead of going into retirement. As Kevin Krajick (1979) pointed out in his article, "Growing Old in Prison," some years ago, "The inmate who has served a true life sentence for one crime committed in his youth is relatively rare."

But every big prison does have a few of them, worn, dusty men who might once have been black or white or brown but whose rightful color now is gray—prison gray from all the years they've lived behind bars. You can see them, tending flower gardens, working in hospitals, sometimes left to their own menial chores away from the younger men who nod at them and call them "Pops," afraid to look too long for fear that the old ones' bad luck will rub off and they, too, will end up old in prison. Somehow these old men have managed to beat the odds, but in reverse; they have "slipped through the cracks" and stayed in prison while their partners in crime got out and resumed their lives in the free world. They've done bad things, no doubt, murders and rapes and robberies and drug deals, but men who've done worse crimes have come after them, served their time, and gone home. Somehow they remain, the old-timers, as permanent as the walls that define their world.

These are the men we call the "long-termers," the odd few for whom a life sentence truly meant life, or as close to it as most prisons are likely to come. There aren't many of them; though with sentencing trends as they are at present, one day there will probably be a lot more. Real long-termers at the Louisiana State Penitentiary at Angola are only 31 in number. As of early 1988, these inmates had served a continuous sentence of 25 years or longer. They are a select group, the present and soon-to-be-inducted members of the "million dollar club," based on recent cost estimates of the National Council on Crime and Delinquency to confine a prisoner for a natural life sentence (which they estimated at 30 years).

A statistical description of these 31 convicts shows that 27 are black and 4 are white. Seventeen were confined for murder and 14 for aggravated rape. The 4 whites were all confined for killing whites; of the blacks, 14 were confined for murder and 13 for rape (10 of the 13 for raping a white female). Nineteen of the crime victims were white and 12 were black. Seventeen of Louisiana's parishes are represented on the list. Orleans Parish, which includes New Orleans, has 9. The inmates ranged in age from 42 to 71; most are in their 50s and 60s, after having been confined an average of 29 years.

Although the longest-serving of them was imprisoned in 1948, most entered in the 1950s and 1960s, when a life sentence in Louisiana meant that inmates served only 10 years and 6 months before going to the Pardon Board. The great majority were granted clemency and released right away. Angola's present warden estimates that no more than 5% of the lifers were kept in prison beyond the arbitrary 10½-year point. How did these 31 men get into the category of "the undeserving" and continue on in confinement?

From prison records and personal interviews conducted with each long-termer, several recurring themes emerged. There are circumstances relating to the prison experience, to the inmate's own personality or state of mind, and to how the outside world remembers him that seemed to have direct bearing on the length of this term of imprisonment.

We found four main circumstances in the long-termers' background that set them apart from other lifers who have won earlier release:

1. An early record of frequent, perhaps serious, prison misconduct.
2. Strong opposition to release by the victim, the community, the court and law enforcement officials.
3. Lack of outside assistance.
4. Lack of serious, continuing effort by the inmate to win his release.

Not all of these circumstances apply equally to each of the 31 men in a precise formula, but a portrait does emerge from their combination that describes how a long-termer is created. The portrait begins with a poor young man (most likely black) who commits a homicide or a rape. He is legally ignorant and is given appointed counsel, who seems to take little interest in his case. He is about equally likely to plead guilty or be convicted at trial; he is given the same life sentence regardless.

When he gets to prison he gets off to a bad start, fighting with other inmates or staff and earning a reputation as a troublemaker. He fights the system long enough to earn a bad name that will follow him into middle age (and perhaps eventually old age as well).

For years he may make only the barest effort to be released. He does his time, works, settles down into the routine of prison life. When it begins to bother him that everyone else has gone home and he is still in prison, he finds that his resources are sorely limited. His family has forgotten him or is unable to help. The only ones who remember him, it seems, are his victims and officials of the legal system. So the long-termer waits, serving 20, 25, 30 years, hardly daring to hope that some day the right set of circumstances will somehow come together and he will go free.

All of these men came to Angola convicted of violent crimes. At the time they entered prison, they ranged in age from 16 to 41. The great majority of them were young, no older than 30. The Angola that they came to, in the '50s and '60s, was a tough, old-fashioned prison farm. There were few "free world" guards. Inmates armed with shotguns and rifles guarded other inmates who worked the fields. Domination of younger, weaker inmates, with or without the cooperation of the inmate guards, was a common practice.

Several of the long-termers spoke of their struggle to survive in this brutal, primitive environment. One man, who came to prison in 1952 to serve one life sentence and then got a death sentence after killing another inmate in a 1954 knife fight, remembers: "If you did not stand up as a man, you would end up being treated as a woman. Getting killed at Angola was a way of life here then."

Another inmate recalls being "brought down the Walk in 1961 and thrown into the jungle. The security captain told me, 'Son, get yourself an ole man, do what he say, and be a good prisoner.'" But he was determined not to be turned into what Angola inmates called a "gal-boy," a prison whore. Instead he fought back, earning a reputation as a bad man to cross. He says today, "I ain't never figured it out. I got lost in the wild and violent ways of Angola during the bad years. You had to fight to survive. I think I hurt myself by trying to keep up with the fittest instead of trying other ways of coping. But I was young, ignorant—but I had no malice in my heart. I had to be macho to survive and maintain my manhood."

Similar attitudes and patterns of behavior show up in several of the long-termers who were young men in those days. At least three

of them killed men in prison, and others received additional time for assault or escape. If you look at their prison records in more recent years, however, you see that many of them have been model inmates over their last 10 or 15 years in confinement. The process of aging among the long-termers as individuals and the generally improved security environment at Angola after 1975 (accomplished by tripling the number of guards) have dramatically reduced the incidence of violent behavior among the inmates in this group.

Not all of the long-termers were trouble-makers. One is a first offender with an excellent work record and no serious disciplinary infractions in 30 years at Angola. Another built a reputation over 31 years as a quiet man, respected by both prisoners and staff. The only write-ups he remembers were many years ago, for "leaving [his] socks on his bed and stuff like that." And another, in 37 years at Angola, had only 13 disciplinary reports.

One common thread connecting the long-termers is that, as they have gotten older, they have been given more freedom of movement and responsibility. Practically all of them are now trusties, except for a half dozen who are so mentally or physically disabled that they cannot work at all. Many of them have held important work assignments, the kind where a man has to show up day after day and do a good job. Most of them, having accumulated enough age and seniority by now to avoid true hard labor, are in prison "retirement," assigned to light duty jobs as orderlies. At 71, the oldest inmate spends his time tending two beds of rosebushes at the Main Prison. It is doubtful that prison authorities now consider him or any other of the long-termers as either dangerous or escape risks. They have lived long enough to overcome the violence that marked their lives as young men.

Despite this evidence of change, there are those who do not see the long-termers as quiet, harmless old men. Frequently victims and their families, as well as prosecutors and law enforcement officials, continue to oppose the efforts of the long-termers to earn release from prison. A few of the inmates draw vehement opposition whenever their cases appear before the Pardon Board or Parole Board. One man's application for clemency was rejected three times in the '70s and again in 1981 because of strong opposition from the community where he killed two deputy sheriffs in 1958. Two other long-termers were rejected for parole, according to the Parole Board chairman, because of strenuous objection from law enforcement and judicial officials, three decades after their crimes. In their interviews some of the inmates found it difficult to believe that there could be such opposition, that principals in their cases could harbor such strong feelings for so long; or even worse, that their reputations could be handed down for the next generation to hate.

The long-termers have few resources with which to counter outside opposition. Almost all of them had appointed counsel, who years ago performed only the most perfunctory role in assisting their clients. At least 16 of the 31 pleaded guilty, on the advice of counsel, to avoid the possible imposition of the death penalty; for several, that was the last they saw of their attorneys. They have had to struggle in the years since to pursue legal appeals or to get their cases into clemency channels.

"Why am I still here? I'd sure like to know," one long-termer said, after serving 25 years for killing another black youth in a knife fight in New Orleans in 1962. "I don't know how or why it works like that. . . . My momma is poor and I can't afford a lawyer, so maybe that is why."

Practically all of the long-termers are poor and most have gradually lost contact with their families. Their parents have grown old and died, their brothers and sisters have stopped visiting, they end up old men, alone. Prison authorities everywhere have long said how important maintaining contact with the outside world is for long-term inmates. But one man has had only 7 visits in 30 years, another 12 visits in 29 years, another 10 visits in 28 years, another 10 visits in 26 years, another 1 visit in 28 years, another 1 visit in 28 years, and yet another no visits in 28 years.

Hearing accounts like these, from man after man, one begins to sense how estranged from the outside world the long-termers feel, how they come to think of prison as their natural home, how they gave up on a free world that long ago lost interest in them.

We heard repeatedly that they had come to prison believing in the "10-6" rule. One man reported, "The DA, the judge, and my lawyer said to plead guilty and I would be there 10 years and 6 months if I kept my record clean. I did, but they never let me go."

Another long-termer said almost exactly the same thing. "The judge, the DA, and the state-appointed lawyer all told me to be good and in 10 years I would be out," the 59-year-old inmate said. "I've done 10 years three times over and I'm still here, and I've done nothing bad since I've been here."

One long-termer who came to Angola in 1960 for aggravated rape said his attorney and the prosecutor told him "if I pled guilty, I'd be out in 10½ years." He took them at their word; he didn't even bother to apply for clemency until he'd been in prison for 12 years and realized he would not be freed. When he was turned down, he didn't apply again until 15 years later.

This is another pattern that one sees with the long-termers: a first application for clemency, rejection, then a long period of confinement before another application is made. One long-termer applied to the Pardon Board for clemency in 1965, after 6 years in prison, was rejected and did not apply again until 1977, when he was recommended for a time cut that was never signed by the governor. When another inmate's first clemency request was rejected in 1961, he waited 20 years to reapply, hoping to build a record worthy of favorable consideration. Another man applied for clemency in 1962 and was denied; he didn't apply again until 1987. Asked why not, he replied, "I just gave up. They wouldn't do nothin' for me no how." When another inmate's first application was rejected in 1973, after a blemish-free record of 11 years at Angola, he says, "I got so disappointed I just didn't care no more."

Call it what you may, passivity, resignation, withdrawal, lack of zeal, or naiveté, the fact is that many of the long-termers simply put the thought of getting out of prison out of their minds. They quit trying to work through the system, went about their jobs quietly, and kept a low profile. There are some exceptions, like one long-termer who has been to the Pardon Board "over 30 times" and has always been denied, but on the whole, the long-termers have been a remarkably accepting lot, at least on the surface. They seem to lack the persistence or the aggressiveness to push for release that other inmates have displayed.

They still want to get out, but many of them express feelings of helplessness in regard to the process necessary to win their freedom. They feel frustrated in dealing with the corrections bureaucracy. Clemency for them is a three-stage process: first, to the Pardon Board for a positive recommendation, then to the governor for his signature, then to the Parole Board for a favorable vote (unless they are among the lucky ones cut to time served). These three steps become like a series of ordeals. Some have never gotten past the first step; others have gotten the Pardon Board's approval, but have not been approved by the governor (particularly in the Louisiana of the 1980s, when commutations have been hard to come by); others have cleared the first two hurdles only to be rejected by the Parole Board.

They sound reflective and despondent when they talk about it. "I don't know what happened," one long-termer says. "I guess it is the system . . . it just leaves people behind. I don't have any support, I don't know anyone who could make a phone call or would know what or how to do anything on my behalf."

One long-term inmate said, "I guess I just didn't try to help myself. I didn't know how and I didn't know anybody important to ask for help. All the others that came here with me have left a long time ago and I figured my time would come too."

Another long-termer came to Angola for aggravated rape in 1961. Asked why others who came in with him and after him had been freed while he remained, he said, "I don't have any answer why I am still here and everyone else has been released. It's an impossible situation that has no answer."

Another man, who served 19 years before asking for a time cut, said, "I do not have any money, no one powerful enough to help. Politics keeps you here and it gets you out. My problem is that I don't know any politicians."

Of all the long-termers interviewed, only one appeared confident of his release: "The President of the United States gave me a pardon and I will be going home May 5, 1989," said this man from his cell, where he has been under the care of the prison's mental health department since 1976.

At least 5 of these 31 Angola long-termers have been released since our research was completed early in 1988. Five of them have been sent home, and doubtless others will be in the next few years as more attention is focused on their situation. Despite the severity of their crimes, it is hard not to feel sympathetic toward the ones who remain, a select few who, because of their personal inabilities (or disabilities) and lack of resources, defy the law of averages and serve three or four or five times as long as other men who have committed similar crimes. The long-termers seem almost like random choices, like the unfortunate woman selected to be stoned in Shirley Jackson's story, "The Lottery." They exemplify to the masses the worst that might happen. The rest of us, seeing what has happened to them, can think of their edifying example and be grateful we have escaped their punishment.

If all of the remaining 31 went home tomorrow, we would not be short of similar examples for long. Their replacements are already approaching, working their way up through the system: nearly 100 inmates who have served more than 20 years; a few hundred more who have served more than 15 years; and literally thousands more who are good prospects, having come in after tougher sentencing laws began to take effect in Louisiana in 1977. Indeed, of the 4,700 men serving time at Angola in 1989, about two thirds are either lifers or men serving such long mandatory terms (in the range of 35 to 140 years) that they, too, will grow old in prison, barring prolific use of executive clemency. As the retired head of the Louisiana Department of Corrections, C. Paul Phelps, said, "As things stand right now, the State of Louisiana is posturing itself to run probably the largest male old-folks home in the country."

The young lifers coming in this year, who will join the "million dollar club" 30 years from now, may well live to see Angola become a prison of old men. The only good thing about that future, from the point of view of the 31 long-termers in this present group, is that it won't matter to them: One way or the other, they'll be out of Angola by then.

REFERENCES

Bureau of Justice Statistics. (1984, June). Time served in prison. Washington, DC: U.S. Department of Justice.

Bureau of Justice Statistics. (1987). *BJS Data Report, 1986*. Washington, DC: Government Printing Office.

Krajick, K. (1979, March). Growing old in prison. *Corrections Magazine*, pp. 33-46.

5

Facing Long-Term Imprisonment

Michael G. Santos

I turned 24 just before the judge sentenced me to 45 years in federal prison. Although I had been held in various jails in the Seattle area for about a year as I awaited trial, this was my first trip to the penitentiary. I did not know what to expect. I heard many stories from the other prisoners I met during that year, so my mind was filled with tales of prison life. And, of course, I remembered the stereotypes of prison life from such films as *Brubaker* and *Stir Crazy*. Would this be it? Would my life be reduced to a prison registration number, being counted periodically as I waited for paint to peel off prison walls and years to pass away? How can a person be left with nothing meaningful to do for 45 years? I was thirsting for life at the same time as I was trying in my mind to untangle the web that had led me to such a sentence. I would scream of injustice, but I was unsure of my ground. I read the presentence report prepared by the government. It said mine was a victimless crime. Does a victimless crime really merit a 45-year prison term? I did not know. Yet those were the questions tormenting me as I waited in the county jail.

Then, early one Saturday morning, the guards shouted at me, "Santos, pack up!" I knew neither where I was going nor how I would get there. I was expecting a visit from my parents that day, but the immediate transfer would prevent me from getting word to them. I asked another prisoner—one with whom I had developed a friendship during my time in the county jail, and one whom I would never see again—to call my father and let him know I was on my way to prison, though I did not know which one. Later I learned my destination was not "Club Fed," or one of the college-campus like prisons for which the Bureau of Prisons (BOP) is becoming known. I was a long-term prisoner, and as such my destination was the United States Penitentiary in Atlanta (USP Atlanta), one of the two oldest penitentiaries in the federal system.

The trip from Seattle to Atlanta was long. My physical movement was restricted by a chain wrapped around my waist that was connected to the manacles around my wrists and the steel cuffs around my ankles. There was nothing to restrict my thinking.

A flood of thoughts (none pleasant) collided in my mind; I felt as if I were drowning in my own brain. I thought of how far away I would be from my family. I felt the burden of realizing the shame and humiliation my actions had brought them. My parents and grandparents gave me every opportunity to bring pride and distinction to our family. I had no reason to sell cocaine. Like a fool, though, I made some wrong decisions that hurt many people and society. Eventually I decided I could not afford to wallow in self-pity; I had to prepare myself for what lay ahead. Yet I did not know *what* lay ahead. All I knew was that I must survive a sentence of 4½ decades. I was on my way to a maximum-security penitentiary, and I tried to develop a strategy to help me endure the imminent prison experience.

A lengthy prison term seemed likely to rip apart my relationships. I was almost certain it would destroy my marriage. I had been married for only a few months before my arrest. Prison would offer no legitimate opportunities for me to contribute financially to my marriage. It would be impossible for me to achieve the intimacy in which marital and domestic problems ought to be discussed. Furthermore, my wife would have needs that prison walls would preclude my fulfilling. I could not be there to hold her, to comfort her, or even to listen to her. The emptiness caused by realizing I would lose a relationship that I thought meant the world to me, and the helplessness to do anything about it, brought forth a cold and dark loneliness in my soul that I had not known was possible, a loneliness made even greater because I assumed it would grow inside me for the duration of my prison term. I counted the equivocal blessing of having no children. On one hand, I was relieved that I would not be abandoning children in addition to a wife I could not support. On the other hand, I felt the sadness in knowing I would be too old to enjoy the experience of having children upon my release.

I spoke with other prisoners at USP Atlanta facing long-term incarceration who did have children. One prisoner, whom I will call Chris, has a 4-year-old daughter and a 5-year-old son. He was beginning a 30-year term and felt helpless because he realized he would be unable to play a significant part in his children's education. He told them he was going away to school, and he worried about the time he would have to tell them he is serving a prison term. Chris recognizes his role as a father is to educate, discipline, and love his children. His prison term, however, will remove him from their entire childhood. The pain of his children's being reared without their father's presence is much more difficult for Chris to bear than his prison sentence.

Another prisoner, Hector, is beginning a 35-year sentence. He has a 6-year-old son who can visit only once each year because of the geographic distance between them. Hector's parents care for his son. The only thing Hector can do is let the child know, through phone calls and a weekly letter, that he has a father and is loved. He cannot hold the boy when he falls off his bicycle or congratulate him on a fine play he makes during a baseball game; he will not be with his son until the boy is a grown man. Hector's prison term is much more difficult because he knows he has a child in the world, yet cannot contribute to his welfare.

Another prisoner, Ron, has a 14-year-old daughter who has experienced severe difficulty since his incarceration began. After Ron received a lengthy sentence, his wife sold all of the family's assets, then abandoned him and his daughter. Up until Ron's arrest, he enjoyed a close relationship with his daughter, but since his confinement, the girl's life has been turned upside-down. Her mother absconded with the family's assets, her father is beyond her reach, and she is without money or a home and is living with an aunt who does not want her. The girl indicates she is severely depressed and frequently writes about taking her own life. Ron took these letters to the prison psychologist, who tried to help Ron secure a transfer to a prison closer to his daughter. Excited at the prospect of a transfer, Ron called his daughter to relay the good news. The case manager controlling Ron's file, however, refused to process the transfer request until his next scheduled unit team meeting, which was 6 months away. The news devastated Ron and shattered the girl, nearly driving her to suicide. Ron calls his daughter up to three times each day just to keep her calm. He is angry because of the obstacles placed before him by the BOP. He is far away from home, and his daughter's life is critically affected by the distance between them. Incarceration is more difficult for Ron and other parents in prison because they cannot give their children the comfort and support they need.

Besides not being able to have children, aging is another very real concern for me and the other prisoners facing long sentences. I began my term in confinement in my early twenties but would not breathe the fresh air of freedom until I was well into my sixties. At 20 years of age, it is difficult to imagine being 30. It is much more difficult for a 20-year-old prisoner to realize that release from prison will not come until several decades pass.

Vincent, another prisoner with whom I spoke, began serving a 30-year sentence when he was 26 years old. He says the reality of the sentence has not yet hit him. Five years is all Vincent can think about. For the first 5 years, Vincent will focus on the legal issues of his case. When 5 years have passed, and if he remains incarcerated with no relief in sight, Vincent says he will be "hitting that wall every minute of the day." Escape will consume his every waking thought. Vincent absolutely refuses to leave prison as a decrepit old man without a life; he says his crime was not severe enough to warrant such a sentence. To Vincent, there is more honor in fighting for freedom, even if it means getting killed in the process, than to spending 30 years in prison, waiting for death. There would be zero opportunity for Vincent to make up for time he has lost in prison; he says he will give them 5 years, but he will not allow the prison system to take 30 years of his life. The thought of growing old in prison is anathema to both Vincent and me, but our long sentences eclipse all thoughts of waiting for release to come.

And what is release? By the time the prison doors open for me, I expect to know no one well, except other male prisoners who have served long prison terms. Even if someone were to come and tell me I could go home immediately, that control of my life would be returned to me, the news would leave me weary. I am growing numb to my surroundings. It is a strange numbness because I never know what will happen. There is a monotonous and regular routine, yet I know it can change abruptly, on an administrator's whim. There is no spark, no passion in life. The feelings and emotions men develop by living in a world with women and children are becoming more absent from my life. I will have neither a home nor a career. Being forced to live in proximity with people I loathe will affect my life and my actions. And there will be violence. How can I escape it? I am young and I will be living in a maximum-security prison. It is inevitable that I will be tried. And I will respond in the manner appropriate for prisons. Although I am not in fear of being robbed or beaten, the constant companionship of thieves, rapists, killers, aggressive homosexuals, and snitches who will say or do anything to save their own hide is far from relaxing. All of these factors exacerbate the tensions of beginning a long prison term. They will not prepare me for release. The coming of the Messiah seems closer than my release from prison.

These thoughts generate anxiety, apathy, and depression. There was a pattern to those first years. I was nervous about what I would find in prison, then I did not care, and then an ocean of depression swallowed me. Such a long sentence did not seem real. How could it? The sentence was nearly twice as long as I had been alive on the planet. I had been out of high school for only 5 years; then suddenly, I was staring down the long end of a 45-year prison term. No violence was even alleged in my case, and it was my first commitment. I listened to numerous violent and repeat offenders around me complaining of sentences only a fraction as long as mine. My thoughts began to turn away from the wrong decisions I made during the recklessness of youth and turn toward the perceived injustices our criminal justice system was perpetuating against me and the friends I was meeting in prison. I was not alone.

There were numerous other prisoners around me. The vast majority were beginning lengthy prison terms for their participation in the illicit drug industry. Their level of cynicism was taller than the skyscrapers in New York City. Corrupt lawmakers and savings-and-loan bandits escape the pains of long-term imprisonment altogether, they complained, but people striving to pull themselves out of poverty regularly receive sentences totally disproportionate to their crimes. They laughed at the so-called "war on drugs," more accurately describing it as a war on people.

One of the consequences of long prison terms is a loss of the prisoners' sense of their own efficacy. Prisoners are told where to live and with whom. They are issued clothing; an indifferent administration prepares their food. They are forced to work in jobs bearing no relation to their levels of skill, to their release dates, or to the types of employment they will receive upon release. The prison staff members tend to feel superior and righteous; the social structure inside the prison proper brings the prisoners feelings of guilt, inferiority, and powerlessness. Time fills the prisoners with resentment and boredom. They lie on their beds, staring at the bunks above them and the walls surrounding them. The prison system has taken their identities; it has removed their abilities to distinguish themselves. It tells the prisoners they cannot be trusted, cannot be given responsibility, and can be given no opportunities to contribute to the welfare of the general community. Physical resistance is met

with a massive show of force. Intellectual resistance is met with ZIP code changes and
more subtle ways of upsetting progress. For
example, those who use brawn to solve their
problems will quickly be restrained with a
team of prison guards. No prison mutiny has
ever been successful. Prisoners who strive to
upset the system through organizational efforts will be transferred to another institution
or given meaningless chores to replace their
contemplative time.

Prisoners adopt individual methods of coping with and adjusting to the pressures of life
in confinement. Once long-term prisoners get
situated in prison cells and are assigned prison
jobs, they develop strategies for making their
stay as light as possible. Most will look for
ways to keep themselves busy mentally and
physically, though a few will retreat into their
own worlds and avoid contact with the prison
system's social network. Many gradually lose
interest in the world outside the prison walls
and focus only on their time inside. They learn
how to survive in prison by making it their
business to know what the administration will
tolerate. They want to know which prisoners
are troublemakers and which prisoners mind
their own business. They want to know which
areas of the prison are tightly secured and
which areas of the prison are loose. Long-term
prisoners will develop daily routines that enable them to achieve their individual goals
while sliding past trouble. Prison is a micro-
cosm of the larger society; what occurs behind
the walls is intensified, exaggerated, and immediate. One prisoner said it is where you
meet shock, hopelessness, helplessness, fear,
depression, hate, extreme sadness, coldness,
and loneliness all at once. It all hits like a
freight train, and no one can help.

Support from family, friends, and educational programs has helped me cope in this
environment. Nearly 7 years have passed since
I started this prison odyssey. I began and completed my undergraduate studies and now am
nearly finished with a master's program I began
independently at Hofstra University. Although
many long-term prisoners lose interest in the
outside world and become increasingly dependent on prison routines, other prisoners
and I search for ways to contribute to and
remain active with the world outside. Besides
a demanding academic program, I also exercise regularly and keep an eye open for potential problems. Other active prisoners write

prolifically, immerse themselves in the law
library, or seek spiritual programs. I find a
busy schedule keeps me away from trouble
and focused on my academic goals; such goals
are meaningless, I realize, to many other prisoners. The prison system is not designed to
inspire progress. Although administrators have
ample sanctions from which they can draw to
punish prisoners who break prison regulations, they neither encourage nor reward those
who make significant progress behind prison
walls.

Prisoners notice that an incentive system is
missing. My studies of prisoners in the BOP
suggest that is the reason such a minute percentage put forth the energy to develop skills
that will enhance their chances for success
upon release. Prisoners see no relationship
between hard work and better living conditions; there is no indication their behavior in
prison can help them advance their release
dates. All prisoners with whom I spoke said
they would pursue zealously educational programs if some type of meaningful incentive
system existed. But there is no quid pro quo,
no tit for tat. Accordingly, prisoners spend
their time learning to live as comfortably as
possible during their stay in prison. They become hustlers, scammers, and artists of the
con. They learn to break rules without getting
caught and take pride in beating the system.
Their behavior is a natural response; it com-
pensates for a social structure that forces prisoners to live under a coercive system which
tells them their efforts are worthless. A long-
term prisoner who aspires to accomplish goals
during incarceration is offensive to the administration because such a prisoner is not
truly a prisoner. His or her mind is free. The
administration demands that prisoners limit
themselves to their functions as prisoners:
doing time without attracting attention or dis-
rupting the system.

Those facing long prison terms recognize
prison is the world in which they will spend
long periods of their lives. They will live without the companionship of the opposite sex;
ties to their families and communities will
separate. Relatives will come into their families through birth and marriage and some
will pass on through death; these events will
happen without the prisoner's participation.
Prison is the least likely place for positive
changes to occur in human beings. It is an
environment where such seemingly effortless

activities as holding onto one's identity and sanity take on a significance of paramount importance. Some prisoners say long prison terms are like drawn-out death sentences. I will just say they are futile and excessive acts of vengeance.

6

Coping With Imprisonment

A Long-Termer's View

Carl Kummerlowe

INTRODUCTION

This *Guidebook* is replete with opinions, perceptions, and suggestions that, theoretically, will affect long-term inmates. These opinions, perceptions, and suggestions are those of correctional staff, correctional consultants, and project staff. Clearly, what is lacking are the voices of the long-termers themselves. To broaden the perspective of this document, a long-term inmate was asked to prepare an essay that would give the reader an appreciation for the "inside" realities of long-term confinement.

The author is well-suited to this task, having served 16 years of a life sentence. Since 1971, he has collected everything about long-term confinement that came to his attention. Due to his interest in and knowledge of long-term imprisonment, he was selected to participate in a study of long-term imprisonment conducted by his home state; respect for his communication skills led to his being asked to author the study's final report.

This essay helps to personalize the issue of long-term confinement; to raise it above the mundane consideration of yet another correctional management problem. Long-term inmates are probably the most improbable group for which to engender concern and positive actions. Their criminal acts have shocked the public's conscience and their sentences reflect the magnitude of their deeds. They are not attractive targets for reform or innovation. However, they do evoke a need to devise an approach whereby the years spent in confinement are not wasted—for the long-term inmate or for the correctional agency. While long-term inmates' needs are very similar to those of short-term inmates, the length of their sentences exacerbates these needs until they may bear slight resemblance to those of short-termers.

Correctional agencies are often ravaged by deep cuts in operating budgets and strapped for resources. There is the potential for a reciprocal relationship between long-termers and correctional agencies, wherein both parties benefit. The achievement of this goal requires insight into long-term confinement. This essay is an attempt to provide the beginning of this insight. Also included in the essay are many

NOTE: Reprinted from *Managing Long-Term Prisoners: A Guide for the Correctional Administrator* (U.S. government document), Fall 1995, pp. 69-79, with permission of the National Institute of Corrections, Washington, DC.

recommendations for improving the management and programming of long-term inmates.

THE MOST CRITICAL ISSUE

The paramount concern of all prisoners is "When will I get out?" The lack of a firm release date constitutes the most difficult adjustment to confinement for all prisoners, especially long-termers. This uncertainty contributes more than any other factor to the debilitating effects of incarceration. For long-term prisoners, almost equal concerns are "What kind of person will I be upon release? Will I be physically and mentally healthy? Will I still have a family and friends to assist me on the outside? Will I have an opportunity to lead a meaningful and useful life?" If satisfactory answers to these questions cannot be found, attempts to cope with the problems of long-term confinement are likely to fail.

An optimum release time exists for the majority of confined individuals. When prisoners are discharged beyond that optimum time, their anxiety increases, despair and depression grow, and hostility and fear fester. As a direct result, those confined beyond that optimum time, the criminal justice system, and even the public may suffer.

For example, a sentence of life without parole is a condition of confinement that many prison officials and all prisoners so sentenced consider beyond that optimum time—for many inmates, a fate worse than death. Lifers without hope of release die a little with each passing day. Some lifers lapse into a state of harmless senility after many years of occupying scarce and costly bed space in highly secure institutions. Others look out for themselves the best way they know how and strive for prestige by engaging in reckless encounters with staff or other inmates. A few, believing they will never get out, fail to channel their energies, take menial prison jobs, and become so institutionalized that they lose their identities. The miracle is that most retain some degree of autonomy, hoping they will some day be released.

Many offenders wish to make amends for acts they have committed and to restructure their lives; sentencing sanctions such as life without parole and long mandatory sentences such as 50 years, no parole, offer little incentive to change.

FAMILY/COMMUNITY RELATIONSHIPS

An important concern for many prisoners, but especially for long-termers, is separation from their families and friends. The pain of separation is often profound, and with the passing of time, the probability of continuing to maintain contact becomes an important concern. As long-termers watch relationships between other prisoners and their families diminish, fears of their own betrayal and complete abandonment arise. Worries about their children's schooling and behavioral problems, the financial situation at home, transportation to visit, and divorce are ever present. In most instances, the spouses of long-term prisoners are their prime source of social and emotional support and represent their main link to the community.

Separation from family may stimulate serious self-doubts about sexual adequacy, harming the long-termers' self-images. Some become severely frustrated from being deprived of normal heterosexual relationships. They may turn to pornographic magazines, obscene mannerisms, self-gratification, or homosexual relationships in an effort to satisfy their natural urges. As the problems associated with maintaining close "free world" relationships are compounded over time, many long-termers lose their desire to remain involved with family responsibilities. Some slowly withdraw from all contact with family and home.

The importance of assisting prisoners in maintaining family and societal relationships is too often overlooked by correctional administrators. Concern about overcrowding, staff limitations, budgetary restraints, security, smuggling of contraband, and lack of facilities may even lead to restrictions on programs and policies that would help prisoners to strengthen family and community ties. Failure to understand the importance of close prisoner-community relationships has sometimes caused unrest and discontent in institutions that house long-termers. In facilities offering open visitation, correspondence, and other channels of communication, prisoner tension and unrest are generally minimized.

Long-termers view numerous conditions of their confinement as detrimental to maintaining family and community ties. Some of the most important of these conditions are discussed below:

1. *Visiting lists that limit the total number of visitors a prisoner may have.* These lists do not consider the size of inmates' families or the extent of their community support groups. Prisoners with large families must often choose to visit only with family members, thereby eliminating community contacts offering religious, employment, and other important social ties. Those inmates with large community support groups are forced to dissolve some of these important relationships at the very time they are most needed. These restrictive limitations serve little practical purpose, are costly and time consuming to administer, foster inmate discontent, and only slightly enhance institutional security. They also are harmful to the general public because they tend to decrease prisoners' chances for success upon release.

2. *Insufficient time for visitation and inadequate visiting facilities.* Immediate improvements could be made in many institutions simply by increasing the number of visiting days allowed and/or the total number of visiting hours per day. These changes would not require significant increases in facilities or staffing.

3. *Restricted access to home visit/furlough programs.* No group of prisoners is likely to benefit more from home visits than long-term inmates, who have been cut off from the "free world" for years. A program of regular family visits can be a re-introduction to family, associates, and the swiftly changing technological advances in society today. These visits help reduce the debilitating effects of extended institutionalization and positively prepare inmates for eventual re-entry into society. Stringent selection criteria should be applied to ensure the safety of the community and the acceptance of the program, but length of sentence alone should not be a reason to exclude any prisoners from participation.

4. *Lack of pre-furlough and post-furlough counseling.* Counseling prior to home visits would help prepare individuals who have been confined for many years for the realities facing them upon their first venture alone into the "free world." Post-furlough counseling might be helpful in evaluating and heading off adjustment problems.

5. *Lack of "day passes" for furlough-eligible inmates.* In some states, inmates are limited to one or two furloughs yearly. As a supplement to these infrequent leaves, the establishment of short duration "day passes" would permit furlough-approved long-termers an opportunity to re-enter the community more often. These passes might be for purposes of community betterment programs (where there is a real need for participation), counseling, and other activities consistent with promoting offenders' reintegration into society.

6. *Lack of extended family visitation programs for those long-termers not yet eligible for home visits.* Extended family visiting is used as a supplement to furlough programs in many countries and not as a substitute for them. They are an integral part of the penal systems in Canada, Sweden, Great Britain, West Germany, Denmark, Belgium, numerous countries in Latin America and Asia, and even a number of communist countries, including the Soviet Union. In the United States this practice is limited to only seven states (Mississippi, California, South Carolina, New York, Minnesota, Connecticut, Washington).

Family visitation as proposed here would be used solely as an alternative to long-termers being permitted to go to their own homes on furlough. It would be established for those inmates who might meet the general criteria for home furlough, but are ineligible for that program for some specific reason, such as no suitable family member residing within the state, insufficient time served on sentence, or nature of offense.

The arguments favoring this visitation concept center on strengthening marriages and family ties. These visits would provide inmates with a strong, healthy home life to return to upon their release. The extensive use of this concept in other nations speaks well for its acceptance and success, and limited experience in the United States has been positive. Extended family visits boost morale, help keep marriages intact, and, as one administrator in California reported, "Are a hell of a tool for the institution—a kind of safety valve that helps let steam out of a potentially explosive situation."

A common response among prison administrators, legislators, and the public regarding this concept is that institutions are already overcrowded and they do not have funding or space to support such a program. In answer to this response, consideration could be given to the utilization of donated house trailers located inside a secure institution area. Prisoners would be permitted to stay there for a specified time with their families. They would be charged a fee sufficient to cover the rental and maintenance for the duration of their stays. The program would therefore be self-supporting without requiring public expenditures for prison facilities.

7. *Insufficient programs supporting community outings for long-term prisoners.* Escorted community programs focusing on service projects, recreational activities, or religious functions afford an opportunity for long-termers to prepare for their return to society. Such programs could be promoted through organizations such as the Jaycees or Lifer's Clubs.

8. *Lack of family counseling and educational support groups.* These programs could cover issues relating to family disintegration under pressure of loneliness, sexual frustration, depleted economics, and stigmatization. Scheduled meetings could be held during regular visiting periods or at other prearranged times. Off-site support programs might also be established in various community settings to provide information, counseling, and other forms of assistance to the spouses of prisoners.

9. *Inadequate programs to meet the specific needs of female prisoners.* Many incarcerated women were the sole or primary caretaker of their children at the time of arrest. The abrupt separation of mothers from very young children may cause damaging consequences to those children in later life. A second problem women may face is the birth of a child during confinement. The establishment

of prison facilities and programs enabling infants to remain with their mothers would give them an opportunity to form an attachment bond, considered essential by many psychologists for normal childhood development. In those institutions lacking such facilities, it is common for infants to be given to relatives, placed in foster homes, or given up for adoption. The needs of the children are seldom considered by correctional agencies. Even most social service agencies make little effort to ameliorate the negative effects of their parents' incarceration on children.

HOUSING CONSIDERATIONS

Lack of space and privacy becomes a significant concern over time. Inmates dislike being forced into intimacy with others chosen by the prison administration. They frequently tend to ostracize other inmates whose crimes may differ from theirs. Racial tensions exist and often flare up within the hostile prison environment. Older prisoners frequently find it difficult to adjust to the young "kids" who bring their loud stereos and music with them. Confrontations occur daily. These problems can only escalate as prisons become populated with disproportionate numbers of inmates who must live together for many years. Long-termers believe many of these problems can be avoided if administrators are willing to recognize and respond to them.

1. *Provide maximum privacy for long-term inmates.* Privacy offers long-termers a way to cope with time. If they can find a "niche" in which to remove themselves from the daily stresses of prison life, long-termers may be able to relieve some of the tension and anxiety that often accumulate with the passage of time.

2. *Provide quiet living areas.* Tension can be effectively reduced if institutions set aside "quiet" housing units for those who are easily irritated by music and television blaring all day and night, as is so often the case. These "quiet" units should be reserved for those who ex-

hibit a willingness to comply with the requirements for quiet.

3. *Establish honor dorms for long-termers as an incentive for good behavior.* Special "honor" housing should be established at every custody level. As inmates progress through the system, perform work and other assignments in a satisfactory manner, and maintain a good disciplinary record, they should be entitled to an upgrading of privileges. These could include carpeting on the floor, curtains at windows, an extension of allowable personal items, a telephone for their units, an extension of curfew hours, and increased visiting periods. Only those inmates who desire placement in this type housing should be assigned there. Serious violations of the conduct established for "honor" residents would result in removal from the unit.

RULES AND REGULATIONS

In correctional systems throughout the nation, hundreds of rules and regulations extend into all areas of inmate life. These rules cover contact with family, access to legal materials, medical services, dress codes, disciplinary hearings, meal schedules, length of hair, sanitation, library, etc. Many of these rules arouse hostility among inmates simply because they do not make sense. Others seem but irritating gestures of authoritarianism that restrict inmates' abilities to make choices. It may appear that these rules are made by people inexperienced with and far removed from the prison setting. Further, they are carried out by people other than those who formulate them, thus allowing degrees of interpretation. Prisoners are sometimes unaware of rules. Moreover, rules and regulations frequently contradict each other and often fail to reflect their intended purposes. In some institutions, procedures developed to meet the needs of the nineteenth century are still actively enforced. So many different directives, institutional regulations, and policies have accumulated over the years that few staff or inmates really know how many of them are to be applied.

Examples of these types of rules and regulations are presented below.

1. Rules That Do Not Make Sense

Procedure may allow visitors to bring food items into the visitation area to be shared with minimum custody inmates. Barbecue pits and picnic benches are provided, and charcoal, lighter fluid, and matches are allowed. However, pots, pans, and other metal or glass cooking and eating utensils may be prohibited. Another example: electric clocks are prohibited, but electric clocks with radios are allowed.

2. Rules That Contradict One Another

Departmental policy might specify that "random" strip searches will be required of minimum custody inmates returning from visits. There may be a contradictory rule at the institutional level that specifies "all" inmates returning from a visit will be strip searched. What rule is to be followed? Generally, staff will implement the more severe rule even though it conflicts with departmental policy.

3. Rules That Are Not Fairly Enforced

In prisons there are an endless number of violations that might result in disciplinary action. The need for such action is not in question here. The sanctions levied are questionable due to the wide range of penalties imposed for identical violations. In a situation in which two inmates are "horse playing" with each other, both are charged for the same rule infraction and each is referred to the institutional court. One might go to court on Tuesday, be found guilty, and given a suspended sentence. The other may go to the same court on Thursday, be found guilty, and given a sentence of 10 days in the "hole." Few states publish case reports for these hearings. This often results in the inconsistency noted above since each new case is treated as if it were the first of its type handled by the court.

4. Rules That Mandate Certain Allowable Items Are Contraband If Not Purchased Through the Prison Store

Long-term inmates usually move to different institutions as they progress through the system. After transfer, they may be required to discard previously purchased items (lamps, hot pots, etc.) because rules at the new institution may declare these items contraband unless obtained from its store. The articles available in one institutional store are seldom the same as those sold in another institution. This imposes senseless financial burdens on long-term inmates who generally can ill afford them.

Short-term inmates often find prison little more than an unpleasant adventure; they can accept or reject the rules that govern their lives. The consequences, except for the most severe infractions, are themselves short-term. Long-termers, however, are not tourists in prison. They will live there for a significant portion of their lives. Rules and regulations for long-term prisoners are a way of life. They may be perceived as irritating, frustrating, senseless, and debilitating, and they frequently strip these inmates of dignity and self-esteem.

Long-termers, who have often been around longer than most staff, can contribute valuable insight into the feasibility of rules before they are issued. This would help prevent incomplete, inconsistent and sometimes senseless rules from being implemented.

All inmates are punished by a loss of freedom; further punitive measures are secondary sanctions that only serve to increase hostility and resentment among inmates.

PROGRESSION THROUGH THE SYSTEM

Nothing contributes more to prisoners' anxieties and insecurities than an unknown future in a strange and hostile environment. It is essential that all prisoners, especially long-termers, be provided with a program of systematic progression (a graduated release plan) through the correctional experience, from date of admission to date of release. Such a plan will assist them in managing their time and accepting their imprisonment with some knowledge of the future. It is unfortunate that most long-termers in today's prisons have no such plan to guide them. In some states the implementation of a realistic graduated release plan will require changes in sentencing and release laws. However, no programs will be meaningful to inmates unless they clearly have some bearing on their eventual release.

The key elements for any graduated release program designed to assist the progress of long-termers through the system should include the following:

1. Inmates Should Be Given Early Notification of Their Tentative Release Dates

Preferably, these dates would be established within three months of initial incarceration. They should be flexible enough to permit modification if circumstances change significantly. They must also meet existing statutory requirements. In those states where some sentences do not have fixed terminal dates, criminal code revisions should be sought. Every sentence, including that of life, should have a release date. (Researchers from many nations have concluded that it is the certainty of punishment and not the length of sentence that deters criminal behavior.)

2. Inmates Should Be Assured That Their Established Tentative Release Dates Cannot Be Altered Except for Specified Reasons

3. Progress Reviews Should Be Conducted Once Every Year

4. General Criteria Should Be Established to Govern Progress Through Each Custody Level

Decisions should always consider placement at the lowest possible custody level commensurate with public and institutional safety. Access to every level should be attainable for every prisoner regardless of length of sentence. Every prisoner should also be considered for community release status following the satisfactory completion of ten calendar years.

5. The Program Plan Should Include Incentive Awards

Exceptional achievement and/or conduct, educational or vocational training, counseling, work performance, community service, etc. should be rewarded through incentives. These awards would permit an earlier advancement into lower levels of custody for those with superior achievement. When applied fairly, incentives are a helpful tool in maintaining an orderly institution.

6. Documentation Should
Be Fair, Accurate, Up-to-Date,
and Reflective of Positive Information

Attention should be given to including all current psychological information, work reports, educational achievements and meritorious acts. Case records should be designed to reflect positive changes and should not emphasize the negative as many currently do.

7. Individualized Treatment Plans
Should Be Established for Every Prisoner

It must be recognized that the requirements of each inmate differ. A plan tailored to meet the specific needs of each individual as he/she progresses toward release is mandatory.

INMATE WORK PROGRAMS

In a nation that has always taken pride in its work ethic, it is difficult to understand why correctional agencies have been so remarkably inattentive to that ethic. The idleness that exists in prisons is one of the most critical concerns for both staff and inmates. Idleness, extended over long periods of time, contributes significantly to the debilitating effects of incarceration. Inmates milling around with nothing to do or sitting in front of a television set watching soap operas are certainly more prone to disorder than those working or studying regularly. Crowding has already overextended the use of monotonous, unskilled, and make-work jobs. These efforts to reduce idleness last only a few hours each day and usually result in discontent and boredom. For reasons such as these, long-term inmates often express serious concern about the current state of prison work programs.

There are some programs, though, that most long-termers believe will succeed, if properly implemented. Some of these may require legislative action; others will require the cooperation of trade unions and the private sector. Functional programs containing features noted below are in effect in several states, and model programs have been tried on a pilot basis in others.

1. Revitalization of Prison Industry

Traditional prison industrial programs have attempted to compete in a restricted marketplace by using cheap, unskilled prison labor. It was believed they would provide work for otherwise idle prisoners, train people in good work habits, give them an opportunity to learn about the job market in the real world, and be competitive because of the inexpensive labor available. In practice, they have been plagued by inferior products, missed delivery deadlines, and cost overruns.

Many long-termers believe these work programs will not be effective until they are independent of the correctional bureaucracy and the estrangement that often develops between industrial managers and correctional administrators is reduced. Sufficient funds must be available to modernize equipment and technology. Product lines will need expansion beyond the traditional license plate and furniture market. Work programs should be structured to function like private industry. Trade union and private business restraints must be removed and laws limiting product sales must be relaxed. Experienced industrial managers and engineers should be recruited as staff managers. These programs must also provide reasonable wages and other worker incentives. Each industry should be self-sustaining.

Even if all of the above were accomplished, industrial programs would still be dependent upon a stable labor force of trained workers. Most prisoners are unskilled and until recently the vast majority were imprisoned only for short terms. Unskilled "short-termers" often exhibit the "I don't give a damn, I'll be out in a little while any way" attitude. Such prisoners comprise an unwilling and inefficient work force. Long-termers, on the other hand, generally welcome opportunities for constructive work as a way to relieve idleness. If they have no specific work skills, their longer sentences make them ideal candidates for training. Once trained, they are capable of providing stability in a constantly changing work force.

Probably the most important element required for an efficient, competitive industrial program is an incentive for inmates to work. A reasonable wage plan offering raises over time and bonuses for exceptional performance are important motivators for increased productivity. "Preferred" housing areas could also contribute to worker efficiency. The most important incentive for long-termers would be "time credits" for work performed, but such credits must be available to all workers regardless of sentence.

Another concept many believe could be successful involves the use of private firms to expand work programs for inmates. Factories funded by private industry could be erected within the institutional walls, or, as has been done in Kansas, near existing correctional facilities. Many of the disadvantages associated with the traditional prison industrial concept would be eliminated in the hands of private industry. Funding would no longer be the state's obligation.

2. Use of Para-Professional Positions at the Institutional Level

Another work opportunity for long-termers who have exhibited positive behavior and adjustment would be para-professional assignments within institutions. In some institutions these positions are filled by inmates rather than civilian staff. These assignments are of a non-security type, mainly in the area of support services. Potential para-professional positions include library aides, maintenance workers, teacher's aides, research assistants, typists, and fire department aides. Inmates trained as para-professionals would afford around-the-clock availability of trained personnel and provide growth opportunities for long-termers.

3. Availability of Career Ladders

There should also be a progression, akin to that in private industry, from lower to higher skill levels. Only actual job openings should be filled, and make-work assignments should be eliminated. Serious consideration must be given to providing work opportunities at all levels of custody. In addition, wage scales must include provisions ensuring retention of pay grades for inmates who have earned lower custody status. Long-termers, due to length of sentence, are seriously affected by incentive payment plans that frequently are reduced when inmates are transferred to lower custody

status and placed on another job. As previously noted, it is long-termers who are most likely to lose contact with family and friends. They must, therefore, be self-supporting. If their choice is to accept lower custody at less wages, they may suffer financial difficulties. If they remain in higher custody so they can be self-supporting, their chances for parole or other forms of release might be negatively affected.

4. Employment of Long-Termers in the Construction of New Prisons

In an effort to meet demands for rapid prison expansion, some correctional agencies employ inmate labor. Long-termers have frequently been called upon to provide stabilization in such work units. They have generally been willing laborers who took pride in their work. Their construction projects were usually on a par with those contracted to "free world" companies. Their low wage scale (10 to 20 times lower than prevailing "free world" wages) permitted the completion of many projects at costs below those estimated by private firms.

In some states, however, long-termers believe they are faced with a dilemma: they are more likely to be retained for the maximum length of their sentences now than just a few years ago. Many believe they have already paid their debts to society and realize a new bed represents a bed that will be occupied, probably by one of them. They also know that short-termers have the best chances for release as a result of intolerable overcrowding. Many long-termers equate being asked to assist with new prison construction with being asked to extend their own imprisonment.

Correctional administrators and policy makers often fail to realize while all prisoners desire freedom, most are willing to work to achieve it and few will willingly work to deprive themselves of it. Although long-termers comprise the most valuable work group in our prisons, in some states their greatest incentive has become a remote possibility. The key to motivating this important work force is incentives, ones that reduce long-termers' fears about extending their confinement.

5. Creation of Community Work Crews

Crews capable of performing a variety of services to state, county, and city governments could expand work opportunities for long-termers. Stability could be achieved through a core of "low risk" long-term inmates. Assignments might include the construction and maintenance of highways, parks, government buildings, and other civic projects. Work should not be limited to menial tasks. Training could be provided where required. All inmates should be paid for their labor and, as a special incentive, housed in community facilities or camps located near job sites. A public that likes to see prisoners work would find them highly visible, performing necessary labor. Both the inmates and the public would benefit.

6. Establishment of Contract Work Centers

Mutually beneficial work programs for long-term inmates are possible between private industry and state correctional agencies. These programs take the form of contract work centers. The contract between the industry and the state calls for the long-term inmates to perform certain services in return for room, board, and prison wages. The correctional agency provides security services. Inmate participants benefit by being allowed to utilize their work skills, while employed full time at jobs resembling those in the "real world." Private industry profits from reduced wages and motivated workers. The correctional agency benefits from reduced costs of confining these inmates.

7. Development of Service and Para-Professional Positions in Community Centers

Carefully chosen long-term inmates should be considered as supplemental staff in para-professional and service functions at community halfway houses and release centers. They are capable of providing a variety of services at minimum cost. In addition, the experience would enhance their transition back into society.

A pilot program of this type has been conducted in Arizona. Six long-term males, including five lifers, were transferred to a pre-release center to work in maintenance, food service, transportation, and teaching. These duties were later expanded to include counseling, research, photographic services, Human Potential Seminars, and flood relief assistance.

After allowing for their room, board, and prison wages of $0.50 per hour, the services they provided (in lieu of hiring additional staff) saved the state an estimated $77,054 during the 23 months the program was operational. They also volunteered 8,000 hours of community service to agencies ranging from alcohol and drug treatment centers to homes for abused women and children. Each participant was able to avail himself of counseling, religious, and educational opportunities not available within the institution. Family ties were strengthened and strong levels of community support resulted from the experience.

8. Need for Work Release Programs

Although long-term inmates as a group are probably the most "needy" when it comes to providing community programs designed to help them make a more successful adjustment from a situation of almost total dependence to complete freedom, they have traditionally been the last group to be placed in such programs. In 1983, 49 states had statutory provisions for implementing community work release programs. However, in some states, long-termers, including lifers, are not eligible to participate in these programs.

Work release programs can help long-termers gradually adjust to life in the community and the responsibilities community living entails. They can serve as a vehicle through which inmates can preserve family and community relationships. They might also eliminate or reduce the degree of psychological and cultural shock that often occurs when long-term inmates are directly released from an institution into the community. The cost savings possible through the utilization of community work release have been well documented. Significant contributions have been made by inmates in areas pertaining to the costs of imprisonment, family support, restitution, state and other taxes, debts, and institutional and program management.

SUMMARY

The concerns of long-term prisoners are many. When will I get out? When I do, what kind of person will I be following many years of exposure to the debilitating effects of imprisonment? Will I be mentally and physically healthy? Will I still have a family and friends in the community? Will I still be able to lead a useful and meaningful life? For those with diminished hope, life contains little meaning and they must adjust to the prospects of a lifetime that will be spent in a harsh and anomalous environment.

Correctional agencies are equipped to deal with some of these concerns. But to do so, they must recognize the unique management concerns presented by long-term inmates. Their foremost concern is the maintenance of family and community ties. Channels for visitation, correspondence, and other means of communication must be less restrictive. Administrators must be supportive of home furlough programs for all inmates, including those with the longest sentences. Community activities and release programs should be available to worthy long-term prisoners. Housing adjustments tailored to meet the specific needs of long-

termers can be implemented. Administrators should direct the formulation of individualized inmate programs designed to meet the specific needs of inmates as they progress through the system. Realistic and meaningful work programs should be established, both inside and outside the institutions. Mental and physical health programs and effective counseling should be implemented. Legislative authority should be sought to implement any of these programs not currently authorized by law.

Finally, correctional administrators must play an active role in educating the public on prison matters. They must recognize that today's long-termers are not tourists just passing through the system. Increasing numbers of long-termers will be confined for many years in oppressive, impersonal prison environments. Administrators must strive to lessen the secondary impacts of incarceration on long-term inmates—their punishment is the loss of freedom.

PART THREE

■ The Effects of

Long-Term Imprisonment

7

The Controversy Over the Effects of Long-Term Incarceration

J. Stephen Wormith

It goes without saying that if we are to examine the treatment and management of long-term prisoners, or if we are to develop sound policies and effective programs, we should understand something about the impact of lengthy incarceration on our clientele. Similarly, if we insist on sentencing offenders to lengthy terms, and especially if we continue on the current trend of giving even longer sentences for serious offenses than has been our tradition, then we should know more about what we are getting into.

This paper was initially conceived as a devil's advocate position for a conference at which the author was prepared to be sacrificed to a group of forensic and mental health specialists participating in a symposium on the effects of incarceration.[1] So, tongue-in-cheek, a provocative title, "The Positive Effects of Incarceration," was chosen and some cursory notes taken in an attempt to counter the inevitable deluge of proclamations citing the deleterious impact of imprisonment and the diatribes condemning its ubiquitous effect. But in the end, it is suggested that such a position be

taken more seriously, for we have yet to learn a great deal about the effects of long-term imprisonment on offender intellect, personality, and attitude. Decidedly, an open-minded, objective point of view will be essential, if we are to make any headway with this intriguing, often perplexing phenomenon.

A PROFILE OF LONG-TERM PRISONERS

In order to provide an appreciation of the number of long-term prisoners and some of their personal characteristics, the following descriptive data are reported. Statistics generated a year ago as part of another study (Wormith, 1983) are cited, so that comparisons may be made and some indication of the growth trends might be gleaned.

A selection criterion based on a sentence length of 21 years or more was established. This includes post-1977 sentences of life—minimum 25 years, life—minimum 10 years, pre-1977 sentences of life—minimum 7 years,

AUTHOR'S NOTE: The statements expressed herein belong solely to the author and do not necessarily represent the position of the Correctional Service of Canada or the Ministry of the Solicitor General. Address requests to the author, Research Division, Ministry of Solicitor General, 340 Laurier Ave. W., Ottawa, Ontario, Canada K1A 0P8.

TABLE 7.1 Canada's Long-Term Incarcerates

	Mid 1983	Mid 1984
All Life Sentences	1,403	1,514
Minimum 25 years	208	263
Minimum 15-24 years	(NA)	147
Minimum 10-14 years	(NA)	970
Minimum 7-10 years	(NA)	134
Indeterminate Sentences	121	130
Dangerous Sexual Offender (DSO)*	47	48
Habitual Offender (HO)*	35	31
Dangerous Offender (DO)*	28	41
Warrant of the Lieutenant Governor (WLG)	11	10
Long-Term Fixed Sentences	120	124
Total Long-Term Incarcerates	1,644	1,768
	(released 58)	(admitted 180)
Total Federal Incarcerates	11,200	11,876
Time Served		
7 years or more	582 (35%)	660 (37%)
1 to 7 years	857	928
Less than 1 year	184	180
Offense		
Murder (First, Second Degree)	1,283	1,393

NOTE: *The assignment of Dangerous Sexual Offender and Habitual Offender status by the Court was abolished in 1977 with the introduction of the Dangerous Offender legislation into the Criminal Code.
(NA) Not available.

the previously employed indefinite sentences of dangerous sexual offenders (DSO) and habitual offenders (HO), their replacement, the dangerous offender (DO) sentence, and all fixed definite sentences of 21 years or more. The 21 years was chosen as a criterion so that all offenders who can be virtually guaranteed a minimum incarceration period of 7 years would be included (i.e., the earliest possible release for a 21 year sentence for a pre-1977 life sentence is 7 years).

In mid-1983, 1,644 or 15% of all federally incarcerated prisoners were identified according to this selection process. In this group, 208 could be described as "very long-term prisoners" in that we can reasonably expect them to be incarcerated for at least 25 years. Approximately one year later, the number had risen to 1,768, 263 of whom were in the 25-year category. A quick examination of the inmate flow illustrates the current build-up. The net increase was due to the release of 58 long-termers in a period when 180 long-term admissions were made. Stated differently, we are currently admitting three times as many long-

term inmates as we are releasing. One can only imagine the numerical and social consequences of such a practice over time. Similarly, the sudden increase in offenders serving very long sentences (i.e., 55 in the last year) is of importance to sentencing and correctional policy makers alike. Since the first offenders sentenced to a minimum of 25 years, barring a pardon, will not be eligible for parole until the twenty first century, we can expect the aggregation to be tremendous.

As a group, most offenders (85%) were serving various versions of life sentences. First or second degree murder represented the most common offense (78%). More than one-third had already served more than seven years. As expected, the majority were held in maximum (55%) or medium (33%) security institutions. Interestingly, 71% were serving their first federal incarceration, while only 3% have more than two previous federal terms. As a group, long-term prisoners are older than the average CSC inmate, having a mean age of 35.8 years. Approximately 8% reported a native ethnic background.

THE GANSER SYNDROME AND OTHER POPULAR POSITIONS

The vast majority of criminological literature bemoans the devastating impact of prison on its inhabitants. Consider the following:

The long-term institutional resident or inmate unless he is of exceptional strength from the beginning, has some fixed external point towards which to orient, or the institution provides stimulation for him, may degenerate in his person to become not only 'mindless' but will-less and guiltless. (Ham, 1976)

Various terms have been coined to describe this pattern, although not without considerable confusion. Regardless, the above description presents the classical picture of what has been described as "institutional neurosis" or that point at which "the individual is adrift on a timeless stream with no beginning and no end" (Vail, 1966). Vail also contends that ultimate tragedy is not that impulse control is gone, but that impulse generation, the capacity to respond to external or internal stimuli which prod the ordinary person, is so dull as to be random in its manifestations and pathetically feeble. Elsewhere, institutional neurosis is described as a "man-made disease," a "mental bedsore" with characteristic signs and symptoms that include:

apathy, lack of initiation, loss of interest more marked in things and events not immediately personal or present, submissiveness, and sometimes no expression of feelings of resentment at harsh or unfair orders. There is also a lack of interest in the future and an apparent inability to make practical plans for it, a deterioration in personal habits and standards generally, a loss of individuality, and a resigned acceptance that things will go on as they are unchangingly, inevitably and indefinitely. (Barton, 1959)

Similarly, the psychiatric literature has waxed eloquent on the psychological consequences of long-term incarceration throughout this century. First described by Ganser in 1898 as a "peculiar hysterical twilight state," the Ganser Syndrome is characterized by the giving of approximate but wrong answers, clouding of consciousness, somatic conversion and subsequent amnesia for previous symptoms (Shorer, 1965). However, confusion abounds concerning this psychopathological disorder. As McKay, Jayewardene, and Reedie (1979) found in their review, evidence for the incidence of occurrence is scanty and varied. This is partly due to the difficulty in obtaining a precise definition and a standard for evaluating reported cases. For example, the syndrome has been cited in patients later diagnosed as schizophrenic (Anderson, Trethowan, & Kenna, 1959) and reported time of onset varies tremendously, ranging from those waiting trial (Shorer, 1965) to those just prior to release (May, Bolgele, & Padino, 1960).

McKay et al. (1979) concluded that although most clinicians agree that an independent and identifiable clinical syndrome does exist, they disagree on the symptom pattern, its interpretation, and frequency of occurrence. As a postscript to the literature on the psychiatric perspective of long-term incarceration effects, the recently adopted diagnostic scheme of the American Psychiatric Association (1980) classifies the Ganser Syndrome as a facetious disorder with psychological symptoms, meaning that the individual assumes a patient's role by means of voluntary, severe, and often psychotic symptoms.

PRISON AND PRISONIZATION

The culprit responsible for these debilitating effects, is of course, the prison, that "total institution" eloquently described by Goffman (1961) as a social hybrid, "part residential community, part formal organization." According to Goffman these establishments are the "forcing houses for changing persons in our society. Each is a national experiment, typically harsh on what can be done to the self." Others saw the total character of prison symbolized by the barrier to social intercourse with the outside built right into the physical plant, such as locked doors, high walls, barbed wire or cliffs (Ham, 1976). These accounts, which ascribe a wide range of inevitable and debilitating effects, may be referred to as the "myth of prisonization." In reality, the evidence for a profound and incapacitating influence, that is both commonplace and severe, is scarce, if existent at all.

As Radzinowicz (1968) said in his report to the Advisory Council on the Penal System to the British Home Office:

> Practically nothing is known about the vital subject of the lasting effects on human personality of long-term imprisonment, yet pronouncements on the subject continue to be made . . . and very long prison sentences continue to be imposed.

More recently, we find little has changed since Radzinowicz's statement. McKay et al. (1979) similarly report an astounding lack of knowledge about the effects of long-term incarceration. Such a state can hardly be unexpected since the area, which has been described as a "methodological nightmare," does not lend itself easily to systematic empirical verification. Hence, McKay et al.'s analysis revealed a less than adequate quality to the research. Specifically, the work suffered from methodological problems, inadequate research designs, unsystematic sampling procedures, poor control comparisons, and disregard for orientation, milieu and security of the setting. Indeed, most accounts are self-report and anecdotal, but they are of riveting intensity.

Social scientists, however, would be well advised to heed Cressey's (1973) curious, but insightful, comments:

> Prison life is made up of social interactions that are confused, entangled, complicated, and so subtle in their effects that any detailed attempts to tell what happens in them sounds like the ravings of a crazy man.

Cressey goes on to say that no man can accurately discern what shapes his life in prison and warns against heeding those who make sweeping generalizations about the penal environment because there are bound to be inaccuracies in such statements. Cressey has also taken the position that the prison itself does not do anything, that it just sits there. What really matters are the "subtle specifics of each prisoner's participation in prison life." Indeed, the prison experience is complex and interactive. It cannot be encapsulated in a few terms, such as "institutionalization" or "prisonization" (Clemmer, 1940) nor can it be explained in a single model, as was attempted

by the importation or deprivation theories (Thomas, 1977; Thomas & Petersen, 1977).

As an illustration of the futility of these simplistic approaches, one need only consider the American criminological research on prison impact that pitted two models against each other. The "importation" view claimed that the personal and background characteristics, with which an offender enters prison, predispose him to a particular manner of prison adaptation, while the "deprivation" position professed that specific prison conditions are responsible for the amount and nature of an offender's prisonization. However, it has been acknowledged that these models do not account for a high proportion of the variance in prisonization among incarcerates (Thomas, Petersen, & Zingraff, 1978) and that a move toward and integration of existing theories is required (Thomas, 1970). Furthermore, recent work by Suedfeld and colleagues (Suedfeld, Ramirez, Deaton, & Baker-Brown, 1982) illustrates the inadequacy of the deprivation model. They examined the personality, intelligence, mood, stress, and creativity of inmates in solitary confinement of five North American federal penitentiaries. Finding few differences from standardization samples, they concluded that solitary confinement is not universally damaging, aversive, or intolerable. Indeed, it is not uncommon for incarcerates to request solitary confinement or isolation as a learned strategy for coping with the environment.

THE EMPIRICAL STUDIES

Whereas theories of importation and deprivation once took the malevolence of prison as their point of departure and conventional wisdom inexorably linked long-term incarceration to deterioration of personality, Flanagan (1982) notes that there has been a profound change in these assumptions. This rather sudden development has been due to the findings of several investigators whose objective tests yielded virtually no convincing evidence that systematic deterioration occurs in any of the physical, psycho-pathological, attitudinal, or cognitive realms of human functioning. One might even go so far as saying that there is a sizeable literature, large enough to command attention and deserving of an explanation, that indicates a positive effect of incarceration for certain offenders. The following is an overview of the more notable studies.

The complexity of imprisonment and the discrepancy of effects is illustrated most clearly in Bukstel and Kilmann's (1980) recent review of 90 experimental studies examining the psychological effects of imprisonment. Their analysis indicated that some prisoners deteriorate in response to confinement, while others show no appreciable change and yet others demonstrate improved functioning. They caution, however, that changes in functioning may also vary according to the phase of the sentence and the time remaining to release, as well as institutional factors such as crowding, prison orientation, and peer group affiliation. In sum, each individual responds uniquely to a complex interaction of variables. The diversity of inmate responses to incarceration is illustrated in Irwin's (1981) recent report in which at least 6 different kinds of adaptation and adjustment are reported. His typology of adjustment styles includes the following: community simulation via an active prison socioeconomic lifestyle; accumulation of material possessions; self-improvement along various dimensions such as physical health, education, trade training and skill development, which, of course, can be prosocial or antisocial; program resistance or radicalization; and psychological withdrawal from the reality of prison. Only by reviewing the incarceration literature can one appreciate the diversity of inmate reactions and, hence, appreciate the importance of approaches such as Irwin's.

A group of British studies comprise the most impressive and thorough examination of the issue. Richards (1978) asked two groups of long-term prisoners to rate a list of 20 problems in terms of frequency and intensity of occurrence. Those who served more than 8 years expressed basically the same problems and rated them as being similar in severity as those who had served less than 18 months. The author concludes that long-term confinement does not necessarily have a progressive or cumulative effect. Interestingly, the most severely rated problems expressed by both groups concerned deprivation of relationships rather than personal threats to mental health.

Similarly, Heskin et al. (Heskin, Bolton, Smith, & Banister, 1974) in one of a series of studies (Banister, Smith, Heskin, & Bolton, 1973; Heskin, Smith, Banister, & Bolton, 1973) found few differences in the attitudes of long-term prisoners who had served an average of 11 years in comparison to those who were just beginning their lengthy sentences and had served only 2.5 years. Using a semantic differential technique, they found similar attitudes towards such conventions as the home, marriage, the law, police, and prisons, although some decline in self-evaluation was detected. The authors concluded that their study shows no evidence that imprisonment is associated with increasing hostility towards the law and its agents. More impressive, however, is one of the only longitudinal studies carried out. Undertaken as part of this research series (Bolton, Smith, Heskin, & Banister, 1976), objective tests of intellectual functioning were re-administered to a group of 154 long-term prisoners. The follow-up did not reveal any psychological deterioration associated with long-term imprisonment. In fact, verbal intelligence showed a significant improvement between testings while hostility decreased over time. The authors concluded that sometimes imprisonment may be associated with beneficial effects and these are rarely, if ever, discussed.

Finally, Sapsford (1978), also in Britain, examined a cross-section of maximum security prisoners serving a life sentence who had been recently admitted or who had served from 6 to 11 years. He found no association with medical reports and psychiatric diagnosis between groups. Although there was some indication that those who had served more time were more introverted, there was no indication of increased apathy, disregard for community events, or loss of interest in release.

Two interesting German studies are particularly noteworthy. Rasch (1981) undertook a comprehensive assessment program of three groups of lifers who had served an average 3, 8.5, or 13.5 years, respectively. Data collection included medical, psychiatric, intellectual, psychological, and attitudinal components. The results were unable to reveal any deterioration in state of health, psychiatric symptoms, or intellect. Furthermore, attitudinal measures and MMPI data indicated a development towards more conventional sentiments and decreased psychopathology as measured by the paranoia and schizophrenia scales of the MMPI.

Elsewhere, Bresser (1974) and Goeman (1977) investigated the life situations and social prognosis of long-term prisoners. Adopting a "phase approach," they were unable to find any evidence of the general personality deterioration hypothesized to occur in the third phase, after 20 years of imprisonment. When dysfunction was observed among long-term prisoners, a long history of personality defects was also revealed. Research such as this dispells the theory that incarceration entails a sequential and invariant series of stages through which all long-term prisoners progress. Individual differences and varying prison conditions are simply too powerful to make any such claims.

PRISON SUICIDE

How might these results be reconciled with common notions about prison effects? Self-reports and clinical observations abound with personal tragedies and accounts of the individual suffering that occurs behind bars (Toch, 1975). One is left with many puzzling questions. How many of these incidents may be attributed to the impact of incarceration, particularly long-term incarceration? Of those that are due to prison, what aspects of imprisonment are responsible?

A close examination of prison suicides may be helpful in addressing these questions. A nationwide survey of inmate suicides in the U.S. between 1952 and 1973 revealed a rate of 17.5 per 100,000 inmates, compared to a rate of 11 per 100,000 people in the general population (Austin & Unkovic, 1977). Although the loss of any human life is tragic, one is left with the question as to what the suicide rate is for those in the community who are comparable to incarcerated offenders in terms of risk factors, such as socio-economic status, and psychiatric history. As an illustration of the latter dimension, an analysis of 14 offender mental health surveys (Bentz & Noel, 1983) generated an incidence of 39% fitting into a diagnostic category representing psychiatric disorder. Such a figure suggests that incarcerated offenders are indeed at greater risk for suicide than the general population. As an aside, however, it is not suggested that this rationale absolves the correctional administrator. To the contrary, it suggests a need for greater attention to prevention and an improved readiness to respond to such contingencies.

A more recent examination of prison deaths is also revealing in that it further challenges some of the common assumptions about prison suicide. The National Center on Institutions and Alternatives (Hayes, 1983; National Center on Institutions and Alternatives, 1982) found more than 50% of the suicides occurred within the first 24 hours of imprisonment and 92% had not yet gone to trial. Ironically, two-thirds of the incidents occurred in isolation, where presumably the offenders were being detained for their own safety. Although these findings provide important information concerning administrative mismanagement and misunderstanding of offender control strategies, they do not provide a convincing argument for the deleterious effects of long-term incarceration. In fact, some studies even suggest that the suicide rate in certain U.S. federal institutions is lower than the general population (Newton, 1980). In sum, there is growing evidence that, as Gibbs (1982) puts it, "the first cut is the deepest." Clearly, the trauma and uncertainty of initial incarceration should not be confused with the effects of long-term imprisonment.

SOCIAL GERONTOLOGY

Social gerontology is another research area of relevance to the investigation of prison effects. It represents possibly one of the few domains in which the traditional folklore is consistent with empirical data. Consider the following convict's observation from *A Thief's Primer* (Jackson, 1969).

There's something else funny that happens to some people; they come down here and their age seems to fix at what it was when they come in. And something else: I don't think they age as much in appearance as they do in the free world. Down here I see guys all the time that are sixty or seventy-five who look like forty to forty-five. Physically they stay younger.

Similarly, another older prisoner claims (Wiltz, 1973):

Your regular hours of eating and sleeping preserve your health. If a man doesn't catch something here, I believe he can live to be 110 or 115 years old.

TABLE 7.2 MMPI Correlations With Time Served, Aggregate Sentence, and Age of Admission ($N = 269$)

	Zero Order Correlations			Time Served Controlling for Aggregate Sentence and Age	
Scale	Time Served	Aggregate Sentence	Age of Admission	Total Sample	Less Recent Admission ($N = 161$)
L	.07	.04	.13*	.03	.02
F	−.28***	−.19***	−.15**	−.18**	−.23***
K	.23***	.21***	.12*	.10	.15*
HS	−.22***	−.16**	.02	−.17**	−.17*
D	−.26***	−.22***	−.01	−.17**	−.17*
Hy	−.16**	−.11*	.06	−.14*	−.15*
Pd	−.14**	−.15**	−.07	−.07	−.06
Mf	−.06	−.07	.16**	−.09	−.18*
Pa	−.20***	−.12*	−.03	−.16**	−.17*
Pf	−.26***	−.24***	−.11	−.14*	−.14
Sc	−.26***	−.22***	−.15**	−.15*	−.17*
Ma	−.12*	−.16	−.16**	.02	−.02
Si	−.20***	−.15**	−.07	−.14*	−.16*

All tests two-tailed.
$*p < .05; **p < .01; ***p < .001$.

These impressions are supported by a number of more rigorous investigations. For example, Reed (Reed, 1978; Reed & Glamser, 1979) studied aging of older prisoners (median age of 60 years) who had served an average of 23 years in a major penitentiary. The authors report that many of the experiences associated with aging in open society including retirement, loss of spouse, and financial insecurity were not present and that traditional physical and emotional deterioration resulting from work and stress was absent. Inmates appeared and reported feeling younger than their chronological age. Traditional milestones of aging such as retirement and widowhood held no meaning and they did not have to make radical adjustments to maintain social status or financial security. It was also noted that the older long-term prisoner was well-informed, interested in politics and made plenty of use of his leisure time. Furthermore, from a gerontological point of view, the study is used to illustrate the importance of social and cultural aspects of aging in contrast to development phenomena and chronological age. Related studies have also shown that older prisoners adjust more readily and can satisfactorily cope with prison life (Wooden & Parker, 1980).

A CANADIAN PSYCHOMETRIC STUDY

Our own work with federal inmates has produced some quizzical findings on the long-term impact of prison. Over the course of five years, consecutive referrals to a specialized psychiatric facility ($N = 269$) were administered a routine psychological test battery that included the MMPI.[2] The prisoners had served an average of 25 months at the time of assessment. There was, however, a wide range of time elapsed since the prisoners' sentences began ($SD = 24$ months). This permitted an examination of the Time Served dimension. Concerning the MMPI and questions of its validity with offenders, the reader is referred to Gearing (1979) who systematically reviewed 71 studies of MMPI applications in corrections. He concluded that the test provides a reasonable classification of psychopathology among offenders and may be particularly valuable in the identification of hostile-assaultive offenders.

The findings reported in Table 7.2 indicate that the inmates who had served more time displayed less deviance on their MMPI profiles. The amount of Time Served at testing was significant and negatively correlated with eight of the ten clinical scales. However, due to the cross-sectional nature of the study, alternative explanations could be suggested. For example, sentence length was also inversely related to psychopathology on all scales except *Mf*. In other words, prisoners with longer sentences displayed less mental disorder. Therefore, it was possible that inmates who had served longer time showed less psychopathology because, having received longer sentences, they were less deviant at the outset. However, when partial correlations were computed, controlling for the effect of Sentence Length, the Time Served—Mental Health relationship was maintained. Similarly, Age upon Admission was moderately correlated with psychopathology, younger offenders displaying greater disorder. Again when Age was partialled out of the correlation, Time Served was still inversely related to Mental Disorder.

It has also been suggested that offenders are at their worst upon admission to the prison system because of the trauma of the judicial process, the separation from family and community, and the sudden change to a prison environment. Therefore, recent admissions were deleted from the sample and the calculations were repeated. Employing a criterion of six months or more of post-sentence incarceration, the initial findings were again upheld, with six of the ten clinical scales being significant.

Furthermore, improvement was not limited to the MMPI. Long serving prisoners also expressed more prosocial attitudes toward the criminal justice system (Andrews & Wormith, 1984) and displayed more socially and psychologically adjusted profiles on the California Psychological Inventory. There was, however, no effect of Time Served on intelligence as measured by thc WAIS. Another curious and potentially important finding was that the inverse relationship was limited to caucasian prisoners. When the sample was divided ethnically, there was absolutely no such effect among Indian and Métis inmates, suggesting that if there is any profit to be gained by incarceration, it is not experienced by the native offender.

The data were further analyzed to examine whether the relationship was due to proximity of expected discharge, and not simply due to absolute amount of time served. There was, however, no relationship whatsoever between

per cent of Time Served and psychopathology on the MMPI. Finally, the contribution of prisoners serving life sentences to the relationship was examined. This analysis was carried out because of the prison folklore that "lifers" represent the most stable element of the prison culture and one could expect them to have served more time. Controlling for time served, lifers did not differ on any of the MMPI scales from prisoners serving fixed sentences. Therefore, their inclusion in the sample could not account for the results.

DIFFERENT APPROACHES LEAD TO DIFFERENT RESULTS

These findings may offer more confusion than explanation in our quest for understanding the prison experience. We can only echo what McKay et al. (1979) found in their review, "One of the strongest impressions to emerge in reviewing long-term confinement literature is the striking discrepancy between personal accounts and the data-based research describing it." On the one hand, one finds experiential, qualitative descriptions that document the severe, sometimes hideous and tragic, effects of incarceration. As diverse as such authors as Jack Abbott (1981), Carl Chessman (1954), Roger Caron (1978), Eldridge Cleaver (1969), and Alexander Solzhenitsyn (1968) might be, their compelling and persuasive writings are clear and consistent in their presentation of long-term confinement. On the other hand, one notes the objective, quantitative studies that generally fail to indicate deleterious effects. These studies, some of which are reviewed herein, have raised many questions about the long held belief that linked long-term incarcerations to personality deterioration (Flanagan, 1982; Walker, 1983).

The shortcomings of both approaches are obvious. Clearly, personal accounts can include an element of bias and many do, which is not unexpected, since the author is often the kept and is describing environmental conditions and their effects that are the responsibility of his adversary, the keeper. Secondly, anecdotal reports can be found to support virtually any hypothesis. For example, if we now have 266 inmates who will spend most of their adult lives in prison and if Statistics Canada (1981) is correct in its projection that 12½% of our population will be hospitalized at least once during their lives for a mental disorder, we can expect that about 30 of these current lifers will require psychiatric hospitalization during their long-term confinements, and some figure greater than 30 if they represent a subset of our national population that is particularly at risk for mental illness (for example, if they disproportionately represent low socioeconomic groups).

Similarly, the data-based research can be criticized for its lack of completeness and its methodological inadequacies. Specifically, simulations are problematic in that they are a far cry from the reality of imprisonment, true experimental efforts are virtually impossible in prison, and the accuracy of a survey is only as precise as the sensitivity of its measurement instruments. Finally, important, but hidden effects may be overlooked by crude methodologies, excessive collapsing of data, and a preoccupation with statistical significance when social significance is staring one in the face.

UNRAVELLING PRISON IMPACT

Prison life is multidimensional and so affects its clientele in different ways at different times. The nuances of offender change, both positive and negative, remain mysterious and complex. This is illustrated by another study in which offender characteristics at different points in time were examined in relation to outcome (Wormith, 1984). A three-year follow-up study of released provincial prisoners revealed that recidivism was more related to offender change during incarceration, rather than the attributes possessed by the inmate at the time of program entry or discharge.

Secondly, some changes correlated with recidivism in a manner contrary to traditional expectation. For example, increased self-esteem during incarceration was correlated with increased recidivism while an increased sense of inadequacy during imprisonment was related to post-release success. The latter finding provided a clue as to how these results might be unravelled. Indeed, reflecting on the incarceration process, one might actually expect that those who develop greater self-esteem in the context of a prison environment would actually become a greater risk for recidivism. With this in mind, the data were reanalyzed, concomitantly looking at how prisoners changed in terms of their criminal orientation and identification. An important and telling interaction emerged. Those inmates whose increase in self-esteem occurred in conjunction with an increase in Identification with Criminal Others, experienced the most severe recidivism. Interestingly, of the remaining 3 groups, those who increased in their criminal identification in prison, while experiencing a falling sense of self-esteem, emerged three years later as the most successful.

These findings suddenly throw the self-esteem construct into a different perspective. In actuality, studies of self-esteem in prison have produced very contradictory results (Newton, 1980), effects over time being described as increasing, decreasing, U-shaped, inverted U-shaped, and even reversed J-shaped (McKay et al., 1979). Indeed, it now appears that self-esteem should be regarded as a double-edged sword because, at least for prisoners, so much depends on the context of its acquisition. This study also illustrates the complexity of prisoner change. Clearly, there are no simple explanations or solutions.

CONCLUSION

In summary, lengthy sentences will have many complicated and diverse effects. For every *Belly of the Beast* (Abbott, 1981) there is another long-term prisoner who becomes a *Bird Man of Alcatraz* (Gaddis, 1955), and another who abandons his life as a former *Go-boy* (Caron, 1978). Similarly, there are countless descriptions, such as the following:

> The long-term institutional resident or inmate unless he is of exceptional strength from the beginning, has some fixed external point towards which to orient, or the institution provides stimulation for him, may degenerate in his person to become not only 'mindless' but will-less and guiltless. (Hayes, 1983)

There are also personal accounts like this:

> In the midst of what is meant to punish and degrade, art and literature and religion revive and flourish. Not in great crowds, but here and there, an artist in one place, a native brotherhood in another, a writer somewhere else. The

sparks fly-up the darkness and are seen by others, our task is to see that they are not put out. (Caves, 1980)

Certainly, there can be, indeed are, deleterious effects of incarceration. A single suicide, or self-mutilation, is tragic, wherever it occurs, regardless of its incidence rate. But to claim these are straight-forward and inevitable consequences of long-term incarceration is simplistic, if not erroneous, and will only divert us from the truly important questions: What are the adverse effects of incarceration? Who will experience them? Why will they experience them? and How can we ameliorate them?

NOTES

1. An earlier version of this paper entitled "The positive effects of incarceration" was presented as part of a workshop on the effects of long-term incarceration (F. Porporino, Chair) at the Second World Congress on Prison Health Care, Ottawa, August, 1983.

2. Data for the MMPI study were collected while the author was at the Regional Psychiatric Centre (Saskatoon), Correctional Service of Canada. Thanks are expressed to Walter Black, Ingrid Draper, Rod Laciuk, Tracy Pytlowany, Dorothy Reid and Eric Smith for their assistance with this study.

REFERENCES

Abbott, J. H. (1981). *In the belly of the beast: Letters from prison*. New York: Random House.

American Psychiatric Association. (1980). *Diagnostic and statistical manual of mental disorders: DSMIII* (3rd ed.). Washington, DC: APA.

Anderson, E. W., Trethowan, W. H., & Kenna, J. (1959). An experimental investigation of simulation and pseudo-dementia. *Acta Psychiatrica et Neurologica Scandinavia, 34*, 1-42.

Andrews, D. A., & Wormith, J. S. (1984). Criminal sentiments and criminal behaviour: A construct validation (User Report #30). Ottawa: Ministry of the Solicitor General.

Austin, W. T., & Unkovic, C. M. (1977). Prison suicide. *Criminal Justice Review, 2*, 103-106.

Banister, P. A., Smith, F. V., Heskin, K. J., & Bolton, N. (1973). Psychological correlates of long-term imprisonment: I. Cognitive variables. *British Journal of Criminology, 13*, 312-323.

Barton, R. (1959). *Institutional neurosis*. Bristol: Wright.

Bentz, W. K., & Noel, I. W. (1983). The incidence of psychiatric disorder among a sample of men entering prison. *Journal of Corrective and Social Psychiatry*, 22-27.

Bolton, N., Smith, F. V., Heskin, K. J., & Banister, P. A. (1976). Psychological correlates of long-term imprisonment: IV. A longitudinal analysis. *British Journal of Criminology, 16*, 38-47.

Bresser, P. H. (1974). "Die Begutachtung zur Sozialprognose 'Lebenslänglicher' und Sicherungsverwahrter." *Juristische Rundschau, 7*, 265-270.

Bukstel, L. H., & Kilmann, P. R. (1980). Psychological effects of imprisonment on confined individuals. *Psychological Bulletin, 88*, 469-493.

Caron, R. (1978). *Go boy: Memoires of a life behind bars*. Toronto: McGraw-Hill.

Caves, B. (1980). Outside and inside: The prison in the life of Canada's native people. *Tawow: Canadian Indian Cultural Magazine, 8*(1), 3-4.

Chessman, C. (1954). *Cell 2455, death row*. New York: Prentice Hall.

Cleaver, E. (1969). *Soul on ice*. London: Cape.

Clemmer, D. (1940). *The prison community*. Boston: Christopher.

Cressey, D. R. (1973). Adult felons in prisons. In L. E. Ohlin (Ed.), *Prisons in America*. Englewood Cliffs, NJ: Prentice Hall.

Flanagan, T. J. (1982). Lifers and long-termers: Doing big time. In R. Johnson & H. Toch (Eds.), *The pains of imprisonment*. Beverly Hills, CA: Sage.

Gaddis, T. E. (1955). *Bird man of Alcatraz*. Manttitach, NY: Rivercity Press.

Gearing, M. L. (1979). The MMPI as a primary differentiator and predictor of behavior in prison—A methodological critique and review of the recent literature. *Psychological Bulletin, 86*, 929-963.

Gibbs, J. J. (1982). The first cut is the deepest: Psychological breakdown and survival in the detention setting. In R. Johnson & H. Toch (Eds.), *The pain of imprisonment*. Beverly Hills, CA: Sage.

Goeman, M. (1977). *Das Schicksal der Lebenslänglichen*. Berlin: Walter de Gruyter.

Goffman, E. (1961). *Asylums: Essays on the social situation of mental patients and other inmates*. Garden City, NY: Doubleday.

Ham, J. (1976). *The forgotten minority—An exploration of long-term institutionalized aged*. Unpublished doctoral thesis, University of Michigan.

Hayes, L. M. (1983). And darkness closes in . . . and a national study of jail suicides. *Criminal Justice and Behaviour, 10*, 461-484.

Heskin, K. J., Smith, F. V., Banister, P. A., & Bolton, N. (1973). Psychological correlates of long-term imprisonment: II. Personality variables. *British Journal of Criminology, 13*, 323-330.

Heskin, K. J., Smith, F. V., Banister, P. A., & Bolton, N. (1974). Psychological correlates of long-term imprisonment: III. Attitudinal variables. *British Journal of Criminology, 14*, 150-157.

Irwin, J. K. (1981). Sociological studies of the impact of long-term confinement. In D. A. Wood & K. F. Schoen (Eds.), *Confinement in maximum custody*. Lexington, MA: D. C. Heath.

Jackson, B. (1969). *A thief's primer*. London: Macmillan.

May, R. H., Bolgele, G. E., & Padino, A. F. (1960). The Ganser Syndrome: A report of three cases. *Journal of Nervous and Mental Disorders, 130*, 331-339.

McKay, H. B., Jayewardene, C.H.S., & Reedie, P. B. (1979). *The effects of long-term incarceration and a proposed strategy for future research*. Ottawa: Solicitor General of Canada.

National Center on Institutions and Alternatives. (1982, August). Jail house suicides are neither remorseful nor depressed. *Psychology Today*, pp. 12-13.

Newton, A. (1980). The effects of imprisonment. *Criminal Justice Abstracts, 12*(1), 134-151.

Radzinowicz, L. (1968). *The regime for long-term prisoners in conditions of maximum security: Report of the advisory council on the penal system*. London: HMSO.

Rasch, W. (1981). The effects of indeterminate detention: A study of men sentenced to life imprisonment. *International Journal of Law and Psychiatry, 4*, 417-431.

Reed, M. B. (1978). *Aging in a total institution—The case of older prisoners*. Nashville: Tennessee Corrections Institute.

Reed, M. B., & Glamser, F. D. (1979). Aging in a total institution—The case of older prisoners. *Gerontologist, 19*, 354-360.

Richards, B. (1978). The experience of long-term imprisonment. *British Journal of Criminology, 18*, 162-169.

Sapsford, R. J. (1978). Life-sentence prisoners: Psychological changes during sentence. *British Journal of Criminology, 18*, 128-145.

Shorer, C. E. (1965). The Ganser Syndrome. *British Journal of Criminology, 5*, 120-131.

Solzhenitsyn, A. (1968). *One day in the life of Ivan Denisovich*. London: Penguin.

Statistics Canada. (1981). *One in eight: Mental illness in Canada*. Ottawa: Supply and Services.

Suedfeld, P., Ramirez, C., Deaton, J., & Baker-Brown, G. (1982). Reactions and attributes of prisoners in solitary confinement. *Criminal Justice and Behaviour, 9*, 303-340.

Thomas, C. W. (1970). Toward a more inclusive model of the inmate contraculture. *Criminology, 8*, 251-262.

Thomas, C. (1977). Theoretical perspectives on prisonization. *Journal of Criminology and Criminal Law, 68*, 135-145.

Thomas, C., & Petersen, D. (1977). *Prison organization and inmate subculture*. Indianapolis: Bobbs-Merrill.

Thomas, C. W., Petersen, D. M., & Zingraff, R. M. (1978). Structural and social psychological correlates of prisonization. *Criminology, 16*, 383-393.

Toch, H. (1975). *Men in crisis: Human breakdowns in prisons*. Chicago: Aldine.

Vail, D. J. (1966). *Dehumanization and the institutional career*. Springfield, IL: Charles C Thomas.

Walker, N. (1983). Side-effects of incarceration. *British Journal of Criminology, 23*, 61-71.

Wiltz, C. (1973). *The aged prisoner: A case study of age and aging in prison*. Unpublished thesis, Kansas State University.

Wooden, W. S., & Parker, J. (1980). *Aged men in a prison environment: Life satisfaction and coping strategies*. Long Beach: Sociology Department, California State University.

Wormith, J. S. (1983, November). *What do we really know about the effects of incarceration?* Invited address presented at Dialogue on Criminal Justice. Biennial Conference of the Canadian Association for the Prevention of Crime, Ottawa.

Wormith, J. S. (1984, November). Attitude and behaviour change of correctional clientele: A three year follow-up. *Criminology, 22*.

8

Long-Term Incarceration Impacts and Characteristics of Long-Term Offenders

An Empirical Analysis

Doris Layton MacKenzie

Lynne Goodstein

The responses long- and short-term inmates make to incarceration and differences in the responses made by distinct subgroups were examined. Prison inmates in three large maximum security institutions reported their levels of stress (anxiety, depression, psychosomatic illnesses, fear), adjustment (prisonization), criminal history, self-esteem, and demographic characteristics. Inmates new to prison who anticipated serving long terms in prison were found to report higher levels of stress and lower self-esteem than did inmates who had already completed long terms in prison. Short-term inmates new to prison reported less depression and fewer psychosomatic illnesses in comparison to new inmates with long sentences. Distinct subgroups of long-term offenders (lifers versus habituals) could be identified on the basis of demographics and past history. However, these groups did not differ in stress, adjustment, or self-esteem. It was concluded that inmates who were new to prison but anticipated serving long sentences experienced the most stress. Inmates who had received long sentences and had already served a lengthy time in prison appeared to have developed a method of coping with the experience.

The past decade has witnessed a burgeoning of prison populations throughout the country, and this figure is expected to increase in coming years (Blumstein & Kadane, 1983). A significant proportion of these inmates are serving lengthy prison sentences that, even after reductions for good time or parole release, generally involve a long term behind bars (U.S. Department of Justice, 1981). Furthermore, there are indications that this segment of the American prisoner population may be increasing at a more rapid rate than those serving shorter terms. This disproportionate increase may result in part from recent

AUTHORS' NOTE: This investigation was supported in part by grant 80-NI-AX-006 from the National Institute of Justice to the Pennsylvania State University.
NOTE: Reprinted from *Criminal Justice and Behavior*, Vol. 12, No. 4, December 1985, pp. 395-414. Copyright 1985 by Sage Publications Inc, and by American Association for Correctional Psychology.

sentencing legislation aimed at removing individuals with serious criminal histories from society for longer periods of time.

A 1983 survey by the National Council on Crime and Delinquency revealed that laws imposing mandatory prison terms for offenders convicted of a number of serious violations are in place in almost every state. Under these provisions, judges have no choice but to impose prison sentences, often of 5 years or more, when defendants are convicted of crimes specified by these statutes. Offenses for which mandatory sentences are imposed generally fall within one of four broad categories—violent crime, habitual crime, narcotics violation, and use or possession of a firearm (Bureau of Justice Statistics, 1983).

Other types of sentencing provisions were explicitly written to incapacitate felons—with extensive criminal histories or who are guilty of extremely serious crimes—by imposing longer sentences. For example, determinant sentencing reforms in Minnesota (Minnesota Sentencing Guidelines and Commentary, 1980), Pennsylvania (Pennsylvania Commission on Sentencing, 1982), and North Carolina (Clark, 1984) were developed with the objective of incarcerating serious offenders for longer terms than they had customarily served under previous statutes.

Laws imposing mandatory incarceration for offenders convicted of a number of serious offenses, such as rape, have been passed in a number of states including Illinois (Illinois Criminal Law Procedure, ch. 38), Connecticut (Connecticut General Statutes Annotated vol. 27: 53a-55), and Pennsylvania (18 Pa. Consolidated Statutes §101). Other determinate sentencing provisions—for example, the Minnesota sentencing guidelines—were explicitly written to incapacitate felons with extensive criminal histories by awarding longer sentences (Minnesota Sentencing Guidelines and Commentary, 1980).

Not only are more defendants being given long sentences under the new provisions, but a wider range of cases have become eligible for these extended terms. For example, under the recently adopted Connecticut sentencing law, a defendant convicted of assault I or burglary I must be given a mandatory minimum of 5 years and could serve as much as a 20-year sentence. In addition, defendants convicted twice of statutory felonies are classified as "persistent dangerous offenders" and are sentenced as Class A felons for a term of between 10 and 25 years (Goodstein, Kramer, & Nuss, 1984). Under the former sentencing law, many of these cases would have received shorter sentences. The same process—of sentencing more individuals convicted of a wider variety of offenses to more time in prison—is occurring in other states with sentencing reform (Cooper, Kelley, & Larson, 1982). Indeed, in a recent study of 10 years of sentencing reform, in all 50 states, Shane-Dubow (1984) reports that 33 states have implemented harsher habitual offender laws; not a single state had decreased penalties for habitual offenders during that period.

An implication of this change in sentencing policy is that the characteristics of the long-term prisoner population may be changing as well. Although extremely long sentences were formerly reserved primarily for individuals convicted of crimes such as murder or kidnapping, it is now possible for an individual convicted repeatedly of robbery or assault to be labeled as a habitual offender and given a long prison term. This increase in the application of habitual offender laws may lead to differences in the characteristics of long-term offenders—increasing the proportion of long-term offenders who are younger, more criminally experienced, and more violent.

In the coming decades correctional management in all probability will be faced with increasing proportions of inmates serving long prison sentences or, as we shall refer to them, long-term offenders (LTOs). Assuming that the proportion of inmates serving long sentences will be increasing, it is important to focus on the modes of adaptation to prison characteristic of that subpopulation. Correctional administrators should be cognizant of the effects of long-term incarceration and should be prepared to develop strategies for counteracting these effects should they prove detrimental.

Additionally, researchers should examine the possibility that different types of long-term offenders manifest different reactions to imprisonment. If, indeed, more LTOs who are younger, more criminally experienced, and more violent are entering prisons, it would be important to determine whether they adjust to prison differently from former LTO types. More fundamentally, it must be determined whether the long-term offender population is made up of homogeneous or heterogeneous groups.

The present study addresses these concerns. Specifically, it asks the following questions:

1. What are the impacts of long-term incarceration on patterns of inmate adjustment to prison?
2. Are there distinct subgroups of LTOs?
3. Do different LTO subgroups respond differentially to incarceration?

Before turning to the methodology used and results obtained in the present study, attention will be focused on the available literature that addresses the above questions.

EFFECTS OF
LONG-TERM INCARCERATION

Inspection of the corrections literature yields numerous references to the potentially detrimental impact of long-term confinement. Anecdotal information points to fears among prisoners that extended incarceration will cause them to become "institutionalized." Prisoners and correctional staff use this term to describe a process involving the following: losing interest in the outside world, viewing the prison as home, losing the ability to make independent decisions, and, in general, defining oneself totally within the institutional context (Cohen & Taylor, 1972; Flanagan, 1980, 1981; Goffman, 1961; Rasch, 1977). This constellation of reactions is assumed to be traumatic to the individual's personality and sense of self and to be a particular source of difficulty when the individual is ready to leave the institution (Bennett, 1974; Clemmer, 1958; Goodstein, 1979; McCorkle & Korn, 1954).

It is noteworthy that, to date, adverse effects of long-term confinement have not been demonstrated in the bulk of the empirical research conducted. Overall, the literature on impacts of long-term confinement in such areas as intellectual ability, personality, physical condition, and interpersonal relations does not demonstrate strong and consistent evidence of broad-scale deterioration. However, it should also be noted that this evidence must be viewed cautiously, as most of the available research in this area has been performed in Great Britain (Banister, Smith, Heskin, & Bolton, 1973; Cohen & Taylor,

1972; Heskin, Bolton, Smith, & Banister, 1974; Richards, 1978; Sapsford, 1978), which has both a lower rate of incarceration and a smaller proportion of racial minority inmates than the United States (Great Britain Home Office, 1978). Thus, generalization of those results to U.S. prisoners would be tenuous.

SUBGROUPS OF
LONG-TERM OFFENDERS

In most of the studies previously cited, long-term offenders were considered to constitute a unidimensional group whose reactions to confinement would form a consistent pattern. The possibility that individuals with different experiential backgrounds react differentially to long-term confinement was not addressed in the investigators' research design. Indeed, the samples studied were probably more uniform with respect to background characteristics than might be found in an equivalent group of U.S. prisoners, because the majority of subjects had been incarcerated for serious "person" crimes such as homicide and sex offenses (Richards, 1978; Sapsford, 1978).

The importance of considering personal characteristics that might lead to differential adjustment patterns has been stressed by several authors recently (Flanagan, 1982; Toch, 1977; for an earlier discussion of this point, see Cohen & Taylor, 1972). Irwin (1981) notes that many offenders enter prison with considerable foreknowledge of the prison environment. Others, also incarcerated for serious crimes, come to prison ill prepared for the experience and thus suffer more. He emphasizes that inmates develop different modes of adaptation to help them adjust to prison life, including affiliation with one's subculture, attempting to maximize choice, "resting," "accommodation," and "withdrawal." It is implied that some of these strategies may be more effective than others in warding off the potential damage of long periods of incarceration.

Flanagan (1982, pp. 82-83) echoes the argument that the American LTO population is made up of groups of individuals with diverse backgrounds and presumably different needs:

Available data on the criminal histories of long-term prisoners indicate that diversity is a hallmark of this group. It includes career criminal robbers in whose lives before imprisonment crime was a daily activity and who adapt to incarceration by continuing careers of deceit and violence. In contrast, other long-term prisoners are essentially noncriminal individuals, whose act of violence was unprecedented and is unlikely to be repeated, and whose interest and perspectives within the prison coincide more closely with those of the officers than with those of fellow inmates. Although murderers make up a large percentage of long-term prisoners, the motives, justifications, and behaviors that are incorporated under the "homicide" label are themselves of broad scope.

The importance of recognizing the existence of subgroups of long-term offenders with different needs and orientations to imprisonment is underscored by recent sentencing reforms that have led to longer sentences for offenders convicted of a wider range of crimes (Cooper et al., 1982). These recent developments may increase the proportion of younger, more criminally experienced and "street wise" inmates within the long-term offender population as a whole.

METHOD

Subjects

A written questionnaire was filled out by 1,270 inmates incarcerated in three prisons. On the average these inmates were 29.8 years of age, serving sentences with a maximum length of 12.5 years. Slightly more of the inmates were black (46%) than were white (42%) or some other race (12%). A substantial majority had completed some high school grade (32%) or had graduated from high school (59%). Approximately half had lived in large cities (55%) before being arrested, whereas few had lived in the suburbs (12%) or country (8%).

Research Sites and Procedure

The three institutions from which data were collected are the following: Stateville Correctional Center, Illinois; Somers Correctional Institution, Connecticut; and Stillwater Correctional Facility, Minnesota. Somers and

Stillwater are mixed medium and maximum security institutions. Stateville is a maximum security prison. All are large institutions (inmate populations more than 1,000) housing adult male felons. The prisons were chosen to be similar in the demographic makeup of the populations.

Questionnaires were administered to inmates in each prison on three successive visits, separated by at least 6 months. This procedure alleviated concern with the influence of contemporaneous events that might result in problems of interpretation if the data are collected at one period of time. For each visit, approximately 250 names were selected through systematic random samples of the institutional populations, drawn immediately prior to data collection. Thus, unless inmates' names were drawn more than once by chance, participants completed questionnaires only once. Those who had previously filled out the questionnaire were eliminated at times two and three, leaving approximately 2,142 inmates who were asked to participate once. Of these, 479 inmates from Somers, 400 inmates from Stillwater, and 391 inmates from Stateville—or 59% of the total—consented to participate.

Inmates were asked to attend questionnaire sessions in groups of approximately 30. After the research was verbally described, a written explanation of the study, a consent form, and a questionnaire were distributed to each inmate. The questionnaires took approximately one hour to complete and each man received $1.50 for coming to the session.[1]

Instruments

Included in the questionnaire were questions regarding the demographic variables of age, race, employment, and school involvement. From the latter two responses a prosocial lifestyle variable was created, with those who attended school or who worked full-time immediately prior to incarceration considered to have had a high prosocial lifestyle.[2] Those who participated in these activities only part-time were considered moderate in prosocial lifestyle, whereas those who had neither worked nor attended school were considered low in prosocial lifestyle.

Inmates were also asked to report their previous experiences with the criminal justice system by indicating number of prior arrests and convictions. Respondents were classified into two groups: (1) those who had no previous experience and (2) those who had previous experience with the criminal justice system. In addition, inmates were asked to report the offense(s) for which they were presently serving time. These offenses were classified on a 7-point scale for severity using state statutes, with a score of 1 being the most severe.

Favorable and unfavorable adjustment patterns during incarceration were expected to be reflected in the following areas: anxiety, depression, psychosomatic-type problems, and self-esteem (see Appendix).

Depression was measured using a short scale (5 items), emphasizing apathy and lethargy, developed for use with a prison population (Coefficient alpha = .78; Goodstein & MacKenzie, 1984). Responses to stress with psychosomatic-type problems were measured by the number of different types of problems reported by inmates (e.g., problems with nerves, headaches, stomach cramps; Goodstein & MacKenzie, 1984). Self-esteem was measured with a 9-item scale (Coefficient alpha = .76) developed by Rosenberg (1965). Fear of others was measured with a summated scale (4 items) developed through a factor analysis procedure using a large number of individual prisonization items (Coefficient alpha = .66; Goodstein & MacKenzie, 1984). A well-researched scale measured prisonization (Thomas & Foster, 1972; Thomas & Poole, 1975; Coefficient alpha = .56). Anxiety was measured using the state version of the State-Trait Anxiety Scale (Spielberger, Gorsuch, & Lushine, 1970; Coefficient alpha = .86). Time served in prison was calculated from respondents' reports of date of entry to prison.

Sentence length was defined as the difference between the date of entry to prison as reported by the respondent and the earliest possible release date, also as reported by the respondent. This is an estimate of sentence length that is argued to be more reliable than the traditional indicators of judicially imposed maximum or minimum sentences due to reductions for good time and parole renewal.[3]

Identification of LTOs

There are two possible methods of identifying those who are LTOs. Each is relevant depending upon the research question to be addressed.

The first method is based upon time actually served in prison, with those who have been in prison 6 or more years considered LTOs. For the present study middle-range inmates were also identified. The division between short and middle range for time served was set at 3 years. Those who had served less than 3 years were considered short; those who had served more than 3 years but less than 6 years were classified as middle.

The second method defines inmates as LTOs on the basis of their received sentence length. Although the criterion is somewhat arbitrary, inmates required to serve at least 6 years in prison, taking into account state provisions for good time and parole, are generally regarded as LTOs (Flanagan, 1980). Study respondents were classified into two categories based upon sentence length. Those who received sentences requiring at least 6 or more years in prison were classified as LTOs; the rest were considered short in sentence length. Table 8.1 illustrates a classification scheme, taking into consideration both time served and sentence length, that can be used to examine various hypotheses. Also included in this table are the numbers of inmates in the sample who fell into each cell.

Research Design

The dimension of time served alone, or a comparison of cell I to cell K (Table 8.1), can be used to examine the impact of a long prison sentence. However, those who are new to prison and will, most likely, serve a long term in prison may differ from those who are new to prison but will not serve a long sentence. The expectation of a long sentence may be particularly stressful, or LTOs may differ from non-LTOs prior to incarceration. In either case comparisons of cells A and E on the variables of interest will permit an examination of possible differences between LTOs and non-LTOs early in their sentences. This would eliminate the possible confound of time served and sentence length.

Comparisons of cell E to cell G (Table 8.1) can be used to address both the issues of the impact of incarceration and possible changes in the type of inmates now being given long

TABLE 8.1 Levels of Analyses of Offenders Classified by Sentence Length and Time Served[a]

		Short	Mid	Long	Total
			Time Served in Prison		
			Cell (n)		
Sentence Length	Short Term	A (655)	B (71)	C (0)	D (726)
	Long Term	E (109)	F (77)	G (90)	H (276)
Total		I (764)	J (148)	K (90)	L (1002)

a. Inmates who failed to respond to either question were omitted from the analysis.

sentences. These analyses will contrast LTOs early in their sentences (early-LTOs) with LTOs late in their sentences (late-LTOs). Differences in the demographics of these groups would suggest recent changes in the type of offenders being given long sentences. Adjustment and attitude differences might then be attributed to either these preincarcerational differences or to time served in prison. Should no differences be found in the demographics of the groups, then differences in attitudes and adjustment variables might be attributed to the impact of incarceration.

To address the question of subgroups of LTOs, those who fall into cell H will be examined. It has been hypothesized that at least two distinct groups of long-term offenders can be found. The *traditional lifer* group is expected to be made up of men who have had little or no previous history of criminal behavior and who previously lived a fairly stable lifestyle. The other group, here called the *habitual offender*, is expected to have had both a previous history of experiences with the criminal justice system and a less stable and socially acceptable lifestyle. If these two groups exist and each adjusts differently, then prior incarcerations or arrests and a prosocial lifestyle prior to prison would be expected to distinguish the two. Hypothesized differences between groups in attitudes and prison adjustment will then be examined.

RESULTS

On the average the early-LTOs had served 1.3 years in prison and were serving sentences requiring 12.1 years in prison.[4]

The late-LTOs had served an average of 10.3 years in prison and were serving sen-

tences with an average length of 15.7 years. The early non-LTOs had served an average of 1.1 years and were serving sentences of 2.5 years in length.

As Table 8.2 indicates, no differences were found between early-LTOs and late-LTOs on the variables of prior arrests, prior incarcerations, education, or the severity of sentence of conviction. In addition, no differences were found in prosocial activities, size of town, or race. As might be expected, at the time of data collection late-LTOs were older than early-LTOs, $t(173) = 4.9, p < .01$.[5]

Compared to late-LTOs, the early-LTOs reported significantly more anxiety, $t(154) = 2.8$, $p < .01$; depression, $t(129) = 3.4, p < .01$; psychosomatic illnesses, $t(187) = 3.1, p < .01$; and fear of other inmates, $t(183) = 2.0, p < .05$ (see Table 8.2). They also reported lower self-esteem than the late-LTOs, $t(124) = 2.7, p < .01$, but there was no difference in prisonization attitudes.

There were no differences between early-LTOs and early non-LTOs in age, education, prosocial activities, or race. The non-LTOs had previously been arrested more often ($M = 3.2$ times) than the early-LTOs ($M = 2.2$ times), $t(243) = 2.5, p < .05$. There was a borderline difference in the number of prior convictions for felonies, with early-LTOs having fewer convictions ($M = 1.4$) compared with non-LTOs ($M = 1.8$), $t(171) = 1.8, p < .10$. As expected, early-LTOs were incarcerated for significantly more severe sentences than the early non-LTOs, $t(223) = 13.5, p < .01$.

The early-LTOs were significantly higher than the early non-LTOs in depression, $t(87) = 2.2, p < .05$, and psychosomatic illness $t(132) = 2.6, p < .05$; but there were no differences in anxiety, self-esteem, fear of others, or prisonization attitudes (see Table 8.2).

TABLE 8.2 Scores of Early-LTO, Early Non-LTO, and Late-LTO Groups on Demographic, Offense-Related, and Prison Adjustment Variables

	Early-LTOs (n = 109)	Late-LTOs (n = 90)	Early Non-LTOs (n = 655)
Demographic Variables	$\overline{X}$	$\overline{X}$	$\overline{X}$
Age in years	29.6	35.4*	28.5
Highest grade in school	11.5	11.7	11.2
Criminal Justice History			
Prior arrests	2.2	2.8	3.2*
Prior convictions	1.4	1.3	1.8*
			(borderline)
Offense severity	1.6	1.5	2.8*
Sentence length (months)	144.7	187.8	29.7
Time served (months)	15.8	125.2	12.9
Prison Adjustment Variables			
Anxiety	55.4	50.3*	55.1
Depression	12.0	9.6*	10.8*
Self-esteem	33.2	36.0*	33.5
Psychosomatic illnesses	3.9	2.6*	3.2*
Fear of others	14.8	13.8*	14.4
Prisonization	27.6	26.9	27.8

*Significantly different from early-LTOs at $p < .05$.

To examine the prison adjustment of subgroups of LTOs, three groups were identified. If the inmates had previously led a high prosocial lifestyle (full-time work or school) and had no prior experience with the criminal justice system through arrests or convictions, then they were classified as traditional lifers. A second group, the habitual offenders, were identified as those who had been previously arrested and/or convicted of a felony offense and who had not been involved in high prosocial activities prior to prison. Those who did not fall in either of these groups were classified as "others." Of the 276 inmates classified as LTOs based on sentence length (cell H, Table 8.1), 61 (22.1%) could be classified as traditional lifers, and 61 (22.1%) could be classified as habitual offenders. The remaining 154 (55.8%) did not fit in either category.

The traditional lifer group did differ from the habitual offender group as hypothesized on race, sentence, age at first arrest, and severity of crime. There were proportionally more whites (63%) in the lifer group and more blacks (54%) or others (70.6%) in the habitual group (36.6% white habitual, 45.9% black lifers, and 29.4% other lifers), $\chi^2 = 6.6$, $p < .05$. More of the lifers had received life sentences

(31%) than the habituals (14%), $\chi^2 = 4.8$, $p < .05$. The habitual group had been significantly younger than the lifers when first arrested (18.5 years and 23.8 years, respectively), $t(102) = 3.9$, $p < .01$; and the habitual group was incarcerated for less severe crimes ($M = 1.6$) than the lifers ($M = 1.3$), $t(97) = 2.2$, $p < .05$.

Despite these differences between the two groups, there was no evidence of differential patterns of adjustment to prison. The groups did not differ in anxiety, depression, self-esteem, psychosomatic illnesses, fear of others, or prisonization. This was also true when the lifers and habituals were separated and compared early and late during their time in prison.

DISCUSSION

The failure to find differences between early- and late-LTOs on the demographic variables does not support the hypothesized change in the types of inmates now being sentenced to prison. There was no evidence that recently sentenced inmates were characteristically different from those who had been sentenced on the average 10 years previously. In addition, the data revealed no increase in the proportion of habitual offenders among the subgroup of early-LTOs compared to late-LTOs.

These findings could be interpreted as an indication that sentencing reform is not having the expected impact of broadening the composition of the long-term offender population. However, we are cautious about making this inference. In the states studied, sentencing reforms had been implemented only shortly before the data were collected: within 3 years in Illinois, 2 years in Minnesota, and 1 year in Connecticut. Considering the time lag between enactment of a sentencing reform and its application to new cases, particularly when serious offenses are concerned, relatively few inmates sentenced under the reforms would have been eligible to participate in the present study. The data for this study were probably gathered too soon to uncover the effect of the new, harsher sentencing laws on the composition of the LTO population. This point is underscored by Shane-Dubow's (1984) finding, mentioned above, that laws specifying increasingly severe penalties for habitual offenders have been adopted in the majority of states within the past several years.

Regardless of whether the proportion of LTOs is increasing in the prisoner population, the present study provides insight into the processes of LTO adaptation to prison. First, it is important to note that the results suggest no sign of deterioration over time among LTOs. In fact, there was evidence that the early period in prison was more stressful for LTOs than later periods. On all the measures of stress—including anxiety, depression, and psychosomatic illness—LTOs reported significantly more problems during their first 3 years of incarceration than LTOs who had served at least 6 years. In addition, early-LTOs' self-esteem was lower during this early period, and they reported greater fear of other inmates.

In contrast, inmates who anticipated shorter prison terms (early non-LTOs) were relatively better able to adjust to prison life during this early phase. Compared to recently admitted LTOs, inmates with shorter sentences remained less depressed and reported fewer psychosomatic illnesses during their first 3 years, although the two groups did not differ on anxiety, self-esteem, or fear of others. The fact that inmates sentenced to shorter terms appeared to be somewhat less traumatized by the transition to institutional life may be due to two factors. First, upon entering prison, they knew that they would be released in the relatively near future. This may have alleviated some of the psychological shock experienced by LTOs who perceive "no light at the end of the tunnel." Second, the greater frequency of prior arrests and convictions suggests that they were more experienced with prison life and hence were better prepared.

These results suggest that the early period of incarceration is particularly stressful for long-term offenders as they make the transition from the outside world to institutional life. No evidence supports the notion of psychological deterioration over time. Instead, with more time served, long-termers appear to develop strategies for coping with prison.

This finding is consistent with most researchers' conclusions that long-term incarceration promotes few demonstrable disabilities (Banister et al., 1973; Flanagan, 1980; Heskin et al., 1974; Sapsford, 1978). In suggesting improvement rather than deterioration over time, it complements Heather's (1977, p. 384) finding that "men at the beginning of their sentences show more personal illness more often than those who had spent longer in prison." Also, Flanagan's (1980) inference that LTOs experience greater psychological stress in the early years of their sentence is corroborated by the present results.

The second major finding of the present study is that distinct subgroups appear to exist within the LTO population. Although the majority of LTOs could not be categorized as either lifers or habitual offenders, according to the criteria selected, substantial minorities could be clearly differentiated into these two groups.

More noteworthy than the simple validation of subgroups of LTOs, however, are the findings concerning the adjustment patterns of these groups. Despite the fact that the habitual offenders were younger, more criminally experienced, and involved in preprison prosocial activities to a lesser degree, they were no more or less likely than lifers to manifest stress reactions, fear of others, or prisonization; nor did the subgroups differ on self-esteem. This finding stands in contradiction to the arguments of those who contend that LTOs who are habitual offenders pose more institutional management problems than lifers (Flanagan,

1981; Irwin, 1981). The implication of this finding is that even if populations of LTOs should become more heavily represented by habitual offenders in coming years, the strategies of adjustment of LTOs as a whole should not be expected to change. Rather, habitual LTOs as well as the traditional lifers would be expected to experience some transitional problems during the initial adjustment period, followed by successful coping and adaptation to prison life.

NOTES

1. Those respondents who were having difficulty reading the questionnaire were offered assistance; the questionnaire was read to those with a low level of literary ability.

2. Illegal activities were not considered employment.

3. Judicially imposed sentence lengths are particularly unreliable in the states studied because of recent change in good time calculations and sentencing laws (Goodstein, Hepburn, Kramer, & MacKenzie, 1984). For example, a 20-year maximum sentence could vary substantially in required time to serve, depending upon the jurisdiction within which the sentence was imposed and the specific laws and administration rules in effect during the offender's prison career.

4. Those who received sentences of life or death were excluded from this average but were otherwise included in the analyses as long-term offenders.

5. T-tests were done using Behrens-Fisher calculations with the Welch adjustment for degrees of freedom.

REFERENCES

Banister, P. A., Smith, F. V., Heskin, K. J., & Bolton, N. (1973). Psychological correlates of long-term imprisonment: I. Cognitive variables. *British Journal of Criminology, 13,* 312-323.

Bennett, L. A. (1974, January). The application of self-esteem measures in a correctional setting: II. Changes in self-esteem during incarceration. *Journal of Crime and Delinquency,* pp. 9-15.

Blumstein, A., & Kadane, J. B. (1983). An approach to the allocation of scarce imprisonment resources. *Crime and Delinquency, 29*(4), 546-561.

Bureau of Justice Statistics. (1983). Setting prison terms. *BJS Bulletin* (NCJ-76218). Washington, DC: Author.

Clark, S. (1984, January). *Determinate sentencing laws: North Carolina.* Paper presented at the National Conference on Sentencing, Baltimore, MD.

Clemmer, D. (1958). *The prison community.* New York: Holt, Rinehart & Winston.

Cohen, C. F., & Taylor, L. (1972). *Psychological survival.* New York: Pantheon.

Cooper, C. S., Kelley, D., & Larson, S. (1982, January). *Judicial and executive discretion in the sentencing process: Analysis of state felony code provisions* (Law Enforcement Assistance Administration contract No. J-LEAA-011-78). Washington, DC: U.S. Department of Justice.

Flanagan, T. J. (1980). The pains of long-term imprisonment. *British Journal of Criminology 20*(4), 148-156.

Flanagan, T. J. (1981). Dealing with long-term confinement. *Criminal Justice and Behavior, 8*(2), 201-222.

Flanagan, T. J. (1982). Correctional policy and the long-term prisoner. *Crime and Delinquency, 28*(1), 82-95.

Goffman, E. (1961). *Asylums: Essays on the social situation of mental patients and other inmates.* New York: Anchor.

Goodstein, L. (1979). Inmate adjustment to prison and the transition to community life. *Journal of Research on Crime and Delinquency, 16*(2), 246-272.

Goodstein, L., Hepburn, J. R., Kramer, J. H., & MacKenzie, D. L. (1984). *Determinate sentencing and the correctional process: A study of the implementation and impact of sentencing reform in three states.* Unpublished report to the National Institute of Justice.

Goodstein, L., Kramer, J. H., & Nuss, L. (1984, April). Defining determinacy: Components of the sentencing process ensuring equity and release certainty. *Justice Quarterly.*

Goodstein, L., & MacKenzie, D. L. (1984). Racial differences in adjustment patterns of prison inmates—prisonization, conflict, stress and control. In D. E. Georges-Abeyie (Ed.), *Blacks, crime, and justice.* New York: Clark Boardman.

Great Britain Home Office. (1978). *Prison statistics; England and Wales (1977).* London: HMSO.

Heather, N. (1977). Personal illness in "lifers" and the effects of long-term indeterminate sentences. *British Journal of Criminology, 17*(4), 378-386.

Heskin, K. J., Bolton, N., Smith, F. V., & Banister, P. A. (1974). Psychological correlates of long-term imprisonment: III. Attitudinal variables. *British Journal Criminology 14,* 150-157.

Irwin, J. K. (1981). Sociological studies of the impact of long-term confinement. In D. A. Ward & K. F. Schoen (Eds.), *Confinement in maximum custody.* Lexington, MA: Lexington Books.

McCorkle, L., & Korn, R. (1954). Re-socialization within walls. *Annals of the American Academy of Political and Social Science, 293,* 88-98.

Minnesota Sentencing Guidelines and Commentary: Training Materials. (1980). Minnesota Sentencing Guidelines Commission.

Pennsylvania Commission on Sentencing. (1982). *Sentencing guidelines manual.* State College: Author.

Rasch, W. (1977). Observations of physio-psychological changes in persons sentenced to life imprisonment. In S. Rzkallan, R. Levy, & R. Zauberman (Eds.), *Long-term imprisonment: An internation seminar.* Montreal: University of Montreal.

Richards, B. (1978). The experience of long-term imprisonment. *British Journal of Criminology, 18*(2), 162-169.

Rosenberg, M. (1965). *Society and the adolescent self image.* Princeton, NJ: Princeton University Press.

Sapsford, R. J. (1978). Life-sentence prisoners: Psychological changes during sentence. *British Journal of Criminology, 18*(2), 128-145.

Shane-Dubow, S. (1984, January). *Sentencing reform in the United States: History, content, and effect.* Paper presented at the National Conference on Sentencing, Baltimore, MD.

Spielberger, C. D., Gorsuch, R. L., & Lushine, R. E. (1970). *Manual for the state—trait anxiety inventory.* Palo Alto, CA: Consulting Psychologists Press.

Thomas, C. W., & Foster, S. C. (1972). Prisonization and the inmate contraculture. *Social Problems, 20,* 229-239.

Thomas, C. W., & Poole, E. D. (1975). The consequences of incompatible goal structures in correctional settings. *International Journal of Criminology and Penology, 3,* 27-42.

Toch, H. (1977). *Living in prison.* New York: Free Press.

U.S. Department of Justice. (1981, April). Prison population still rising. *Justice Assistance News,* p. 1.

APPENDIX

Depression Scale

	Adjusted Item to Total Correlation
At times I worry too much about things that don't really matter.	0.49
Sometimes, recently, I have worried about losing my mind.	0.68
I often feel angry these days.	0.65
In the past few weeks, I have felt depressed and very unhappy.	0.70
These days I can't help wondering if anything is worthwhile any more.	0.69

Response choices:

> Not at all; Somewhat; Moderately so; Very much so

Fear of Victimization

	Adjusted Item to Total Correlation
The odds of getting hurt while you're pulling time here are pretty high.	0.64
I worry a lot about getting beaten up or attacked before I get out of here.	0.53
One of the worst things about being in prison is that you never know when somebody might try to really hurt you.	0.56
You can't help feeling like a caged animal in a place like this.	0.57

Response choices:

> Strongly Disagree (1) to Strongly Agree (5).

Psychosomatic-Type Problems

Subjects were asked to indicate which of the following problems they had in the *past 3 months*.

> Nerves; stomach cramps, aches, nausea; headaches; breathing problems; skin rashes; dizziness; tiredness; irregular heartbeat; difficulties in sleeping; pain in chest; muscle tension; general poor health.

Scored as a sum of the number of different problems indicated.

9

Reexamining the Cruel and
Unusual Punishment of Prison Life

James Bonta

Paul Gendreau

It has been widely assumed that prison is destructive to the psychological and emotional well-being of those it detains. However, this assumption has rarely been critically examined. The present report evaluated the evidence pertaining to the effects of imprisonment. Studies on the effects of prison crowding, long-term imprisonment and short-term detention, solitary confinement, death row, and the health risks associated with imprisonment provide inconclusive evidence regarding the "pains of imprisonment." Rather, the evidence points to the importance of individual differences in adapting to incarceration. As the use of incarceration is unlikely to decrease in the near future, research on its effects is urgently needed and a situation-by-person approach may be the most fruitful research strategy.

Historically, prisons have been described as barren landscapes devoid of even the most basic elements of humanity (cf. Sykes, 1958) and detrimental to the humanity of the offender (Rector, 1982). Perhaps one of the best known descriptions of the inhumanity of prison is Cohen and Taylor's (1972) description of long-term inmates in a British maximum security prison. Such notions about prison life have been pervasive whether from the perspective of investigative journalists (Mitford, 1973) or academics writing for basic criminology texts (see Fox, 1985).

Mitford (1973), in her very effective polemical style, painted a scathing indictment of prisons. Not only does imprisonment strip offenders of civil liberties, but also prison reforms are nothing but rhetoric and rehabilita-

AUTHORS' NOTE: Authorship is alphabetical and the opinions expressed in this paper do not necessarily represent Ministry policy. Reprint requests should be addressed to the first author, Chief Psychologist, Ottawa-Carleton Detention Centre, 2244 Innes Road, Ottawa, Ontario, Canada K1B 4C4. He is also Adjunct Research Professor, Psychology, Carleton University and Clinical Associate Professor, Psychology, University of Ottawa. The second author is Professor, Division of Social Sciences, University of New Brunswick at Saint John, P.O. Box 5050, 'A', Saint John, N.B., Canada E2L 4L5, and consultant, Saint John Police Force. We would also like to thank Don Andrews for his critique of an earlier draft of this manuscript. NOTE: Reprinted with permission from *Law and Human Behavior*, Vol. 14, No. 4., 1990, pp. 347-372. Copyright 1990 by Plenum Publishing Corporation.

tion initiatives are despotic. Goffman (1961) also has been equally harsh in his assessment of the prison as a "total institution."

Careful empirical evaluations, however, have failed to uncover these pervasive negative effects of incarceration that so many have assumed. Mitford (1973) and Cohen and Taylor (1972) did not provide empirical evidence for psychological or behavioral deterioration. We need to be reminded that even Goffman (1961) did not collect data directly from prisons. His conclusions were based upon a review of the prison literature combined with data gathered from "asylums." Furthermore, earlier reviews of empirical studies also failed to uncover the widespread harm that is presumed inherent to prisons (Bukstel & Kilmann, 1980; Walker, 1983).

For some, the quantitative data, gathered as much as possible under conditions of objectivity, must not be believed. The failure of such data to confirm popular expectations has led to a number of responses. One is an increased dependence upon a phenomenological approach (e.g., Flanagan, 1982), or, at the very least, a shift from quantitative psychology to a process that examines prison existence in a qualitative and interpretative manner (see Sapsford, 1983).

Another expression of disbelief in the data comes from critics (Mohr, 1985) who have argued that the failure to find damaging effects of incarceration has been due to the "false reality" of the researchers concerned. This false reality has apparently been ascribed to the fact that government researchers have vested interests in reporting results uncritical of the penal establishment.

A final concern, in this case emanating from researchers who have not yet embraced phenomenology, has been that much of the research has reached a "dead end." Historically, incarceration research examined informal social organizations within prisons and did not speak persuasively to the actual effects of imprisonment itself. In addition, the methodological problems in much of the early work were considerable and a number of researchers have been rather critical of the early simplistic approaches to imprisonment research (Porporino & Zamble, 1984; Wormith, 1984). That is, much of the early research was guided by the "all or none" views of the deprivation (Clemmer, 1940; Sykes, 1958) and the early importation theorists (Irwin & Cressey,

1962). Thus, the complex nature of incarceration was not addressed.

In the past, most prisons were maximum security, and psychoeducational programming was minimal. Daily prison life featured 20-hour lock-up for a few and highly regimentized and monotonous work duties for the rest. Until recently, approaching the examination of prison life from a uniform perspective made eminently good sense. Now, however, the realities of prison life are far different. It is now appropriate to reexamine the effects of incarceration with special attention to the specific conditions of confinement. Although prisons may appear similar on the surface, closer examination finds them varying widely in security, living conditions, and the degree of programming.

Prison overcrowding, almost unknown in the early 1970s, is now very evident. Today, both very long-term and short-term periods of incarceration have dramatically increased. The number of offenders incarcerated is over 700,000 (U.S. Department of Justice, 1988). Current government crime control strategies, in the United States at least, will likely ensure that imprisonment will be the preferred option for the time being (Currie, 1989). In addition, one of the most extreme forms of prison life, solitary confinement, is still frequently employed.

Thus, research examining the effects of prison life is critically important. More knowledge must be generated and analyses of prison life must take into account the deprivation and importation literature, while also recognizing the great variety of structures and experiences that incarceration currently includes.

SELECTION AND ORGANIZATION OF STUDIES

This review focuses on quantitative studies about effects of imprisonment. Qualitative or phenomenological studies were not included. To be included in the review, a study was required to employ objective measures of the variables of interest and to evaluate the relationship between them by means of statistical tests.

Thus, the majority of studies were of a correlational or quasiexperimental nature. The only truly experimental studies (i.e., random assignment) were found in the solitary confinement literature. Some studies appeared to straddle both the quantitative and qualitative camps. In these instances, we made a judgment call and only included them for discussion where appropriate.

The studies were identified with the aid of a computer search of the prison adjustment and penal literature. Other reviews (e.g., Bukstel & Kilmann, 1980; Gendreau & Bonta, 1984; Wormith, 1986) and a review of recent criminological journals identified additional studies.

We viewed imprisonment as an independent variable and the behavioral and psychological observations of inmates as dependent variables. This organization appeared to work well with the studies dealing with specific conditions of confinement (e.g., solitary confinement). There is, on the other hand, a voluminous and frequently reviewed literature that has the independent variable, imprisonment, less clearly defined and investigates dependent variables such as attitude and self-esteem changes. These later studies were not included in the present review.

Finally, a further comment on the dependent variables in the review is in order. Our interest was on the evaluation of assumed negative effects due to incarceration, and, therefore, we reviewed topics that were most likely to evidence such effects. We did not review the literature on rehabilitation and educational programs in prisons (see Gendreau & Ross, 1987) because their stated purpose is to actively promote positive behaviors. In general, negative effects were behaviors that threatened the physical welfare of the offender (e.g., aggressive behavior, suicide) and indicators of physiological stress levels (e.g., elevated blood pressure) and psychological distress (e.g., depression).

We examined specific aspects of confinement, namely, crowding, long-term imprisonment, solitary confinement, short-term detention, and death row. We make one departure from this format and provide a commentary on the health risks associated with imprisonment, which follows from our discussion of prison crowding. In our review of the prison crowding literature, we were able to use meta-analytic techniques because there were both an identifiable theoretical perspective and sufficient studies that could be subjected to analysis. With respect to the other aspects of confinement, either there were too few studies (e.g., death row) or they consistently failed to show negative consequences (e.g., solitary confinement), or, as in the case of long-term confinement, the cross-sectional methodology with multiple groups did not make the data amenable to meta-analytic techniques.

Crowding

Crowding is invariably perceived negatively. It is seen by many correctional managers as *the* major barrier to humane housing of offenders despite an estimated 170,000 additional new beds since 1980 (*Corrections Digest*, 1986). This population explosion has prompted court interventions (Angelos & Jacobs, 1985; Call, 1983), sentencing reforms (Kennedy, 1985), and innovative classification systems intended to reduce prison populations (Clements, 1982).

Researchers view crowding as a complex phenomenon. Stokols (1972) distinguished *density*, a physical condition, from *crowding*, a psychological condition involving the individual's perception of constraints imposed by limited space. Loo (1973) further differentiated physical density into *spatial density* (number of people constant but the available space varies) and *social density* (space is constant but the number of people vary). For example, prison renovations might reduce the amount of space available to a number of inmates (spatial density), but the effects of this spatial rearrangement on the inmates may differ from the effects of a sudden influx of new inmates into the institution (social density).

Despite these distinctions, corrections research has been inconsistent in the use of the concepts of crowding and spatial and social density. Studies have described crowding as both an independent and dependent variable, and the distinction between social and spatial density has infrequently been noted.

Most researchers agree that crowding describes a psychological response to high population density which is often viewed as stressful (Altman, 1978; Paulus, 1988). Although high population density is a necessary condition for crowding, it is not a sufficient condition, and other variables may be required to produce the perception of crowding. Sundstrom (1978) described crowding as a sequential process resulting from an interaction of person variables, high population density, correlates of high density (e.g., increased noise levels), and situational variables (e.g., duration of exposure).

Following Sundstrom's (1978) model, we would expect that the behaviors observed under high population densities would vary in intensity and variety with length of exposure. For example, under brief exposure we may see elevated blood pressure, followed by reports of anxiety as exposure increases, and ending with violent behavioral outbursts under prolonged exposures. To test this hypothesis, a longitudinal design is required, and, to the best of our knowledge, there is only one study that has approximated this goal (Ostfeld, Kasl, D'Atri, & Fitzgerald, 1987). Indirect support of the model may be gathered from comparisons of the relative strength of the relationships between population density and a variety of outcomes. That is, we would expect that reports of physiological and psychological stress would be relatively easy to come by and that the findings would be robust, whereas observations of violent behavior would be more infrequent and equivocal.

To explore this model, we undertook both a qualitative and quantitative review of the prison crowding literature. Studies that provided sufficient statistical information on the relationship between population density and the dependent variable were subject to a meta-analysis. The dependent variable was arranged into three categories: physiological, psychological, and behavioral. Some studies reported more than one measure within a category. In these situations, we gave priority to systolic blood pressure for the physiological category, a paper-and-pencil measure of perceived crowding described by Paulus (1988) for the psychological category, and misconduct for the behavioral category. These measures were the most frequently used. We would have liked to categorize the measures of crowding into aggregate, social, and spatial density, but to have done so would have drastically reduced our samples in each cell.

The strength of the relationship, or effect size, was measured by Cohen's d (1977) and calculated using the statistical conversion formulas described by Glass, McGaw, and Smith (1981). In our analysis, d indicated the size of the difference in standard units between crowded and noncrowded conditions. Standardizing the measures (d) allowed us to compare results from different studies. For studies that reported nonsignificant results, d was set at zero. The results of this meta-analysis are shown in Table 9.1.

As can be seen from Table 9.1, physiological and psychological stress responses (Outcomes A and B) were very likely under crowded prison conditions. The majority of studies employing such measures found significant results. The one inconsistent finding was the *inverse* relationship between crowding and blood pressure ($d = -.70$) reported by McCain, Cox, and Paulus (1980). This may have been a spurious result because there was no relationship between blood pressure and crowding for the institution in question for the previous year (1978). If this size effect is removed from the calculation of the mean, then we obtain a mean of $d = .51$ for Outcome A, which is quite consistent with the model. In the case of behavioral acting-out, the strength of the relationship diminished to the point of being relatively insignificant as the studies ranged in effect size from $-.90$ to $+.87$.

While the results outlined under Outcomes A and B seem straightforward, some clarification is required. That is, although physiological stress in response to population density was the rule, reports of psychological stress concomitant with physiological stress were not always observed and, for the most part, rarely studied. When the two were observed together, the relationship was usually dependent upon other variables. In 1973, Paulus, McCain, and Cox reported (no data were presented) that social density was related to a physiological measure of stress (palmer sweat) but not to a subjective appraisal of feeling crowded. However, in a subsequent study (Paulus, Cox, McCain, & Chandler, 1975), which considered length of exposure, there was an increased perception of feeling crowded for inmates in dormitories (high social density) but not for inmates in cells (low social density). Other studies have noted the moderating effect of length of exposure on physiological and psychological measures of stress (D'Atri, 1975; D'Atri, Fitzgerald, Kasl, & Ostfeld, 1981; McCain, Cox, & Paulus, 1976; Paulus, McCain, & Cox, 1978, 1981).

In the one longitudinal study reported in the literature, Ostfeld and his colleagues (1987) followed 128 inmates through their incarceration to release and postrelease. Physiological and psychological measures were taken at regular intervals and controls were introduced for other confounding variables such as weight

TABLE 9.1 Effect Size of Outcome for Prison Crowding[a]

		Outcome		
Study	*Sample*	*A*	*B*	*C*
D'Atri (1975)	34 adults (M)	1.19		
D'Atri & Ostfeld (1975)	91 adults (M)	1.06		
	126 adults (M)	1.05		
D'Atri et al. (1981)	37 adults (M)	.79		
Ostfeld et al. (1987)	128 adults (M)	.54	n.s.	
McCain et al. (1976)	64 adults (M)		.53	
Paulus et al. (1975)	121 adults (M)		.34	
McCain et al. (1980)	206 adults (M)	n.s.		
	183 adults (M)	n.s.	.82	
	87 adults (M)	−.70		
	121 adults (M)	n.s.		
	212 adults (M/F)		.51	
Ray et al. (1982)	115 juveniles (M)	n.s.		
Ruback & Carr (1984)	561 adults (F)			.37
Jan (1980)	4 adult prisons (M/F)			.43
Megargee (1977)	1 adult prison (M)			.87
Nacci et al. (1977)	37 adult prisons (M/F)			.47
Bonta & Kiem (1978)	1 adult prison (M)			n.s.
Bonta & Nanckivell (1980)	1 adult prison (M)			−.52
Clayton & Carr (1984)	21,500 adults (?)			n.s.
	1,203 adults (?)			.70
Porporino & Dudley (1984)	24 adult prisons (M)			−.90
Ekland-Olsen et al. (1983)	14 adult prisons (M/F)			n.s.
N of studies		10	5	11
Means		.39	.44	.13
SD		.62	.30	.52

a. A = Physiological measures (blood pressure, heart rate); B = Psychological measures (reports of crowding, discomfort); C = Behavioral measures (assaults, misconducts). Samples may employ male (M) or female (F) inmates or both. Sometimes the composition of the sample was unclear (?).

and criminal history. They found changes in blood pressure associated with population density but no statistically significant changes for anxiety, hostility, and depression.

These studies, nevertheless, suggested a positive relationship between social density and physiological indicators of stress and subjective reports of discomfort. Indications of physiological stress appear as immediate consequences to high social density, and it is possible that with increased exposure to such a situation other cumulative consequences such as psychological distress may follow (Paulus et al., 1975).

It is most important, however, from a policy perspective, to evaluate whether or not population density is related to severe, disruptive behavior that may jeopardize the physical safety of the inmates. The findings as shown in Table 9.1 do not support an overall relationship between crowding and disruptive inmate behavior.

Megargee (1977) was the first to empirically study the relationship between crowding and reported disciplinary infractions. He collected data over a 3-year span at a medium security prison for youthful offenders (aged 18 to 25). Spatial density was more highly correlated with institutional misconduct than was social density, but social interaction factors (e.g., friendship ties) may have played an important role. Density, without distinction to spatial or social density, and disciplinary infractions are, according to some investigators, positively related (Cox, Paulus, & McCain, 1984; Jan, 1980; Nacci, Teitelbaum, & Prather, 1977; Paulus et al., 1981; Ruback & Carr, 1984), but no such association was found by others (Bonta & Kiem, 1978; Bonta & Nanckivell, 1980; Clayton & Carr, 1984; Ekland-Olsen, Barrick, & Cohen, 1983; Porporino & Dudley, 1984).

From our appraisal of the empirical literature we cannot conclude that high population density is always associated with aggressive behavior. Most researchers agree that other variables play important moderating roles (Bonta, 1986; Cox et al., 1984; Ellis, 1984). One important moderator variable is age of the inmates. The relationship between misconduct and population density has been more pronounced in institutions housing young offenders (Ekland-Olsen et al., 1983; Jan, 1980; Megargee, 1977; Nacci et al., 1977). Even in studies that failed to uncover a general positive relationship, the introduction of age as a moderator showed a correlation between population density and misconduct (Bonta & Kiem, 1978; Bonta & Nanckivell, 1980; Clayton & Carr, 1984; Ekland-Olsen et al., 1983). In the Ekland-Olsen et al. study (1983), when institutions with a relatively young population (median age of 27) were selected for analysis, a highly significant correlation was found ($r = .58$ or a $d = 1.43$). The authors concluded that age is a much better predictor of disciplinary infractions than prison size.

Only one study (Gaes & McGuire, 1985) discounts the importance of age. Gaes and McGuire (1985) assessed a variety of predictors along with age and under these conditions age became relatively less important. The authors observed that most studies of overcrowding and misconduct typically assess few variables and may overestimate the importance of any one variable.

Interpreting the behavioral consequences of prison overcrowding is further confounded by the use of aggregate level data. As Table 9.1 clearly shows, almost all the studies under Outcome C are aggregate level data. The problem with this level of analysis is that many other factors (e.g., age, release policies) may play more important roles than population density. Clayton and Carr (1987) have shown that aggregate data analysis overestimates the relationship between crowding and behavior (a point already made in the preceding paragraph). In their study investigating the relationship between prison overcrowding and recidivism (2 years postrelease), age was the critical variable. The only other study that used recidivism as an outcome measure was by Farrington and Nuttall (1980), and they found a significant relationship between crowding and postrelease recidivism. However, Gaes (1983) has suggested that other extraneous variables (e.g., age, staff-inmate ratios) could better account for the results.

Although age has consistently been identified as an important moderating variable, explanations of why this is so have not been carefully researched. Are the young simply impulsive, lack coping skills, and more easily susceptible to stress? MacKenzie (1987) found oppositional or "assertive" attitudes and fear of victimization rather than coping ability as most relevant to misconducts. Clearly further research on this issue is desirable.

The identification of person variables as moderators in the experience of prison crowding raises the enduring issue of importation versus deprivation. That is, are the behaviors observed in prison reflective of behavioral patterns that were present prior to incarceration or a response to the deprivation of liberties imposed by confinement? As Freedman (1975) wrote, "crowding has neither good nor bad effects but rather serves to intensify the individual's typical reactions to a situation" (p. 89). Thus, the disciplinary infractions observed in crowded prisons may be the result of either high population densities or a continuation of behaviors that existed before incarceration, or both. As Ruback and Innes (1988) have remarked, there are no studies that have partitioned inmates with violent histories from nonviolent inmates. This is very important because it is usually the maximum security settings that are crowded, and they are also the settings most likely to house violent inmates. The possibility of an interaction can be seen in Smith's (1982) account of how assertive inmates became more aggressive and the passive inmates more submissive under crowded conditions.

There are other factors, besides person variables, that may influence aggressive behavior in crowded prisons. For instance, crowded prisons may be poorly managed (Gaes, 1985). Although prison populations may fluctuate widely, corresponding changes in the number of supervisory staff, counselors, and programs rarely occur. When the population is large, there are fewer correctional staff to monitor behavior and provide inmates with the opportunities to learn adaptive coping skills. The management of prisons and prison systems may account for some inmate disturbances. A case in point is the occurrence of sudden changes in the population membership (Ellis, 1984). Porporino and Dudley (1984), in reviewing evidence from 24 Canadian penitentiaries, found high inmate turnover more important than population density in the prediction of inmate disruptions. The authors speculated that inmates are required to deal with newly arrived inmates more frequently and this may be extremely stressful. For example, in the 1980 New Mexico prison riot, the inmate population was not at its peak but there was a sudden influx of new inmates in the months preceding the riot (Colvin, 1982).

Another factor appears to be the chronicity of the situation (Megargee, 1977). That is, as sentence length or exposure to crowded situations increase so does the risk for misconduct (Bonta & Nanckivell, 1980; Nacci et al., 1977). This is a tentative conclusion because of other confounding factors such as age and type of institution (Jan, 1980; Paulus, 1988).

In summary, crowded prisons may produce physiological and psychological stress among many inmates. More disruptive effects however, depend upon moderating person variables such as age, institutional parameters (e.g., sudden shifts in the inmate membership), and the chronicity of the situation. In addition, aggressive behavior may be a cumulative effect of high population densities. More research into the parameters that govern this effect is required.

Two theoretical models have been advanced in an effort to explain the inmate's response to prison overcrowding. The social-interaction demand model favored by Paulus and his colleagues (Cox et al., 1984; Paulus, 1988) assumes that social interactions interfere with goal attainment and increase uncertainty and cognitive load. That is, it is the nature of the social interactions that may produce negative effects and high population densities are important only to the degree that they affect social interactions. The second model is based on a cognitive social-learning model (Bonta, 1986; Ellis, 1984; see also Cox et al., 1984, for a critique of this model).

This latter model places greater emphasis on individual differences (person variables) and stresses two processes: attribution and learned coping behavior. Increases in population density produce not only changes in social interactions but also changes in noise level, temperature, etc., and these in turn produce physiological arousal. When inmates attribute this arousal to violation of their personal space rather than some other factor they then report feeling crowded. Once the attribution is made, existing coping behaviors are activated, with the goal to reduce arousal and feelings of crowding.

Except for MacKenzie's (1987) findings, penal researchers have found that coping behavior plays a significant role in the inmates' response to incarceration and that inmates vary in the effectiveness of their coping behaviors (cf., Zamble & Porporino, 1990). Clements (1979) has suggested that coping behavior may be influential in the inmates' adaptation to prison overcrowding, although some of these behaviors, such as assault and suicide (Cox et al., 1984; Megargee, 1977), are clearly not adaptive. Unfortunately, poor coping skills are all too prevalent among inmate populations and this is reflected in their disruptive behavioral responses to high population densities. However, other behaviors can alleviate crowding-induced arousal and at the same time be adaptive. For example, classroom attendance (Jan, 1980; Lawrence, 1985) and psychological interventions (Karlin, Katz, Epstein, & Woolfolk, 1979) have been shown to decrease feelings of being crowded. Besides searching for ways to control the prison population growth we can also develop programs to teach individual inmates more effective skills to cope with high prison populations.

Health Risks

As we have seen with the prison crowding literature, it is not uncommon to observe physiological and psychological distress associated with high population densities. Such outcomes are also commonly associated with stress and physical disorders. In fact, many studies of prison overcrowding will use illness complaints as a dependent measure. Thus, we now turn our attention to a related topic and ask ourselves if imprisonment threatens the health of the confined.

Most of the research has dealt with the identification and description of illnesses reported by prisoners (cf., Novick & Al-Ibrahim, 1977). Available data fail to clearly indicate whether inmates display more or less health risks than the general population. When threats to health come from suicide and self-mutilation, then inmates are clearly at risk. Though it is widely believed that the risk of homicide is greater within prison than in the community, the evidence is mixed. In Canadian penitentiaries, the homicide rates are close to 20 times that of similar-aged males in Canadian society (Porporino & Martin, 1983). In the United States, deaths due to homicide are actually less likely within prison (Ruback & Innes, 1988). With respect to self-injurious behavior, the results are more consistent. Inmate suicides for a 20-year period in the United States were at a rate of 17.5 per 100,000 inmates in contrast to 11 per 100,000 people in the general population (Austin & Unkovic, 1977). Self-mutilations are at an even higher rate (Ross & McKay, 1979).

When one examines the incidence of physical illnesses, the findings are less conclusive. One of the classic studies comes from Jones (1976) who surveyed the health risks of Tennessee prisoners and compared them where possible to probationers and data existing on the general adult male U.S. population. The patterns of results are rather complex but, by and large, a variety of health problems, injuries, and selected symptoms of psychological distress were higher for certain classes of inmates than probationers, parolees, and, where data existed, for the general population.

In contrast to Jones (1976), a number of other researchers have failed to find deleterious effects on health. Goldsmith (1972) followed 50 inmates over a 2-month period and found no major health problems as assessed by physical examinations. On a larger inmate sample ($N = 491$), Derro (1978) found that only 12% of the symptoms reported on admission related to a significant illness. This is an important point because many studies "count" health care contacts without differentiating the nature of the contact. Inmates may seek the aid of health care professionals for reasons other than a physical illness.

Two studies also reported a significantly lower incidence of hypertension among inmates compared to the general population. Culpepper and Froom (1980) found the incidence of hypertension among a prison population at 6%. In another study (Novick, Della-Penna, Schwartz, Remlinger, & Lowenstein, 1977), the incidence of hypertension among 1,300 inmates was 4.5%. We remind the reader, however, that this finding relates to the effects of incarceration in general and not to specific conditions such as prison crowding where the results are different (Gaes, 1985).

One of the problems with the interpretation of the above data has been that there is so little use of adequate control groups especially with respect to age and race (see Ruback & Innes, 1988, for a notable exception). Also, Baird (1977) found that many prisoners with physical complaints were displaying a variety of health risks well *before* incarceration. As a case in point, Bentz and Noel (1983) found that upon entering prison, inmates were reporting a higher incidence of psychiatric disorder than a sample of a rural population in North Carolina. This finding is also of interest in light of Gibbs' (1987) claim that incarceration aggravates psychological symptomatology (we will say more about this in the discussion on short-term detention).

A final consideration is that many prisons may actually be conducive to good health. In a number of cases, illness complaints have either decreased with time served (MacKenzie & Goodstein, 1985) or remained unchanged (Wormith, 1986). In most prisons, inmates have regular and nutritious diets, access to recreational exercise, and opportunity to sleep. Furthermore, offenders can obtain fairly immediate health care. Because of this last possibility, health risks could easily be overreported in prisons with extensive health services and thus bias some of the research findings.

In summary, the current findings recall Glueck and Glueck's (1950) comparison of 500 delinquents with 500 nondelinquents: In training school, the boys were generally healthy and physically fit, whereas in the community, as a result of their adventurous lifestyles, they were prone to more serious accidents. More than 35 years later, Ruback and Innes (1988) make this same observation based upon information from adult inmates. Thus, as far as physical health is concerned, imprisonment may have the fortuitous benefit of isolating the offender from a highly risky lifestyle in the community.

Long-Term Incarceration

In 1984 there were approximately 1,500 offenders serving life sentences in Canadian prisons (Wormith, 1984) and with recent legislation defining minimum sentences (25 years) without parole for first and second degree murder, those numbers are expected to increase significantly. Similar trends have also been noted in the United States, where mandatory and lengthy prison terms have been widely implemented (cf., Cullen & Gilbert, 1982). What happens to these people as a result of such lengthy sentences? Most of the research has focused upon time spans not longer than 2 or 3 years, and our knowledge regarding offenders serving sentences of 5, 10, or more years is less adequate.

Using cross-sectional designs, Heskin and his colleagues measured inmates' performances on cognitive tests (Banister, Smith, Heskin, & Bolton, 1973), personality measures (Heskin, Smith, Banister, & Bolton, 1973), and attitudinal scales (Heskin, Bolton, Smith, & Banister, 1974). Four groups of prisoners, all sentenced to at least 10 years, were studied. The average time served was 2.5 years for the first group of inmates, 4.9 years for the second group, 6.9 years for the third, and 11.3 for the last group. No differences were found among the groups in intellectual performance, although there was a decline in perceptual motor speed on the cognitive tasks (Banister et al., 1973). On the personality and attitudinal tests, there were increases in hostility and social introversion (Heskin et al., 1973) and decreases in self-evaluations and evaluations of work and father (Heskin et al., 1974).

Subsequently, Bolton, Smith, Heskin, and Banister (1976) retested 154 of the original 175 inmates in the Heskin research (average retest interval was 2 years). Their findings showed no evidence of psychological deterioration. In fact, verbal intelligence improved over time and hostility decreased. The findings with respect to hostility are in contrast to the cross-sectional studies, but, as the authors noted, there was a significant drop-out rate. Furthermore, the initial testing occurred during a period of institutional tensions, which may have produced artificially high hostility scores.

Sapsford (1978) administered a psychometric test battery to 60 prisoners sentenced to life imprisonment. The prisoners formed three groups: (1) reception (newly received), (2) middle (6th year of sentence), and (3) hard core (average sentence served was 14 years). Some matching was attempted but it is not clear the extent to which the procedure was successful. From the results, only three inmates could be described as having failed to cope with their sentence. The only deteriorating effects observed were increases in dependency upon staff for direction and social introversion. In fact, depression and anxiety were lower for inmates serving longer sentences.

Reed's (1978) geriatric prisoner research also has relevance to the issue. His aged prisoners (mean age of 60 years), with an average sentence served of 23 years, reported fewer life problems than their peers in the outside community. Furthermore, they reported active interests and feeling younger than their age.

Similarly, Richards (1978) also failed to note negative differences between British prisoners who had served at least 8 years of their sentence and inmates who had served more than 10 years. The two groups were matched on age at sentencing and type of offense. The inmates were asked to rate the frequency and severity of 20 different problems that may be initiated by incarceration (e.g., missing social life, sexual frustration). The results showed no differences in the perception of problems by the two groups, and there was agreement by the inmates that coping could be best accomplished by relying on "myself."

Utilizing Richards' (1978) problem-ranking task, Flanagan (1980a) assessed American inmates who had served at least 5 years and compared his results to those reported by Richards (1978). He found that the American inmates perceived similar problems to those reported by the British prisoners in that they also did not perceive the problems as particularly threatening to their mental health. Furthermore, they preferred to cope with their sentences on their own rather than seek the aid of others. In another study, Flanagan (1980b) compared misconduct rates of 701 short-term prisoners (less than 5 years) and 765 long-term inmates. Even after controlling for age, the misconduct rate among the long-term inmates was approximately half that of the short-term offenders.

Rasch (1981) assessed lifers who had served 3, 8.5, and 13.5 years and found no deterioration in health, psychiatric symptoms, or intellect. The results of MMPI testing documented decreased pathology over time, replicating Sapsford's (1983) findings. Another German study, cited by Wormith (1984), apparently found similar results. Moreover, when long-term inmates (20 years) displayed pathology, such behaviors were apparent long before incarceration.

A series of studies conducted by Wormith (1984, 1986) observed a differential impact from long-term incarceration. In the first study (Wormith, 1984), 269 inmates who had served from 1 month to 10 years were administered a psychometric test battery. Once again those inmates who had served the most time displayed significantly less deviance. This relationship remained even after the introduction of controls for sentence length, age upon admission, and race. Improvement over time was also noted on attitudinal measures and nonpathological personality characteristics. Finally, changes in intelligence did not vary with length of incarceration.

The second study by Wormith (1986) consisted of a random sample of 634 male prisoners stratified according to sentence length and time served. Long-term inmates (8 years to life), compared to short-term inmates, demonstrated better adjustment on measures of self-reports of emotions and attitudes (e.g., anger) and institution discipline. On measures of criminal sentiments, long-term offenders displayed a U-shaped function while short-term offenders became more antisocial. As expected, long-term inmates had deteriorating community relationships over time but made more use of institutional programs (e.g., education), which was likely important for a successful adaptation to prison life.

MacKenzie and Goodstein (1985) reported findings similar to those described by Wormith (1984, 1986). Long-term inmates (more than 6 years served) found the earlier portion of their sentences more stressful, but with time they learned to cope effectively. Of particular interest was their differentiation of two subgroups of long-term offenders. Using prison experience as a discriminating factor, they identified two groups, inmates with minimal prison experience (lifers) and inmates with extensive prison experience (habituals). Both groups showed the same adjustment patterns, contrary to the expectation that habituals would evidence disruptive behaviors. Similar findings with respect to female offenders have also been reported by MacKenzie, Robinson, and Campbell (1989). In fact, long-term inmates were more bothered by boredom and lack of activities than by anxiety.

Most of the above studies have been cross-sectional. A publication by Zamble and Porporino (1990) on how inmates cope with prison assumes importance for two reasons. First, it is longitudinal. Of their sample ($N = 133$), 30% were serving sentences of more than 10 years. They were assessed within 1 month of admission and 1½ years later. Zamble and Porporino found no *overall* indication of deterioration of coping skills over time, even for inmates serving their first incarceration. As well, there was no increase in identification with "criminal others" and their "view of the world" did not change. The authors surmise that as prisons, by and large, constrain behavior and do little to encourage changes in behavior one way or the other, inmates typically undergo a "behavioral deep freeze." The outside-world behaviors that led the offender into trouble prior to imprisonment remain until release.

Secondly, it is important to emphasize that Zamble and Porporino do not in the least deny the fact that individual differences are meaningful. They reported that how some inmates coped with incarceration correlated with postprison recidivism. For example, some of the significant factors were changes in perceptions of prison life, degree and type of socialization with incarcerated peers, planning for the future, and motivation regarding work and educational goals. We will return to this point later.

In summary, from the available evidence and on the dimensions measured, there is little to support the conclusion that long-term imprisonment necessarily has detrimental effects. As a caution, however, Flanagan (1982) claims that lifers may change upon other dimensions that have yet to be objectively measured. For example, family separation issues and vocational skill training needs present unique difficulties for long-term inmates (Wilson & Vito, 1988). Unfortunately, cross-sectional designs and until recently, small subject populations have been characteristic of these studies.

Solitary Confinement

Solitary confinement is "the most individually destructive, psychologically crippling and socially alienating experience that could conceivably exist within the borders of the country" (p. 243). So wrote Jackson (1983) in his scathing denouncement of the use of solitary confinement for prisoners. The commonly accepted definition of prison solitary confinement is maximum security lock-up, usually for punitive reasons. Sensory stimulation is very limited. The inmate may have a book to read and access to a half hour of "recreation" (alone). Conditions of prison solitary should not be confused with other forms of protective segregation (cf., Gendreau, Wormith, & Tellier, 1985) where admission is usually voluntary, and the inmate has access to programming, TV, and so forth. No doubt, if any prison experience is evidence of cruel and unusual punishment, then surely that experience is prison solitary.

In contrast to the popular notions of solitary's negative effects, there exists an extensive experimental literature on the effects of placing people (usually volunteer college students) in solitary, or conditions of sensory deprivation, which has been ignored in the penology literature. It should be noted that the conditions in some of the sensory deprivation experiments are more severe than that found in prison solitary (cf., Gendreau & Bonta, 1984). In fact, this literature (cf., Suedfeld, 1980; Zubek, 1969) has much relevance to prison solitary confinement. Considerable research has also been undertaken with prisoners themselves (Gendreau & Bonta, 1984), and many of these studies are, methodologically, the most rigorous of all the prison studies. Therefore, conclusions drawn from this source are especially informative.

Experimental studies (Ecclestone, Gendreau, & Knox, 1974; Gendreau, Freedman, Wilde, & Scott, 1968, 1972; Gendreau, Horton, Hooper, Freedman, Wilde, & Scott, 1968; Gendreau, McLean, Parsons, Drake, & Ecclestone, 1970; Walters, Callaghan, & Newman, 1963) have found few detrimental effects for subjects placed in solitary confinement for periods up to 10 days. All but one of these studies employed random assignment and most employed a double blind assessment of dependent variables. Perceptual and motor abilities were not impaired, physiological levels of stress were lower than for the control groups, and various attitudes toward the environment and the self did not worsen. Individual differences have also been observed. Experience with prison life, conceptual ability, anxiety, diurnal adrenal levels, and EEG patterns were related to some of the results reported, although it should be noted that results are based upon very small sample sizes. Some of

the experimental studies even reported beneficial results (cf., Suedfeld, 1980). In certain respects, the prison literature (Gendreau et al., 1972) is quite consistent with the experimental sensory deprivation laboratory data (e.g., Suedfeld, 1980; Zubek, Shepard, & Milstein, 1970).

In contrast to the studies that used volunteer subjects, Weinberg (1967) looked at 20 inmates who were involuntarily placed for 5 days in solitary confinement. Using measures such as cognitive and personality tests, language usage, and time estimation, he, too, found no deleterious effects. Suedfeld, Ramirez, Deaton, and Baker-Brown (1982), also studying inmates involuntarily in solitary confinement, also failed to find detrimental effects. Their data were collected from five prisons in Canada and the United States, and they found that, in general, inmates found the first 72 hours the most difficult but after that they adjusted quite well. The authors reached this conclusion: "Our data lend no support to the claim that solitary confinement . . . is overwhelmingly aversive, stressful, or damaging to the inmates" (p. 335).

In contrast, Cormier and Williams (1966) and Grassian (1983) recorded signs of pathology for inmates incarcerated in solitary for periods up to a year. No objective measures or control groups were used. In the former study, most of the inmates exhibited substantial pathology prior to solitary. In the second study, all subjects were involved in a class action suit against their keepers at the time of the interview, and the author actively encouraged more disclosure when the inmates were not forthcoming with reports of distress. Similarly, the experimental literature on sensory deprivation demonstrates that once controls for set and expectancies are introduced, bizarre experiences, under even the most severe conditions (immobilization and sensory deprivation for 14 days), were minimal for the majority of subjects (e.g., Zubek, Bayer, & Shepard, 1969).

The real culprit may not necessarily be the condition of solitary per se but the manner in which inmates have been treated. There is evidence suggesting that this is the basis for most inmate complaints (Suedfeld, 1980; Vantour, 1975). Jackson (1983) himself acceded to this fact. When inmates are dealt with capriciously by management or individual custodial officers, psychological stress can be created even in the most humane of prison environments. Therefore, solitary confinement may not be cruel and unusual punishment under the humane and time-limited conditions investigated in experimental studies or in correctional jurisdictions that have well-defined and effectively administered ethical guidelines for its use.

We must emphasize that this is *not* an argument for employing solitary and certainly not for the absurdly lengthy periods as documented by Jackson (1983). Gendreau and Bonta (1984) have outlined several research issues that urgently need to be addressed. Some of these are studies investigating individual tolerance of solitary confinement, its possible deterrent effect, and a compelling need to find alternatives to humanely restrain those who are a danger to themselves and others while incarcerated. With rare exceptions (Barak-Glantz, 1983), the necessary research has not been conducted.

Short-Term Detention

In 1972, nearly 4,000 jails in the United States processed 1 million male and female offenders per year (Miller, 1978). The offenders were charged with a variety of crimes and approximately 75% of them were awaiting trial. Despite the extensive use of jails, little is known about the effects of short-term detention. Perhaps this is the area that requires most attention, as it is the initial adjustment phases that are important in assessing the impact of incarceration. For example, 50% of suicides occur in the first 24 hours of imprisonment (Hayes, 1983).

A common belief is that waiting for trial and sentencing produces a considerable amount of anxiety (Cholst, 1979; Dy, 1974; Gibbs, 1982; Schneider, 1979). More specifically, anxiety increases as the trial and sentencing dates approach and then decreases after sentencing when the uncertainty surrounding trial has passed.

A study by Dyer (reported in Krug, Scheier, & Cattell, 1976) is difficult to evaluate because of the lack of information provided. Dyer administered an anxiety scale to adolescent females and found a decrease in anxiety over time in detention. However, no information regarding the number of subjects, the setting, and the interval between tests was provided.

Oleski (1977) administered the same scale to 60 male inmates (ages 18 to 26) in a Boston city jail. All were awaiting trial and all had limited prior prison experience. The tests were administered 1 week after admission and again 8 weeks later. Anxiety levels were found to be higher at posttest.

Bonta and Nanckivell (1980) administered the same anxiety scale used in the previous studies to four groups of inmates selected without age and court status limitations. Group 1 inmates were remanded into custody and sentenced by the time they were retested. Group 2 were still awaiting sentencing. Group 3 inmates entered the jail already sentenced, and Group 4 was a control group for the effects of testing. The test was administered within 1 week of reception and again 3 to 4 weeks later. No changes in anxiety over time or after sentencing were observed.

Gibbs (1987) assessed psychopathology among 339 jail inmates. The inmates were asked to rate symptoms prior to incarceration, 72 hours into confinement, and again 5 days later. He found symptoms to increase between preincarceration and 72 hours of imprisonment and interpreted this finding as showing that detention per se affects symptoms. However, the interpretation is not entirely convincing. First of all, symptomatology prior to incarceration was based upon the inmates' recollections of their difficulties before detention and thus subject to memory and reporting biases. Second, at the 5-day retest, symptoms actually diminished, and third, the finding that those without prior hospitalizations did worse was a puzzling finding and not consistent with the prison as stress model.

There is another intriguing, albeit tangential, aspect to the short-term detention literature, and that is the use of short-term detention as a deterrent. Three common strategies are "Scared Straight," "boot camp," and shock probation programs. The assumption is that prison life is aversive in some form or other and that exposure to it will decrease the probability of future criminal behavior, particularly for impressionable young offenders.

The classic evaluation of "Scared Straight" by Finckenauer and Storti (1978) found only one of nine attitudinal measures significantly changed for juveniles as a result of brief exposure to hardened prisoners and no reduction in recidivism (Finckenauer, 1979). Other variations on the original program have also found no overall deterrent effect (Buckner & Chesney-Lind, 1983; Lewis, 1983), although some individual differences were noted. Similarly, there is now general consensus that shock probation (i.e., short prison terms prior to probation) has also failed to demonstrate significant deterrent effects (Boudouris & Turnbull, 1985; Friday & Peterson, 1973; Vito, 1984). There is even one report (Vito, Holmes, & Wilson, 1985) suggesting that shock probation for a subgroup of probationers increased recidivism!

Some jurisdictions have received media attention by employing quasimilitary, boot camp regimes for offenders. In the only evaluation with a follow-up that we are aware of—although more will be forthcoming in the near future (MacKenzie, personal communication) —juveniles taking part in such a program did not have reduced reconviction rates compared to nonparticipatory youths (Thornton, Curran, Grayson, & Holloway, 1984). Curiously, older adolescents reported an easier time in the program compared to their previous experiences with incarceration.

Death Row

Once an issue of little importance, the pragmatics of how best to deal with inmates awaiting capital punishment is now of particular concern. The rate of death penalty commitments between 1981 and 1983 ranged from 228 to 264 per year in the United States, and these rates are expected to remain in the same range (Cheatwood, 1985). Since the rate of executions is far lower, a considerable number of offenders are on death rows waiting out lengthy appeal applications. In fact, psychiatrists are now being asked to assess the death row inmate's appreciation of the appeal process and competency for execution (Kenner, 1986). In 1985, nearly 1,500 inmates were in this situation (Cheatwood, 1985). The growing numbers have led to crowded conditions on some death rows, and, in one incident, apparently motivated two condemned prisoners to take hostages as a sign of protest (*The Citizen*, 1986).

Very little evidence is available on how inmates adjust to death row. Perhaps the first study reported is that by Bluestone and Mc-Gahee (1962). They interviewed 19 inmates (18 men and one woman) awaiting execution

at Sing Sing prison. Expecting to find intense anxiety and depression, they found none. Gallemore and Panton (1972) tested 8 men awaiting execution at reception and several times thereafter up to a period of 2 years. Five men showed no observable deterioration upon the measures employed whereas 3 reported symptoms ranging from paranoia to insomnia. In a further study of 34 inmates on death row, Panton (1976) compared their MMPI profiles with a large prison sample. Death row inmates showed increased feelings of depression and hopelessness. Severe disturbances (e.g., psychosis) were not observed.

Johnson (1982) interviewed 35 men on death row and found them concerned over their powerlessness, fearful of their surroundings, and feeling emotionally drained. Younger inmates were more susceptible to these concerns. However, no comparison group was employed and the prevalence of these feelings among inmates in general is unknown.

Smith and Felix (1986) conducted unstructured psychiatric interviews of 34 death row inmates. Most of their sample exhibited well-intact defenses regarding their alleged guilt. Only 7 inmates evidenced a depressed mood that might have required further counseling intervention. Debro, Murty, Roebuck, and McCann (1987) interviewed 25 death row inmates and found that *all* slept well and felt relatively good about themselves. None requested or received tranquilizers. Finally, in a rare study of death row inmates who had their sentences commuted to life imprisonment, 23 inmates (46%) showed no change in personality functioning as measured by the MMPI (Dahlstrom, Panton, Bain, & Dahlstrom, 1986). Furthermore, 18 (36%) showed an improvement while only 9 (18%) deteriorated.

This literature, inadequate as it is, is meaningful for what it fails to produce—evidence of severe psychological reactions to a tragic fate. Why this is so is unclear. Some (Bluestone & McGahee, 1962; Smith & Felix, 1986) have suggested that death row inmates have particularly well-developed defense mechanisms, but this hypothesis has been based solely on subjective clinical impressions. In fact, it may be those associated with the condemned inmate (family, prison staff, etc.) that suffer more (Smykla, 1987). The limited data are a testimony to the ability of men to cope with the worst of consequences.

SUMMARY AND CONCLUSIONS

When it comes to scholarly inquiry in the field of criminal justice, a pernicious tendency has been to invoke rhetoric over reality and affirm ideology over respect for empirical evidence. We have witnessed this sad state of affairs in the debates over the effectiveness of rehabilitation, personality and crime, and the relationship between social class and criminal behavior (Andrews & Wormith, 1989; Cullen & Gendreau, 1989).

If we are to make progress in understanding what it is our prisons do to inmates, then we must respect the available evidence. We do not discount the importance of phenomenology in assessing prison life; this line of inquiry does provide valuable insight (e.g., Toch, 1977). But, if we stray too far from the epistemic values that are crucial to a vigorous social science then we run the risk of making disastrous policy decisions. Therefore, if we are to have a more constructive agenda we must face the fact that simplistic notions of the "pains of imprisonment" simply will not be instructive and will mitigate against the inmate's well-being.

The facts are that long-term imprisonment and specific conditions of confinement such as solitary, under limiting and humane conditions, fail to show any sort of profound detrimental effects. The crowding literature indicates that moderating variables play a crucial role. The health risks to inmates appear minimal. Unfortunately prisons, in a way, may minimize some stress by removing the need to make daily decisions that are important for community living (Zamble & Porporino, 1990).

If we approach prison life with sensitivity, however, we will foster a much more realistic and proactive research and policy agenda. Our literature review revealed considerable support for this notion. We repeatedly found that interactions between certain types of individual differences and situational components explained a meaningful percentage of the variance. To illustrate, we found that age, changes in the prison population, and the chronicity of the situation had profound influences on the responses of inmates to high population density. There also appear to be some cognitive and biological individual differences that may influence adjustment to solitary confinement.

In regard to the above, it is important that the assessment of environments reach the same level of methodological sophistication as the assessment of individuals. There have been some promising developments toward that end. Wenk and Moos (1972) have developed the Correctional Institutions Environment Scale; Toch (1977), the Prison Preference Profile; and Wright (1985), the Prison Environment Inventory. These are initial steps and it is hoped that research along these lines will continue.

Our final comments are in regard to theory development. To date, the incarceration literature has been very much influenced by a "pains of imprisonment" model. This model views imprisonment as psychologically harmful. However, the empirical data we reviewed question the validity of the view that imprisonment is *universally* painful. Solitary confinement, under limiting and humane conditions, long-term imprisonment, and short-term detention fail to show detrimental effects. From a physical health standpoint, inmates appear more healthy than their community counterparts. We have little data on the effects of death row, and the crowding literature indicates that moderating variables play a crucial role.

On a brighter note, the stress model does provide a positive agenda for ameliorative action. In the long-term incarceration literature, researchers (Zamble, 1989; Zamble & Porporino, 1988, 1990) have found that some inmates cope successfully with prison but others do not and that the type of coping is modestly related to future recidivism. Furthermore, on the basis of their analysis, if emotional distress is reported by inmates, it is more often early on in their incarceration. It is at this point that they may be receptive to treatment. The implications for the timing of prison-based treatment programs is obvious. The crucial point is that on the basis of this evidence, we can now develop a variety of cognitive-behavioral and/or skills training programs that could assist prisoners in dealing with their experiences in the most constructive manner possible. There is accumulating and persuasive evidence, moreover, that certain types of offender programming strategies in prison can reduce subsequent recidivism (Andrews, Zinger, Hoge, Bonta, Gendreau, & Cullen, 1989). This proactive agenda, we wish to emphasize, was not forthcoming from those who viewed prisons as invariably destructive. Unfortunately, their recommendations were for almost total deinstitutionalization, which is not only an extreme view, but also one that is totally unpalatable given North American cultural values and the current sociopolitical reality (see Currie, 1985; Glazer, 1989).

In our view, a social learning perspective (cf. Bandura, 1977) provides a more comprehensive explanation of the evidence. Social learning theory examines behavior (attitudes, motor actions, emotions) as a function of the rewards and punishments operating in a prison environment. There is an explicit acceptance of person variables moderating the responsivity to imprisonment. Several questions emerge from this perspective: *Who* perceives prisons as stressful? *What* aspect of imprisonment shapes behavior? And *how* do individuals respond to imprisonment? Answers to these questions would provide insight into the individuals who do not perceive their environments as stressful while imprisoned and what aspects of imprisonment attenuate the prison experience. In addition, this perspective would clarify the links between emotions, attitudes, and behavior.

From this review, we also see a clear research agenda. Further efforts to understand the effects of prison overcrowding should focus on individual levels of analysis along with multiple measures of the three outcome variables (emotions, attitudes, and behavior). Longitudinal designs (e.g., Zamble & Porporino, 1990) should be the rule. The inherent difficulties in interpreting aggregate level data appear only to confuse our understanding of the impact of crowded conditions on the individual. We need to know under what conditions an individual feels crowded, becomes emotionally distressed, and copes with this distress in a maladaptive manner. For example, Ruback, Carr, and Hopper (1986) suggested that perceived control is a possible mediator. The solution to prison overcrowding is not to embark on a prohibitively expensive prison construction program (Funke, 1985) but rather to alter the rate of intake and release (Skovron, 1988). One way of accomplishing this task is to increase community correctional treatment programs that would allow the diversion of inmates away from prisons (Bonta & Motiuk, 1987). Despite the reluctance of many correctional administrators to develop such programs, there appears to be considerable public support not only for community treatment initiatives (Skovron, Scott, & Cullen, 1988) but for rehabilitation in general (Cullen, Skovron, Scott, & Burton, 1990).

The application of longitudinal designs using data collected at the individual level is also needed in the other areas we have discussed. This is especially so with long-term imprisonment and health risks where the data suggest that if anything, the prison system may actually prevent deterioration. However, only longitudinal designs will allow us to make such a conclusion with any high degree of certainty. If future research leads us to the same conclusion, then the next step would be to identify the system contingencies that support such an environment, for certainly we can learn something positive from this type of result. Finally, and remarkably, we know so little about the psychological impact of a system that houses over a million individuals: the jails. Here, almost any type of reasoned research would be a step in the right direction.

All of the above is easier said than done. The host of issues that need to be researched seem infinite. The methodological complexities in examining both person and situation interaction are pronounced. But, it appears to us to be a positive agenda in order to gain knowledge addressing a vital question.

REFERENCES

Altman, I. (1978). Crowding: Historical and contemporary trends in crowding research. In A. Baum & M.Y.M. Epstein (Eds.), *Human response to crowding* (pp. 3-29). Hillsdale, NJ: Lawrence Erlbaum.

Andrews, D. A., & Wormith, J. S. (1989). Personality and crime: Knowledge destruction and construction in criminology. *Justice Quarterly.*

Andrews, D. A., Zinger, I., Hoge, R. D., Bonta, J., Gendreau, P., & Cullen, F. T. (1989). *A clinically relevant and psychologically informed metaanalysis of juvenile correctional treatment programs.* Paper presented at the Research Seminar of National Associations Active in Criminal Justice, Ottawa.

Angelos, C., & Jacobs, J. B. (1985). Prison overcrowding and the law. *Annals of the American Academy of Political and Social Science, 478,* 100-112.

Austin, W. T., & Unkovic, C. M. (1977). Prison suicide. *Criminal Justice Review, 2,* 103-106.

Baird, J. A. (1977). Health care in correctional facilities. *Journal of the Florida Medical Association, 64,* 813-818.

Bandura, A. (1977). *Social learning theory.* Englewood Cliffs, NJ: Prentice Hall.

Banister, P. A., Smith, F. V., Heskin, K. J., & Bolton, N. (1973). Psychological correlates of long-term imprisonment: I. Cognitive variables. *British Journal of Criminology, 13,* 312-323.

Barak-Glantz, I. L. (1983). Who's in the "hole"? *Criminal Justice Review, 8,* 29-37.

Bentz, W. K., & Noel, R. W. (1983). The incidence of psychiatric disorder among a sample of men entering prison. *Corrective & Social Psychiatry and Journal of Behavior Technology, 29,* 22-28.

Bluestone, H., & McGahee, C. L. (1962). Reaction to extreme stress: Impending death by execution. *American Journal of Psychiatry, 119,* 393-396.

Bolton, N., Smith, F. V., Heskin, K. J., & Banister, P. A. (1976). Psychological correlates of long-term imprisonment: IV. A longitudinal analysis. *British Journal of Criminology, 16,* 36-47.

Bonta, J. (1986). Prison crowding: Searching for the functional correlates. *American Psychologist, 41,* 99-101.

Bonta, J., & Kiem, T. (1978). Institutional misconducts in a jail setting: Preliminary findings and a note of caution. *Crime & Justice, 6,* 175-178.

Bonta, J., & Motiuk, L. L. (1987). The diversion of incarcerated offenders to correctional halfway houses. *Journal of Research in Crime and Delinquency, 24,* 302-323.

Bonta, J., & Nanckivell, G. (1980). Institutional misconducts and anxiety levels among jailed inmates. *Criminal Justice and Behavior, 7,* 203-214.

Boudouris, J., & Turnbull, B. W. (1985). Shock probation in Iowa. *Offender Counseling, Services, and Rehabilitation, 9,* 53-61.

Buckner, J. C., & Chesney-Lind, M. (1983). Dramatic cures for juvenile crime: An evaluation of a prison-run delinquency prevention program. *Criminal Justice and Behavior, 10,* 227-247.

Bukstel, L. H., & Kilmann, P. K. (1980). Psychological effects of imprisonment on confined individuals. *Psychological Bulletin, 88,* 469-493.

Call, J. E. (1983). Recent case law on overcrowded conditions of confinement. *Federal Probation, 47,* 23-32.

Cheatwood, D. (1985). Capital punishment and corrections: Is there an impending crisis? *Crime and Delinquency, 31,* 461-479.

Cholst, S. (1979). The effects of long-term detention. *International Journal of Offender Therapy and Comparative Criminology, 23,* 210-213.

Citizen, The. (1986, March 18). Killers release hostages after death row siege.

Clayton, O., & Carr, T. (1984). The effects of prison crowding upon infraction rates. *Criminal Justice Review, 9,* 69-77.

Clayton, O., & Carr, T. (1987). An empirical assessment of the effects of prison crowding upon recidivism utilizing aggregate level data. *Journal of Criminal Justice, 15,* 201-210.

Clements, C. B. (1979). Crowded prisons: A review of psychological and environmental effects. *Law and Human Behavior, 3,* 217-225.

Clements, C. B. (1982). The relationship of offender classification to the problems of prison overcrowding. *Crime and Delinquency, 28,* 72-81.

Clemmer, D. (1940). *The prison community.* New York: Rinehart.

Cohen, J. (1977). *Statistical power analysis for the behavioral sciences.* New York: Academic Press.

Cohen, S., & Taylor, L. (1972). *Psychological survival.* Harmondsworth, UK: Penguin.

Colvin, M. (1982). The New Mexico prison riot. *Social Problems, 29,* 449-463.

Cormier, B. M., & Williams, P. J. (1966). *Excessive deprivation of liberty as a form of punishment.* Paper presented at the meeting of the Canadian Psychiatric Association, Edmonton.

Corrections Digest. (1986, June). *17,* 1-2.

Cox, V. C., Paulus, P. B., & McCain, G. (1984). Prison crowding research: The relevance of prison housing standards and a general approach regarding crowding phenomena. *American Psychologist, 39,* 1148-1160.

Cox, V. C., Paulus, P. B., & McCain, G. (1986). Not for attribution: A reply to Bonta. *American Psychologist, 41,* 101-103.

Cullen, F. T., & Gendreau, P. (1989). The effectiveness of correctional rehabilitation. In L. Goodstein & D. L. MacKenzie (Eds.), *The American prison: Issues in research policy* (pp. 23-44). New York: Plenum.

Cullen, F. T., & Gilbert, K. E. (1982). *Reaffirming rehabilitation.* Cincinnati: Anderson.

Cullen, F. T., Skovron, S. E., Scott, J. E., & Burton, V. S. (1990). Public support for correctional treatment: The tenacity of rehabilitative ideology. *Criminal Justice and Behavior, 17,* 6-18.

Culpepper, L., & Froom, J. (1980). Incarceration and blood pressure. *Social Services and Medicine, 14,* 571-574.

Currie, E. (1985). *Confronting crime: An American challenge.* New York: Pantheon.

Currie, E. (1989). Confronting crime: Looking toward the twenty-first century. *Justice Quarterly, 6,* 5-26.

Dahlstrom, G. W., Panton, J. H., Bain, K. P., & Dahlstrom, L. E. (1986). Utility of the Megargee-Bohn MMPI typological assessments: Study with a sample of death row inmates. *Criminal Justice and Behavior, 13,* 5-17.

D'Atri, D. A. (1975). Psychophysiological responses to crowding. *Environment and Behavior, 7,* 237-252.

D'Atri, D. A., Fitzgerald, E. F., Kasl, S. V., & Ostfeld, A. M. (1981). Crowding in prison: The relationship between changes in housing mode and blood pressure. *Psychosomatic Medicine, 43,* 95-105.

D'Atri, D. A., & Ostfeld, A. M. (1975). Crowding: Its effects on the elevation of blood pressure in a prison setting. *Preventative Medicine, 4,* 550-566.

Debro, J., Murty, K., Roebuck, J., & McCann, C. (1987). Death row inmates: A comparison of Georgia and Florida profiles. *Criminal Justice Review, 12*, 41-46.

Derro, R. A. (1978). Administrative health evaluation of inmates of a city-county workhouse. *Minnesota Medicine, 61*, 333-337.

Dy, A. J. (1974). Correctional psychiatry and phase psychotherapy. *American Journal of Psychiatry, 131*, 1150-1152.

Ecclestone, J. E. J., Gendreau, P., & Knox, C. (1974). Solitary confinement of prisoners: An assessment of its effects on inmates' personal constructs and adrenal-cortical activity. *Canadian Journal of Behavioural Science, 6*, 178-191.

Ekland-Olsen, S., Barrick, D., & Cohen, L. E. (1983). Prison overcrowding and disciplinary problems: An analysis of the Texas prison system. *Journal of Applied Behavioral Science, 19*, 163-176.

Ellis, D. (1984). Crowding and prison violence: Integration of research and theory. *Criminal Justice and Behavior, 11*, 277-308.

Farrington, D. P., & Nuttall, C. P. (1980). Prison size, overcrowding, prison violence, and recidivism. *Journal of Criminal Justice, 8*, 221-231.

Finckenauer, J. C. (1979). *Justice awareness project: Evaluation report #2*. Newark, NJ: School of Criminal Justice, Rutgers.

Finckenauer, J. C., & Storti, J. P. (1978). *Justice awareness project: Evaluation report #1*. Newark, NJ: School of Criminal Justice, Rutgers.

Flanagan, T. J. (1980a). The pains of long-term imprisonment. *British Journal of Criminology, 20*, 148-156.

Flanagan, T. J. (1980b). Time served and institutional misconduct. Patterns of involvement in disciplinary infractions among long-term and short-term inmates. *Journal of Criminal Justice, 8*, 357-367.

Flanagan, T. J. (1982). Lifers and long-termers: Doing big time. In R. Johnson & H. Toch (Eds.), *The pains of imprisonment* (pp. 115-128). Beverly Hills, CA: Sage.

Fox, V. G. (1985). *Introduction to corrections*. Englewood Cliffs, NJ: Prentice Hall.

Freedman, J. L. (1975). *Crowding and behavior*. New York: Viking.

Friday, P. C., & Peterson, D. M. (1973). Shock of imprisonment: Comparative analysis of short-term incarceration as a treatment technique. *Canadian Journal of Criminology, 15*, 281-290.

Funke, G. S. (1985). The economics of prison crowding. *Annals of the American Academy of Political and Social Science, 478*, 86-89.

Gaes, G. G. (1983). Farrington and Nuttall's "overcrowding and recidivism." *Journal of Criminal Justice, 11*, 265-267.

Gaes, G. G. (1985). The effects of overcrowding in prison. In M. Tonry & N. Morris (Eds.), *Crime and justice* (Vol. 6, pp. 95-146). Chicago: University of Chicago Press.

Gaes, G. G., & McGuire, W. J. (1985). Prison violence: The contribution of crowding versus other determinants of prison assault rates. *Journal of Research in Crime and Delinquency, 22*, 41-65.

Gallemore, J. L., & Panton, J. H. (1972). Inmate responses to lengthy death row confinement. *American Journal of Psychiatry, 129*, 81-86.

Gendreau, P., & Bonta, J. (1984). Solitary confinement is not cruel and unusual punishment: People sometimes are! *Canadian Journal of Criminology, 26*, 467-478.

Gendreau, P., Freedman, N. L., Wilde, G. J. S., & Scott, G. D. (1968). Stimulation seeking after seven days of perceptual deprivation. *Perception and Motor Skills, 26*, 547-550.

Gendreau, P., Freedman, N. L., Wilde, G. J. S., & Scott, G. D. (1972). Changes in EEG alpha frequency and evoked response latency during solitary confinement. *Journal of Abnormal Psychology, 79*, 54-59.

Gendreau, P., Horton, J. G., Hooper, D. G., Freedman, N., Wilde, G. J. S., & Scott, G. D. (1968). Perceptual deprivation and perceptual motor skills: Some methodological considerations. *Perceptual and Motor Skills, 27*, 57-58.

Gendreau, P., McLean, R., Parsons, T., Drake, R., & Ecclestone, J. (1970). Effects of two days monotonous confinement on conditioned eyelid frequency and topography. *Perceptual and Motor Skills, 31*, 291-293.

Gendreau, P., & Ross, R. R. (1987). Revivication of rehabilitation: Evidence from the 1980s. *Justice Quarterly, 4*, 349-407.

Gendreau, P., Wormith, S. J., & Tellier, M. C. (1985). Protective custody: The emerging crisis within our prisons? *Federal Probation, 49*, 55-63.

Gibbs, J. J. (1982). The first cut is the deepest: Psychological breakdown and survival in the detention setting. In R. Johnson & H. Toch (Eds.), *The pains of imprisonment* (pp. 97-114). Beverly Hills, CA: Sage.

Gibbs, J. J. (1987). Symptoms of psychopathology among jail prisoners: The effects of exposure to the jail environment. *Criminal Justice and Behavior, 14*, 288-310.

Glass, G. V., McGaw, B., & Smith, M. L. (1981). *Meta-analysis in social research*. Beverly Hills, CA: Sage.

Glazer, S. (1989). Can prisons rehabilitate? *Congressional Quarterly's Editorial Research Report, 2*, 430-433.

Glueck, S., & Glueck, E. (1950). *Unravelling juvenile delinquency*. New York: Commonwealth Fund.

Goffman, E. (1961). *Asylums: Essays on the social situation of mental patients and other inmates*. Garden City, NJ: Anchor.

Goldsmith, S. B. (1972). Jailhouse medicine—Travesty of justice? *Health Services Report, 87,* 767-774.

Grassian, S. (1983). Psychopathological effects of solitary confinement. *American Journal of Psychiatry, 140,* 1450-1454.

Hayes, L. M. (1983). And darkness closed in . . . a national study of jail suicides. *Criminal Justice and Behavior, 10,* 461-484.

Heskin, K. J., Bolton, N., Smith, F. V., & Banister, P. A. (1974). Psychological correlates of long-term imprisonment: III. Attitudinal variables. *British Journal of Criminology, 14,* 150-157.

Heskin, K. J., Smith, F. V., Banister, P. A., & Bolton, N. (1973). Psychological correlates of long-term imprisonment: II: Personality variables. *British Journal of Criminology, 13,* 323-330.

Irwin, J., & Cressey, D. R. (1962). Thieves, convicts, and the inmate culture. *Social Problems, 10,* 142-155.

Jackson, M. (1983). *Prisons of isolation: Solitary confinement in Canada.* Toronto: University of Toronto Press.

Jan, L. J. (1980). Overcrowding and inmate behavior: Some preliminary findings. *Criminal Justice and Behavior, 7,* 293-301.

Johnson, R. (1982). Life under sentence of death. In R. Johnson & H. Toch (Eds.), *The pains of imprisonment* (pp. 129-145). Beverly Hills, CA: Sage.

Jones, D. A. (1976). *The health risks of imprisonment.* Lexington, MA: D. C. Heath.

Karlin, R. A., Katz, S., Epstein, Y. M., & Woolfolk, R. L. (1979). The use of therapeutic interventions to reduce crowding-related arousal: A preliminary investigation. *Environmental Psychology and Nonverbal Behavior, 3,* 219-227.

Kennedy, E. M. (1985, March). Prison overcrowding: The law's dilemma. *Annals of the American Academy of Political and Social Science, 478,* 113-122.

Kenner, W. D. (1986). Competency on death row. *International Journal of Law and Psychiatry, 8,* 253-255.

Krug, S. E., Scheier, I. H., & Cattell, R. B. (1976). *Handbook for the IPAT anxiety scale.* Champaign, IL: Institute for Personality and Ability Testing.

Lawrence, R. (1985). Jail education programs: Helping inmates cope with overcrowded conditions. *Journal of Correctional Education, 36,* 15-20.

Lewis, R. V. (1983). Scared straight—California style: Evaluation of the San Quentin squires program. *Criminal Justice and Behavior, 10,* 204-226.

Loo, C. (1973). Important issues in researching the effects of crowding in humans. *Representative Research in Psychology, 4,* 219-226.

MacKenzie, D. L. (1987). Age and adjustment to prison: Interactions with attitudes and anxiety. *Criminal Justice and Behavior, 14,* 427-447.

MacKenzie, D. L., & Goodstein, L. (1985). Long-term incarceration impacts and characteristics of long-term offenders: An empirical analysis. *Criminal Justice and Behavior, 13,* 395-414.

MacKenzie, D. L., Robinson, J. W., & Campbell, C. S. (1989). Long-term incarceration of female offenders: Prison adjustment and coping. *Criminal Justice and Behavior, 16,* 223-238.

McCain, G., Cox, V. C., & Paulus, P. B. (1976). The relationship between illness complaints and degree of crowding in a prison environment. *Environment and Behavior, 8,* 283-290.

McCain, G., Cox, V. C., & Paulus, P. B. (1980). *The effect of prison crowding on inmate behavior.* Rockville, MD: U.S. Department of Justice.

Megargee, E. I. (1977). The association of population density, reduced space, uncomfortable temperatures with misconduct in a prison community. *American Journal of Community Psychology, 5,* 289-299.

Miller, E. E. (1978). *Jail management: Problems, programs and perspectives.* Lexington, MA: Lexington Books.

Mitford, J. (1973). *Kind and unusual punishment.* New York: Knopf.

Mohr, J. W. (1985). The long-term incarceration issue: The banality of evil and the pornography of power. *Canadian Journal of Criminology, 27,* 103-112.

Nacci, P. L., Teitelbaum, H. E., & Prather, H. (1977). Population density and inmate misconduct rates in the federal prison system. *Federal Probation, 41,* 26-31.

Novick, L. F., & Al-Ibrahim, M. S. (1977). *Health problems in the prison setting.* Springfield, IL: Charles C Thomas.

Novick, L. F., Della-Penna, R., Schwartz, M. S., Remlinger, E., & Lowenstein, R. (1977). Health status of the New York City prison population. *Medical Care, 15,* 205-216.

Oleski, M. S. (1977). The effect of indefinite pretrial incarceration on the anxiety level of an urban jail population. *Journal of Clinical Psychology, 33,* 1006-1008.

Ostfeld, A. M., Kasl, S. V., D'Atri, D. A., & Fitzgerald, E. F. (1987). *Stress, crowding, and blood pressure in prison.* Hillsdale, NJ: Lawrence Erlbaum.

Panton, J. H. (1976). Personality characteristics of death row prison inmates. *Journal of Clinical Psychology, 32,* 306-309.

Paulus, P. B. (1988). *Prison crowding: A psychological perspective.* New York: Springer-Verlag.

Paulus, P., Cox, V., McCain, G., & Chandler, J. (1975). Some effects of crowding in a prison environment. *Journal of Applied Social Psychology, 5,* 86-91.

Paulus, P., McCain, G., & Cox, V. (1981). Prison standards: Some pertinent data on crowding. *Federal Probation, 45,* 48-54.

Paulus, P., McCain, G., & Cox, V. (1973). A note on the use of prisons as environments for investigation of crowding. *Bulletin of the Psychonomic Society, 6,* 427-428.

Paulus, P., McCain, G., & Cox, V. (1978). Death rates, psychiatric commitments, blood pressure, and perceived crowding as a function of institutional crowding. *Environmental Psychology and Nonverbal Behavior, 3*, 107-116.

Porporino, F. J., & Dudley, K. (1984). *Analysis of the effects of overcrowding in Canadian penitentiaries.* Ottawa: Solicitor General Canada.

Porporino, F. J., & Martin, J. P. (1983). *Strategies for reducing prison violence.* Ottawa: Solicitor General Canada.

Porporino, F. J., & Zamble, E. (1984). Coping with imprisonment. *Canadian Journal of Criminology, 26*, 403-421.

Rasch, W. (1981). The effects of indeterminate sentencing: A study of men sentenced to life imprisonment. *International Journal of Law and Psychiatry, 4*, 417-431.

Ray, D. W., Wandersman, A. W., Ellisor J., & Huntington, D. E. (1982). The effects of high density in a juvenile correctional institution. *Basic and Applied Social Psychology, 3*, 95-108.

Rector, M. G. (1982). Prisons and crime. *Crime and Delinquency, 28*, 505-507.

Reed, M. B. (1978). *Aging in total institution: The case of older prisoners.* Nashville: Tennessee Corrections Institute.

Richards, B. (1978). The experience of long-term imprisonment. *British Journal of Criminology, 18*, 162-169.

Ross, R. R., & McKay, H. B. (1979). *Self-mutilation.* Lexington, MA: Lexington Books.

Ruback, R. B., & Carr, T. S. (1984). Crowding in a women's prison: Attitudinal and behavioral effects. *Journal of Applied Social Psychology, 14*, 57-68.

Ruback, R. B., Carr, T. S., & Hopper, C. H. (1986). Perceived control in prison: Its relation to reported crowding, stress, and symptoms. *Journal of Applied Social Psychology, 16*, 375-386.

Ruback, R. B., & Innes, C. A. (1988). The relevance and irrelevance of psychological research: The example of prison crowding. *American Psychologist, 43*, 683-693.

Sapsford, R. J. (1978). Life sentence prisoners: Psychological changes during sentence. *British Journal of Criminology, 18*, 128-145.

Sapsford, R. J. (1983). *Life sentence prisoners: Reaction, response and change.* Milton Keynes: Open University Press.

Schneider, M. A. (1979). Problems in short-term correctional settings. *International Journal of Offender Therapy and Comparative Criminology, 23*, 164-171.

Skovron, S. E. (1988). Prison crowding: The dimensions of the problem and strategies of population control. In J. E. Scott & T. Hirschi (Eds.) *Controversial issues in crime and justice* (pp. 183-199). Newbury Park, CA: Sage.

Skovron, S. E., Scott, J. E., & Cullen, F. T. (1988). Prison crowding: Public attitudes toward strategies of population control. *Journal of Research in Crime and Delinquency, 25*, 150-169.

Smith, D. E. (1982). Crowding and confinement. In R. Johnson & H. Toch (Eds.), *The pains of imprisonment* (pp. 45-62). Beverly Hills, CA: Sage.

Smith, C. E., & Felix, R. R. (1986). Beyond deterrence: A study of defenses on death row. *Federal Probation, 50*, 55-59.

Smykla, J. O. (1987). The human impact of capital punishment: Interviews with families of persons on death row. *Journal of Criminal Justice, 15*, 331-347.

Stokols, D. (1972). On the distinction between density and crowding. *Psychological Review, 79*, 275-279.

Suedfeld, P. (1980). *Restricted environmental stimulation: Research and clinical applications.* New York: John Wiley.

Suedfeld, P., Ramirez, C., Deaton, J., & Baker-Brown, G. (1982). Reactions and attributes of prisoners in solitary confinement. *Criminal Justice and Behavior, 9*, 303-340.

Sundstrom, E. (1978). Crowding as a sequential process: Review of research on the effects of population density on humans. In A. Baum & Y. M. Epstein (Eds.), *Human response to crowding* (pp. 31-116). Hillsdale, NJ: Lawrence Erlbaum.

Sykes, G. (1958). *The society of captives: A study of a maximum security prison.* Princeton, NJ: Princeton University Press.

Thornton, D., Curran, L., Grayson, D., & Holloway, V. (1984). *Tougher regimes in detention centres.* London: Prison Department, Home Office.

Toch, H. (1977). *Living in prison: The ecology of survival.* New York: Free Press.

U.S. Bureau of Justice Statistics (1988). *Report to the nation on crime and justice.* Washington, DC: Author.

Vantour, J. A. (1975). *Report of the study group on dissociation.* Ottawa: Solicitor General Canada.

Vito, G. F. (1984). Developments in shock probation: A review of research findings and policy implications. *Federal Probation, 48*, 22-27.

Vito, G. F., Holmes, R. M., & Wilson, D. G. (1985). The effect of shock and regular probation upon recidivism: A comparative analysis. *American Journal of Criminal Justice, 9*, 152-162.

Walker, N. (1983). Side-effects of incarceration. *British Journal of Criminology, 23*, 61-71.

Walters, R. H., Callaghan, J. E., & Newman, A. F. (1963). Effects of solitary confinement on prisoners. *American Journal of Psychiatry, 119*, 771-773.

Weinberg, M. M. (1967). *Effects of partial sensory deprivation on involuntary subjects.* Unpublished doctoral dissertation, Michigan State University.

Wenk, E. A., & Moos, R. H. (1972). Social climates in prison: An attempt to conceptualize and measure environmental factors in total institutions. *Journal of Research in Crime and Delinquency, 9*, 134-148.

Wilson, D. G., & Vito, G. F. (1988). Long-term inmates: Special needs and management considerations. *Federal Probation, 52*, 21-26.

Wormith, J. S. (1984). The controversy over the effects of long-term imprisonment. *Canadian Journal of Criminology, 26*, 423-437.

Wormith, J. S. (1986, August). *The effects of incarceration: Myth-busting in criminal justice.* Paper presented at the 94th Annual Convention of the American Psychological Association, Washington, DC.

Wright, K. N. (1985). Developing the prison environment inventory. *Journal of Research in Crime and Delinquency, 22*, 259-278.

Zamble, E. (1989). *Behavior change during long-term impairment.* Paper presented at the Annual Meeting of the Canadian Psychological Association, Halifax, Nova Scotia.

Zamble, E., & Porporino, F. J. (1988). *Coping behavior and adaptation in prison inmates.* New York: Springer-Verlag.

Zamble, E., & Porporino, F. J. (1990). Coping, imprisonment, and rehabilitation: Some data and their implications. *Criminal Justice and Behavior, 17*, 53-70.

Zubek, J. P. (Ed.). (1969). *Sensory deprivation: Fifteen years of research.* New York: Appleton-Century-Crofts.

Zubek, J. P., Bayer, L., & Shepard, J. M. (1969). Relative effects of prolonged social isolation and behavioral and EEG changes. *Journal of Abnormal Psychology, 74*, 625-631.

Zubek, J. P., Shepard, J. M., & Milstein, S. L. (1970). EEG changes after 1, 4, and 7 days of sensory deprivation: A cross-sectional approach. *Psychonomic Science, 19*, 67-68.

10

The Unintended Effects
of Long-Term Imprisonment

Nigel Walker

There was a time when the worst thing that was said about imprisonment was that it did no good to the offender or his victims. Like most sweeping statements this was subject to quite a few exceptions; but it made a good slogan for penal reformers. Nowadays they have a better one: prison does more harm than good.

But this paper is not about the art of slogan-making. It is an attempt to distinguish the various kinds of harm which imprisonment is sometimes said to inflict on prisoners, and to see what the evidence—if any—is like. I have added "if any" because now and again what has been taken for evidence turns out to be nothing of the sort.

The focus of this paper is on long- or medium-term incarceration under ordinary conditions: not, that is, under the extreme conditions of "death rows", gulags, concentration camps or solitary cells. Nor does it try to deal with the harm done to prisoners' dependents. In passing, however, it is worth noting how little research into this topic has been published since Pauline Morris (1965). She was concerned mainly with the difficulties faced by wives, and did not study their children, an omission which needs to be remedied.[1] As for women prisoners, it is hard to find any systematic study of the ways in which they are affected by substantial periods of incarceration; and no such study seems to have been reported in Britain.

PHYSICAL HEALTH

A subject about which we have remarkably little that can be called evidence is the effects which British penal establishments have on their inmates' physical health. There have been occasional *causes célèbres* in which prisoners have claimed that their illnesses or injuries have been left untreated, or treated incompetently, during their detention. At intervals of roughly a decade there have been campaigns against the Prison Medical Service: one is proceeding at the moment. Noticeably lacking, however, has been any attempt to answer with scientific comparisons the most relevant question. This is not how many of the claims of inadequate medical treatment are true but whether such claims are likely to be true with greater frequency than under the National Health Service. Not that it would be easy to make such comparisons. Properly matched samples of prisoners and controls from general

NOTE: Reprinted with permission from *Problems of Long-Term Imprisonment*, Anthony E. Bottoms and Roy Light, Eds., pp. 183-199. Copyright 1987 by Ashgate Publishing Limited.

practice would be difficult both to design and to collect.

A slightly easier question to answer is whether prisoners are more likely, while inside, to suffer from physical illness or injury than while outside. Yet I know of only one researcher who has addressed this question; and he did his work in Tennessee. Nevertheless, Jones (1976) is worth studying as an example of research design. Essentially, it was a comparison of the medical records of: adult males in Tennessee State Penitentiary; adult males on parole in Tennessee; and adult males on probation in Tennessee. He wisely excluded: chronic conditions, since these might have been present before the men were imprisoned, paroled or put on probation; prisoners who had served less than six months, in order to eliminate most, if not all, the illnesses which might have originated before admission; and non-acute disorders, since these were less likely to be reported by men who were at liberty. Research based on medical records is open to at least one serious criticism. It is unlikely, in Tennessee or elsewhere, that medical attention is equally accessible to prisoners and to their free controls, or, if accessible, of the same standard. In some, probably all, prisons it is easier to "report sick" than it is to attend one's general practitioner's surgery. Sick-bays are more comfortable than cells, and a visit to them "makes a break." The ways of life of parolees and probationers may make resort to medical practitioners less easy or attractive than it is for prisoners. Costs may also enter into the matter. Even if Jones's findings are accepted as likely to be sound, it cannot be assumed that the same differences would be observable between the medical histories of British prisoners, parolees and probationers, under a different prison system and a different health service.

Yet with all these reservations both the method and the findings are of interest. Jones's penitentiary inmates were apparently subject to four types of disorder much more often than his parolees or probationers: "acute respiratory" disorders; "acute or chronic digestive" disorders; "acute infectious or parasitic" disorders; and "acute injuries." The English Prison Medical Service makes considerable efforts to keep such disorders at a minimum. In the 1970s, mass miniature radiography detected the occasional case of pulmonary tuberculosis, but there was seldom if ever any indication that it had been contracted from infection within prison (see Home Office Prison Department, 1977, p. 58; 1978, p. 49; 1979, p. 42). No outbreaks of legionnaire's disease in prisons have been reported, perhaps because their ventilation and plumbing systems are not hospitable to the organism. As for digestive disorders, a great deal of attention is paid to prisoners' diets. Conditions in some prison kitchens are good, in some much less good. One small outbreak of food poisoning by Salmonella was reported in 1980 (Home Office Prison Department, 1980, p. 52); but if newspapers can be relied upon such incidents seem commoner in NHS hospitals. Diets have been blamed not for malnutrition but for producing excess fat. In 1986 the Harvey (1986) Working Party recommended a reduction in the fat content of prison food, and the addition of more sources of vitamin D, as well as more attention to diets for religious and other minorities. But prisoners' preferences for foods, which are not always healthy, mean that care and tact is needed when diets are being improved.

Immunisation against poliomyelitis is offered to prisoners who have not already had it, as are other kinds of immunisation when it seems necessary. Parasitic infestations (which are said to be less common than in the United States) are likely to be detected at or soon after reception, and do not seem to be a problem in training or dispersal prisons.

AIDS

Since auto-immune deficiency syndrome (AIDS) has been the focus of recent concern, especially in North American prisons, some facts about the English experience are relevant. So far, only one inmate of an English prison has been found to be suffering from the full-blown condition: an intravenous drug-abuser. Although there is no compulsory screening of high-risk groups (for ethical reasons) between 30 and 40 inmates have been detected as HTLV III positive, but it is unlikely that any acquired the virus while in prison. However that may be, they are carefully segregated. What the future may bring, of course, is another question. Perhaps, to quote the President of the United States out of context, "we ain't seen nothing yet."

ILLICIT USE OF DRUGS

Another dangerous infection, however, is hepatitis B. In 1984 (Home Office, 1985, p. 70) sporadic outbreaks of this in English prisons were reported, and some 200 chronic hepatitis carriers were detected. (Vaccination was offered to staff who seemed to be particularly at risk.) As in the case of AIDS, one of the likely modes of transmission is the sharing of unsterilised needles among drug users (others are anal intercourse and—much less likely in prisons—blood transfusions). This, and other risks to health, are among the strongest reasons for trying to prevent intravenous or parenteric drug abuse.

Discoveries of illicit drugs (chiefly cannabis but occasionally heroin, cocaine and other substances) are required to be reported to the Prison Department; but illicit drug use is not mentioned as a problem in the Department's annual reports even in connection with outbreaks of hepatitis B. I have so far found no publication, official or unofficial, which deals specifically with illicit drug use in British prisons; but two unpublished documents, prepared by the Prison Officers' Association (POA) and the Prison Medical Association (PMA) in 1985, testify to the extent of the problem. The POA (1985) memorandum is based on a questionnaire completed by 75 branches (that is, about 55 per cent of all branches). Only 12 said that illicit drug use was *not* a problem in their establishments, and seven of those 12 said that there was evidence of *some* illicit use. The memorandum claims that many discoveries of drugs had not been officially reported to the Prison Department's headquarters as instructions require (for example, that only one such discovery was reported by Liverpool Prison in 1954 whereas in reality there were 54). But the highest numbers of notified discoveries were at Albany, Long Lartin and Ford: the problem is clearly not confined to prisons for short-termers. The PMA (1985) memorandum (which was submitted to the Social Services Committee of the House of Commons) does not refer to the POA report, but paints an equally startling picture. In Brixton, for example, heroin abusers refuse to be transferred to the hospital wing because in the other parts of the prison they can get heroin, syringes and needles. The memorandum emphasises "the permissive attitude to

alcohol and drug consumption by prisoners" in "the more liberal regimes of the dispersal prisons."

The POA's report also reflects permissiveness when it says that some officers believe that "drugs can have a calming effect on the establishment." In general, however, it emphasises the overconfidence which results from drug abuse, making some users hard to control. The main smuggling routes seem to be permitted visits, home leaves and food supplied to remand prisoners; and the memorandum stresses both the inadequacies and the difficulties of search procedures. The Swedish prison system now employs search squads with special training and equipment and powers (Edholm & Bishop, 1983). The impression given, however, by the two English memoranda is that governors are reluctant to allow strict searches because they are likely to antagonise both inmates and visitors. In Long Lartin, for example, sniffer dogs are used only in the workshops.

Whatever degree of tolerance seems best in this or that establishment, there is a strong case, in the interests of physical health, for thorough screening of self-injectors—not to mention practising homosexuals—for the hepatitis B virus—not to mention the AIDS virus—and segregating carriers in special units. Such procedures are admittedly open to the objection that they not only alarm identified carriers but also label them, with social consequences which can be serious. Yet such objections must be weighed against the risks to which other prisoners are exposed, without their consent, by close association with unidentified carriers.

PHYSICAL INJURIES

Injuries need more thorough study than David Jones in Tennessee was able to devote to them. They may be: deliberately self-inflicted; the result of assaults, usually by other prisoners, but occasionally by staff; accidental, although some "accidental" injuries are really the results of assaults about which the victims prefer to remain silent, or are not believed. Comparison with the injuries of "outsiders" is made almost impossible by the substantial proportion of assaults not reported to the police; and there are similar difficulties in comparing frequencies of accidental injuries at work, inside and outside penal establishments. We do not know whether prisoners in general are more likely to be the victims of assaults, or accidental injuries, while imprisoned than while at liberty: only a victim survey would tell us this.

Actuarial information of so general a kind, however, would be of less practical value than some of the things we already know about prison assaults. For example, it is generally agreed that certain categories of inmate are at most risk: informers, child-victimisers, defaulters on "inside" debts, and, probably, ex-policemen and ex-prison officers. These categories are recognised as prima facie cases for protection, either under Rule 43 or otherwise. Secondly, we can be fairly sure, on the evidence of disciplinary proceedings, that the incidence of assaults is higher than average in establishments for young adults, and consistently higher than average in some of the closed prisons for long- or medium-sentence men, such as Albany, Camp Hill, Gartree and Parkhurst. On the other hand, it does not seem to be true, at least on similar evidence, that assaults are more frequent, per head of prison population, in the larger establishments or the more overcrowded ones (Farrington & Nuttall, 1980).

MENTAL DISORDER

There is no sound evidence that periods of incarceration—long or short—under ordinary conditions of the kind experienced in British prisons result in mental disorders. A prison sentence is sometimes the first occasion on which an offender becomes the subject of a positive psychiatric diagnosis; but much more often it is found that he or she has a history of in-patient or out-patient treatment.

There are debatable exceptions. A disorder, for example, which used to be mentioned by psychiatric writers in connection with long-term incarceration was the Ganser Syndrome: a transient state of clouded consciousness in which only approximate answers are given to questions, and which is sometimes accompanied by somatic conversion features and subsequent amnesia for the episode. McKay et al. (1979) are probably justified in dismissing the evidence for its connection with incarceration as "scanty," and the definition of it as contro-

versial. The same is probably true of other so-called prison psychoses.[2] Of more interest is depression. When this occurs soon after reception it is usually no more than an understandable reactive state—a response to the prospect of separation from family and liberty. Sometimes, however, it is a chronic mood which the offender has hitherto kept at bay by means of alcohol or other drugs, and which reasserts itself when he is deprived of the drug. In Canadian penitentiaries, Porporino and Zamble (1984, p. 413) found, amongst inmates who had served about six months, that depression was significantly ($p < 0.001$) associated with poor education. Interestingly, it was not associated with the length of the sentence to be faced. (The same seemed true of anxiety.) In English prisons acute cases are treated with anti-depressants, but most have to cope on their own (see below).

SUICIDE AND SELF-INFLICTED INJURY

Although it is a minority of the depressed who commit or attempt suicide, and not all who do are noticeably depressed beforehand, depression seems to be the only predictor of suicide worth consideration (apart from threats of, and previous attempts at, suicide). Certainly researchers' attempts to find other predictors of prison suicides have yielded nothing worth the name. Suicides are more likely to take place at an early stage of incarceration, and there is no real evidence to support the theory that there is a minor peak towards the ends of long sentences (Burtch & Ericson, 1979, p. 40; Home Office, 1985; Jenkins, 1982). On the other hand, Burtch and Ericson (1979, pp. 35-40) found that suicide was somewhat more likely amongst lifers (in Canadian penitentiaries) than among fixed-termers (lifers accounted for only 6 per cent of the inmate population, but 16 per cent of the suicides). Whether the same can be said about self-inflicted non-suicidal injuries is unclear from the very little that has been published about them. The prevention of suicide is certainly a responsibility which is taken very seriously by prison staff, and prisoners who are regarded as suicide risks are put under special surveillance. The most effective form of surveillance is the sharing of cells or dormitories with other prisoners: but there are always short periods when the prisoner is left alone. In any case, enforced cell-sharing with a suicidal prisoner is an imposition which is hard to justify. The 1985 report of the Chief Inspector of Prisons made a number of recommendations on this subject which are being considered by the Prison Department (Home Office, 1985).

VULNERABILITY

Yet even when imprisonment cannot be blamed for the mental disorder, those who suffer from it present the staff with special problems and responsibilities. However mild the illness or the personality disorder it is unsafe to rule out the possibility that it will worsen as a result of incarceration. That apart, some disorders, particularly those involving low intelligence, make those who suffer from them liable to exploitation by the cunning. Other disorders, and especially aggressive personality disorders, represent dangers for fellow prisoners, and a focus of anxiety for staff. Repeated surveys have shown that the percentage of the English prison population with some degree of mental disorder is very substantial (see Gunn, 1977; Gunn et al., 1978). Only a fraction of this group is accommodated in units with specially adapted regimes; and there seems to be no prospect of dealing with the whole problem in this way, or at least in the foreseeable future, whether within the prison system or under the National Health Service. The Prison Rules provide that:

1. the medical officer shall report to the governor on the case of any prisoner whose health is likely to be injuriously affected by imprisonment or any conditions of imprisonment . . .
2. the medical officer shall pay special attention to any prisoner whose mental condition appears to require it, and make any special arrangements which appear necessary for his supervision or care (Rule 18).

It seems unlikely that this Rule is wholly effective in the overcrowded conditions of most local prisons. Whether it is effective in closed training or dispersal prisons is a question which only the medical officers there can answer.

PSYCHOLOGICAL EFFECTS

It is the psychological rather than the psychiatric effects of long detention which have been the subject of most concern, but also the most exaggeration. It was Goffman's (1961) influential book *Asylums* which drew much-needed attention to the nature of "total institutions" and the ways in which inmates adapted to them. Unfortunately he was guilty of sleight of hand, juggling with the literature of mental hospitals, penal establishments, concentration camps, barracks and even public schools and nunneries in order to attribute "mortifying" practices to every kind of total institution, and so argue that "the processes by which a person's self is mortified are fairly standard in total institutions" (Goffman, 1961, p. 14). Another conjuring trick was achieved in Cohen and Taylor's (1972) *Psychological Survival*. This had the merit of being based on close acquaintance with prisoners in the high-security wing of Durham Prison. It has been widely read as evidence of the inmates' psychological deterioration, although in fact all that it documents is their *fears* of deterioration: fears, moreover, which were probably encouraged by the discussions and reading material with which Cohen and Taylor's "classes" provided them.

Nevertheless, the concept of "institutionalisation," or the special variety sometimes called "prisonisation," must be taken seriously, and especially where long-term prisoners are concerned. It raises two problems: how to tell when it is happening, and what to do about it. Telling when it is happening is a task for psychologists rather than sociologists or psychiatrists; and it is psychologists who have developed ideas for measuring it. Since institutionalisation is a protean notion, which takes quite different shapes in different hands, psychologists have wisely dissected it into aspects of personality which seem capable of being measured, or at least assessed, without being confused with each other.

MENTAL SKILLS

Thus the Durham University team, whose work on this subject has received deserved attention abroad as well as in Britain, subjected adult male prisoners to batteries of intellectual and attitudinal tests at an early stage of their sentences, and after they had served, on average, about 19 months. The testers found "no evidence of psychological deterioration. On the contrary, verbal intelligence showed a significant increase between first and second testing, and there were significant reductions in hostility, which were associated with increasing emotional maturity" (Bolton et al., 1976, p. 47). A critic could point out that even by the time of their second testing the subjects had served less than two years of their current sentences; and that this did not guarantee that there would be no deterioration after, say, five or ten years, although it lays the onus of proof upon anyone who argues that there would. Providing proof, or disproof, would be a lengthy as well as a difficult business. As the Durham team realised, it is not sufficient to test "cross-sectional" samples; that is, samples of prisoners who have spent different fractions of long sentences inside. It cannot be assumed that their personalities or experiences inside have been well matched. It is necessary to achieve a "longitudinal" study, in which the same prisoners are tested, and with the same tests, after serving short, medium and long periods inside. Even then, many will have been moved around the prison system. Some will have been transferred to hospitals. Some will have been paroled. Some may have died. That is why so few, if any, longitudinal follow-ups are really long.

PRISONERS' INTERESTS AND PROBLEMS

A natural consequence of the Durham psychologists' findings, the earliest of which were published in 1973, was that prison psychologists turned their attention to other possible manifestations of institutionalisation. In 1978 Sapsford and Richards published separate and quite different studies of long sentence men in English prisons. Richards's (1978) work was done in an establishment with the reputation of being "an easy nick." His subjects were eight lifers and three fixed-termers who were in the first 18 months of their sentences; these were compared with seven lifers and four fixed-termers who had served at least eight years. He asked them to rank a list of 20 problems in order of severity. His findings "ran counter to the assumption [easily drawn, for example, from the work of Goffman, 1961] that it is the internal conditions of an institution which dominate inmates' experience of an institution" (Richards, 1978, p. 168). It is worth noting, by the way, that "being afraid of going mad" and "feeling suicidal" were "problems" which both groups ranked lowest of all.

Sapsford's (1978) subjects were all homicidal lifers in a larger maximum-security prison; and he deliberately excluded fixed-termers. They consisted of three matching groups: 20 very recently received under sentence, 20 in their sixth year who had not yet been interviewed for parole review by the Local Review Committee, and a "hard core" of ten who had passed the average date for release (at that time eleven years) and therefore faced the possibility of serving a very long time. Youths aged under 17 and men aged over 49 were deliberately excluded. Like those of Richards, Sapsford's samples were cross-sectional: but they were larger and better chosen. He used not only well-tried tests but also information from the lifers' files. He found, among those who had served longer periods: a greater tendency to talk and think about the past rather than the future; greater introversion—less interest in social activities and "outgoing behaviour" (an ironic choice of words); more dependence on routine even in petty matters, and less ability to take trivial decisions; no significant decrease in interest in the outside world, but less actual involvement in relations with outsiders (the two long-serving groups had nearly all lost contact with their wives or girlfriends, for example); amongst the hard-core men a greater tendency to see themselves as aligned with the staff (Sapsford did not imply that this was undesirable); but this tendency was not reflected in the staff's view of the hard-core men.

"COPING"

As Sapsford (1983, Chap. 4) later acknowledged, some of these changes should perhaps be regarded not as involuntary processes but as men's ways of coping with the psychological strains of long detention.[3] Prison sociologists recognised long ago that inmates consciously or unconsciously find ways of adapting to their situations, and that these ways differ according to their personalities and histories. If these adaptations lessen the stress they can be called "coping strategies." There are more ways than one of classifying them. While studying the inmates of Albany, King and Elliott (1977) found one method of classification which seemed to them to "capture the fundamental aspects of criminal identity and prisoner response." This was Irwin's (1970) typology, and it must be said in its favour that, unlike most sociologists, Irwin himself had "done time" in an American penitentiary. Like Irwin, King and Elliott (1977, p. 238) make the point that adaptations to prison are "fluid": "Though there is an element of strategic choice about these adaptations, the choices are not mutually exclusive. Most prisoners probably adapt in different ways at different times and many follow elements of several adaptations at one and the same time." Because there is this degree of choice—conscious or unconscious—on the prisoner's part, it seems likely that coping strategies are something that can be influenced by staff. If so, it seems that this should be an objective of policy, and that ways of achieving it should be studied more thoroughly than they have been in British prisons.

For the moment, it is probably sufficient to outline the main strategies which King and Elliott found among Albany inmates. Although everyone with an interest in this subject should read the whole of Chapter 8 of King and Elliott (1977), it is convenient here to cite Mott's (1985, p. 30) summary:

(i) *uncertain negative retreat*—difficulties in coping both with the staff and the other inmates;

(ii) *secondary comfort indulgence*—simply enjoying the comforts of the prison;

(iii) *jailing*—considerable involvement in the inmate social system with access to, and marketing of, contraband items;

(iv) *gleaning*—frequent contacts with specialist treatment staff, attending many educational courses in the hope of acquiring useful qualifications;

(v) *opportunism*—exploiting both the inmate social system and the specialist staff and educational resources;

(vi) *"doing your bird"*—never attracting staff or inmate attention, but respected

by both, while enjoying the comforts of the regime.

Obviously some of these strategies are more desirable than others from the point of view of management as well as mental health. Two points, however, should be kept in mind. However desirable this or that strategy—for example, "gleaning"—may be from the staff's point of view, and however much it may seem to be in the prisoner's own interest—gleaning is again the best example—some strategies are ruled out by the capacities or personalities of individual prisoners, and attempts to force them in an apparently desirable direction may misfire.

Coping with depression in the early stages of a long prison sentence is another matter. Acute depressions can be alleviated by anti-depressant drugs; but these are not usually prescribed for what can be called "realistic gloom." It is left to non-medical staff to offer what help they can. Whether any special training would improve the quality of their help is doubtful. Claims[4] have been made for the technique called "cognitive therapy," which deals with pathological depression by attacking the patient's distorted perception of his situation; but it is not easy to apply this to a prisoner whose appraisal of his situation is only too realistic.

REVERSIBILITY

The other point of prime importance was also made by Sapsford (1978, p. 143). Undesirable changes in a prisoner should be considered as deterioration only if they prove irreversible after his release. In 1983 Coker, who had followed up 239 released lifers, most of them from "the lowest socio-economic group and poorly educated" (the sort whom one would expect to be most vulnerable to permanent deterioration) wrote:

These men showed no evidence of deterioration as a result of their long years in prison, in so far as this can be measured. In general, after a short period of resettlement, sometimes accompanied by restlessness, they obtained and kept work and accommodation—satisfactory by their own standards as well as those of the Probation Service and the Home Office—and many married or remarried and made new homes. In some cases men improved upon their previous levels of employment. Additionally, these lifers revealed, generally, a fierce desire for independence and a capacity to manage their own lives competently, though some valued an opportunity to discuss matters with the probation officer (Letter in *British Journal of Criminology*, 1983, pp. 307-308; but see also Coker & Martin, 1985).

In other words, even if these men had experienced the changes found by Sapsford amongst his lifers, most of the changes seem to have been reversed. That is not to say that they are unimportant, or that no effort need be made to counter them: some of the changes which have been described have an undesirable effect on the "quality of life" of long-term prisoners. What is quite unjustifiable, however, is the prevalent assumption that they persist for long periods after release, or are permanent.

INDISCIPLINE

Individual breaches of discipline are only a little commoner in closed training prisons than in locals, if we can judge by the punishments recorded in Tables 10.2-10.8 of the annual prison statistics, although no doubt there are differences between degrees of enforcement in different prisons. It is remand centres, detention centres and youth custody centres— all for the young—which stand out. Concerted indiscipline, on the other hand, does seem commoner in establishments for long-termers: few, if any, of the reported riots of recent years have happened in other kinds of establishments. Research workers have tried to identify signs and symptoms which could be used to alert staff to the likelihood of a riot: their efforts were reviewed in the CRC report (Home Office, 1984, pp. 96ff). They have focused either on the measurable attitudes of inmates immediately before rioting began, or on the personalities of troublesome or subversive inmates. Neither line of research seems to have yielded very useful findings. Smith (1980) suggests that when the "degree of antagonism" and "support for disruptive action" increase *rapidly* to high levels a major breakdown in con-

trol is likeliest; but he added that an experienced governor might well be a better predictor.

RECIDIVISM

Imprisonment, however, has some intended aims, and the most important of these is obviously the reduction of the volume of crime. The efficacy of long sentences in deterring potential offenders is outside the scope of this paper, which is concerned with what imprisonment does to the imprisoned. As for incapacitation, there is no doubt that substantial periods of detention achieve some reductions in crime rates, although estimates of their importance vary. Critics of long sentences cannot deny their effectiveness as a means of postponing an offender's next crime—at least against a member of the free public. What such critics do condemn is the detention of offenders for longer than their proven offences deserve (whatever "deserve" means), if the sole object of the extra period of detention is the prevention of an offence which the individual is not certain to commit. I have argued elsewhere (Walker, 1982) that even this criticism has been carried to fallacious lengths: but this is not the place to pursue the point, which is of more relevance for sentencing and parole.

More germane to our present concern is the question whether long, or fairly long, sentences are particularly effective in deterring or otherwise discouraging prisoners from reoffending after release. More precisely, are such sentences followed by lower reconviction rates than are shorter sentences, and if so can this be attributed to the extra length? At first sight the reconviction tables in the annual prison statistics for England and Wales seem to show that the answer is "yes," at least so far as adult men are concerned. The longer the nominal length of the sentence from which they are released, the lower the percentage reconvicted over the next two years. Unfortunately these tables make no allowances for differences in age (reconviction rates decline with age), types of offence (sexual offenders, for example, have rather low reconviction rates) and previous records (the shorter these are the better the reconviction rate). Nor do they distinguish ex-prisoners who were on licence for some of the follow-up period from those who were not; and being under licence seems to have a beneficial effect on reconviction rates. It is not easy to justify the crude and misleading form in which these tables are published.

In fact it is by no means certain that longer sentences are followed by lower reconviction rates, when allowance is made for the important variables. It did not seem to be so in the case of Californian burglars (see Jaman et al., 1972). But the best of the North American evidence still seems to be the inadvertent experiment which resulted from the decision of the U.S. Supreme Court in the *Gideon* case. Large numbers of inmates had to be released from penitentiaries before their normal dates. In Florida, Eichman (1966) matched 110 of them with another 110 who had served their normal time, and followed up both groups for about two years. Neither group was under supervision during the follow-up. Sixty per cent of the "Gideon group" had served less than 18 months, compared with 47 per cent of the others. Yet the reconviction rate of the Gideon group was lower than that of the "controls" (14 per cent compared with 25 per cent).

I know of no British study which has tried to relate time actually spent "inside" to subsequent reconvictions. Yet data must be available which could be used to improve on the American studies which have been cited. The Florida "experiment" used, perforce, a rather early "cut-off point": 18 months. The Californian research chose 45 months as its cut-off stage, simply because it was the point at which its sample split into equal halves. It would be better to choose at least two cut-off points, in case there is a curvilinear association between time inside and reconviction.

"SCHOOLS FOR CRIME"?

All we have at the moment, so far as British prisoners are concerned, is the finding by Nuttall et al. (1977, p. 69), in their study of parole, that there were differences in "failure-rates" according to the parolees' previous criminal records and their previous experiences of imprisonment. This can be read as support for Sidney Smith's often repeated claim that penal establishments are "schools for crime." Most of the support for this rests on the impressions of those in charge of prisoners or ex-prisoners, and on autobiographical writings by ex-prisoners. What is said is that inmates form friendships with persistent offenders, and learn techniques of offending

from them; and that independently or together these friendships and techniques lead them into the commission of further offences.

An alternative possibility, however, is that these merely make it easier to trace their offences to them, and to lay hands on them. An important fact—especially when the known facts are so few—is that the persistent offenders whom prisoners encounter inside are offenders who have not been competent enough to avoid conviction. High post-release conviction rates may be the result of learning incompetent techniques or of committing offences in concert with incompetent accomplices. Given the low clear-up rates for most of the types of offence for which men are imprisoned, this is by no means an implausible hypothesis.

What all this amounts to is that we have, as yet, no sound evidence for claiming either that longer periods of detention result in lower reconviction rates or that association with recidivists results in a higher rate of offending, as distinct from a higher rate of detection and conviction; and the distinction is all-important.

GRIEVANCES

Imprisonment not only exposes prisoners to the influence of other inmates. It also places them to some extent at the mercy of staff. The rules and standing orders which prohibit or restrict activities that would be unhindered in the world outside can be applied generously or with bureaucratic strictness. They may even be used punitively against an inmate who has made himself unpopular with staff. It is very hard for officers to steer a middle course between laxity and strictness, although many succeed in learning to do this successfully. What has an effect that must be undesirable is rule-enforcement which prisoners see as unnecessary or vindictive. "Unlawful or unnecessary exercise of authority" by an officer is a disciplinary offence, which is spelt out as "deliberately acting in a manner calculated to provoke a prisoner" or as the use of unnecessary or undue force. How often it occurs is hard to tell: it is only exceptionally that it receives publicity, for example in the aftermath of the Hull riots. Without denying the importance of major incidents, it should be recognised that it is the trivial but repeated instances which have more effects on the attitudes of larger numbers of prisoners, and which fertilise the antagonism of prisoners towards "screws." A similar antagonism can easily be observed in other authoritarian settings, such as a conscript army, where the noncommissioned officers who enforce rules—as distinct from decisions—are more unpopular than their superiors who make the rules. In prison an individual occasionally—whether through mishandling or because of his personality—becomes more or less unmanageable; and it is these cases which attract proper concern. What we do not yet know is the extent to which antagonism to prison officers, in its extreme or its endemic form, lingers on after release, and colours ex-prisoners' attitudes to other agents of the law. Nobody seems to have compared ex-prisoners with other convicted offenders in this respect.

BATHWATER AND BABIES

Research in British prisons—chiefly by psychologists—has done much to deflate the sweeping exaggerations—chiefly by sociologists—about the ill-effects of normal incarceration. Yet every exaggeration has, by definition, a small hard core of truth, which can be overlooked in the process of deflation. There *are* live babies in the bathwater. I have tried to locate them before they are thrown away. Some of them are unanswered questions which call out for more and better research. Some are questions that have not yet been clearly and precisely posed. But a few are questions that have been answered, at least with enough clarity to enable us to discuss what needs to be done about the answers.[5]

BIBLIOGRAPHICAL NOTE

The literature on the unwanted effects of incarceration has been reviewed with differing degrees of thoroughness by several authors. Mott (1985) devotes two chapters to the main findings of British research, but lets some researchers off more lightly than others. McKay et al. (1979) provide an extensive bibliography, together with critical chapters which discuss policy implications from the Canadian point of view (Wormith's [1984] article in the *Canadian Journal of Criminology* seems largely based on the unpublished and more extensive work by McKay et al.) So far as psychological research is concerned, by far the best review is Bukstel and Kilmann (1980), which sorts out the wheat from the chaff, and summarises the research that seems to stand up to methodological criticism. The best review of research into prison suicides is Burtch and Ericson (1979).

NOTES

1. Monger (1970) was a small-scale study, and has never been published. Monger et al. (1981) was largely based on reports in files, and not on a project designed to assess effects on children. Roger Shaw, however, has completed a study of prisoners' children, carried out whilst he was a Teaching and Research Fellow at the Institute of Criminology, University of Cambridge (Shaw, 1987).

2. As Professor Gunn confirms (in a personal communication) the cases which used to be described as "prison psychoses" are debatable. Sometimes they occur in extreme situations, such as prisoner-of-war camps. Even when this is not so "no proper scientific data have been adduced to demonstrate whether the psychiatric problems are in fact directly attributable to the imprisonment or would have happened anyway." And, of course, as is said later in this paper, some people are psychiatrically "vulnerable." I have seen reactive depressions in academics on sabbatical in very foreign countries.

3. This chapter has an excellent discussion of the psychodynamics of coping; but does not offer as clear a classification of coping "styles" as do King and Elliott (1977). Sapsford's (1978) empirical study of lifers had not been designed with this in mind.

4. See, for example, Beck et al. (1977), reporting a controlled trial in which out-patients who underwent Beck's type of cognitive therapy showed greater improvement than those treated pharmacologically, although both groups showed improvement. Like all forms of psychotherapy, however, cognitive therapy seems to make considerable demands on time: in this experiment each patient underwent 20 weekly sessions, each of 50 minutes duration.

5. I am very much indebted to Professor Anthony Bottoms, Professor David Canter, Professor Richard Ericson, Professor John Gunn, to the Director of Prison Medical Services, to the Prison Medical Association and the Prison Officers' Association for helpful comments and references; but they are not responsible for the use I have made of them.

REFERENCES

Beck, A. T., et al. (1977). Comparative efficiency of cognitive therapy and pharmacotherapy in the treatment of depressed out patients. *Cognitive Therapy and Research, 1*(1), 17-37.

Bolton, N., et al. (1976). Psychological correlates of long-term imprisonment. *British Journal of Criminology, 16,* 38-47.

Bukstel, L. H., & Kilmann, P. R. (1980). Psychological effects of imprisonment on confined individuals. *Psychological Bulletin, 88,* 469-493.

Burtch, B. E., & Ericson, R. V. (1979). *The silent system: An inquiry into prisoners who suicide and an annotated bibliography.* Toronto: Centre of Criminology, University of Toronto.

Cohen, S., & Taylor, L. (1972). *Psychological survival.* Harmondsworth, UK: Penguin.

Coker, J., & Martin, J. P. (1985). *Licensed to live.* Oxford: Basil Blackwell.

Edholm, L., & Bishop, N. (1983). Serious drug misusers in the Swedish prison and probation system. *Prison Service Journal, 55,* 14-16.

Eichman, C. (1966). *The impact of the Gideon decision upon crime and sentencing in Florida* (Monograph No. 2). Tallahassee: Florida Division of Corrections.

Farrington, D. P., & Nuttall, C. (1980). Prison size, overcrowding, prison violence and recidivism. *Journal of Criminal Justice, 8,* 221-231.

Goffman, E. (1961). *Asylums.* New York: Anchor.

Gunn, J. (1977). Mental disorder and criminality. *British Journal of Psychiatry, 130,* 317-329.

Gunn, J., et al. (1978). *Psychiatric aspects of imprisonment.* London: Academic Press.

Harvey, J. B. (1986). *Review of the dietary scale in penal establishments in England and Wales.* (unpublished, obtainable from the Home Office Prison Department).

Home Office. (1984). *Managing the long-term prison system: The report of the control review committee.* London: HMSO.

Home Office. (1985). *Report on suicides in prison.* London: Home Office.

Home Office Prison Department. (annually). *Report of the prison department.* London: HMSO.

Irwin, J. (1970). *The felon.* Englewood Cliffs, NJ: Prentice Hall.

Jaman, D., et al. (1972). Parole outcome as a function of time served. *British Journal of Criminology, 12,* 5-34.

Jenkins, J. S. (1982). Suicide in prisoners: an overview. *Prison Medical Journal, 23,* 33-41.

Jones, D. (1976). *The health risks of imprisonment,* Lexington, MA: Lexington Books.

King, R., & Elliott, K. W. (1977). *Albany: The birth of a prison—End of an era?* London: Routledge & Kegan Paul.

McKay, H. B., et al. (1979). *The effects of long-term incarceration: And a proposed strategy for future research.* Ottawa: Ministry of the Solicitor-General for Canada.

Monger, J. (1970). *Prisoners' children: a descriptive study of some of the effects on children of their fathers' imprisonment.* (unpublished, lodged in Barnett House Library, University of Oxford)

Monger, M., et al. (1981). *Through-care with prisoners' families* (Social Work Study No. 3). Nottingham: University of Nottingham.

Morris, P. (1965). *Prisoners and their families.* London: Allen & Unwin.

Mott, J. (1985). *Adult prisons and prisoners in England and Wales 1970-1982: A review of the findings of social research.* London: HMSO.

Nuttall, C., et al. (1977). *Parole in England and Wales* (Home Office Research Study No. 38). London: HMSO.

Porporino, F. J., & Zamble, E. (1984). Coping with imprisonment. *Canadian Journal of Criminology, 26*(2), 403-421.

Prison Medical Association. (1985). *The misuse of drugs, with special reference to treatment and rehabilitation of misusers of hard drugs.* Submission to the Social Services Committee of the House of Commons (unpublished).

Prison Officers' Association. (1985). *Report into drug abuse in penal establishments in England and Wales.* (unpublished).

Richards, E. (1978). The experience of long-term imprisonment. *British Journal of Criminology, 18,* 162-168.

Sapsford, R. J. (1978). Life sentence prisoners: Psychological changes during sentence. *British Journal of Criminology, 18,* 128-145.

Sapsford, R. J. (1983). *Life sentence prisoners: Reaction, response and change.* Milton Keynes: Open University Press.

Shaw, R. (1987). *Children of imprisoned fathers.* London: Hodder and Stoughton.

Smith, J. Q. (1980). The prediction of prison riots. *British Journal of Mathematical and Statistical Psychology, 33,* 151-160.

Walker, N. (1982). Unscientific, unwise, unprofitable or unjust? *British Journal of Criminology, 22,* 276-284.

Wormith, J. (1984). The controversy over the effects of long-term incarceration. *Canadian Journal of Criminology, 36,* 423-437.

PART FOUR

■ Adaptation and Survival

Among Long-Term Inmates

11

Adaptation and Adjustment Among Long-Term Prisoners

Timothy J. Flanagan

Long-term prisoners are a growing segment of the State and Federal correctional population that poses formidable challenges for administrators. Inmates with terms of 10, 20, 30, or more years tax the imagination and resources of correctional systems to the fullest. The challenge is to develop a plan of productive work, education, and meaningful activity for persons who will spend much of their adult lives in confinement.

Several complications make the dilemma of the long-term prisoner even more troublesome. First, long-term prisoners (however defined) are a diverse group of individuals, who differ in criminal history and sophistication, propensity for violence, social background, and response to imprisonment. Prescriptions designed to "manage" long-term inmate populations that ignore this diversity are destined to be irrelevant—perhaps even dysfunctional.

The serious crimes and lengthy prior records of many long-term prisoners also make this group unattractive in terms of public and political support for innovative policies. Public protection demands that tolerance for correctional innovations and risk-taking varies inversely with the seriousness of potential recidivism, so a predominant theme in the management of long-term prisoners will be the provision of secure custody.

The current situation in American corrections is that we have little insight or empirical evidence on "better" methods of managing long-term prisoner populations. This is ironic in light of two considerations. First, other nations have devoted substantially more resources to the problem of long-term confinement. More than 20 years ago, for example, the British Home Office was commissioned to report on the basic elements of a regime for the confinement of long-term prisoners. Studies of long-term confinement have also been issued by the Council of Europe and by prison administrators and the judiciary in West Germany, Italy, Canada, the Scandinavian nations, Hungary, and Australia. In many of these nations, the "long-term prisoner population" is minuscule in comparison to the U.S., and the definition of long-term confinement is very different.

Second, the dearth of empirical study in the U.S. is ironic because we use long-term confinement at comparatively high rates. The Bureau of Justice Statistics reported that the average length of sentences to State prison for felony defendants sentenced in 1986 was nearly 7 years. The average sentence for murder and

NOTE: Reprinted from *Federal Prisons Journal*, Vol. 2, No. 2, Spring 1991, pp. 45-51, issued by the Federal Bureau of Prisons.

negligent manslaughter defendants was about 18 years; these figures do not include the more than one-quarter of such defendants who received sentences of life imprisonment or death. The same study estimated that the actual time to be served in confinement for these defendants was more than 7 years for murder and negligent manslaughter defendants, more than 5 years for defendants sentenced for rape, and nearly 5 years for robbery defendants. These offense categories made up nearly 40 percent of the State prisoner population in 1986. The tremendous influx of drug offenders into State and Federal corrections systems in recent years, coupled with statutory changes that lengthen prison terms for serious offenses, ensures that the number and proportion of long-term prisoners in State and Federal prisons will continue to increase in years to come.

My objectives in this article are fourfold. First, I will try to make sense of the growing body of research on the *adjustment and adaptation* of long-term prisoners to confinement that has accumulated in the last 2 decades. Second, I wish to highlight the *special or unique problems* of long-term prisoners that merit attention in discussions of prison adjustment and program planning. Third, I will sketch what is known about *how long-term prisoners cope or adapt.* Finally, I will offer for discussion some ideas, informed by the research base at hand, about how best to *manage* long-term inmates. Let me anticipate my conclusion—we can do better than we've done in the past—but better management of long-term prisoners requires a commitment to experimentation (i.e., openmindedness) and taking a long view of long-term incarceration.

ADJUSTMENT AND ADAPTATION

There has been a fundamental shift in our thinking about the adjustment of long-term prisoners to incarceration during the last 2 decades. Early thinking about lifers and long-termers assumed that the effects of extended incarceration were relatively predictable and profoundly negative. Long-term incarceration was inexorably linked to deterioration of the personality, growing dependence on the highly controlled regime of institutional life, and increasing levels of "prisonization" or commitment to an oppositional inmate value system. In this view, often articulated in inmate ac-

counts and the reports of early prison researchers, few long-term inmates would survive the experience without substantial and irreparable damage.

In the past 2 decades, investigators who have forayed into prisons in several nations to document and quantify the nature and extent of deterioration suffered by long-term inmates have reached unexpected conclusions. Whether focused on physical impairment, intellectual deterioration, abnormal personality changes, attitudinal shifts, or behavioral manifestations, modern researchers have found "the evidence for a profound and incapacitating influence, that is both commonplace and severe, is scarce, if existent at all" (Wormith, 1984). The consistency with which these findings of "no systematic effect" as a consequence of long-term confinement have accumulated is remarkable. A few examples will suffice.

Rasch studied the *physical condition* of West German lifers and concluded that, as time served increased, "the state of health did not deteriorate in a serious or constant manner" (1977, p. 275). Although the prisoners reported numerous afflictions during the medical interviews, there were no statistically significant increases in serious ailments across time-served groups, and sleep disturbances and loss of appetite diminished as time served increased. Reed and Glamser's (1979) study of older prisoners (who had served an average of 23 years) concluded that "prisoners are reasonably healthy. The availability of regular meals, rest, and medical care exceeds that which is available to many adults, and the effects of economic factors are greatly reduced in a prison setting." While aging prisoners present typical geriatric problems, the researchers found that "much of what is viewed as part of normal aging does not take place in the prison setting." Other researchers have reported stability or actual decreases in illness complaints over time. A recent review concluded that "as far as physical health is concerned, imprisonment may have the fortuitous benefit of isolating the offender from a highly risky lifestyle in the community" (Bonta & Gendreau, 1990, p. 357).

Several investigators have focused on deterioration in *intellectual functioning* as a result of long-term confinement. These studies have also indicated no evidence of systematic decline in intellectual capacity, measured by standard intelligence tests, as a consequence of long-term imprisonment. *Personality deterioration* has also been investigated. In contrast to early descriptions of the "Ganser Syndrome" and related disorders attributed to long-term incarceration, recent studies suggest that personality changes in long-term prisoners are mild. Some investigators reported increases in inner-directed hostility, as well as increased introversion, flatness of affect, and dependency upon staff. In other studies, the findings on measures such as self-esteem and self-concept have been conflicting. As with studies of physical and intellectual functioning, this body of research generally fails to document widespread and serious deleterious results.

In contrast to the dimensions discussed above, studies of *attitudinal change* among long-term inmates report observable changes, though not in the expected direction. Attitudes towards prison staff have been found to improve as time served increases, attitudes toward the criminal justice system do not change dramatically, and emotions such as anger and hostility appear to subside.

The evidence concerning *psychopathological changes* during the long sentence is inconsistent. Several studies have utilized the Minnesota Multiphasic Personality Inventory (MMPI) and other measures of psychopathology, and the findings have been mixed. Although Rasch reported "no evidence" of psychotic symptoms in the West German lifer sample, an Austrian study found that after 4-6 years of confinement, many long-term prisoners manifest symptoms of a "functional psychosyndrome," including inadequate emotions, obsessional ideas, infantile and regressive behavior, and growing insecurity (Sluga, 1977). A study of British lifers found a "remarkably high incidence of personal illness," but the incidence was *inversely* related to time served. More recent studies of American and Canadian long-term inmates have found no evidence of increasing psychopathology, and some have concluded that "prisoners with longer sentences displayed less mental disorder" (Wormith, 1984, p. 341).

Finally, several investigators have examined *behavioral responses* of long-term prisoners. The primary indicators of behavioral adjustment that have been studied are involvement in institutional disciplinary violations and the frequency of requests for medical services. A note of caution is in order. The most

well established correlate of involvement in disciplinary violations is the inmate's age: older inmates have significantly lower rates of institutional misconduct. Of course, time served and age are highly correlated. The challenge is to disentangle the separate effects of age and time served in understanding behavior patterns of long-term and short-term prisoners.

My investigation of the rate of involvement in prison disciplinary infractions among long-term and short-term prisoners indicated that short-termers' rates were double those of long-termers. Even when I controlled for age and restricted the analysis to the first years in prison, I found that long-termers had significantly fewer disciplinary infraction rates. More recently, Toch and Adams' (1989) massive study of inmate adjustment found that young long-term inmates had very *high* rates of disciplinary involvement, but that these declined over time. Toch and Adams suggested that age was a better predictor of institutional adjustment than sentence length.

In a comprehensive study of coping and adaptation among Canadian prisoners, Zamble and Porporino (1988) found that after indicators of coping skills are taken into account, "sentence length does not predict any important measure of adaptation in prison, from disciplinary history to depression." Accordingly, Zamble and Porporino warned that current classification policies—in which sentence length plays a critical role in determining the assignment of offenders to institutions—are misguided. Under such classification systems, they argue, many inmates who *do not need* close supervision are assigned to maximum security institutions.

To summarize, our thinking about the effects of long-term confinement has come full circle from the early "deterioration" model. It would be unwise to accept these findings uncritically, however. Other sources, particularly inmate accounts and ethnographic studies of prisons, suggest that the "pains of imprisonment" are quite real and that long-term inmates feel them acutely. There are several reasons to be cautious about accepting the conclusion that long-term imprisonment exacts no toll on inmates.

First, all of the studies mentioned above recognize that responses to confinement vary tremendously, so it is axiomatic that some long-term prisoners suffer. Second, the studies are based primarily on cross-sectional analyses of inmates who have served varying lengths of time. Comparing across groups of inmates who have served 2, 7, and 12 years in prison illustrates differences, but these designs are incapable of detecting *changes* over time. Investigating change over time requires research that follows inmates through their prison careers. To date, Zamble and Porporino's study is the only one that used such a design, and they were only able to follow their subjects for the first 16 months of confinement. However, they reported that "by the last interview we had seen the emergence of some effects that are probably characteristic of long-term imprisonment. The changes in socialization are signs of coldness and self-containment of men who have long been cut off from intimate contacts with other people. Psychological survival was the goal and they did manage to cope, but the cost was considerable" (1988, p. 122). Finally, and most importantly, there is reason to believe that long-termers face problems and challenges that are different from those faced by inmates serving shorter terms, and these stresses may not be adequately measured by the studies described above.

PROBLEMS OF
LONG-TERM PRISONERS

Long-term confinement presents special stresses and amplifies noxious elements of incarceration into major problems. Studies of long-term inmates in Great Britain, Canada, and the United States indicate that long-term prisoners ascribe greater importance to problems associated with incarceration per se than to deprivations associated with the prison environment (Richards, 1978; Zamble & Porporino, 1988; and Flanagan, 1980a, respectively). I've described the "special stresses of long-term prisoners" in several general categories: external relationships, relationships within the prison, fear of deterioration, indeterminacy, and the prison environment. Recent studies by Zamble and Porporino with Canadian prisoners and by Mitchell (1990) with British lifers confirm several of these problem areas.

In terms of external relationships, loss of contact with family and friends outside the prison is a source of stress for *all* inmates, but for long-term inmates the fear that these relationships will be *irrevocably* lost creates unique concerns. While relationships with spouses, family members, girlfriends, and others may withstand enforced estrangement for a few years, the prospects for maintaining these relationships over the long term are dim. Some long-term inmates seek to "freeze" a mental picture of life on the outside—and their role in it—as an aid in protecting the ego, but the gradual attenuation of relationships is a threat to this strategy. Maintaining external relationships is vital to coping with long-term imprisonment, but the price is high, because this reminds the prisoner that the world outside is changing.

Within the prison, developing personal relationships is often no less troublesome. I have characterized these stresses as problems of commonality and continuity. The long-term inmate, especially an older long-termer, may have little in common with the younger, boisterous short-term inmate whose conversation centers on the triumphs and good times that await him upon return to the streets. Continuity is a problem because inmate friendships are often severed by transfers and releases. Unlike the situation of the short-termer, who can "wait it out," there is no wholly satisfactory way for long-termers to resolve the dilemma of prison friendships. Zamble and Porporino found that "many long-term inmates began to develop a more solitary lifestyle after a while," part of what they have termed the "behavioral deep freeze."

Concern with deterioration is another source of stress. Cohen and Taylor (1972) wrote that the long-termers with whom they worked were obsessive and highly self-conscious about outward signs of deterioration. The features of the prison that provoke these concerns include the fact that prisoners are routinely offered unfavorable definitions of themselves by others, that it can be difficult to mark time in an environment where there is an abundance of time to fill and limited opportunities to fill it, and that limited personal choice in the restricted world of the prison provides few opportunities for prisoners to practice effective coping.

Two additional sources of stress are the indeterminacy of sentences and chronic exposure to noxious features of the prison environment. Goodstein found that the type of sentence had virtually no effect on adjustment, but other researchers suggest that indeterminacy regarding release date, especially among long-termers, causes significant problems (Cohen & Taylor, 1972; Flanagan, 1980a; Mitchell, 1990). Finally, features of the prison environment may be at odds with features conducive to serving a long sentence. Toch (1977a) reported that many long-term inmates prize *structure in their environment*—"a concern with environmental stability and predictability, a preference for consistency, clear-cut rules, orderly and scheduled events, and impingements." Under these circumstances, it is not surprising that some long-term inmates actually prefer the fortress-like "big house" prisons, where experienced inmates and veteran staff achieve a mutual coexistence based on formality and consistency.

As noted earlier, many of these stresses and problems would be difficult to measure with the standard psychometric instrumentation used in recent research. The most informative research in this area has productively blended this approach with ethnographic analyses that enable us to view long-term incarceration from the inmate's perspective.

ADAPTATION AND COPING STRATEGIES

How do lifers and long-term prisoners respond to the constellation of problems they face? Are they able to adapt or do they simply endure? Do some fall apart? We know that many long-term inmates successfully negotiate prison pressures, but the strategies employed are neither easily deduced nor readily classifiable.

Unkovic and Albini (1969) suggested that lifers adapt by taking on a "philosophy of minimum expectation," a fatalistic perspective that establishes the release date as a time boundary. Sapsford (1978) also found that restricting future time perspectives was a common strategy among British lifers, and Flanagan reported these "barrier effects" among American long-termers. The adoption of a "here and now" perspective reduces uncertainty and ambiguity about the future; this resembles coping strategies used by physically disabled patients.

I've suggested that focusing on the "here and now" is a central attitudinal element of a perspective toward doing time that many long-term inmates adopt. The perspective is reinforced through affiliation with other long-

termers. Key elements of the perspective are maturity, predictability of action, and the "prison sense" that comes from years of experience in serving time. This perspective also has behavioral implications that may be highly functional in enabling the prisoner to cope.

These behavioral manifestations include active avoidance of "trouble" within the prison and attempts to use time profitably rather than simply serving time. Long-term inmates avoid trouble through prescriptions such as "mind your own business," "adjust to authority," "choose your associates wisely," and "remain alert to cues in the physical environment." In addition, many long-termers express a desire to use prison time "to gain tangible improvements in skills, and a better chance to negotiate life following release" (Toch, 1977b, p. 287). Zamble and Porporino referred to this motivation to change, which they found was highest in the early period of the sentence, as a "window of opportunity" for staff to direct inmates into productive programs. Mitchell reports that lifers pursue educational and training programs in prisons for several reasons: to improve post-release employability, to pass the time, and because contact with civilian instructors was a "means of retaining a sense of awareness of life outside the institution" (Mitchell, 1990, p. 201).

Toch's research in the environmental psychology of prisons suggests a related adaptive strategy. Some inmates identify "niches" within the prison—environments that often feature lower social density, escape from the tumult of general population, nonconfrontational interactions with staff, and group identity among participants. In many cases, educational, training, and work programs are highly prized "sanctuaries" that provide respite for the inmate.

Cohen and Taylor suggested that the coping style used by long-term inmates was determined primarily by the prisoner's attitude toward authority. Offenders whose pre-prison relationship with authority was based on confrontation will likely continue to rebel for many years. Those who lived by "bending, fixing, and rigging" rules on the outside continue to attempt to subvert authority inside. Cohen and Taylor suggested that long-termers shift their adaptive strategies until they find one that is most functional in their environment.

How well do long-term prisoners cope? A recent comprehensive study of coping among Canadian inmates, which included special attention to long-term prisoners, suggests that ineffective coping skills is a key reason that offenders end up in prison. Moreover, according to Zamble and Porporino, prisons do little to capitalize on the "window of opportunity" presented by the disequilibrium of incarceration; as a result, inmates' poor coping skills do not improve much over time. In part, they argue that this is because the motivation for change decays rapidly. After a few weeks in prison the "window of opportunity" is replaced by "monotony and boredom," which serves to "lower arousal levels and lull people into lassitude and stolid adherence to the daily routine" (1988, p. 114).

Zamble and Porporino attribute the lack of improvement in coping to the "behavioral deep freeze" of incarceration. They assert that "most offenders arrive in prison with poor coping ability. Imprisonment then deprives them of experience with the normal environment, and thus limits their further experience with conditions they must deal with on the outside. Most of us learn to cope better through accumulated experience, but prisoners are deprived of much of that experience. As a result, they do not learn to cope satisfactorily with conditions in the outside world." Zamble and Porporino's pessimistic conclusion is that "prison *affects* men strongly, but in the long run it *changes* them hardly at all" (1988, p. 152, emphasis added).

CAN WE DO BETTER?

Along with more and better research on the adjustment of long-term prisoners and the impact of long-term confinement, a small but growing body of policy-oriented literature on the management of long-term prisoners has developed. The traditional argument in this area was the "concentration vs. dispersal" dispute. That is, is it more effective to concentrate lifers and long-termers in a single facility, or is it better to disperse them throughout a correctional system? As the Home Office Advisory Council on the Penal System observed more than 2 decades ago, "much of the history of penal administration is taken up with the constant dialectic between these two methods" (1968, p. 13). Citing the American expe-

rience with Alcatraz, the Advisory Council concluded that the problems of concentration outweighed the benefits and recommended a dispersal policy.

Facilities of the type discussed by the Advisory Council typically focus not on the environment appropriate for long-term prisoners but rather on the disturbed or disruptive inmate. But should specific institutions be designated as "long-term inmate prisons"? Previously, I have argued that three principles should guide our decisionmaking with respect to long-termers. Since removal from society is the primary sanction that falls most heavily on long-term prisoners, the overriding objective of correctional policy as it relates to long-termers should be reduction of the "secondary sanctions" inherent in imprisonment. These secondary sanctions are the features of prison life that Sykes discussed as the "pains of imprisonment" (Flanagan, 1982, 1985). In pursuit of this goal, the principles of long-term prisoner management ought to be:

- Maximizing opportunities for choice.
- Creating opportunities for the prisoner to pursue a meaningful life in prison.
- To the extent possible, enhancing the permeability of the institution so that the offender does not lose all contact with the outside world.

These objectives can be pursued in a variety of administrative arrangements. They can help define the qualities of programs or living units within an institution, or they could serve as the blueprint for the development of a separate facility for long-term prisoners. Several examples of programs directed to the needs of long-term prisoners are available, and many such programs incorporate one or more of these principles. A review of several "long-termer programs" by the National Institute of Corrections (1985) included a broad-based Long-termer's Program at the Utah State Prison, the "Cabbage Patch Program" at the Somers Correctional Institution in Connecticut, and others. Palmer's (1984) description of the Life-Servers Program at the Warkworth Institution in Canada explicitly focuses on several of these objectives. Cowles and Sabath (1989) instituted several different programs directed to the needs of long-term prisoners in the Missouri correctional system in recent years.

Further development of these kinds of programs can be informed by the findings of Zamble and Porporino's Canadian research. Their findings suggest that such programs for long-term inmates should begin as soon as offenders arrive in prison, and that much of the program content should be focused on enhancing offenders' coping skills and reinforcing the motivation to change.

Thinking about productive correctional experiences for long-term prisoners also requires a different perspective. We have a person who will spend a career with us in prison, and career planning for these inmates is in order. Toch (1977b) introduced the concept of the career perspective, and I have commented that "it is incumbent on the correctional system to work with the offender to plan a worthwhile career, one that will be beneficial both to the offender and others, and that will be transferable and capable of supporting the offender upon his eventual release. Moreover, there is no reason why, during their long imprisonment, many long-term prisoners cannot make a substantial contribution to society through help provided to other inmates." Toch and Adams provided several examples of mutual help among inmates and proposed an extension of this model to build coping competence among disruptive prisoners (1989).

The British Home Office (Mitchell, 1990) has instituted a series of policies that incorporate the career planning model for long-term inmates in a system-wide fashion. Mitchell, in his recent book *Murder and Penal Policy*, reports that this "Revised Strategy," which was adopted in response to an increasing number of life sentence prisoners, is based on certain underlying principles: treating life term inmates as a separate group, but integrating lifers with other prisoners; providing lifers with a sense of purpose and direction; career planning, which involves goal setting, revision, and progression, and makes use of the variety of settings and programs available within the prison system; recognition of the heterogeneity of the lifer group; and flexibility of security designations. Mitchell recognized that "a crucial factor in the success of the Revised Strategy is the extent to which lifers are motivated to use their sentence constructively . . ." (1990, p. 293). The implementation of the Revised Strategy has not been without difficulties (for example, Mitchell reports that many long-termers deeply resent the "compulsory in-

tegration" with short-termers), and Mitchell makes a number of suggestions that highlight the crucial role of correctional staff in administering the Strategy.

In sum, I return to my "anticipated conclusion" that we've learned a great deal about the impact of long-term imprisonment as a result of research during the last 2 decades, and some jurisdictions have begun to act on that knowledge. To learn more, we need to experiment with different approaches to the management of long-term prisoners. We need to think about designs for long-term inmate-oriented facilities, implement the plans, and carefully document the results. We will learn from the failures as well as the successes, provided that we are open-minded about the problem and patient enough to await results.

REFERENCES

Bonta, J., & Gendreau, P. (1990). Reexamining the cruel and unusual punishment of prison life. *Law and Human Behavior, 14*(4), 347-372.

Cohen, S., & Taylor, L. (1972). *Psychological survival: The experience of long-term imprisonment.* New York: Pantheon.

Cowles, E., & Sabath. M. (1989). *Handling long-term offenders: The Missouri project.* Jefferson City: Missouri Department of Corrections and Human Resources.

Flanagan, T. J. (1980a). The pains of long-term imprisonment: A comparison of British and American perspectives. *British Journal of Criminology, 20*(2), 148-156.

Flanagan, T. J. (1980b). Time-served and institutional misconduct: Patterns of involvement in disciplinary infractions among long-term and short-term inmates. *Journal of Criminal Justice, 8*, 357-367.

Flanagan, T. J. (1982). Correctional policy and the long-term prisoner. *Crime and Delinquency, 28*(1), 82-95.

Flanagan, T. J. (1985). Sentence planning for long-term inmates. *Federal Probation, 49*(3), 23-28.

Home Office, Advisory Council on the Penal System. (1968). *The Regime for long-term prisoners under conditions of maximum security.* London: HMSO.

Mitchell, B. (1990). *Murder and penal policy.* New York: St. Martin's Press.

Palmer, W. R. T. (1984). Programming for long-term inmates: A new perspective. *Canadian Journal of Criminology, 26*(4), 439-458.

Rasch, W. (1977). Observations on the physio-psychological changes in persons sentenced to life imprisonment. In S. Rizkalla, R. Levy, & R. Zauberman (Eds.), *Long-term imprisonment: An international seminar*. Montreal: University of Montreal.

Reed, M. B., & Glamser, F. D. (1979). Aging in a total institution: The case of older prisoners. *Gerontologist, 19,* 354-360.

Richards, B. (1978). The experience of long-term imprisonment: An exploratory investigation. *British Journal of Criminology, 18*(2), 162-169.

Sapsford, R. J. (1978). Life-sentence prisoners: Psychological changes during sentence. *British Journal of Criminology, 18,* 128-145.

Sluga, W. (1977). Treatment of long-term prisoners considered from the medical and psychiatric points of view. In Council of Europe, *Treatment of long-term prisoners*. Strasbourg: Council of Europe.

Toch, H. (1977a). *Living in prison: The ecology of survival*. New York: Free Press.

Toch, H. (1977b). The long-term inmate as a long-term problem. In S. Rizkalla, R. Levy, & R. Zauberman (Eds.), *Long-term imprisonment: An international seminar*. Montreal: University of Montreal.

Toch, H., & Adams, K. (1989). *Coping: Maladaption in prisons*. New Brunswick, NJ: Transaction Books.

Unkovic, C., & Albini, J. (1969). The lifer speaks for himself: An analysis of the assumed homogeneity of life-termers. *Crime and Delinquency, 15*(1), 156-161.

Wormith, J. S. (1984). The controversy over the effects of long-term imprisonment. *Canadian Journal of Criminology, 26,* 423-437.

Zamble, E., & Porporino, F. (1988). *Coping, behavior, and adaptation in prison inmates*. New York: Springer-Verlag.

12

Women Lifers

Assessing the Experience

Elaine Genders

Elaine Player

Life imprisonment is the most severe penalty that can be imposed by the British courts for violation of the criminal law. Since the abolition of the death penalty in 1965 it has been the mandatory sentence for murder, as well as the maximum sentence for a number of other serious offenses, including manslaughter, armed robbery, arson, rape, kidnapping, and causing an explosion.[1] Since the Homicide Act 1957 the number of lifers in the prison system has steadily increased: There were 133 men serving life in 1957 in comparison to 2,427 in 1988; in the women's system the population expanded from 7 to 76 during the same period.

Although efforts have been made in the past decade to compensate for the previous academic and political neglect of women in the criminal justice system, our knowledge and vision of those women subjected to the most severe penal sanction remain partial and obscure. There is, for example, no published information about the social backgrounds of women lifers, their previous criminal careers, or even the length of time they typically remain in custody. Those studies that have been conducted on life sentence prisoners have unanimously ignored the female population (Rasch, 1981; Sapsford, 1983; Smith, 1979).

The procedures and rules that govern the serving of life sentences apply equally to men and women, yet inevitably they have been designed with the majority male population in mind. The question that needs to be addressed is whether these strategies are appropriate to the women's system. The purpose of this chapter is to focus attention upon one particular phase of a woman's life sentence: the initial period of assessment in the Main Center. This chapter, which draws primarily upon intensive fieldwork carried out during a 2-day visit to H-wing Durham in December 1987, consid-

AUTHORS' NOTE: This is a revised version of a paper delivered at the 19th Cropwood Conference and published in *Women and the Penal System* Cropwood Conference Series No. 19, Cambridge (1988). We gratefully acknowledge the co-operation and assistance given to us by the staff and inmates in HMP Durham, H-wing. In addition we thank those members of the Prison Department, who provided us with useful comments on an earlier draft of this paper. The views expressed however, are entirely our own and we accept sole responsibility for them.

ers the functions that the Main Center is expected to serve for women lifers, examines the role played by the staff, explores how the women themselves experience the initial stages of an indeterminate sentence, and concludes by reviewing possible directions for change.

H-WING DURHAM—
THE MAIN CENTER FOR WOMEN

All women sentenced to life imprisonment are initially allocated to H-wing Durham unless they have particular medical or psychiatric needs, in which case they may be located at Holloway. H-wing is a separate maximum security unit situated within the walls of the local male prison and is the only establishment within the female system designated as suitable to hold convicted category A prisoners. At the time that research was carried out for this chapter, H-wing accommodated 25 life sentence prisoners, only 2 of whom were assigned category A status, and 11 inmates, including one category A prisoner, who were serving determinate periods of imprisonment.

The decision to allow a lifer back into the community is ultimately the responsibility of the Home Secretary, who may grant release on license if recommended to do so by the Parole Board.[2] The length of time persons may serve in prison is dependent upon two main criteria: whether they are judged "safe" to return to the community and whether they have served enough "time for the crime." Thus, there is an assessment of tariff and an assessment of risk. A major function that Durham serves with regard to female lifers is to carry out an assessment of each prisoner in order to prepare reports for the first parole review. Typically, these are written by the governor, the medical officer, the chaplain, the prison probation officer, and a uniformed officer. Other staff, such as the visiting psychologist, also submit reports if they have particular knowledge of the woman concerned.

The purpose of these reports is twofold: first, to give a clear assessment of a prisoner's suitability for release, either in the short or long term; second, to assist in the development of a career plan. Reporting officers are essentially expected to identify "areas of concern" that reflect an element of risk, both while the woman is in prison and in the event of her eventual release.

A recent circular instruction (procedural directive), issued to prison staff by those departments in headquarters responsible for lifers, identifies the main areas that are expected to be covered in the reports.[3] Some information is required about the woman's attitude toward her offense, especially in those cases where guilt continues to be denied. The question raised is whether the woman has any insight into the problems that underpinned her behavior in the commission of her crime.

The woman's conduct and behavior in prison are also expected to be addressed, especially the quality and value of her relationships with other prisoners and with prison staff. Particular cause for concern in this area is thought to exist where a woman fails to face up to the "realities of the sentence" by becoming completely withdrawn and declining to think constructively about the future. Such cases are considered to be unlikely candidates for release, if only because they are providing little or no opportunity for prison staff to assess the degree of risk they might pose to the outside community. Finally, the reports are expected to include some comment upon the situation regarding the woman's family and her outside contacts.

The context within which these assessments are carried out at Durham is primarily determined by two features of the unit: its size and its level of security. The fact that H-wing is a category A facility ensures that conditions of security are rigorous and ever-present. Ironically, all women, regardless of their escape risk, are subject to the same level of routine security and supervision. Electronically locking double grills on windows and closed-circuit television cameras covering the entrance represent the obvious signs of detention. In addition to the high perimeter security, the women's physical movement is also strictly curtailed by the small size of the unit and the fact that all activities occur within the confines of this fortress. Women do not leave the unit to go to work, to education classes, or to use the gym. It has its own chapel, library, hospital, and visiting room. The only outdoor facility is a small concrete yard in which the women may take their daily exercise. Opportunities to leave this environment are rare. The scale of the unit, designed to accommodate only 40 women, further ensures that the range of work and educational provision is extremely limited. There are no vocational training courses, and only two categories of work are available. The vast majority of women are employed in the workshop, manufacturing textile products, and a small number undertake cleaning duties around the wing. The workshop has succeeded in becoming a profit-making enterprise; consequently, the need to maintain an efficient production line is accorded a high priority when decisions are made about how the women spend their time.

Attendance at education classes is subordinated to the requirements of manning the workshop. A maximum of eight women are permitted to attend education classes during the day, which largely focuses on remedial classes and Open University course work. Although a purpose-built education block has been recently opened in the main part of the prison, this has not been made available to the female prisoners, despite the fact that the Senior Education Officer wanted to offer this facility and welcomed the prospect of introducing some coeducational courses. Day and evening classes for women prisoners are held on H-wing and accommodated in two rooms that are officially designated as association rooms.

Ironically, because of the small scale of the unit, providing education is a relatively expensive enterprise. The supply of two teachers for a maximum of eight women represents a disproportionate use of resources by the female wing. In addition, because of the limited availability of education classes, a number of women had become involved in correspondence courses or individual study programs, which they undertook in their own time, and which may also be relatively expensive on a per capita basis.

The combination of high-profile security within a small unit conspires to produce both an environment that denies privacy and an atmosphere that is routinely described as claustrophobic. The diminutive proportions of the visiting room, for example, ensure that the physical proximity of the two guarding officers is not easily forgotten. The fact that, as a consequence of visits, the women are often required to submit to a strip search further reinforces the intimate intrusiveness of security measures.

The all-embracing quality of captivity is similarly manifest within the hospital. In 1981 the Prison Inspectorate advised the governor to consider how the hospital might be more conveniently relocated from the fourth floor to the ground floor of the wing. The inspectors also commented that the three cells which constituted the hospital accommodation were "not particularly suitable" for such use. Currently, the hospital remains in the same location, approached by steep, narrow gangways and stairs. But what is perhaps most striking about it is that there is nothing structurally or environmentally distinctive about the accommodation that would allow it to be perceived as a sanctuary and thus differentiated from other parts of the wing. In consequence, women recover and convalesce from major surgery in exactly the same milieu as when they are in the main body of the unit. The situation is perhaps best illustrated by the fact that within this area, alongside cells designated for hospital use, are the segregation cells used for isolating women for disciplinary purposes.

THE ROLE OF THE STAFF AND THE PROCESS OF ASSESSMENT

The ways in which the officers on H-wing identified their duties and perceived the nature of relationships both among inmates and between inmates and staff produced a series of ironies and contradictions that again reflect upon the size and security of the unit. The ratio of staff to prisoners is relatively high. There are 26 uniformed officers; one assistant governor (grade 5), who has overall responsibility for the unit; one probation officer; and one full-time teacher. In addition, the senior medical officer visits the wing daily and a visiting psychologist attends once a week. Among the uniformed staff only two had ever held permanent jobs in other prisons and only two had received specific training for working with lifers, although it was said that all officers on the wing would eventually receive such training.

The officers' descriptions of the women were imbued with conflicts. On one hand, the staff demonstrated concern for the women and compassion for their problems and, on the other, expressed cynicism and questioned their integrity. Officers recognized that a constant fear for many women lifers was the possibility that their young children would be adopted and that they would lose all parental rights and risk never seeing their families again. For women who did remain in contact with their children, staff spoke of the "heartrending" process of separation after visits and the consequent difficulties this created for the women in settling down to prison routines. Yet, at the same time, officers depreciated the extent to which the women's concern for their families was genuine. It was argued that many of these women had selfishly neglected their children in the past and that, once inside the prison gates, it became convenient and self-serving to idealize their outside lives and present themselves as paragons of virtue. Similarly, when women spoke of feeling depressed about their loss of contact with their children, staff maintained that this was typically an overstatement and that they were not suffering from depression but were "just miserable."

In general, the officers on H-wing felt that the women did not talk openly about the problems they experienced, aside from those related to the care and welfare of their children. Most of them were said to be more concerned with the day-to-day running of the wing than with matters concerned with the outside world. The picture painted by the staff was one in which the women were totally self-oriented and obsessed by petty details that had assumed a disproportionate importance. A frequently cited example of this was the apparent inability of the women to deal with minor ailments without resorting to medical referral:

> When they get a cold they can't cope with a couple of paracetamol, like they would outside. It gets blown up out of all proportion and they're not satisfied until they've seen the doctor.

It was not only the women's problems that tended to be diminished by the staff, but also the nature of their relationships with one another on the wing. In spite of, or perhaps because of, the small size of the unit, officers argued that relationships tended to be superficial and instrumental. It was claimed that there was not one "genuine" friendship on the wing and that, in general, the women used and exploited one another, leading unerringly to arguments and petty wrangling.

Lesbian relationships were perceived as attempts by the women to reexperience a sense of closeness and intimacy and, as such, were defined by the staff as an inevitable aspect of long-term imprisonment. Most women serving long sentences were said to "pass through a phase" of lesbian activities, although the majority were thought not to be gay outside and later regretted and were ashamed of the experience. The intensity of these relationships was said by staff to occasionally cause difficulties by generating extreme feelings of jealousy and engendering suicidal thoughts when they broke up. Despite the view that such relationships inevitably engendered breaches of prison discipline, there was little support for any potential changes that might provide the heterosexually oriented women with alternative opportunities for close relationships and sexual expression. Mixed-sex prisons, for example, were thought to be undesirable and unworkable. Staff maintained that they had enough problems being located within the boundaries of a male prison without allowing male and female prisoners to come into contact with one another. Conjugal visits were similarly dismissed on the ground that, although they might work abroad, they would only lead to a spate of manipulative behavior by unattached women, who would get engaged to men in the local prison and then demand conjugal rights.

The officers described their own relationships with the women as informal but professionally distant.

> You can have a laugh and a joke with them, but you've always got to be wary. What I'm saying is—you can be friendly but not too familiar, because the time may come when you've got to give them an order or put them on report.

> Experience teaches you that when it comes down to it you can't trust them. You get to learn that you don't give them the benefit of the doubt because it comes back on you. Don't get me wrong, they all have their good points, but you can't talk to them in confidence because they could use it against you.

In general, the staff identified their task primarily as maintaining discipline, ensuring security, and providing the necessary physical and material care. They did not see themselves as having a proactive role to play in talking to the women about their problems or in discussing their offenses. Should a prisoner choose to talk to a member of staff, then the officer would be willing to listen, but it was for the woman to approach the staff and not the other way around. One way in which the uniformed staff did believe they could play an important rehabilitative role was in setting a personal example of appropriate feminine conduct. Many prisoners were said to have led disorganized and deviant lifestyles outside, and prison officers maintained that their own appearance and demeanor presented the women with an alternative role model based upon a clean, tidy, and law-abiding life.

> I think we can show them that there is another way to live. We come into work looking smart and tidy, we might talk about things we've been doing at home, and it makes them realize that there is another way of going about things.

The designation of H-wing as a lifer Main Center, and therefore responsible for the detailed assessment of all life sentenced prisoners, was not interpreted by the officers as having a major structural impact on their working lives. The task of assessing each woman in the preparation of her parole reports was seen primarily as a management function. Their own involvement was deemed to be extremely marginal in that, although the governor took into account their views about a prisoner, the assessment decisions were his own.

> When I joined, I thought the job would be much more welfare-oriented. In fact, what I do most of the day is nothing. It's called 'supervision,' but what it amounts to is me standing around watching other people working.

The emphasis placed upon security tasks left a number of the officers feeling underemployed, dissatisfied, and bored. Plans to introduce a personal officer scheme on the wing were generally welcomed by the staff, who saw it as an opportunity to have a closer and more purposeful working relationship with the women.

This brief study suggests, however, that the process of assessing women lifers at Durham is imbued with three fundamental problems. The first is one of definition and generic to all such evaluations. A primary purpose of as-

sessment is to estimate the nature and degree of risk a woman poses to both the prison authorities and the outside community. Yet the definition of risk in these circumstances is notoriously difficult to pin down (Hawkins, 1983). Also, the evaluation of risk is known to be influenced by a range of extraneous factors, such as the stage an individual has reached in her sentence, which bear no relation whatsoever to the intrinsic dangerousness of the prisoner (Maguire, Pinter, & Collis, 1984).

Second, the value of the assessment process in assisting in the development of a lifer career plan is somewhat less compelling for women than for men. In the male system the number of dispersal prisons, the range of vocational and educational opportunities, and the gradations of security classification provide opportunities for choice in allocation and a varied passage through the system. For women, however, the reality is somewhat different. From Durham a woman will be sent to one of two closed training prisons, her allocation being contingent upon the availability of vacancies and the geographical location of her home. Although the assessment process at Durham may be influential in determining the time at which a woman moves on to another establishment, it does not play a significant role in deciding which prison this will be. The primary contribution the assessment process makes to the development of a career plan is in identifying particular problems and assets that a woman lifer might have.

In relation to this, the third difficulty that the assessment process at Durham faces is the lack of a systematic approach to counseling as a means of gathering relevant information about the women. Although H-wing is afforded the facilities of a visiting psychiatrist and psychologist, the nature and direction of this input did not appear to structure the assessment process. Soon after their arrival, all women were seen for an initial psychiatric assessment. The main purpose of this is to review the possibility of a misallocation on medical grounds, in other words, to consider again whether, under the terms of the 1983 Mental Health Act, the woman is suffering from a mental illness and should therefore be transferred to a suitable hospital accommodation. Alternatively, it should consider whether she is in need of other forms of medical treatment, which may be available at Holloway.

Referral to the visiting psychiatrist during the course of sentence at Durham is possible but not routine. Typically, it would seem that the women themselves have to initiate a request for a psychiatric consultation and establish a case for so doing. At the time of the study, two women were seeing the psychiatrist. A similar pattern was found for referrals to the psychologist. All new arrivals were said to undergo a psychological assessment, consisting of a series of IQ and personality tests. Referrals for individual consultations were possible, and we were informed that a social skills course had also been run by the psychologist. However, the fact that the psychologist was attached to another prison and only attended H-wing one day each week severely restricted the extent of the services available, and in practice it would seem that most women lifers at Durham were unaffected by these specialist agencies.

As has already been mentioned, the uniformed staff on H-wing, who have the most regular and frequent contact with the women, felt excluded and marginal to the whole process of assessment. Neither the management nor the officers felt that they had received sufficient training or professional support in developing appropriate procedures. Indeed, the uniformed staff revealed an inherent dilemma in how they conceptualized their role. On one hand, they spoke about the need for more counseling and therapeutic facilities, and they included themselves as valuable yet underutilized resources in this respect; on the other, they diminished the problems that the women expressed and displayed a reticence to take on a more proactive role. None of this, however, need necessarily be inconsistent with the structural position the staff found themselves in. Clearly, fundamental principles of humane containment insist that a woman confronting the early stages of a life sentence requires some assistance in adjusting to her dramatic change of circumstances and future life prospects. Yet prison staff are faced with a notable lack of leadership to demonstrate how they should intervene. What they do have, however, is a clearly defined system for maintaining security and control. Within this context, displays of deviant behavior are perceived as threatening and therefore dysfunctional to the regime, rather than symptomatic of underlying problems and therefore functional to the process of assessment.

THE WOMEN'S EXPERIENCE

The major deprivations of imprisonment were identified by Gresham Sykes as the loss of liberty, the loss of possessions, the loss of autonomy, the loss of privacy, and the loss of heterosexual relations (Sykes, 1958).

The experience of imprisonment for women serving determinate sentences has previously been discussed elsewhere in the context of the first three of these deprivations (Genders & Player, 1987). The women lifers in Durham expressed similar concerns about the consequences their loss of liberty had for maintaining their relationships with people outside the prison. But among the life sentence prisoners, a far greater emphasis was placed upon those deprivations that emanated from the material conditions of custody. The loss of personal possessions rarely figured among the concerns expressed by the women at Durham. This was not because they had not suffered such privation. Indeed, if anything, their losses could be seen as even more permanent and irretrievable than those of the women serving determinate sentences. Instead, their lack of concern for lost possessions reflected their dissociation from the outside world and its accompanying artifacts. The loss of liberty for the life sentence women was associated with their drastically reduced contact with the physical reality of the outside world:

> I went for an interprison visit a couple of months ago. It was just amazing. I realized I hadn't seen a tree or a car for a year. The thing is I don't know when I'll see them again. You wouldn't believe it, but seeing anything of the outside world is so rare in here. It really affects you, too. The women in here have a shower and get themselves all done up with makeup and that just to go over to the dentist in the main prison. It's like going out on the town. It's a big expedition.

They felt acutely, too, their loss of liberty within the prison environment. They described graphically the feelings of claustrophobia and despair generated by the miniature scale of the unit and the inevitable restrictions placed upon their freedom of physical movement. Such feelings were intensified by the sure knowledge that they would remain within the same conditions for at least 3 years and possibly longer.

There's hardly any natural daylight in here and it's so cramped—the exercise yard is tiny. There's not enough room in my cell to sit straight at my desk to study. There's just no physical space. It's so important to have space—what we need is more fresh air, more light, more exercise, and more space—space to cook and sew, space to do things that we'd normally do at home.

But, perhaps most significantly, they missed their freedom to act naturally and express their emotions:

You have no outlet for your emotions in here. If you're too noisy you're told to shut up. If you're quiet you're asked what's up.

The prison context affords very little privacy, and in Durham the women are confined together, for long periods at a time, in a small unit that permits few opportunities for seclusion. As in other prisons, their activities are also under constant surveillance by staff. Of particular concern to the women was the censorship of all mail, both in and out of the prison, and the close supervision of visits. Together, these measures were said to severely inhibit meaningful communication with family and friends and to deny the women any opportunity to reveal their emotions to those closest to them.

You can't really say anything in your letters because they're all censored and there's always the knowledge that the staff gossip about what's in them.

It's so difficult to reassure your family on visits that you're all right, because the staff are always there just a few feet away. I hate visits because of the pressures they create. I try to reassure them but it's so hard. It's not fair on my mother—she hasn't done anything wrong. I just don't see why my family should have to do my life sentence with me.

You can't talk to your family—not properly. There are so many constraints when visits are so closely supervised. It's no good for women when their children come to visit. You're an emotional wreck for days building up to the visit, and then when it comes, you can't relax and you can't be how you want to be. But it's afterwards that's the worst because it's gone, it's a great anticlimax—and you regret all the things you didn't say.

You slowly lose touch with your family in here because they don't see the real you any more.

The women felt that additional assaults upon their personal privacy were made by having to ask the staff for sanitary napkins and by the lack of integral sanitation and the consequent procedure of slopping out.

The most keenly felt invasion of privacy, however, was the process of strip-searching, the frequency of which was, they believed, because H-wing housed three category A prisoners.

One of the worst things about this place is the complete and utter lack of privacy. You get strip-searched about once every 2 weeks. It's so degrading. As an older woman it's especially awful when you're stripped by some of the young officers here—some of them try to be sensitive about it but not all of them. . . .

For the women in the first stages of life imprisonment at Durham, the outside world had become a distant place, over which they no longer felt that they had any influence. Their lack of autonomy was described in terms of their reliance upon staff as gatekeepers to the various services and facilities within the prison walls.

The staff treat you as a retarded 5-year-old—but they have the keys. So you have to bite your tongue and keep your head. It's hard to contend with this. This total dependence upon other people for everything. The food in here is terrible and we're not even allowed to buy vitamin tablets. I resent this dependence upon staff when I know that I could do things better myself.

You have no control over your own
health in here. You're totally reliant upon
the medical services. They've been here
so long that they don't see the problems
any more. You get cockroaches and mice
in here and sometimes the sluices
overflow. You wouldn't live in these
conditions at home. All we can do is
complain about it.

The lack of autonomy was most painfully
experienced by the women in relation to their
feelings of total powerlessness over their own
destiny. As life sentence prisoners, their lives
inside the prison were characterized by uncertainty. They neither knew, nor felt they had
any control over, how long they would remain
at Durham, or even to which prison they would
eventually be allocated. Most important, however, they could have no certain knowledge of
when they would be released. Their greatest
fear was that they might be forgotten by those
they described as the "faceless machinery" at
the Home Office, in whose hands such decisions were seen to rest. What they did know
was that their futures rested upon the recommendations made by staff from H-wing, and
that their behavior was subject to constant
assessment. What they did not know was what
was expected of them or by what criteria their
behavior was being judged:

No-one has ever sat down and said 'You
know why you're here and what's going
to happen.' I don't know what's the right
and wrong thing to do.

The structural location of Durham H-wing
within a large male prison ensured that the
women were not totally deprived of contact
with men. Despite the fact that there were no
communal facilities or activities, some degree
of communication was possible by prisoners
of both sexes shouting to one another out of
the windows. Although the loss of heterosexual relations was not included among the primary concerns of the women lifers, it became
apparent on closer questioning that it constituted an issue that elicited strong and conflicting emotions. A number of the women had
received their life sentences for murders that
had emanated from oppressive and violent
relationships with men. For such women, imprisonment was seen as providing a retreat
from their previous world and an opportunity

to reflect upon and reassess their history of
personal relationships. Thus, not all of the
women welcomed the opportunities for "window" relationships and, in some cases, the
attentions of the male prisoners were felt to be
intrusive, threatening, and demeaning.

At the same time, however, considerable
consternation was expressed by the women
about the lack of "normal contact" with men
and the implication of such deprivation for
their future sexual relationships. One of their
major concerns was that they would forget
how to socialize with men, lose their sexual
attraction, and be unable to form heterosexual
relationships on their release. The absence of
male company was also held responsible for
much of the lesbian activity that occurred on
H-wing. For the most part, sexual relations
between the women were regarded not as a
reflection of sexual preference but as the consequence of a desperate attempt to find emotional comfort:

The women in here—all of us—need comfort and someone to hold. We need to feel
close to someone. That's why some of
them turn to lesbianism. They're not
really that way inclined, they're just
using each other to satisfy their immediate emotional needs. Then they have real
problems when they get out of prison.
Can you imagine telling a man you love
that you've slept with a woman?

The experience of women life sentence prisoners was also accompanied by an overwhelming fear of deterioration in their physical health
and psychological well-being. They variously
complained of a cessation of menstruation and
an increase in premenstrual tension; and they
suffered skin complaints and weight problems,
which they attributed to the lack of fresh air
and poor diet. But of greatest concern was the
seemingly high number of hysterectomies that
were carried out and the consequent anxiety
that a gynecological referral generated in the
women. The women's fears of psychological
deterioration related mainly to their inability
to think positively about themselves, to their
dread of institutionalization and loss of self-
identity, and to their inability to conceive of a
future after prison.

From what has been described so far, it is
perhaps not surprising that low self-esteem
was manifest among the women. Not only did

they lack confidence in themselves as people, but they also felt personally devalued as women. For most, this process had been set in motion by events prior to imprisonment, but the prison environment also served to expedite and reinforce a derogatory status. The degree of personal derogation that could be experienced was graphically portrayed in the words of one woman, who had recently become engaged to a male lifer with whom she had become acquainted through prison correspondence:

> I felt that I had to settle for him even though we don't really know each other, because I couldn't marry a man who hadn't been through the same experience. It couldn't work because he'd never understand such a big part of my life. There would always be a barrier there. Could you imagine telling someone you loved what you'd done and what you'd been through in prison? He'd never want you after that and he'd never be able to trust you or love you. Even if he could still love you, it couldn't be equal.

Their capacity, psychologically, to survive a life sentence was an issue under serious review by the women at Durham. The major anxiety was that they would lose all motivation and sense of self-identity through a process of institutionalization. They recognized, with some trepidation, the signs of such deterioration in others:

> I had a real fright when I first arrived and saw the mental state of some of the women in here. They can't think beyond the prison and they can't talk about anything important anymore. It's like they've had all the fight knocked out of them. There's something about the place that takes all the maturity away from you. You retreat into a childhood state. It's so easy to lose sight of your real self. If you slot in with the system you lose your self and your mind. The system cracks people. It takes all their spirit and independence away. It's terrifying. It really is.

Such fears are not unrealistic, given not only the function Durham performs in the assessment of life sentenced prisoners but also the fact that the regime rewards quiet, resigned, cooperative, and settled behavior.

Some of the women approached the problem stoically, expressing their intention to "keep an eye on themselves" and maintain their interest in the outside world. These women were determined to fight the psychological pressures borne out of the monotony of the regime, their dependent status within the prison system, and the uncertainties associated with the indeterminacy of their sentence. But one woman, who was further into her sentence, was demonstrably less confident:

> Institutionalization is the biggest problem in this place. Everything becomes magnified in here. I have difficulty in staying asleep. I worry over small issues and I know that I'm getting obsessional. I'm worried about my compulsive behavior. I'm always forgetting things now. I have to write myself notes about things all the time.

What was most striking about the lifers at Durham, however, was their apparent inability to formulate their progress through the system, envision their release, or anticipate any future life after their imprisonment:

> I can't see a life after this. People tell me it's Christmas. I believe it but I can't see it. I've got no concept of the future.

> I can't plan anything. It would be a weak link and would make me vulnerable. My only plan is to keep in touch with myself and to survive this sentence.

> I don't care about myself. I just take each day at a time.

> I don't know what the future holds. I can't see that far ahead.

Staff were perceived primarily as symbols of authority, their paramount function being that of containment and control. For the most part, the women were not hesitant to approach them with straightforward practical problems, although they expressed little confidence that officers would take any action on their behalf. Their personal anxieties, however, they kept to themselves. Social relations between inmates and staff were characterized as suspicious and lacking in trust. As life sentence prisoners, they feared that any confidences shared with staff would not be respected and that any anxieties they displayed would have deleterious consequences for their future prospects of allocation and release.

Similarly, sharing their problems with other prisoners was not an option the women were inclined to exercise. Those who claimed to have friends with whom they discussed their problems were few and far between. The highly artificial environment of H-wing, where behavior is constantly reviewed and rewards conferred on the basis of "appropriate" conduct, inevitably led the women to exercise caution:

> It's ruthless. You can't trust anyone. You can't show your weak spots in case you get them thrown back at you later.

The women referred to their social environment as a "jungle" where everyone was on top of each other all the time, every woman fighting for herself and for her own space. Within this context, fellow prisoners were described as immature, bitchy, untrustworthy, and unsupportive. Their relationships were perceived as superficial, nebulous, questionable, and short-lived. In this respect, the women's portrayal of their relationships with one another was not dissimilar to that which staff attributed to them.

Many women derived considerable comfort from the knowledge that their families had remained supportive of them, yet they were reticent to show them any indication of their personal concerns and anxieties. This was due partly to the desire to protect their families from being burdened with such issues, and in part to the lack of privacy afforded by supervised visits. Although outside organizations, such as the Womens' Resource Center or NACRO, provided an important source of support to some of the women, this was usually of a practical rather than emotional nature.

It would be misleading, however, to suggest that they accepted their situation with total passivity. The women placed considerable emphasis upon the value of education because it provided them with an interest and allowed them to experience a sense of achievement. They also claimed that it kept them in touch with the realities of the outside world. Beyond education, however, the women coped with their anxieties by repressing them. Ironically, they felt there was no strategy for coping, other

than that which the assessment procedures defined as a "cause for concern."

CONCLUSION

The strategies and procedures currently available for coping with life sentence prisoners have been designed primarily for the male population. Facilities in the male system permit a degree of choice and flexibility in planning lifer career paths, but the range of options is far more limited for women. The assessment process at Durham, though influential in determining *when* a woman is relocated, plays little if any part in affecting *where* she is allocated. The primary purpose of the assessment process for women, therefore, is to identify "areas of concern" and evaluate the level of risk that individual prisoners present, both inside and outside the prison walls. Thus, the objective of any resulting career plan is to focus staff attention upon the particular problems of the individual woman.

The structural conditions that exist on H-wing and the working patterns of both the professional and uniformed staff raise problematic questions about the efficacy of this process. In order to assess someone's attitudes and behavior certain conditions are necessary. It must be possible for individuals to express their attitudes, display their behavior, and thus reveal their problems. This would necessitate a milieu in which the women are both encouraged to expose their emotions and anxieties and provided with appropriate facilities and forums in which so to do. An important quality of this environment would be that it minimizes the women's sense of vulnerability and maximizes their sense of protection and safety. This would require, first, the removal of those features of incarceration that impose a level of deprivation beyond what is necessarily concomitant with the fact of imprisonment. Within the context of H-wing, this would call for a reappraisal of the need to confine the women within such restricted physical conditions, subject them to such closely supervised visits, and expose them to frequent strip-searches. Second, for this environment to exist, staff would need to adopt a facilitative role that not only treats but also defines certain manifestations of deviant behavior as symptomatic of underlying problems. This would require a response to disruptive behavior that utilizes not only disciplinary procedures but also communicative skills that enable the women to reveal and reflect upon the reasons for their conduct. Finally, a process or assessment based upon therapeutic principles would imply a provision of treatment in its widest sense. Clearly, if the purpose of assessment is to identify "areas of concern," then it should follow that the system is able to provide a supportive structure within which the women may seek resolution.

NOTES

1. The Homicide Act 1957 abolished hanging for all except a very restricted category of offenses. The Murder (Abolition of Death Penalty) Act 1965 abolished all executions for a trial period and this was made permanent in 1969.

2. Persons sentenced to life imprisonment remain subject to recall to prison at any time during the rest of their life if their conduct gives cause for concern.

3. Home Office (1986). Prison Department Circular Instruction 2/86, issued by P2 (responsible for adult male lifers) and P4 (responsible for female lifers and male young lifers detained in Youth Custody Centres).

REFERENCES

Genders, E., & Player, E. (1987). Women in prison: The treatment, the control and the experience. In P. Carlen & A. Worrall (Eds.), *Gender, crime and justice*. Milton Keynes: Open University Press.

Hawkins, K. (1983). Assessing evil. *British Journal of Criminology, 23*, 101-127.

Maguire, M., Pinter, F., & Collis, C. (1984). Dangerousness and the tariff. *British Journal of Criminology, 24*, 250-268.

Rasch, W. (1981). The effects of indeterminate detention: A study of men sentenced to life imprisonment. *International Journal of Law and Psychiatry, 4*, 417-431.

Sapsford, R. J. (1983). *Life sentence prisoners*. Milton Keynes: Open University Press.

Smith, D. (Ed.). (1979). *Life sentence prisoners* (Home Office Research Study No. 51). London: HMSO.

Sykes, G. (1958). *Society of captives: A study of maximum security prisons*. Princeton, NJ: Princeton University Press.

13

Long-Term Incarceration of Female Offenders

Prison Adjustment and Coping

Doris Layton MacKenzie

James W. Robinson

Carol S. Campbell

The characteristics, adjustment, and coping of female offenders serving three types of prison sentences were compared: (1) newly entered inmates with short sentences, (2) newly entered inmates with long sentences, and (3) inmates with long sentences who had been incarcerated for a long term. Few differences were found among the groups in demographic characteristics and prior experience with the criminal justice system. The inmate groups did appear to experience different problems and to cope with their experiences in different manners. The newly entered inmates were more apt to be members of "play" families and they were more concerned about safety. The newly entered short-termers reported less control of events in the environment. Those who had served long terms in prison reported more situational problems such as boredom, missing luxuries, and lack of opportunities. There were no differences in the groups in anxiety and coping problems. The results suggest that long-term incarceration for these offenders is associated with increased concern with realistic problems reflecting limitations of the environment, but not with deterioration or an inability to cope.

AUTHORS' NOTE: An earlier version of this article was presented at the American Society of Criminology Annual Meeting in Montreal, Canada, November 1987. We would like to acknowledge the help and cooperation of Deputy Warden Nellie Fanguy, the staff, and the inmates at the Louisiana Correctional Institute for Women. Requests for reprints should be addressed to the senior author at the National Institute of Justice, 633 Indiana Ave., NW, 8th Floor, Washington, DC, 20531. Opinions expressed in this article are those of the authors and not necessarily those of the U.S. Department of Justice or the Louisiana Department of Corrections.
NOTE: Reprinted from *Criminal Justice and Behavior*, Vol. 16, No. 2, June 1989, pp. 223-238. Copyright 1989 by Sage Publications, Inc, and by American Association for Correctional Psychology.

Women inmates have been called the "forgotten offenders," and this label is even more appropriate for the long-term female offender (Unger & Buchanan, 1985). In comparison to the total population of offenders their numbers are small. Most research focuses on male prisoners. There are problems faced by the female prisoner that are unlike those faced by males; consequently, the research on male inmates cannot automatically be generalized to women prisoners. The environment of prison for women may be more cruel and deprived for them than is the environment of the male prison for males. In part, this cruelty may be due to the small numbers of women in prison; because there are few women prisoners, there are not many places to which they can be transferred. Opportunities, activities, and even social interactions are severely limited. Their relationships with their children are often destroyed, and this may be a more severe deprivation than it is for the male parent (Baunach, 1985; Unger & Buchanan, 1985).

Although these problems may be difficult for any female offender to handle, a long term in prison frequently amplifies the problems. While male long-term inmates may be transferred to take advantage of program opportunities or to be closer to their families, this is frequently not possible for the female offender. Most states have only one prison for female offenders; therefore, the long-term female offender will spend many years in one prison (Rafter, 1989). In such a situation there are few ways to escape from personality conflicts or to find comfortable niches (Toch, 1977). Additionally, the females, who may suffer more than males from separation from their children, cannot be transferred to a location closer to their families.

On the other hand, there is some evidence that male and female prisons differ in ways that make each environment more comfortable for each respective group. For example, Harris and Wright (1985) found a substantial difference in the environments of male and female prisons, but the way in which they differed was related to the expressed needs of the specific inmate population. Thus, there was a congruence between the needs and the environment even though the needs of the groups differed.

One difference between male and female prisons is the establishment of affectional relationships in female prisons. Frequently this is through the use of "play" families (Giallombardo, 1966; Ward & Kassebaum, 1965). The families are organized voluntarily by mutual agreement among inmates and may or may not represent homosexual relationships. Members of the families are given titles (e.g., mother, child, aunt, father); in some cases these titles indicate homosexual relationships (e.g., husband and wife), in others the titles indicate help and caring (e.g., mother and daughter).

Research on long-term offenders has been meager and research on female long-term offenders is almost nonexistent (Flanagan, 1984; Unger & Buchanan, 1985). Research on long-term male offenders has focused on describing their characteristics, identifying their problems and needs, examining the effects of extended imprisonment, or identifying policy and management issues (Flanagan, 1984). Research examining offender characteristics has found few consistent demographic differences between long-term and short-term male offenders other than what would be expected (e.g., serious nature of the crime and sentence length).

Studies of the effects of long-term confinement have not documented the commonly expressed view that such confinement will lead to deterioration (Flanagan, 1984). In fact, MacKenzie and Goodstein (1985) found that those who suffered most were new to prison but anticipated serving long terms in prison. These researchers speculated that male offenders who have served a long time in prison may have developed a method of coping with the environment that leaves them less susceptible to stress.

In an examination of the needs and problems of long-term male prisoners, Richards (1978) found the problems rated most severe by inmates were related to the deprivation of relationships in and with the outside, rather than to the deprivations of prison life itself. There was strong agreement in problem ratings of long-termers who had served a short time in prison and long-termers who had served a long time in prison. This led Richards to conclude that long-term confinement did not have cumulative effects on the daily experience of problems in the situation. The problems that were rated most severe did not seem to be indicative of extreme psychological disturbance. Later research by Flanagan (1980), replicating Richards's work with U.S. prisoners, reported similar results.

In summary, there is relatively little research on female long-term offenders. Research examining male long-term offenders shows little evidence of demographic differences between long- and short-termers. Also, the needs and problems of newly entered long-termers and those who have been in prison for a while are very similar (Richards, 1978). Both groups suffer most from their lack of relationships with the outside. Neither group appears to have severe psychological problems. However, those who are newly entered and who anticipate serving a long term in prison seem to experience more stress than do other inmates (MacKenzie & Goodstein, 1985).

This research examines the characteristics of female offenders incarcerated in a southern prison for women. Three groups of offenders are examined: those who have served a short period of time in prison and who expect to serve a short term in prison, those who have served a short term in prison but who expect to serve a long term in prison, and those who expect to serve a long term in prison and who have already served a long time in prison.

The three female offender groups are compared on demographic characteristics and experiences with the criminal justice system. Additionally, the inmates were examined to determine whether they differed in their problems, needs, and stress while in prison. It was hypothesized that the inmate groups would differ in their adjustment to prison. The long-term prisoners who had served a long time in prison were expected to be most concerned with social stimulation, activity, and freedom because of the extreme monotony and lack of opportunities in the environment. In contrast, it was anticipated that those who had served a short term in prison (whether long- or short-term prisoners) would be more concerned with safety, emotional feedback, and support. These inmates were expected to be more stressed and, therefore, to need an environment that was emotionally supportive. However, like the findings in previous studies for male inmates, it was expected that female inmates who were new to prison, but who anticipated serving a long term in prison, would experience the highest levels of anxiety. It was anticipated that both groups would suffer from problems that could be attributed to the deprivation of relationships with the outside.

METHOD

Subjects

Subjects were 141 of a total of 360 inmates incarcerated in Louisiana's only prison for adult female offenders. The mean age of those in the sample was 30.0 years ($SD = 7.1$), the majority were first offenders (57%), and most were nonwhite (65.7%). These characteristics were similar to those of the population (mean age = 31.0 years; 59.2% first offenders; 63.1% nonwhite). There was some difference between the sample and the population in the most serious crime for which the woman was serving time (χ^2 goodness-of-fit [$df = 4$] = 18.6, $p < .05$). In comparison to the population, more of the sample inmates were convicted of murder (32.5%), theft (38.9%), or robbery (14.3%), and fewer were convicted of drugs and other nonviolent crimes (14.3%) and other violent crimes (0%). The percentages for the population were 29.2 for murder, 29.9 for theft, 11.9 for robbery, 21.1 for other nonviolent crimes, and 8.8 for other violent crimes.

Sentence Length Groups. Three categories of inmates were identified, using time served in prison and sentence length. Those who had been in prison for less than 2 years and had sentences of less than 48 months were considered the short-sentenced newly entered inmates ($n = 37$). The long-sentenced, newly entered inmates ($n = 20$) had also been in prison for less than 2 years but had sentences of 96 months or more. The final group ($n = 18$) was made up of those who had received long sentences (96 months or more) and who had been in prison for a long term (at least 48 months). The remaining inmates who did not fit any of these categories were dropped from the analyses.

Procedure

All inmates in the prison were asked to volunteer to participate on two successive Saturdays. Coffee and cookies were offered as an incentive to participate. Each inmate was given a questionnaire that took approximately one hour to complete. Inmates in solitary confinement were given questionnaires in their cells.

Visits, work, or sleep were given as reasons for not participating.

Instruments

The first part of the questionnaire included standard demographic items and criminal history information. The second section of the questionnaire included measures of stress and prison adjustment. Three scales were used to examine the coping and adjustment of the offenders: Prison Preference Inventory (PPI), Control of Events, and Perceived Problems and Needs. These scales were selected in order to determine whether the offenders differed in their environmental needs (Harris & Wright, 1985; Toch, 1977), in the problems they encountered in prison (Richards, 1978), or in their ability to control events in their lives while in prison. Previous research with males has indicated that lack of control in prison is associated with higher levels of stress (MacKenzie, Goodstein, & Blouin, 1987). How stressed they were in the environment was examined with self-reports of anxiety. Furthermore, they were asked if they were members of play families to examine whether they differed in their use of a play family to help them cope with imprisonment.

Prison Preference Inventory. The environmental preferences of the inmates were measured with Toch's (1977) Prison Preference Inventory (PPI). In this 56-item forced-choice scale inmates were asked to indicate their preference for 30 statements (e.g., I'd prefer, "Guards who act the same way every day" versus "Housing that keeps out noise"). For the remaining 26 items inmates were asked to circle the item of the pair that would bother them more (e.g., I would be more bothered by "too much time to think" versus "too much talk and noise"). Altogether, there were eight environmental concerns: Support, Emotional Feedback, Activity, Safety, Structure, Social Stimulation, Freedom, and Privacy. Scores for each scale were calculated by adding one point to the scale score each time a choice was made for the scale item. There were seven items for each scale matched with each other item for a total range of 0 to 14 points for each scale.

Anxiety. Anxiety was measured with the state version of the State-Trait Anxiety Scale (Spielberger, Gorsuch, & Lushene, 1970).

Control of Events. The events that the inmates could control in their life were measured by the Control of Events Scale. This was based on the scale developed by MacKenzie and Goodstein (1985). Additional items were added to the original scale. Inmates were asked to respond on a 5-point scale (*definitely yes* to *definitely no*) whether, "If you wanted to, could you." This statement was followed by statements such as "find a way to make an emergency phone call" or "change jobs in here." There were a total of 17 items with five response choices for a total scale range from 17 to 85. A high score on this scale indicated little control of events.

Play Family. Interviews with staff during the planning stage of the research revealed that many of the inmates were members of "play families." It was felt that this might be a coping method of some groups of inmates and so an item was included in the questionnaire. The item asked inmates to respond yes or no to the question "Are you in a 'play' family?"

Perceived Problems and Needs. The perceived problems and needs of offenders were measured using the 20-item scale developed by Richards (1978) to measure the needs of long-term male inmates. Three additional items were added (see Appendix). For each item inmates were asked to indicate how severe each problem was for them to handle (scale of 1 = *very easy* to 4 = *very difficult*). The factor structure of the 23 problem statements was identified by means of a principal components factor analysis. The eigenvalues and an examination of the scree plot suggested that two factors could be extracted. A varimax rotation was used. The results of this factor analysis are presented in the Appendix.

A factor score was computed for each inmate, using the standardized raw score for each scale weighted by the coefficient produced in the factor analysis. Therefore, each inmate received two scores, one for each factor. The meaning of the factor scores is described below.

Fifteen items loaded above 0.4 on factor one. These items appear to be related to difficulties in the prison situation both because of limitations of the situation (interesting jobs and activities) and interactions with the outside world (luxuries and social life). The standardized factor scores ranged from −2.12 to 2.0. An inmate high on this factor is expressing problems with boredom, privacy, lack of activity, and interactions with the outside. This was called the *Situational Problems Scale*.

The second factor extracted in the analysis is different from the first. The items loading highest on this factor are problems related to suicide, self-confidence, feeling sorry for oneself, or being mad at the world. Standardized scores on this factor ranged from −1.1 to 3.16. Inmates high on this scale, called the *Coping Difficulties Scale*, appear to be having severe problems in coping with the situation. Rather than focusing on the problems in the situation, these inmates show signs of being unable to cope.

In addition to using the items from Richards's perceived needs and problems scale for the Situational Problems Scale and the Coping Difficulties Scale, the items were used to form the two scales Richards had identified: an Inside Scale, including the items related to problems within the prison; and an Outside Scale, including the items related to the inmate's deprivation of relationships in and with the outside.

RESULTS

Shown in Table 13.1 are the demographic characteristics and the criminal justice system experiences of the three groups of inmates identified on the basis of their sentence length and time served: those with short sentences who were newly entered (short term, short time, or STST); those with long sentences who were newly entered (STLT); and those with long sentences who had been in prison for a long term (LTLT). The STST group was compared to the STLT group and the STLT group was compared to the LTLT group using *t* tests.[1] The former was to examine whether the two groups who had served a short period of time but who expected to serve different lengths of time in prison differed in their initial adjustment to prison. The comparison of the STLT group and the LTLT group was made to iden-

tify how inmates may change over time in their adjustment to prison and whether inmates with long sentences who have recently entered the prison differ from those who came in previously.

As can be seen in Table 13.1, the samples were similar in age, education, and race. The LTLT inmates did have significantly fewer children than did the STLT inmates, $t(36) = 2.8$, $p < .01$. Surprisingly, there were no differences in the groups in the number of prior arrests or convictions. As expected, the newly entered with short sentences had received significantly shorter sentences than the newly entered with long sentences $t'(17) = -10.3$, $p < .001$. There was also a significant difference in the sentence length for the two long-term groups; the LTLT group had longer sentences than the STLTs, $t'(11.5) = -2.39$, $p < .05$. The STST group had served significantly less time than the STLT group, $t'(30) = -2.3$, $p < .03$, and the LTLT group had served significantly more time, $t'(20.3) = -10.9$, $p < .001$ (see Table 13.1). As expected, there were differences in crime types for the three groups. Most of the STST group was serving time for theft or other nonviolent crimes. In comparison, most of the inmates in the groups with long sentences were serving time for murder. There was a difference in crime type between the two groups with long sentences. The second largest category of offenses for the STLT group was for theft (21.1%), whereas the second largest category for the LTLT group was robbery (22.2%). Other than this difference, the STLT and the LTLT groups were similar in crime types.

A comparison of the rank orders of the means of the environmental concerns in the PPI is shown in Table 13.2. The higher the rank order, the more important this concern was considered to be by the inmates. There was only one significant difference in the scores: The LTLT groups ranked Safety significantly different and of less concern than did the other long-sentence group, $t(26) = 2.4$, $p < .05$.

The means and standard deviations for Anxiety, Control of Events, Situational Problems, and Coping Difficulties of the three groups are shown in Table 13.3. There were no significant differences in anxiety or coping problems. The STST group reported significantly less control than the STLT group, $t(46) = 2.4$, $p < .05$, and the LTLT group reported signifi-

TABLE 13.1 Demographic Characteristics and Criminal Justice System Experiences of Women Inmates Varying in Time Served and Sentence Length

| | Short Sentence | | Long Sentence | | | |
| | Newly Entered (n = 37) | | Newly Entered (n = 20) | | Long Term in Prison (n = 18) | |
Demographics						
Mean Age (SD)	29.2	(6.4)	31.0	(5.6)	33.8	(7.2)
Mean Education (SD)	10.7	(2.3)	10.7	(2.4)	10.8	(2.8)
Race (%)						
White	37.8		20.0		22.2	
Black and Other	62.2		80.0		77.8	
Mean Number of Children (SD)	1.9	(1.8)	2.3	(1.6)	1.1*	(1.1)
Criminal Justice System Experiences						
Mean Prior Arrests (SD)	1.7	(2.4)	1.5	(2.3)	0.8	(1.5)
Mean Prior Convictions (SD)	0.9	(1.7)	0.6	(1.2)	0.7	(1.4)
Sentence Length (in years) (SD)	2.6*	(1.1)	17.2	(6.1)	27.1*	(12.2)
Number of Lifers	0		2		8	
Mean Time Served (in months) (SD)	8.7*	(6.1)	13.4	(8.2)	80.3*	(24.9)
Crimes Type (%)						
Murder	10.8		63.1		61.2	
Theft	32.4		21.1		5.6	
Robbery	10.8		5.3		22.2	
Other Nonviolent	46.0		10.5		11.1	

*Significantly different from newly entered with long sentences at $p < .05$.

TABLE 13.2 Rank Order of Means of the Concerns of Women Inmates Serving Short and Long Sentences

| | Short Sentence Newly Entered (n = 24) | | Long Sentence | | | |
| | | | Newly Entered (n = 15) | | Long Term in Prison (n = 13) | |
Concern						
Support	9.7	(1)	10.1	(1)	9.5	(1)
Emotional Feedback	8.7	(2)	8.1	(2)	8.7	(2)
Activity	6.8	(3)	7.3	(3)	7.2	(4)
Structure	6.3	(5)	6.9	(4)	7.5	(3)
Safety	6.5	(4)	6.0	(5)	3.8	(8)*
Freedom	5.7	(7)	5.6	(6)	6.6	(5)
Social Stimulation	5.9	(6)	5.3	(7)	4.8	(7)
Privacy	5.1	(8)	5.1	(8)	5.2	(6)

NOTE: Numbers in parentheses are rank orders for each type of sentence.
*Significantly different from newly entered with long sentences at $p < .05$.

cantly more situational problems than the STLT group, $t(28) = -2.3$, $p < .05$.

Also shown in Table 13.3 are the means for the Inside Scale and the Outside Scale. As shown, there were no significant differences for the groups.

DISCUSSION

Similar to what has been found with male inmates, few differences were found in demographics among the three different groups of female inmates. The prisoners who had been

TABLE 13.3 The Adjustment to Prison of Women Inmates Varying in Sentence Length and
Time Served

| | Short Sentence Newly Entered | | Long Sentence | | | |
| | | | Newly Entered | | Long Term in Prison | |
Adjustment Measure	M	(SD)	M	(SD)	M	(SD)
Anxiety	46.6	(8.7)	49.2	(15.0)	46.6	(9.5)
Control of Events	50.1*	(14.2)	39.9	(13.4)	47.3	(13.3)
Situational Problems	−0.24	(1.0)	−0.19	(0.9)	0.50*	(0.7)
Coping Problems	0.05	(0.8)	0.32	(1.4)	−0.11	(1.0)
Inside	17.5	(5.2)	18.7	(9.2)	17.7	(6.1)
Outside	21.3	(6.9)	21.4	(7.4)	23.4	(6.6)
Play Family Member (%)						
Yes	71.9		76.5		31.3	
No	28.1		23.5		68.8	

*Significantly different from newly entered with long sentences at $p < .05$.

in prison for a long period of time did have fewer children, but this is most likely due to the time spent in prison.

The three groups did not differ in their previous experiences with the criminal justice system. As expected, based on the selection criteria, they differed in sentence length and mean time served on the current sentence. The short-sentenced groups differed in both sentence length and time served on current sentence, and there was a difference in the sentence lengths of the two long-sentenced groups. Also, these groups differed in the crime types. The largest percentage of both long-sentenced groups were murderers. However, the newly entered (STLT) had a larger number of thieves and the long-termers (LTLT) had more robbers and vice versa. Thus, the LTLT group appeared to include inmates with more serious crimes.

There were few differences in the environmental concerns of the groups as measured by the Prison Preference Inventory. These scores are also similar to those found by Harris and Wright (1985) for a sample of female inmates in New York. The only real difference among the groups was that the LTLT group was much less concerned about safety than the STLT group.

There could be many reasons for the difference in the groups in the ranking of safety; for one, those who have been in prison for a while may have learned that the environment is not really dangerous, though the newly entered inmate may think that it is. Or those who have

been in prison for a while may learn ways to cope with the environment that makes it appear less dangerous. Another possibility is that the environment is actually more dangerous for the newly entered inmate who has not yet developed a friendship network. However, an examination of the adjustment of the inmates to prison does not suggest that the newly entered women experience more stress than other inmates. There are no differences in the groups in the degree of anxiety.

There is some evidence that the groups adjust to prison differently. For example, the newly entered with short sentences report that they have significantly less control of events than do those who are also new to prison but who have long sentences. Those who had short sentences were found to have served less time in prison than the group with long sentences, so this difference in control could be a function of time in prison. However, this control difference was not evident between the two groups with long sentences.

Whether the reported control of events is actual or perceived is somewhat uncertain. On one hand, some inmates in prison may actually have the ability to "get things done." For example, one inmate may be able to talk a social worker into allowing an emergency phone call, but another inmate may not. One inmate may work in a location where she has access to a phone, though another does not. It is also possible that some inmates believe they can accomplish a task when in actuality they may not be able to do it. Anecdotally, it is often said that the "model" prisoner is the lifer. It may be that the inmates with longer sentences adjusted to prison in a manner that gave them more control of events.

The groups also differ in their involvement with play families. A large percentage of those who are new to prison admit to being involved with play families. This changes for those who have been in the prison for a longer period of time. The majority of these inmates do not acknowledge being in a play family. Play families may be a coping mechanism that helps the newly arrived inmate adjust to prison. The newly arrived inmate who is concerned with safety may feel more secure as a member of a family. Play families may not be as important for adjustment later in a woman's prison career.

There was a difference between the two groups with long sentences in their reported needs and problems. Those who had served a long term in prison reported many more problems related to the environmental situation than did those who were new to prison. Thus, it appears that the severity of the problems increases for the women serving long terms in prison. It has been suggested that the prison environment for women may be extremely difficult because of the small number of women incarcerated. Transfers to prisons closer to families may be severely limited, as may the latitude for activities, jobs, educational opportunities, and social interactions. The difficulties presented by these restrictions may accumulate so that the women who have served a long time in prison suffer more than those who have just entered.

What is interesting is that this does not seem to be similar for coping problems and anxiety. There were also no differences in the Richards Inside and Outside scales. We speculate that the problems reported and those most pertinent to these women were those that had to do with the situation. They suffer realistically because they cannot interact with their loved ones, social stimulation is lacking, they miss men and social life, they want more to do, and they wish they could get an interesting job. Such needs are practical, immediate, cumulative, and obvious in the situation. Suffering becomes more severe as the amount of time in the environment increases.

On the other hand, they do not appear to be having problems coping with the environment. We speculate that the difference is in whether the environment is overwhelming to the inmate. If she is overwhelmed she may begin to focus on herself—fear of going mad, thoughts of suicide, worried about becoming a vegetable, anger—which may be symptomatic of severe coping difficulties. Such problems may reflect individualistic factors for all groups of inmates and not be related to time served and sentence length. An examination of the factor analysis in this study and the two Richards scales (Inside and Outside) suggests that this may be what occurred for male inmates in the Richards study. That is, the problems are not inside the prison versus outside the prison, but rather are related to the individual and the situation. Those that reflect the individual aspect are an indication of an inability to cope effectively with the situation and are related to a situation that overwhelms the individual. In such a situation the individual focuses on her own adjustment and feelings rather than the actual environmental situation. From this perspective, the Coping Difficulties Scale reflects a stress response to the environment, and the Situational Problems Scale reflects difficulties in the situation. Thus, differences among the long-sentenced inmates are in the situational problems, not in their coping ability.

In summary, the time factor seems to be important in the adjustment of women to prison. Those who are new to prison suffer less from situational problems. They may use play families to help support them in their initial adjustment. They are more concerned with safety issues than they will be later in their sentence. They are not necessarily stressed beyond their ability to cope. This research does not suggest that the characteristics of women entering prison recently with long sentences are any different from those of women who entered prison in the past. Neither are there easily identified demographic differences between inmates with short sentences and those with long sentences.

NOTE

1. The Behrens-Fisher calculations with the Welch adjustment for degrees of freedom were done for *t'* tests if the variances were found to be heterogeneous.

REFERENCES

Baunach, P. J. (1985). *Mothers in prison*. New Brunswick, NJ: Transaction Books.

Flanagan, T. J. (1980). The pains of long-term imprisonment: A comparison of British and American perspectives. *British Journal of Criminology, 20*(2), 148-156.

Flanagan, T. J. (1984). *Research on long-term incarceration: A review and assessment* (Report). Kansas City, MO: Correctional Services Group, Inc.

Giallombardo, R. (1966). *Society of women: A study of a women's prison*. New York: John Wiley.

Harris, J. W., & Wright, K. N. (1985, November). *Beyond physical differences: How female inmates differ from male inmates in adjustment to prison.* Paper presented at the annual meeting of the Society of Criminology, San Diego, CA.

MacKenzie, D. L., & Goodstein, L. I. (1985). Long-term incarceration impacts and characteristics of long-term offenders: An empirical analysis. *Criminal Justice and Behavior, 12*, 395-414.

MacKenzie, D. L., Goodstein, L. I., & Blouin, D. C. (1987). Personal control and prisoner adjustment: An empirical test of a proposed model. *Journal of Research in Crime and Delinquency, 24*, 49-68.

Rafter, N. H. (1989). Gender and justice: The equal protection issue. In L. I. Goodstein & D. L. MacKenzie (Eds.), *The American prison: Issues in research and policy* (pp. 89-109). New York: Plenum.

Richards, B. (1978). The experience of long-term imprisonment. *British Journal of Criminology, 18*, 162-169.

Spielberger, C. D., Gorsuch, R. L., & Lushene, R. E. (1970). *Manual for the state-trait anxiety inventory.* Palo Alto, CA: Consulting Psychologists Press.

Toch, H. (1977). *Living in prison*. New York: Free Press.

Unger, C. A., & Buchanan, R. A. (1985). *Managing long-term inmates: A guide for the correctional administrator* (Report to the National Institute of Corrections). Washington, DC: U.S. Department of Justice.

Ward, D., & Kassebaum, G. (1965). *Women's prison*. Chicago: Aldine.

APPENDIX

Richards's Needs and Problems Scale

		Varimax Rotated Factor Pattern	
		Factor I	Factor II
Situational Problems			
(O)	Wishing that time would go faster	0.47591	0.39653
(In)	Wishing you had more privacy	0.50464	0.28305
(O)	Feeling that your life is being wasted	0.57124	0.28978
(O)	Missing little "luxuries," e.g., your favorite food, your own clothes	0.64884	−0.02386
(In)	Keeping out of trouble	0.46381	0.25715
(O)	Missing social life	0.51528	0.35369
(O)	Missing somebody	0.52199	0.05407
(In)	Getting annoyed or irritated with other inmates	0.48608	0.35762
(O)	Longing for a time in the past	0.41868	0.22079
(O)	Feeling sexually frustrated	0.58215	0.00193
(O)	Worrying about how you will cope when you get out	0.58267	0.20804
(In)	Being bored	0.48779	0.30986
(A)	Wishing you had more choice	0.70165	0.24919
(A)	Wishing you could get an interesting job in prison	0.71121	0.10130
(A)	Feeling that you need opportunities	0.79982	0.09249
Coping Difficulties			
(In)	Being worried about becoming a vegetable	0.19345	0.57869
(O)	Being afraid of dying before you get out	0.19852	0.56428
(In)	Feeling suicidal	−0.12592	0.69532
(In)	Losing your self-confidence	0.26059	0.70423
(In)	Feeling sorry for yourself	0.18207	0.71579
(In)	Feeling angry with yourself	0.37982	0.68301
(In)	Feeling angry with the world	0.16551	0.76039
(In)	Being afraid of going mad	0.15955	0.78798

NOTE: O = Richards's original outside items; In = Richards's original inside items; A = items added in this study.

14

Behavior and Adaptation in Long-Term Prison Inmates

Descriptive Longitudinal Results

Edward Zamble

A comprehensive set of measures of behavior, emotional states, and cognitions was gathered longitudinally for a sample of long-term prison inmates across more than 7 years from the beginning of their terms. Over time they became more involved in work and other structured activities, and less involved in casual socializing with other inmates, but their rates of contact with people on the outside were maintained. These changes were accompanied by evidence of improved adaptation, including considerable decreases over time in dysphoric emotional states, and also decreases in stress-related medical problems and the number of disciplinary incidents. Although these beneficial effects cannot easily be interpreted as the effects of long-term imprisonment, the entire pattern of results provides strong evidence against expectations of widespread or generalized deleterious effects.

Changes in prisoners' behavior, cognitions, and emotional adjustment ought to be one of the major questions in criminological research. However, most studies of the effects of imprisonment concentrate on the undesirable effects predicted by prisonization theory (Clemmer, 1958; Thomas & Peterson, 1977). Unfortunately, this narrow focus on socialization has often excluded measures of general psychological functioning or adaptation. There

also have been serious methodological faults in prisonization studies, and the results have been inconsistent and contradictory, as previous reviews (e.g., Bukstel & Kilmann, 1980) have shown.

Thus the amount of reliable and rigorous information on the psychological effects of imprisonment is small (McKay, Jayewardene, & Reedie, 1977). A few careful studies do stand out, such as the work of Bolton, Smith,

AUTHOR'S NOTE: This research was supported by a grant from the Social Science and Humanities Research Council of Canada. The work was much facilitated by the assistance of Jennifer Cumberland. The author is grateful to William Palmer for helpful editorial criticism and also to several institutional psychologists and the Research Division in the Correctional Service of Canada for their active cooperation. Correspondence may be addressed to Edward Zamble, Department of Psychology, Queen's University, Kingston, Ontario, Canada K7L 3N6.

Heskin, and Banister (1976) and Sapsford (1978, 1983). Contrary to the expectations of prisonization theory, the evidence from these indicates that marked psychological deterioration is not a necessary consequence of imprisonment.

However, there are several limitations in previous studies. Many have included biased samples of long-term prisoners, selected after attrition by selective release. This selection procedure is especially problematic given the limitations of the cross-sectional designs employed (Farrington, Ohlin, & Wilson, 1986). The research can also be criticized for using insensitive measures (Flanagan, 1982) and for covering only a limited range of psychological functioning.

In a recent study, our research group attempted to avoid most of these criticisms through an extended longitudinal investigation of how offenders cope with the problems they encounter, both in prison and on the outside (Zamble & Porporino, 1988, 1990; Zamble, Porporino, & Kalotay, 1984). We included a wide variety of measures of behavior, cognitions, and emotional experience, and examined changes over a 1½-year period in prison. These measures failed to show a generalized pattern of emotional damage from imprisonment, and, except for a reduction in dysphoria and a loss of apparent motivation for change, psychological functioning was remarkably stable over time in prison. Much of the pattern of results has been confirmed by other investigators (Toch & Adams, 1989).

Unfortunately, although periods of 1 or 2 years are sufficient to establish what happens with most prisoners, they are too short to give conclusive evidence about the effects of much longer terms of imprisonment. Therefore, the investigation reported here was designed as a longitudinal extension of the previous work.

METHOD

Subjects

Five years after the completion of the previous study, the 41 subjects in the original "long-term" group were traced with the aid of the Correctional Service of Canada. Of the original group, 26 had remained in prison in the Ontario region, and all but 1 of these agreed to participate in the new study. All but

4 subjects were serving life terms for some category of homicide; the mean time served in the current term was 7.1 years ($SD = 0.4$). Their mean age was 37.5 ($SD = 10.3$). Only 3 had reached the point of eligibility for full parole, and 2 of these had begun gradual release programs, so there is no indication of bias by selective releases.

Materials and Procedures

A variety of measures were taken, intended to index a wide range of behavior, cognitions, and emotional states. A structured interview, based on the protocol included in Zamble and Porporino (1988), was used as the principal instrument for information on current behavior. It included questions dealing with time use, patterns of activities, and chronic problems experienced. There were also questions in other areas, such as contact with the outside and expectations of release. In addition to questions used previously, a number of new items were added to provide information on the special experiences and problems of long-term prisoners.

A battery of written questionnaires was also administered, including several instruments to assess emotional state, such as the Beck Depression Inventory (Beck, 1967), the Beck Hopelessness Scale (Beck, Weissman, Lester, & Trexler, 1974), the State Anxiety Inventory (Spielberger, Gorsuch, & Lushene, 1970), and the Coopersmith Self-Esteem Inventory (Coopersmith, 1967). A revised version (Levenson, 1975) of Rotter's (1966) Locus of Control Scale was used to measure generalized attributions of control. Criminal attitudes and belief systems were measured with the Criminal Sentiments Scale (Andrews & Wormith, 1983). The Prison Problems Scale (Porporino, 1983; Zamble & Porporino, 1988) was also included to assess generalized perceptions of environmental stress. All of these questionnaires had been used previously for the same subjects (Zamble & Porporino, 1988; Zamble et al., 1984), so changes over time could be assessed.

In addition to the data obtained directly from subjects, institutional files provided information on disciplinary and medical events during the term. Files were also checked to provide confirmation and elaboration of information from subjects; in the two cases where there were significant discrepancies, both the inmate and institutional staff were consulted to resolve the apparent conflicts.

Procedure

After being located, each subject was seen individually to obtain written consent to participate. Typically, the interview was done prior to the administration of the questionnaires. After both were completed, files were searched.

RESULTS

Progress Toward Release

Twenty-two of the 25 subjects had started their terms in maximum security institutions. However, subsequent placements varied greatly, and at the time of the study 4 were still in maximum-security, 15 were in medium-security, and the other 6 were in minimum-security institutions. The majority had begun the progression of steps toward release; for example, 13 had been allowed some temporary leaves. Seven were working at jobs on the outside at least several days a month, returning to their institution after work.

Despite progress toward release, most subjects still had a period of time before full parole. The mean time that subjects said that they expected to serve before full parole was 2.0 years. The reality was likely longer, because the recorded dates of eligibility ranged from about 1 to 17 years.

Behavior Patterns

Time Use and Socialization. Despite the prospects of foreseeable release, most inmates were still leading lives dictated by institutional routines. Table 14.1 shows means for selected behavioral measures for the three interviews of the earlier study and the present (fourth) interview. (Values may differ from previous reports, because they are based on the present sample rather than the larger original set.)

As can be seen, the time spent working was by far the largest proportion of reported activities, and it had increased significantly from the beginning of the term (first interview), $t(24) = 3.03, p < .01$. The proportions of time in other categories did not change significantly from the first interview. However, the level of socializing had risen from initial values by the time of the second interview (about 4 months after the beginning of the term), and the decline from there to the final value was statistically significant, $t(24) = 3.01, p < .01$.

Although the amount of time socializing fell during the term, the average number of friends did not change significantly over time. The majority of subjects had acquired a few close friends, mostly other long-term prisoners, both for basic social needs and also for practical purposes such as protection. Similarly, at the time of the present study there was no evidence of an increasing number of social isolates—if anything, *fewer* subjects said that they preferred to spend time on their own.

When subjects had the choice of going out onto the range or staying in their cells, they increasingly chose the latter, and the amount of optional cell time was significantly higher than at the beginning of the term, $t(24) = 2.49$, $p < .05$. The most frequent reason given for the change was the choice of activities that could be done better in their cells, such as studying, hobbycraft, or watching television. (Inmates could purchase televisions from canteen funds.) Thus, it appears that subjects had chosen to spend their time in routines of their own devising, instead of the unstructured or aimless activities that typify institutional socializing.

Their conscious and deliberate policy of withdrawing from the flow of institutional social activity was apparently in response to the emotional and practical problems created by entanglements in casual prison relationships, as noted by two thirds of the sample (e.g., "With too many people there are always conflicts. Most of the guys in here are legends in their own minds." "The more involvement . . . the more problems. . . ."). Most subjects were acutely aware of the greater consequences of institutional charges for long-term inmates, so they avoided the risks by minimizing their involvement in the confusion and uncertainties of commonplace patterns of prison socializing.

Outside Contacts. In contrast to reduced social activity within the prison, outside contacts did not decrease systematically over time in prison. The number of letters received (and sent) had increased considerably over the early part of the term because of the time it took for

TABLE 14.1 Measures of Specific Behavior Across Time in Prison

Variable	Interview			
	1	2	3	4
Time use categories—mean percentage of time specified in				
Work	29	31	35	37
Sports and hobbies	08	08	10	11
Socializing	20	23	17	14
Passive activities	26	26	23	22
Visits and letters	06	04	04	06
Employment				
Percentage with institutional job	—	96	96	92
Mean rating of job (0-100)	—	67.3	80.6	83.1
Socializing in prison				
Mean number of "close friends"	1.6	2.6	1.6	1.9
Percentage with no (0) friends	44	24	36	38
General preferences for socializing				
Percentage staying "on my own"	44	28	52	28
Percentage with a few friends	40	60	40	56
Percentage in a larger group or floating	16	12	8	16
Mean percentage of optional time spent in cell	34	25	42	51
Percentage saying no (0) optional time in cell	25	21	8	10
Outside contacts				
Mean number of visits received (month)	0.6	1.2	1.4	2.6
Percentage with no (0) visits	50	48	36	8
Mean number of letters received (month)	4.6	13.0	13.6	7.8
Percentage with no (0) letters	16	12	8	16
Mean frequency reading or listening to news	9.1	9.2	10.5	10.0
Frequency of missing people from outside				
Percentage "always" or "most of the time"	81	72	76	64
Percentage "sometimes"	14	16	12	32
Percentage "rarely" or "never"	5	12	12	4

mail to catch up with institutional assignments. However, the average number of letters did not change significantly from then until the time of the present study, although a nonsignificant decrease is visible in Table 14.1. The lack of a significant decrease in the number of letters is somewhat surprising, because alternative channels of communication, particularly telephones, had become increasingly accessible during the term. The majority of subjects had at least weekly calls with family, and several mentioned it explicitly as a reason for reductions in the number of letters.

At the same time, there was a significant increase from the beginning of the term in the number of visits received, $t(24) = 2.43$, $p < .05$. Over the years, the families of some inmates had moved closer to where they were imprisoned, so visits became easier. At the same time, the majority of subjects had established institutional conduct records good enough to qualify them for family trailer visits, another innovation developed during their terms. The opportunities for such extended visits were an incentive for family members to travel long distances to the institutions.

Similarly, there was little change in the frequency of missing people from the outside. Although some relationships were weakened or dissolved, new relationships were established and, indeed, some inmates increased contact with the outside while in prison. For example, two subjects had been married during their terms, and at least three others had reestablished links with previously estranged family members. In general, the level of emotional ties with people on the outside had been maintained.

These results may be surprising in light of some expectations, but they are internally quite consistent and also consonant with other data from this study. Long-term imprisonment need not result in the loss of outside relationships.

Thoughts and Feelings

Emotional State. Table 14.2 presents data concerning subjects' emotions and cognitions. There were sizable and systematic decreases in emotional dysphoria across the series of measurements. Scores on the Beck Depression Inventory fell significantly from the beginning of the term to the time of the present study, $t(24) = 3.71$, $p < .001$; the current mean fell within the range considered normal. State Anxiety Inventory scores also decreased significantly, $t(24) = 3.83$, $p < .001$, and Hopelessness Scale scores approached a significant decline, $t(24) = 2.03$, $p < .06$. Complementarily, Self-Esteem scores rose significantly, $t(24) = 3.92$, $p < .001$.

Corresponding results can be seen in the self-reported frequencies of specific emotional states. There were significant decreases from the beginning of the term in both depression, $t(24) = 4.48$, $p < .001$, and anxiety, $t(24) = 3.08$, $p < .01$. There were changes as well in the frequencies of other emotional states. Guilt feelings fell considerably from the beginning of the term, $t(24) = 2.23$, $p < .05$, and the majority of subjects reported none at all at the time of the present study. Thus, in general, the extent of subjects' dysphoric emotional states decreased over the term.

Boredom also decreased from the beginning of the term, $t(24) = 2.75$, $p < .05$, consonant with descriptions from subjects that they had learned how to involve themselves in a variety of activities to avoid being bored. Of the emotional states examined, only anger and loneliness did not change consistently and significantly.

Cognitions. In contrast to the changes in emotions over the term, there was little difference in appraisals (see Table 14.2). In general, subjects did not see their lives in prison as significantly more desirable or rewarding after several years, nor did they see fewer problems than previously.

Over time, a higher proportion of the sample was able to cite some positive aspects of their lives in prison, $Z = 2.40$, $p < .01$. However, about one third of the examples specified were improvements resulting from transfer to lower security institutions (e.g., "There's less tension here, and more freedom"). Otherwise, the most frequently cited positive aspects were consequences of progress through the system or greater access to people from the outside. Thus, the change in this measure reflects objective improvements in respondents' situations, rather than any change in how they perceived or evaluated conditions in the system. This point is substantiated by subjects' assessments of the overall quality of their lives in prison, which did not change over time.

Unexpectedly, the one questionnaire measure of general cognitions that changed significantly was the Criminal Sentiments Scale, indicating that attitudes toward the criminal justice system actually became more prosocial over time, $t(24) = 3.11$, $p < .01$. However, there was no significant decrease in the subscale of Identification with Criminal Others. Several explanations for these findings are plausible, but none is conclusively indicated by the data.

Other questions measured specific cognitions about personal objectives and time framing. Although most subjects said that they lived day by day rather than planning their time over days, about two thirds were able to state a goal for their term, most commonly educational objectives. Interestingly, the proportions did not vary much over the four assessment occasions. This finding is in contrast to our earlier reports, based on a random sample with a preponderance of inmates with shorter terms (Zamble & Porporino, 1988), in which it appeared that the majority of inmates lost their motivation for self-improvement within a year or so.

Time framing did show some changes. It was in practice impossible to differentiate reliably between thoughts of the "future outside" and the "future before the end of the term," because the gradualness of the release process obscured the distinction, so these two categories were summed to yield a total frequency of thoughts of the future. This measure showed a significant increase over the term, $t(24) = 2.29$, $p < .01$.

Answers to qualitative questions were also consistent with an increased concern with the future. For example, subjects' daydreams were largely composed of (pleasant) imaginings and "rehearsals" for their lives after release. Again,

TABLE 14.2 Measures of Emotions and Cognitions Across Time in Prison

Variable	Interview			
	1	*2*	*3*	*4*
Mean score on Beck Depression Inventory	14.5	11.3	10.4	9.0
Percentage scoring ≥ 15 ("mildly depressed")	48	36	24	21
Mean score on Hopelessness Scale	5.9	3.7	4.7	3.5
Mean score on Spielberger State Anxiety Inventory	49.0	45.3	43.3	38.5
Percentage > 46 (norm for anxiety patients)	64	48	40	29
Mean score on Coopersmith Self-Esteem Scale	5.0	—	7.6	7.9
Mean weekly frequency reported for:				
Depression	3.4	3.2	2.0	1.4
Anxiety	3.0	2.8	2.1	1.2
Anger	1.8	2.4	2.6	1.1
Guilt feelings	1.8	1.4	0.6	0.6
Boredom	3.0	3.1	3.3	2.1
Loneliness	—	4.8	4.5	3.7
Mean score on Prison Problems Scale	—	61.3	59.8	54.2
Mean score on Internal-External Scale	30.2	—	30.1	30.5
Attitudes toward criminal justice system				
Prosocial	73.6	—	74.8	85.3
Identification with criminal others	17.6	—	16.0	15.7
Mean general rating of quality of life (0-100)	32.2	38.3	38.6	42.0
Percentage rating quality of life < 50	68	50	44	42
Percentage specifying "No (0) positive things here"	48	32	40	8
Total number of problems mentioned (22 possible)	6.7	10.9	11.1	6.7
Percentage with goal to accomplish in prison	80	72	60	64
Percentage with educational goal	64	64	48	56
Percentage with goal of reform or behavior change	4	4	8	4
Percentage who say they plan time in prison	12	24	12	20
Percentage self-classified as "gleaners"—attempting to make most of time and benefit from term	44	—	40	56
Time framing				
Mean frequency thoughts of future (days/month)	2.7	15.0	—	—
Mean frequency thoughts of future in prison	—	—	6.8	11.9
Mean frequency thoughts of future outside	—	—	11.6	13.1
Mean frequency of thoughts of past	2.8	12.3	12.8	10.9

this pattern is in contrast with the findings of our previous study, where most subjects seemed to have a strong focus on the immediate present. It is not clear whether the difference resulted from long-term imprisonment or from the closeness of release. However, there had been little evidence in the earlier results (based predominantly on shorter-term inmates) of realistic planning for the future, even among those for whom release was imminent.

Disciplinary and Medical Measures

Many of the changes described in the previous sections support the conclusion that inmates' adaptation improved during the term.

Other relevant information, not subject to the problems of self-report, can be found in institutional files.

The number of disciplinary offenses was used as an index of adaptation to institutional rules. In the system, charges are filed by institutional staff but are judged by independent adjudicators, so convictions rather than charges were used.

For comparisons across time, the data were grouped into five blocks. Each of the first two blocks included information for 1½-year periods, starting from the beginning of the term. The last two blocks also covered 1½ years each, counted backwards from the time when the data were obtained. Because the total length of time surveyed varied across subjects, the length of the middle block also varied; therefore, data were prorated to estimate values for 1½ years. The number of disciplinary convictions was significantly lower in the last period than at the beginning of the term, $M = 0.6$ versus $M = 2.4$, $t(24) = 2.75$, $p < .05$.

Data from medical files were divided into the same five periods as disciplinary incidents. The total number of new initiations, that is, requests for medical attention exclusive of follow-ups, showed a nonsignificant tendency to decline, from a mean of 16.4 in the first period to 7.4 in the last, $t(24) = 1.92$, $p < .07$. However, data from more restricted categories of medical usage also were examined. Using the number of requests for attention to stress-related problems, for example, sleep disturbances, headaches, or tension, a progressive decline over the five periods was visible, and the change from the first to the last period was significant, $M = 6.8$ versus $M = 1.6$, $t(24) = 2.19$, $p < .05$.

Given that the total number of problems can be inflated by inclusion of trivial complaints, the number of days for which medications were prescribed for stress-related complaints was also calculated. This measure was intended as a weighted index of seriousness of the presented problems, as judged by the attending physician, and included only prescription medications and not "over the counter" remedies. The decline over time in this measure was quite substantial, $M = 71.7$ versus $M = 5.8$, $t(24) = 2.94$, $p < .01$.

Finally, as an approximate measure of the most serious consequences of stress, the number of days on which subjects received psychotropic medications were counted. Only prescription medications whose primary use is for treatment of psychiatric symptoms were included. Although the use of such medications is, of course, only partially related to stress, there was a significant decrease from the start of the term, $M = 38.0$ versus $M = 3.6$, $t(24) = 2.35$, $p < .05$.

In sum, there were decreases during the term in stress-related medical symptomatology. It is unlikely that the differences resulted from changes in the willingness to use medical services generally, because there were no visible changes in other subcategories (e.g., requests for attention to accident-caused conditions or infections). Moreover, the evidence

here is quite consistent with the improvement in mood states presented above.

DISCUSSION

In several ways, the present results support and extend the findings of recent studies of coping and adaptation in prison. For example, the reduction in dysphoria over time after the very high levels at the beginning of the term has been documented by Zamble and Porporino (1988) and Toch and Adams (1989). The lack of change in a variety of specific behaviors is also consistent with previous results. It would appear that the beginning of the term induces considerable psychological discomfort but that the constancy of the prison environment leads to a slow and gradual amelioration. At the same time, the environment does not induce widespread behavior change, supporting the earlier characterization of imprisonment as a "behavioral deep freeze" (Zamble & Porporino, 1988).

However, perhaps the most striking overall result was the total absence of any evidence for general or widespread deteriorative effects. Subjects did not become social isolates inside of prison, and neither did they lose contact with the outside. Most did not sink into despair or rebellion, but rather their emotional states, health, and conduct in the institutions generally *improved* over time.

Some individuals showed maladaptive behavior patterns, and remained in maximum-security, even several years into their terms. A cross-sectional study of inmates in maximum-security at that time would have shown them to have more problems than a new cohort beginning their terms, because of the biasing effect of the selection process. However, given the longitudinal perspective available here, one can see that the cross-sectional conclusion would be erroneous. When we follow a group of men over time, we find much more evidence of improvement than of deterioration.

Despite the consistency of findings, a plausible ground for reservations is that this study included only three subjects with *extremely* long terms, such as those assigned for first-degree murder in Canada, that is, life with no possibility of parole before 25 years. If prisoners are subjected to such terms, where release is too far off for it to work as either a goal or an incentive, it is possible that they will suffer damage. The current study does not allow easy generalization to such long periods. Nevertheless, the present data, covering more than 7 years and including a comprehensive set of measures, provide strong discomfirmation for expectations of widespread deleterious effects from imprisonment for periods up to about a decade.

The current findings also shed some light on how men adapt under the circumstances of long-term imprisonment. Some of the most visible changes were in the area of socializing within prison. The majority of subjects largely withdrew from the diffuse social networks that are typical of inmate interactions. Instead, they spent much of their discretionary time in their cells, and when they did socialize, it was primarily with one or two close friends. Their socializing was centered more on these interactions or on relationships with people on the outside.

Changes were also evident in several other areas. Most subjects' activities seemed to be planned around long-term goals, and their thoughts were largely concerned with their lives after release. In effect, they sometimes seemed to be living within a world of their own, inside the prison but separate and apart from its ordinary discourse. Most of the men in this study created niches for themselves (Johnson, 1987; Toch, 1977), but their niches were often defined in terms of routines and behaviors, rather than physically. If their bodies were in prison, their cognitive focus was elsewhere.

As part of this process, they became more adaptive within the prison environment. They avoided the entanglements that result from involvement with other inmates, and they began to monitor, analyze, and control their own behavior better. As a result, they began to make progress through the system, albeit slowly. At some point, they would likely have entered a self-reinforcing cycle, where the improvement in conditions motivated continued work on monitoring and controlling their behavior. After some time in this cycle, they could realistically look forward to release. Thus, unlike short-term inmates, their motivation for self-improvement did not disappear.

One might therefore conclude that motivation is maintained much better for long-termers. However, it is not certain that motivation remained constant over the term, and there may have been a decrease in the middle, especially after the loss of appeals about 3 years into their terms (Palmer, 1984). The data may show only a recovery of motivation at the end of the term, as release became more salient. Some aspects of the data, for example the continuous pattern of educational enrollment, would argue against any phasic interpretation, but one cannot say for sure what occurred in the 5-year gap between measurements.

Still, one might ask why there were changes in behavior in the first place. Although any conclusions are only speculative at this time, it is plausible to argue that there were several factors working in concert. The first is simple maturation. It has frequently been argued that offenders are retarded in their social development and that their social behavior resembles that of adolescents. If this is so, then there is certainly room for maturational changes.

Even if there were no deficits, one would normally expect some developmental changes in a period as long as that studied here. Such changes could result from growth in adaptive abilities for the younger inmates, or from the loss of strength or energy for destructive behavior in older inmates (Toch & Adams, 1989); both would lead to reductions in maladaptive behavior in prison. Given the available evidence, it is difficult to judge the relative importance of these two types of effects, although it was the author's clinical impression that the most substantial changes during the term were among the younger subjects.

It might be argued that the changes seen here were entirely maturational and that their appearance in prison was incidental. However, our own previous evidence, with a sample of predominantly short-term inmates (Zamble & Porporino, 1988, 1990), showed very little evidence of growth. The present sample did not include an abnormally high proportion of younger inmates (who would show growth more than others) or older inmates (who would show loss of capabilities more than others). We are faced with the question of why maturational effects were visible in this study and not with prisoners serving shorter terms.

The most plausible explanation lies in the special conditions of long-term imprisonment. Unlike the very weak contingencies between behavior and consequences that the system presents to most prisoners, misbehavior really does result in tangible reductions in the quality of life for long-term prisoners. Even though the contingencies are only inconsistently enforced, over a period of years the institutional consequences of proscribed or disruptive behaviors are sure to be triggered. Although a short-term inmate may suffer punishments for misbehavior, the end is always in sight, and it is possible to drift through a term by annihilating a finite succession of minutes, that is, by "doing" time. In contrast, long-term inmates, and especially lifers, see an indefinitely long period in which even an unresponsive bureaucracy has time to take into account their (mis)behavior.

The most powerful contingency of all was undoubtedly the granting of release. Because release was not assured within any reasonable length of time, it had become a goal to direct subjects' behavior, and most oriented their thoughts and actions around this goal. They monitored and controlled their behavior more than previously, they planned and directed their actions toward events in the future, and they avoided behavior that might interfere with their prospects of release. During the course of the interview, they often explicitly discussed this orientation.

The subjects in this study were in for the long term and, consequently, were controlled by events far in the future. If our definition of mature behavior includes considering the consequences of one's actions, then we might say that they were led to some degree of maturity by their experiences in prison. As part of this process, they likely began to define themselves differently, that is, as persons living in prison rather than offenders doing time. The changes in goal orientation, self-perceptions, other cognitions, and the consequences of their behavior probably all interacted to produce the results seen here. Thus, the special conditions of imprisonment for long and indefinite periods may actually promote the development of more mature ways of coping and behaving.

Nevertheless, this hypothesized connection should not be seen as justification for the use of long-term imprisonment, for it is likely that greater changes could be produced much more quickly and less expensively by use of a treatment program explicitly focusing on changing cognitions and improving coping skills. Unfortunately, until prison systems acknowledge the superiority of effective treatment over passive custody, such comparisons remain to be tested.

REFERENCES

Andrews, D. A., & Wormith, J. S. (1983). *Criminal sentiments, criminological theory, and criminal behavior: A construct validation.* Unpublished manuscript, Carleton University, Ottawa.

Beck, A. T. (1967). *Depression: Clinical, experimental and theoretical aspects.* New York: Hoeber.

Beck, A. T., Weissman, D., Lester, D., & Trexler, L. (1974). The measurement of pessimism: The Hopelessness Scale. *Journal of Consulting and Clinical Psychology, 42,* 861-865.

Bolton, N., Smith, F. V., Heskin, K. J., & Banister, P. A. (1976). Psychological correlates of long-term imprisonment. *British Journal of Criminology, 16,* 38-47.

Bukstel, L. H., & Kilmann, P. R. (1980). Psychological effects of imprisonment on confined individuals. *Psychological Bulletin, 88,* 469-493.

Clemmer, D. (1958). *The prison community.* New York: Holt, Rinehart & Winston. (Original work published 1940)

Coopersmith, S. (1967). *The antecedents of self-esteem.* San Francisco: Freeman.

Farrington, D. P., Ohlin, L. E., & Wilson, J. Q. (1986). *Understanding and controlling crime: Toward a new research strategy.* New York: Springer-Verlag.

Flanagan, T. (1982). Lifers and long-termers: Doing big time. In R. Johnson & H. Toch (Eds.), *The pains of imprisonment* (pp. 115-128). Beverly Hills, CA: Sage.

Johnson, R. (1987). *Hard time: Understanding and reforming the prison.* Monterey, CA: Brooks/Cole.

Levenson, H. (1975). Multidimensional locus of control in prison inmates. *Journal of Applied Social Psychology, 5,* 342-347.

McKay, H. B., Jayewardene, C. H. S., & Reedie, P. B. (1977). *Report on the effects of long-term incarceration and a proposed strategy for future research.* Contract report for Ministry of the Solicitor General of Canada, Ottawa.

Palmer, W. R. T. (1984). Programming for long-term inmates: A new perspective. *Canadian Journal of Criminology, 26,* 439-457.

Porporino, F. J. (1983). *Coping behaviour in prison inmates: Description and correlates.* Unpublished doctoral dissertation, Queen's University, Kingston.

Rotter, J. (1966). Generalized expectancies of internal versus external control of reinforcement. *Psychological Monographs, 80* (No. 609).

Sapsford, R. J. (1978). Life-sentence prisoners: Psychological changes during sentence. *British Journal of Criminology, 18,* 128-145.

Sapsford, R. J. (1983). *Life-sentence prisoners: Reaction, response, and change.* Milton Keynes: Open University Press.

Spielberger, C. D., Gorsuch, R. L., & Lushene, R. E. (1970). *Manual for the State-Trait Anxiety Inventory.* Palo Alto, CA: Consulting Psychologists Press.

Thomas, C. W., & Peterson, D. M. (1977). *Prison organization and inmate subcultures.* Indianapolis, IN: Bobbs-Merrill.

Toch, H. (1977). *Living in prison: The ecology of survival.* New York: Macmillan.

Toch, H., & Adams, K. (1989). *Coping: Maladaptation in prisons.* New Brunswick, NJ: Transaction Books.

Zamble, E., & Porporino, F. J. (1988). *Coping, behavior, and adaptation in prison inmates.* New York: Springer-Verlag.

Zamble, E., & Porporino, F. J. (1990). Coping, imprisonment, and rehabilitation: Some data and their implications. *Criminal Justice and Behavior, 17,* 53-70.

Zamble, E., Porporino, F. J., & Kalotay, J. (1984). *An analysis of coping in prison inmates* (Programs Branch User Report No. 1984-77). Ottawa: Ministry of the Solicitor General of Canada.

15

The World of Prisoners' Wives

Laura T. Fishman

I get so mad when I look at how the TV stereotypes prisoners' wives. These movies that were done in the fifties really make me mad. They show the wives as playing one guy against another guy. They show the wives as either cheats or as illiterates who are browbeaten and cringe from their husbands. You never see the woman who makes it even though her husband is in prison. They're shown as either know-nothings or tramps. Every time I watch I get angry inside.

—A Prisoner's Wife.

Male criminality is a vital issue with which prisoners' wives struggle at home, with their children and parents, and in their communities. Wives must enter into painful interpersonal negotiations about what is or is not acceptable about their husbands' behavior. The purpose of these negotiations is to limit opportunities for encountering stigmatization and to normalize both their husbands and themselves.

Earlier research on wives of alcoholics and batterers has shown that wives are likely to hold a traditional view toward their roles as wives and mothers.[1] What has been learned about prisoners' wives fits well with what is known about "traditional" women who endure their marriages no matter how unsatisfactory they may be. They readily accept its permanence, the view that a "woman's place is in the home," that men ought to be the breadwinners, and the belief that males ought to be heads of their households. Their marital expectations are similar to those of the women

from similar social backgrounds: stable, conventional lifestyles. They want their husbands to work. They want material goods. They want companionship. Unfortunately, neither they nor their husbands have, as a rule, the kinds of skills that would enable them to pursue this kind of conventional lifestyle. Instead, they often find themselves living fast; fast living provides men with a means of avoiding the pressures and difficulties involved in settling down.

To cope with this contradiction, wives expected that through love and forbearance, they would be able to induce their men to settle down to a traditional and conventional lifestyle. In this context, accommodations served as attempts to normalize their husbands' behavior and prevent their getting into trouble with the law as well as to integrate their husbands into their households. Similar to spouses of prospective mental patients (see, e.g., Mayo, Havelock, & Simpson, 1971; Sampson, Messinger, & Towne, 1962; Yarrow, Clausen,

NOTE: Reprinted, with changes, from *Women at the Wall: A Study of Prisoners' Wives Doing Time on the Outside*, pp. 261-262, 268-277, by permission of the State University of New York Press. Copyright 1990 State University of New York.

& Robbins, 1955), these wives were reluctant to contact the police or social agencies even though they found their husbands' behavior intolerable. Instead, the majority of women believed that their husbands would get arrested eventually and anxiously awaited this event.

What is particularly interesting here is that, almost universally, it is *women* who must cope with *men's* problems. Throughout their lives, these women have been faced with difficulties arising from male criminality. These problems do not end when husbands are incarcerated. They do not simply vanish when the men disappear behind prison walls. Husbands continue to have a significant impact on their wives' daily lives which is as important as that generated by dramatic encounters with police, courts, and prisons. Prisoners' wives are not simply "separated" from their husbands—although they share similarities with others facing "crises of separation." They must also continually deal with the problems of minimizing opportunities for stigmatization, particularly in prison towns and in the various prisons. Old timers also often face hostility from their families, who feel betrayed by husbands' histories of imprisonment.

The accommodative strategies these wives adopt are those suggested by their own backgrounds and social groups. While the social pressures with which prisoners' wives must cope depend, in some measure, on whether or not they live in crime-tolerant communities, all wives have a sense that they are "different" from those around them. It is this sense of differentness that underlies their stance toward the larger social world and toward the criminalization process.

LIVING ALONE

Whether men are voluntarily or involuntarily separated from their families, their wives find that they must adjust to their husbands' physical absence. In order to make this adjustment successfully, wives must be willing to shift roles and take up many of their husbands' responsibilities. They must often also maintain their husbands' place in the family circle by correspondence, telephone calls, and visiting. Within this context, prisoners' wives must therefore be able to gain a measure of independence in making decisions. While en-

forced separation engenders hardships, it also seems to provide its own unique opportunities for women to begin playing a larger role in directing their own lives.

While most women experienced problems typical of those faced with enforced separation (social, emotional, and sexual deprivation, financial difficulties, and child management), a significant number also reported difficulty coming to terms with the prospective duration of the separation and a feeling of being, themselves, imprisoned. Although not widely discussed in the literature, this phenomenon is reminiscent of Swan's (1981) concept of "transfer of punishment." While some wives might have identified with their husbands' situations or felt that they themselves were being punished, it is also likely that some, in effect, created their own prisons by putting their lives "on hold" until their husbands could return.

STIGMATIZATION AND FEELINGS OF SHAME

The stages in the criminalization process—from arrest, to sentencing, incarceration and release—set up a series of changes in the roles these wives found themselves enacting: "wives of accused," "prisoners' wives," and finally "wives of ex-convicts." The current literature has primarily documented the extent to which stigma is displaced to wives enacting roles of "wives of accused" and of prisoners. It has been assumed that whenever wives fill these roles they become stigmatized unless they live in crime-familiar communities. The present study supports earlier research findings that wives who reside in crime-familiar communities do not appear to encounter stigmatizing situations (Koenig & Gariepy, 1985; Schneller, 1978; Schwartz & Weintraub, 1974). However, the wives in this study reported numerous stigmatizing situations when they lived in prison towns.

These results suggest that at the time of their husbands' arrest and initial incarceration, shame and stigmatization were not central but rather situational issues in wives' lives. They were more likely to worry about the possibility of stigmatization within their communities than actually to experience it. Feelings of shame appeared to dissipate quite rapidly, since these women had more pressing concerns to handle (e.g., their husbands' legal affairs, their own lives, their households, and their children).

Wives' perceptions of stigmatization when dealing with the prison systems were found to be of crucial importance. Their accounts revealed that the extent to which they felt shamed and discredited varied with the kinds of house rules prisons established for visiting. Responses of prison guards were perceived to be stigmatizing by most wives.

The findings presented here, therefore, extend Goffman's (1961) observation that, upon admission to a total institution, inmates are subjected to a series of abasements, degradations, humiliations, and profanations of their selves. Wives, too, are subjected to mortification by such contaminative exposure as forced interpersonal contact with other prisoners' wives, searching of their possessions, strip searches, closely supervised visits, and so forth. Their self-respect was assaulted whenever they interacted with prison guards who categorized wives as "the good wife" or as "the whore," and who discriminated among them on this basis, making derogatory statements, or treating them in a disrespectful manner. House rules for visiting and the treatment by prison staff were perceived as ever-present reminders that wives shared their husbands' stigmatized status.

The findings add to a growing literature that argues that imprisonment of husbands had deleterious effects on the wives. On the basis of the present study, it is concluded that prison policies believed functional for the institution can have dysfunctional consequences for prisoners' wives. Specific prison policies can set the wives up for encounters that they find extremely distasteful. For instance, the policy permitting prisoners to visit and maintain contacts with their wives includes "house" rules for visiting that restrict the women's behavior. The wives claimed that these rules and regulations created situations in which they felt personally diminished. Even the policy permitting prisoners to have "legal goods" made wives vulnerable to stigmatizing and punitive encounters with prison personnel.

Wives came to believe that they were treated as criminals and punished for wanting to see their husbands in order to reaffirm their marital ties. If one can assume that visits serve to preserve prisoners' marital ties, then those security measures that include demeaning or degrading actions should be closely examined.

Such security measures do not, according to many wives, encourage families to maintain close ties but inadvertently work against the family keeping close contact with its imprisoned member.

Although stigmatization was not central to their lives, wives attempted to insulate themselves from it by controlling information about their husbands' situation, by employing accommodative strategies to reduce its effects or turn them aside, and by participating in a normal round of life. Wives also actively avoided labelling themselves as "wives of accuseds" and "wives of prisoners." They had a stake in maintaining their identities as "normal" in order to sustain their relations with others and to reinforce their own notions that they are "ordinary" wives and mothers. Participating in a conventional lifestyle not only provided a sense of normalcy, but allowed them to resist stigmatization. Other wives resisted the application of stigmatizing labels by simply terminating their affiliation with their officially-labeled husbands and dropping out completely. Those not committed to being prisoners' wives resisted learning how to make the psychic adjustments needed to perform this role.

LARGER IMPACT OF PRISON ON WIVES' LIVES

Recent research suggests that prison systems may not be as closed as previously assumed. Many studies have specifically focused on the extent to which prisoners are able to maintain relationships with their families on the outside. Some attention, although fragmentary, has been given to the kinds of contacts that prisoners maintain with their wives.

The findings presented here, however, elaborate upon these earlier research findings. The present research has specifically examined the role played by patterns of interaction—such as courtship, business arrangements, sharing household decisions, and performing personal services—during prison visiting. For instance, prison romances and renewed courtships flourished as a result of prison policies allowing women to perform personal services for their men and to deliver approved material goods and/or contraband to them. Both forms of interaction provided the husbands with opportunities to enact dominant roles, while the women could defer. These accounts also revealed that these same patterns of interaction could produce their own stresses and strains. Courting could erupt into arguments revolving around husbands' jealousies and anxieties about their wives' infidelity or their decision to limit the supply of contraband or other goods they delivered to the prison.

Several investigators have suggested that maintaining family ties contributes positively to successful rehabilitation (Homer, 1979; Holt & Miller, 1972; Irwin, 1970; Glaser, 1969). Accordingly, many prison systems have established visiting policies that encourage ties with family and friends. However, the findings reported here suggest that interactions between inmates and their wives are perhaps not optimal. Constant surveillance and frequent disruptions may inhibit all but superficial communication. Also, these interactional patterns recounted by the wives suggest that an air of idealistic romanticism pervades these visits. Conversations rarely included realistic appraisals and plans for the future.

The wives also had considerable contact with their husbands through telephone conversations and home visits, modes of communication that substantially alleviated some of the difficulties associated with separation. While telephone conversations often strengthened marital ties, home visits even more dramatically improved family morale, since they were intensely and almost entirely pleasurable. In particular, they served to promote feelings of well-being for both husbands and wives, reinforcing marital and family commitments. Telephone calls and visitation further provided the wives with a respite from their own sense of imprisonment.

Despite the obvious benefits of such communication, it should not be overlooked that, more often than not, men used telephone contacts to place restrictions on their wives, to make demands and to maintain their authority and dominance. Also, a significant proportion of these men used the telephone to check up, periodically and unpredictably, on their wives' activities. In response, the wives reported that they had no lives of their own and were forced to create "prisons" for themselves.

It should also be noted that, despite the several positive aspects of home visits, these furloughs did not appear to accomplish their intended function as dress rehearsals for later reintroduction into the community, with its attendant duties and responsibilities. On the contrary, husbands were carefully shielded, by their wives, from domestic pressures, stresses, demands, and responsibilities. Moreover, the nature of such visits might well have perpetuated idealized or unrealistic expectations of how life together would be in the future.

The current literature indicates that prisoners' attitudinal and behavioral changes are more closely related to men's adaption to the prison environment than to how they perform once they have been released (see Ekland-Olsen, Supancic, Campbell, & Lenihan, 1983; Irwin, 1970). It is significant that the wives believed that their husbands had undergone sufficient attitudinal and behavioral changes to be released and to lead conventional lives. Prison visiting was a time when the wives searched for clues indicating significant behavioral and attitudinal change. The findings suggest that prison, an institution that emphasizes punishment, unintentionally encourages men to be contrite and repentant, to make promises never to get into trouble again and to make future plans with their wives for release and renewal. In turn, most wives believe that these promises are viable, unaware that they have been made in response to prison life, and not as a consequence of a realistic appraisal of what the men could achieve later. Certainly, the fact of imprisonment makes it impossible for husbands to engage in criminal activities which had been the root of many domestic quarrels on the outside. In the absence of such conflict-producing episodes, it makes sense that relations between the spouses would be less strained and that wives would be more willing to believe that their husbands had reformed. However, the reports of wives whose husbands had been imprisoned previously (old timers) make it clear that such perceptions were frequently naive or idealistic. Old timers were far less likely than neophytes to believe that their husbands had truly reformed and would lead conventional lives upon their release.

MALE CRIMINALITY, INVOLUNTARY SEPARATION, AND POVERTY

In many respects, the experiences these prisoners' wives encountered during involuntary separation parallel those of single mothers who live at the edge of subsistence. Prisoners' wives share many experiences with women whose husbands are absent due to separation, desertion, divorce, and so forth.[2] The women interviewed recounted numerous problems centered around finances, loneliness, anxiety and stress, stigmatization, and child management. Rather than feeling "liberated," they were emotionally and socially isolated, as well as overloaded with demands on their time and energy.

Some wives also derived real benefits from their husbands' imprisonment. These women mentioned release from marital disruptions and its impact on their roles as wives and mothers, feelings of a sense of personal autonomy, and increased control over their lives, household finances, and children. Many reported that they felt increasingly competent to cope, as wives and mothers, with difficult circumstances.

Most wives revealed that financial insecurity and hardships were not unfamiliar to them. Most did not experience a drop into poverty upon their husbands' removal from their households, although this phenomenon was reported by square janes. Rather, most of the wives had lived at the edge of subsistence during their growing years and their marriages simply meant a continuation of persistent financial hardships. Within this segment of the population of poor, single mothers, transition in family status (i.e., their husbands' enforced separation from their households) appeared to have little bearing on their continuing impoverishment. The observation that a fundamental cause of poverty among female-headed households is due to familial changes (e.g., divorce, widowhood, etc.) perhaps is more relevant for middle-income white women than lower-income white women.[3]

The literature on the poverty of women offers a related and important factor to explain the increasing poverty among female-headed households: the male flight from responsibility. Ehrenrich (1983) claims that the majority of men who are not living with their wives and children have abdicated their familial responsibilities. Study upon study (see, e.g., Anderson-Khleif, 1982; Arendell, 1986; Hewlett, 1986; Nazzari, 1980; Pearce, 1978; Rodgers, 1986; Sidel, 1986; Stallard, 1983; Weitzman, 1985) reveal that most divorced men neither financially support nor directly care for their children after separation or divorce. There is little doubt that this analysis of women and poverty

is valid, but it is not the whole story. Although Ehrenrich and others speak of the males' abdication of family responsibility after divorce, the present research suggests that this abdication, for at least this segment of the American population, occurs during the early years of marriage.

According to wives' accounts, their husbands' pursuit of a fast-living lifestyle and criminal escapades can be equated with an abdication of familial responsibility. They also reported that prior to arrest and imprisonment their men further abdicated their responsibility by being unemployed or intermittently employed and thus contributing little income to their households. In response, wives reported that they received some form of governmental assistance and/or participated in some form of quasi-illegal and/or illegal activities in order to make ends meet.

Furthermore, the findings strongly suggest that imprisonment is an important family structural change that has been ignored by literature. Wives' accounts showed that imprisonment inadvertently kept most wives at the edge of subsistence while legitimating the male flight from economic support of their wives and children. Imprisonment thus reinforced male irresponsibility. Most women in the study believed that their incarcerated husbands did not suffer the hardships that characterized their own lives; their husbands did not have to worry about children or how the bills were going to be paid, or the food placed on the tables. They had many and sometimes more of the comforts of living than the wives and children. They had the time and energy to pursue various personal interests and activities. And finally, unlike their wives, the prisoners had constant companionship. The gap between the experiences of these women and their husbands continued to widen as the years passed.

Imprisonment thus sets men up to persist in their flight from commitment insofar as men who are paroled from Vermont prisons are quite likely to reencounter unemployment, underemployment and life at the margins of society. It is not surprising that a significant number of paroled men become further entrenched in such irresponsible behavior as participation in the cycle of unemployment, fast-living and criminal activities.

Prisoners' wives reported that such hardships as increased parenting responsibilities, providing their incarcerated husbands with material goods, the financial costs of communicating with their incarcerated husbands, and loneliness created a socioemotional impoverishment directly related to familial structural change that occurred after their husbands' imprisonment. Nevertheless, although most women found themselves carrying burdens that they expected their husbands to assume, they were strongly committed to their marriages. Several factors emerge from the wives' accounts that provide some important insights into the wives' marital commitments.

These wives remained in their marriages because they had few other alternatives, particularly if they had children. Most of the women who considered dissolving their marriages reported that, if they did so, they would remain hopelessly impoverished. They usually had few financial resources, few marketable skills, and little community or family support to lift themselves out of poverty.

Many wives maintained the belief that they would, some day, be taken care of by their men and thus did not need to prepare themselves to be fully independent. They believed that their husbands should and would support the family financially and that their own equally important contribution should center around caretaking.

During involuntary separation many wives gained insight into the actual inequalities of the gender roles in the family. However, this did not encourage them to dissolve their marriages. Wives of prisoners knew that they had more to lose economically and emotionally through divorce and thus they had more at stake in marriage. Wives reported that these burdens—especially the financial burdens—they carried during imprisonment were heavy and far outweighed any benefits that they might have gained from the temporary separation from their husbands. These insights and experiences reinforced their determination to establish stable and conventional lifestyles for themselves and their children, no matter what the costs. Whatever conventionality they achieved during this period, however, was perceived as temporary. Most wives believed that such a lifestyle could only be secured upon their husbands' release from prison and subsequent employment. Increasingly, their husbands' return seemed attractive to these women because it might provide a more secure economic foundation for a con-

ventional lifestyle. In this sense, then, imprisonment inadvertently functions to keep married women "in their place"; that is, married.[4]

Nevertheless, the extent to which the women in the study population were resistant to extricating themselves from their marriages was startling. These women, therefore, challenge the public image of prisoners' wives as women who walk out on their husbands the first time they get arrested and imprisoned. The accounts of these women also contradict the public image of prisoners' wives either as stoic women who passively and helplessly stand by their troublesome husbands, or as fast livers. Rather, they are seen as traditional wives who actively manipulated their environments, continuously attempting to establish stable conventional lives for themselves. In so doing, they displayed both a remarkable variety and similarity of coping strategies.

Throughout this book, an attempt has been made to explain, illuminate, and generally make sense of the careers of prisoners' wives as they do their own time on the "outside." The women who participated in this study wanted to be a part of it in order to "tell it like it is" to people who would come to know exactly who they were—and the texture of their struggles.

NOTES

1. The following investigators point out that battered wives tend to be traditional women who have adopted the roles of wives and mothers as primary identities. Thus even when they are gainfully employed, they are strongly motivated to succeed in their domestic roles. Most battered women do remain economically dependent on their husbands, a dependency that provides a strong motivation to cope with violence: Ferraro and Johnson (1983), Dobash and Dobash (1979), and Walker (1979).

2. For an extensive documentation of the hardships wives encounter due to husband absence, see the more current literature: Arendell (1986), Berman and Turk (1981), and Weiss (1979).

3. Claude (1986) makes a similar observation in her discussion of the impoverishment of black women. She suggests that for black women poverty is often independent of family patterns. Given this context, there does not appear to be any significant increase in the poverty of black women when they assume the status of female head of their households. They are likely to be poor before a change puts them into a female-headed household. Claude concludes that the feminization of poverty fails to

take into account that the experiences of lower-class black women are somewhat different from those of middle-income white women.

4. A similar observation is made by Arendell (1986). She observed that divorced women were in agreement that any satisfactions that they derived from their status as divorcees paled in comparison to the stress caused by the emotional and economic effects of divorce. She then draws the conclusions that divorced women are more likely to look to remarriage than to themselves if they want to achieve secure lives for themselves and their children.

REFERENCES

Anderson-Khleif, S. (1982). *Divorced but not disastrous: How to improve the ties between single-parent mothers, divorced fathers, and the children.* Englewood Cliffs, NJ: Prentice Hall.

Arendell, T. (1986). *Mothers and divorce: Legal, economic, and social dilemmas.* Berkeley: University of California Press.

Berman, W. H., & Turk, D. C. (1981). Adaptation to divorce: Problems and coping strategies. *Journal of Marriage and the Family, 43,* 179-189.

Claude, J. (1986). Poverty patterns for black men and women. *The Black Scholar, 17,* 20-23.

Dobash, R. E., & Dobash, R. (1979). *Violence against wives: A case against the patriarchy.* New York: Free Press.

Ekland-Olsen, S., Supancic, M., Campbell, J., & Lenihan, K. (1983). Postrelease depression and the importance of familial support. *Criminology, 21,* 253-274.

Ehrenrich, B. (1983). *The hearts of men: American dreams and the flight from commitment.* Garden City, NY: Anchor.

Ferraro, K., & Johnson, J. (1983). How women experience battering: The process of victimization. *Social Problems, 30,* 325-335.

Glaser, D. (1969). *The effectiveness of a prison and parole system.* New York: Bobbs-Merrill.

Goffman, E. (1961). *Asylums: Essays on the social situation of mental patients and other inmates.* Garden City, NY: Doubleday.

Hewlett, S. A. (1986). *A lesser life: The myth of women's liberation in America.* New York: Warner Communications.

Holt, N., & Miller, D. (1972). *Explorations in inmate-family relations.* Sacramento: Department of Corrections Research Division.

Homer, E. L. (1979). Inmate-families ties—Desirable but difficult. *Federal Probation, 43,* 47-52.

Irwin, J. (1970). *The felon.* Englewood Cliffs, NJ: Prentice Hall.

Jackson, J. (1954). The adjustment of the family to the crisis of alcoholism. *Quarterly Journal of Studies on Alcohol, 15,* 562-586.

Koenig, C., & Gariepy, L. (1985). *Life on the outside: A report on the experiences of the families of offenders from the perspective of the wives of offenders.* Chilliwack, BC: Chilliwack Community Services.

Mayo, C., Havelock, R., & Simpson, D. L. (1971). Attitudes towards mental illness among psychiatric patients and their wives. *Journal of Clinical Psychology, 27,* 128-132.

Nazzari, M. (1980). The significance of present-day changes in the institution of marriage. *Review of Radical Political Economics, 12,* 63-75.

Pearce, D. (1978). The feminization of poverty: Women, work, and welfare. *The Urban and Social Change Review, 11,* 28-36.

Rodgers, H. R., Jr. (1986). *Poor women, poor families.* New York: M. E. Sharp.

Sampson, H., Messinger, S., & Towne, R. D. (1962). Family processes and becoming a mental patient. *American Journal of Sociology, 68,* 88-98.

Schneller, D. P. (1978). *The prisoner's family: A study of the effects of imprisonment on the families of prisoners.* San Francisco: R. and E. Research Associates.

Schwartz, M. C., & Weintraub, J. F. (1974). The prisoner's wife: A study in crisis. *Federal Probation, 38,* 20-26.

Sidel, R. (1986). *Women and children last—The plight of poor women in affluent America.* New York: Viking.

Stallard, K., et al. (1983). *When mothers go to jail.* Lexington, MA: Lexington Books.

Swan, L. A. (1981). *Families of black prisoners: Survival and progress.* Boston: G. K. Hall.

Walker, L. (1979). *The battered women.* New York: Harper & Row.

Weiss, R. S. (1979). *Going it alone: The family life and social situation of the single parent.* New York: Basic Books.

Weitzman, L. (1985). *The divorce revolution: The unexpected social and economic consequences for women and children in America.* New York: Free Press.

Yarrow, M. R., Clausen, J. A., & Robbins, P. R. (1955). The social meaning of mental illness. *Journal of Social Issues, 11,* 6-10.

PART FIVE

■ Correctional Responses and
the Management of Long-Term Prisoners

16

The Good Old Days in the Joint

Hans Toch

Like other senior citizens, long-term inmates like to indulge in reminiscences. Such inmates tell us that prison have become jungles populated by unprincipled, predatory "punks" who are at best tactless and at worst violent. In former days, they say, convicts respected each other, "kept their hands out of your pockets," and did their time with discretion. Guards were also dependable and basically nonintrusive; some guards treated you "very fairly," others kept their distance.

These comparisons of the status quo to the "good old days" parallel chronologies by sophisticated observers of prisons (e.g., Irwin, 1970, 1980) but must nevertheless be accepted with caution. One problem is that the stories recur over decades of research, which suggests that one generation's stability becomes another's chaos, and vice versa. Second, the stories are similar to those of inmates in other sorts of institutions. For example, graduate schools tend to be recalled as congenial, and mentors as wise. Mentors, in turn, tended to relay experiences involving rigorous-but-scintillating apprenticeships.

A common denominator in such accounts is that the narrator's memory has gilded attributes he or she currently values. Progenitors gain stature in ways we now appreciate. Pris-

ons offer commodities—structure and privacy —of the kind older inmates like (Toch, 1977). Younger inmates (including old inmates when young) have predilections that may be quite different. The "young punk" in the senior citizen's story could be the senior citizen when he was carefree and aggressive, loud and invasive.

A sanitized past is also a type of history that is useful to inmates. For one, it helps to validate grievances. When one says "things are lousy but have been improving" this takes the steam out of condemnations. "Prisons were okay, but now they stink" invites sympathy. We expect inmates to hate prisons, because we know that prisons are punitive. But if prisons have always been punitive, it is hard to see what inmates have to complain about at any point in the sequence. Only "things have been getting worse" can attract interest to complaints.

Another contention we find in senior citizen accounts is the refrain, "I am an Old Convict." When an inmate tells us this he means, "I am a product of the system," or "prison has made me what I am." If we believe the inmate's charge, we are invited to see prisons as emasculating people (Cohen & Taylor, 1972), making them violent (Abbott, 1981), or teaching them crime (Bondeson, 1989). We may be

AUTHOR'S NOTE: The author is Distinguished Professor, School of Criminal Justice, University at Albany, State University of New York.
NOTE: Reprinted from *The Prison Journal*, Vol. 80, No. 1, Spring/Summer 1990, pp. 1-8. Copyright 1990 by Sage Publications, Inc.

impressed because an inmate has declared himself emasculated, violent, or criminal, which looks disarmingly self-effacing. We forget that the attribution in the statement also makes the inmate not responsible for his conduct.

Prisoner accounts may be valid despite such facts, but over time composite reminiscences become suspect, because the trend they depict (cumulatively downhill) is implausible. Moreover, when we accept retrospectives that say "prisons are getting worse" and others that say "I used to be decent and normal, but prison has warped me," we are asked to abandon hope for prisons. For if prisons harm people, they harm more people more seriously if they get worse.

IS IT PRISONS THAT GET WORSE, OR PRISONERS?

To make sense of prisoners' accounts, we must ask where change would occur, if it occurred. When some people say "the prison" they mean the criminal justice system in which prisons are embedded. For others (e.g., DiIulio, 1987), prison means correctional administrators and their philosophy of management. But for prisoners, prison means prison. It means mostly (1) the amount of time to be served and (2) the people with whom one must live while serving time. Other attributes of prison—food and accommodations, services and programs, guards and civilians—also matter, but become a more or less taken-for-granted backdrop of institutional life.

To say "prisons are worse than they used to be" implies that doing time is getting harder and sentences feel longer. It means that the inmates one is surrounded by are more difficult to deal with. But if one thinks of oneself as being harmed, one may forget the other side of the picture, which is that one is part of someone else's environment.

While inmates may think of themselves as harmless, they know that other convicts are the critical feature of their environment. However, some observers find this view unappealing because they want something other than prisoners to blame for prison conditions. And it would weaken conspiracy theories even further to assume that prisons can feel bad if inmates who do the feeling have changed while the prison has stayed the same.

THE PRISON CRISIS

Unfortunately, today the accounts of veteran inmates ring true. Today's prisons are crowded and this makes them worse. We see this change from an inmate-centered perspective because crowding increases the chances for inmates to infringe on each other, which means that doing time would be harder—especially for older inmates, because they are easily infringed upon. (Crowding cuts into programs as well, but older inmates are less apt to cite this fact than younger inmates who feel they lack education and skills.)

It also appears as if the ability of prison staff to control prisoners is diminished in disquieting ways. This impression is supported by a variety of facts, such as the proliferation of gang violence in some of our prisons (Jacobs, 1977), the increased use of administrative segregation (including maxi-maxi settings) and of protective segregation, allegations of endemic drug traffic, and so forth. Such developments make it inviting to agree with senior citizens that prisons must be populated by a new breed of convict, who is hard to control, impairs the stability of prisons, and contaminates the environment.

Destabilizing attributes of inmates are hard to define, but it is again younger inmates who would possess these attributes to a greater extent than older inmates. This means that as prison populations get younger, older inmates should find prisons even more difficult to deal with, and eventually, so should rambunctious younger inmates. Another inmate background variable that could play a similar role is past institutional history, because offenders who have grown up in reformatories might tend to thrive on the stuff of prison underworlds. The well-publicized influx of drug offenders, who provide a market for intoxicants, would also benefit convict rackets.

More stringent sentencing practices contribute to crowding, but the significance of the trend for prison milieus is not obvious. Though long-term inmates are notoriously well behaved (Flanagan, 1983), this might change if inmates with long sentences happen to be young offenders with juvenile records and reformatory confinement.

There are other complexities we must consider as we think about what makes prisons worse. Some trends run two ways rather than unidirectionally. For example, crowding may breed violence (Paulus, 1988), but violence makes a prison feel more crowded (Ellis, 1984). Inmates who act out invite punitiveness, but the contrary also holds, that is, custody-orientation lowers punishment thresholds. Over time, the result can be that guards and inmates play "cops and robbers," and the game keeps escalating. Inmate violence also spawns cycles. Some conflicts lead to fights; some fights spark new conflicts; and the losers—or losers' friends—retaliate.

RESILIENCE AND PERCEPTIONS

The most germane set of complexities with respect to inmates-as-environment relates to the checkered nature of influences and responses to influences by different prisoners. We mentioned that older inmates prefer different types of prison from younger inmates. A prison that is a good place to do time for senior citizens would bore younger inmates. A prison that is lively enough for the young is much worse: It shows that one group of inmates is capable of destroying the milieu of another group by creating an environment satisfactory to itself.

In other words, some inmates have strong impacts on other inmates, but such impacts are not symmetrical, meaning that some groups can harm other groups more than they can be harmed in turn. A "bad" prison from an outsider's perspective is a prison in which the benefits derived by some are outweighed by the harm they do to others. But what is a "bad" prison from an insider's perspective depends on which side of the fence one is on.

Three facts are relevant to the prisoners' experience of degenerating prisons:

1. One fact is that the more taxed a person is by his environment, the more apt he may be to see that environment as "bad." The more resilient the person, the less jaundiced his perspective is likely to be.

2. Given a constant environment (no change), increased resilience may inspire a perception of "improvement," but lessened capacity to cope may translate into the conviction that "things are getting worse."

This means that as we learn to cope, we reinterpret our failures and blunders as incur-

sions by the setting in which we learn. A summary statement such as "the place was tough but it loosened up, and now things are fine," suggests an apprenticeship that has been completed. "Things were really rough for a while" denotes a crisis, and it is not clear whether the blame lies with us, or the world.

This gets us to our third fact, which is that all of us shape our environments while we experience them. Sometimes we do a lot of shaping, but at other times we come to benefit (or suffer) from the shaping of others. Transitions from shaper to shapee roles are often not perceived but can be attributed to the environment, as in the case of long-term inmates. We know—but the inmates do not—that:

a. Young long-termers at the inception of their sentence are among the most troublesome inmates in the prison;

b. Old long-termers in the late stages of their sentence are among the best-behaved prisoners; and

c. These two groups are often the same people at two points in time.

TRACKING ENVIRONMENTAL CONGRUENCE AND DISCORDANCE

As we look at the same people over time, we can see junctures at which the settings in which the people live "fit" them better than at other times. By "fit" we can mean many things, including a fit between aptitudes or skills and the challenges that settings pose. When we get better at negotiating life, we need settings that grow with us, and when we decline, we need a lowering of the pressures that we face. It may be true that when the going gets tough, the tough get going, but it is also true that under the same circumstances the nontough often get hurt.

A second point has to do with the fact that settings do consist of people—meaning that in social environments such as prisons, one group is the milieu in which another group functions. The tough who "get going" may be the milieu of the nontough who get shouldered aside, and suffer in consequence. A disjuncture or mismatch would be a situation in which one group thwarts another group's goals, or becomes victimized by them. One aspect of this mismatch is experienced as a "destructive milieu" and the other as a feast. The two perceptions, of course, come hand in hand, depending on the source of the assessment. The scenario of the fox in the henhouse spells Armageddon for hens and temptation for the fox.

A third point is that resilience and vulnerability may evolve or not evolve. Given two tough groups, the first can stay tough and the other not, creating a mismatch over time. The same mismatch can be created where one group is a succession of toughs or tough cohorts that come and go, while the second is a group that starts tough but mellows and ripens into victimhood. This fate typically befalls our long-term inmates. Such offenders often start out surrounded by young short-term inmates and continue to be surrounded by them (or their successors) as they age. This process starts as a "match" and becomes a "mismatch" over time. This contingency is even more strongly the case where resilient inmates increase in resilience (i.e., get tougher) and vulnerable inmates gain vulnerability (get nontougher), as is likely to occur where "weakness" feeds on predation in prisons.

This victimization sequence is very worrisome, and its relevance is obvious to administrators. But less horrendous scenarios are also relevant, in that they can have long-term impact. For example:

1. The level of challenges in an educational program may be pegged to fast learners and leave slow learners behind.
2. Treatment may be aimed at "hard nuts" but may frustrate the progress of those who recover more quickly.
3. Long-term punishment may cause inmates to make serious resolves to reform, but confinement may persist beyond the juncture where resolves can take hold.

Inmates may change at rates faster or slower than do responses to the changes in the inmates. Worse still, no response may occur at all, or responses may occur in directions opposite to those that are desirable.

INMATE CLASSIFICATION

What do these ruminations about change have to do with the management of prisons and the handling of long-term confinees? Principally, these concerns have to do with the classification process. Classification viewed in this way can be translated to mean promoting matches between prisoners and prison settings, or avoiding mismatches between them (Toch, 1977). In general terms, this perspective leads to recommendations such as the following:

1. Classification analysts must be sensitive to any junctures at which mismatches between inmate needs and prison resources have occurred, and to junctures at which inmates appear well matched with settings. Such knowledge must be cumulated across inmates, settings, and classification analysts.

This means that classification would become a science if we start pooling knowledge instead of thinking about the work classifiers do as specific to the inmates they are classifying and the settings they are classifying them into (Wright, 1987).

2. Classification must consider not only the shape of the inmate assigned but that of the other inmates in the setting in which the inmate is placed. The goal must be to ensure that strengths and weaknesses of the inmates are evenly matched.

It is fortunate that at least one attribute of settings is easy to compile, and this consists of the sum of individual classifications of inmates in the settings who compose one another's milieu. This can be done, ideally, where classifiers are assigned to specific settings, as in unit management (Glaser, 1964). One could add, of course, that:

3. The *mix* of people in a setting is a particularly crucial variable, which is susceptible to classification and manipulation.

The point here is to find "mixes" that produce some desirable ends, such as surrounding wilder inmates with more mature inmates who may sober them up (Mabli, Holley, Patrick, & Walls, 1979). Where mixes produce undesirable ends—such as would be the case with too many wilder inmates—they can be adjusted. For example:

4. Classification can be used to encourage out-migration of inmates who have become vulnerable to peer encroachment, or have developed the capacity to encroach on their peers, until an acceptable inmate "mix" is attained.

CLASSIFICATION OVER TIME

A different set of prescriptions emerges when we consider the careers of individual inmates over time. The first proposition would be that:

1. Classification might be a cross-sectional process with short-term inmates, but it must be repeated over time with long-termers, whose changing vulnerabilities one must gauge.

Another way of saying this is that:

2. Static offender attributes have to be superseded as classification criteria where they are uncorrelatable with personal change, as they are among most long-term offenders.

And that, instead:

3. Classification adjustments must be made for inmates who experience increases or decreases in (a) capabilities or coping competence and (b) vulnerability or coping deficits.

The goal of this process would be to adjust environmental challenges or pressures so that they keep rough pace with changes in the inmate. An inmate who temporarily undergoes a personal crisis, for example, could be sequestered in a low-pressure setting for a short time (Toch, 1975). An inmate who has acquired new skills (say, through vocational training) could be assigned work in which the skills are utilized. The point being that:

4. Changes of assignment for an inmate should have something to do with changes in the inmate, so that stability

of experience becomes an option with accommodation to emerging needs.

LONG-TERM INMATES AS CLASSIFICATION TARGETS

I have implied that long-term inmates could be classified and dealt with differently at different stages of their sentence. A young inmate could be grouped with young short-term prisoners, rather than with long-term inmates in the twilight of their careers. This does not mean, of course, that the inmate's length of term is irrelevant. Sentence length is relevant but has different connotations at different junctures of a career. For example, a long-term inmate when he first arrives in prison must invariably deal with the prospect of his term. He may do so by appealing his case, expressing rage, immersing himself in day-by-day living, denial (pretending his sentence does not exist), or becoming depressed. These adjustment strategies each have different implications for the programming of the inmates.

The same point holds throughout the prisoner's term. The inmate at the end of his sentence, for example, may have to digest problems such as those of significant others who are no longer significant, neighborhoods that have become unfamiliar, and strange (if any) job prospects. The inmate at this stage of his career needs prerelease assistance, but such assistance must be different from that provided to short-term prisoners, who have less drastic adjustment problems and return to a world with which they are familiar.

These are short-term classification concerns, in that they relate to discrete stages of the long-termer's sentence. But to respond to a long prison career in stage-by-stage fashion is like baking a pie one slice at a time. Life is a continuum, and one must make any assignment with one eye on the person's previous assignment and the other on the next step the person might take.

How long a view one can afford, of course, hinges on one's ability to predict and control changes. Two-stage sequences can always be planned by making Stage 2 contingent on responses to Stage 1. One typically tells an inmate, "When you get the equivalency diploma, you can take college courses," or "When you handle this setting, we can try you in population." Longer projections are riskier and iffier, and they become increasingly hypothetical the longer they extend. Long-term projections risk being overly optimistic (e.g., "After you finish the remedial education course, you go to high school, college, graduate school, and get a Ph.D. before you get out"), or they can be insufficiently dynamic ("After 5 or 10 years as porter, you might try stamping license plates for a change of pace, and then . . .").

The object of the game of classification is to sequence prisoner assignments so that experiences dovetail and build on each other. We must ask, "How does this assignment enable the person to do more or better at something he values?" or "How does this prevent or retard incapacitation?" If possible, each step the inmate takes should yield improvement or escape from anticipated harm. We must recall that a long sentence is an in-house career for the inmate, and that the dictionary defines a career as the "pursuit of consecutive progressive achievement." The fact that a career must be an institutional career should not deprive it of the potential for yielding increments of status and personal improvement.

Career planning is essential and it must involve the inmate himself in reviewing his short-term and longer-term options. The deployment of contracting between inmates and staff is attractive, but contracting cannot be used to cover long prison terms. In thinking about long prison terms, one must expect to accommodate changes, including changes in the inmate's goals and perspective. Career moves occur among persons in the free world after thoughtful reviews. They can similarly occur in prison, and they can "dead-end" vocational or educational sequences in midsentence. Classification must be flexible at such junctures, and it must assist the inmate to evolve new sets of plans. Classification can in fact promote reassessments and it can invite the inmate to review his life from time to time. It would make sense, for example, to trichotomize long prison sentences into opening games, mid games, and end games, and to try to schedule review-planning sessions at the inception of each segment.

ENGINEERING
THE SOCIAL ENVIRONMENT

Classification must be concerned not only with what the inmate does but also with whom

he does it, and with whom he lives while he does it. This aspect of classification ostensibly has no counterpart in the free world, where we select cohabitants, and sometimes divorce them. But in the free world cohabitants can be tangibly victimized, and interventions (such as police action) may separate victims (e.g., spouses or children) from aggressors. Counseling is also used in the free world to address incompatibilities and can be similarly used in prisons.

What makes prisons unique is that they assign people to live with each other and thereby engineer environments, including settings in which exploitation and conflicts arise. This assignment process confers the obligation on authorities to monitor the outcome of groupings, particularly for socially disadvantaged members of the community. Where social disadvantages change over time, monitoring must occur over time, and because one man's advantage is another's disadvantage, monitoring presupposes not only the classification of some inmates with respect to other inmates but also their reclassification over time.

We started with the point that long-term inmates can become disadvantaged in mainline settings, where younger prisoners set the tone. This contingency can be accommodated by controlling the mix in such settings (Mabli et al., 1979), but at some junctures the strategy may not suffice, because veteran inmates can no longer tolerate the stimulation levels of mixed-age groups and need a lower-pressure setting, such as one for victim-prone or elderly inmates.

Unit-managed prisons are another solution because they permit us to implement more refined classification systems aiming at compatible inmate groups, compatible programming, and congruent staffing (Levinson & Gerard, 1973). One assumption in unit management is that "the placement of an offender in a particular living unit is contingent upon a need for the specific type of treatment program offered" (Levinson, 1982, p. 245). The most treatment-oriented units have been therapeutic communities (Toch, 1980) that rely on inmates to exercise beneficent influence on each other. The process works particularly well when inmates have similar problems. This rationale requires sorting inmates into fairly homogeneous categories, using instruments such as the Quay Adult Internal Management System (Quay, 1983), which yields types such as the "manipulator," the "inadequate-withdrawn," and the "neurotic-anxious." The Prison Environment Preference Inventory (Toch, 1977) is another example of a classification device that is aimed at inmate groupings. This instrument lets us pair inmates who need a similar environment, such as one that provides low interaction levels (high privacy), a predictable regime (high structure), and concerned staff (high feedback).

The profile I am alluding to is one that we often find among "old cons," and it is largely age-related. This means that it is not (as some contend) a prison product—one that results from intimidation and brainwashing.

Institutionalization is a problem, but it typically arises where inmates' needs are ignored or squelched in institutions. If we retain older inmates in settings that do not match their needs, the inmates can be harmed in this way, or "institutionalized." Overstimulation is stressful, as is its opposite, understimulation, which is likely to become a problem for the inmates early in their terms. Both types of problems can be avoided, however, through the use of classification over time. With flexible programming we can adjust environments to evolving needs, and long sentences can be served with dignity. If this were to be achieved, we might encounter inmate biographies very different from those we customarily hear when we do prison research.

REFERENCES

Abbott, J. H. (1981). *In the belly of the beast.* New York: Vintage.

Bondeson, U. V. (1989). *Prisoners in prison societies.* New Brunswick, NJ: Transaction Books.

Cohen, S., & Taylor, L. (1972). *Psychological survival: The experience of long-term imprisonment.* Harmondsworth, UK: Penguin.

DiIulio, J. J. (1987). *Governing prisons.* New York: Free Press.

Ellis, D. (1984). Crowding and prison violence: Integration of research and theory. *Criminal Justice and Behavior, 11,* 277.

Flanagan, T. J. (1983). Correlates of institutional adjustment among state prisoners. *Criminology, 21,* 29.

Glaser, D. (1964). *The effectiveness of a prison and parole system.* Indianapolis: Bobbs-Merrill.

Irwin, J. (1970). *The felon.* Englewood Cliffs, NJ: Prentice Hall.

Irwin, J. (1980). *Prisons in turmoil.* Boston: Little, Brown.

Jacobs, J. B. (1977). *Stateville: The penitentiary in mass society.* Ithaca: Cornell University Press.

Levinson, R. B. (1982). Try softer. In R. Johnson & H. Toch (Eds.), *The pains of imprisonment.* Beverly Hills, CA: Sage.

Levinson, R. B., & Gerard, R. E. (1973). Functional units: A differential correctional approach. *Federal Probation, 31,* 8.

Mabli, J., Holley, C., Patrick, C., & Walls, J. (1979). Age and prison violence: Increasing age heterogeneity as a violence-reducing strategy in prisons. *Criminal Justice and Behavior, 6,* 175.

Paulus, P. B. (1988). *Prison crowding: A psychological perspective.* New York: Springer-Verlag.

Quay, H. C. (1983). *Technical manual for the behavioral classification system for adult offenders.* Washington, DC: National Institute of Corrections.

Toch, H. (1975). *Men in crisis: Human breakdowns in prison.* Chicago: Aldine.

Toch, H. (1977). *Living in prison.* New York: Free Press.

Toch, H. (Ed.). (1980). *Therapeutic communities in corrections.* New York: Praeger.

Wright, K. N. (1987). *Improving correctional classification through a study of placement of inmates in environmental settings.* Binghamton, NJ: Center for Social Analysis.

17

Administrative Perspectives on Management of Long-Term Prisoners

EDITOR'S INTRODUCTION

The brief essays in this chapter were published under the title "Reports from the Field" in the Spring-Summer 1990 issue of *The Prison Journal*. In a special issue of that journal devoted to issues and research on long-term incarceration, I felt it essential that the perspectives of correctional leaders charged with managing growing numbers of long-term offenders be included. I asked several well-known, experienced correctional leaders to write short "policy briefs" on long-term imprisonment. They were asked to comment on the administrative and policy challenges posed by an increasing number and proportion of long-term inmates in state and federal prisons, and to describe programs, policies, and information needed to face this challenge.

When these essays were written, Thomas A. Coughlin III was commissioner of the New York State Department of Correctional Services for more than 10 years. J. Michael Quinlan was director of the Federal Bureau of Prisons; today, he is publisher of *Corrections Alert*, a publications of Corrections 2000, Inc. Richard L. Dugger was secretary of the Florida Department of Corrections when his essay was written; today he is Superintendent of the Putnam

Correctional Institution in that state. Kenneth L. McGinnis was director of the Illinois Department of Corrections when this essay was published; today he heads the Michigan Department of Corrections. Finally, the description of management of long-term prisoners in the United Kingdom was prepared by the staff of Her Majesty's Prison Service.

These reports from the field share several themes. First, these correctional leaders recognized in 1990, as we do even more acutely today, that pressure from legislatures, the judiciary, and the public to increase the number of offenders sentenced to long prison terms would yield growing numbers of long-termers. Second, these same developments could substantially change the composition of the long-term inmate group, especially increasing the number of drug offenders sentenced to long terms. Third, these administrators recognize that long-term prisoners present unique challenges in terms of adjustment, career planning, and aging that must be met by prison systems. These "Reports from the Field" provide an invaluable perspective on long-term incarceration from the ground level and offer a challenge to contemporary correctional leaders to design productive and secure regimes for long-term inmates.

NOTE: Reprinted from *The Prison Journal*, Vol. 80, No. 1, Spring/Summer 1990, pp. 109-119. Copyright 1990 by Sage Publications, Inc.

Problems and Challenges Posed by Long-Term Offenders in the New York State Prison System

Thomas A. Coughlin III

During the past decade, statutory changes and enhanced law enforcement efforts focusing on drug crimes have caused the prison population in New York State to increase at a rapid pace. On December 31, 1980, the prison population in New York State was 21,632. By December 31, 1989, the under custody population had climbed to 51,245; a 137% increase.

In addition to the overall increase in size of the prison population, there has been a concurrent increase in the number of offenders serving long prison terms. While definitions of a long-term offender vary, New York defines inmates who will spend a minimum of 5 years in prison as long-term offenders.

On December 31, 1980, there were an estimated 6,421 inmates in the prison population who had minimum sentences of 5 years or more. By December 31, 1989, that number had risen to 17,169.

This increase in the number of long-term offenders has occurred for two basic reasons. First, public sentiment has favored longer prison terms for serious offenders. Second, the legislature, in response to public demands, has passed legislation requiring longer prison terms for certain classes of offenses.

For example, the Second Felony Offender Law, enacted in 1973, provided for mandatory prison terms and increased the minimum period of confinement for such offenders. In similar fashion, the Violent Felony Offender (VFO) Law, passed in 1978, increased minimum terms of confinement for specified violent offenses.

The effects of these legislative enactments were not immediately felt within the prison system; however, over a period of years, the effect was one of increasing the proportion of long-term inmates in the prison population.

A correctional administrator must be aware of any special problems posed by population subgroups such as long-termers and develop strategies for addressing these problems. In New York, we have found few differences between long-term and short-term inmates in terms of their needs. Our strategy, therefore, has been one of providing programming options for all inmates to allow them to develop their own coping strategies.

However, we do recognize that long-term inmates may face problems qualitatively different from short-term inmates. An examination of these differences does not, however, suggest the need for any major changes in administrative direction.

PRINCIPAL PROBLEMS FACED BY LONG-TERM OFFENDERS

There are two basic problem areas that appear to be more relevant to long-term inmates than to short-term inmates: (1) initial adjustment to the idea of long-term confinement and (2) developing activities or interests that allow one to cope with long-term confinement. Most other problems that inmates face, such as maintaining family contact, medical problems, and educational deficiencies, are shared by long-term and short-term inmates and are addressed through a variety of services available to all inmates.

Initial Adjustment. The initial problem faced by offenders entering the prison system with long sentences is adjusting to the idea that they will be incarcerated for a very long time. The New York State Department of Correctional Services experience with this problem is that long-term offenders tend to "settle in" fairly quickly without too much trouble and develop a perception of "reality" of the prison being their "home."

The basic pattern of adjustment involves denial of the situation at first. Then, the inmates become more realistic about where they are and begin to deal with the problems posed by long-term confinement. As a matter of fact, once long-term inmates "settle in," they are generally easier to manage than short-term inmates.

One indication that an inmate may have adjustment problems is the need for mental health services. Of the 51,245 inmates under custody at the end of 1989, 2,118 had extended classifications indicating the need for mental health services. Of those inmates requiring mental health services, only 912 had minimum sentences of 5 years or more.

We have found then, through experience, that long-term inmates do not appear to need any type of specialized counseling to assist them in adjusting to the reality of long-term confinement. Any problems that do arise appear to be individual in nature and have been handled effectively on a case-by-case basis within the framework of existing services.

Coping With a Long Period of Incarceration. A problem faced by all inmates in prison is the development of a strategy for doing time. For short-term inmates, release from confinement is an attainable goal in the not-too-distant future.

On the other hand, release from confinement for long-term inmates is not a realistic goal for some time. For example, many inmates serving life sentences may have to serve 15 or more years before release is even possi-

ble. Therefore, long-term inmates may have to develop strategies for coping with confinement different from their short-term counterparts.

Two examples illustrative of coping strategies unique to long-termers can be found in two inmate organizations, one composed of male inmates and the other composed of female inmates. Each of these groups focuses on issues relevant to coping with long-term confinement.

For females, the Long Termers' Committee at Bedford Hills Correctional Facility is the oldest inmate organization at that facility. The committee began as an advocacy group lobbying for issues relevant to their long-term status, such as good-time off the minimum sentence.

The committee has since evolved into a support group. In fact, the group currently has a grant from the Presbyterian Church that supports the selling of crafts outside the prison and yarn to inmates inside the prison. At the present time, 20 inmates serve on the actual committee, and there are a total of 120 inmate participants in the Long-Termers' group.

As a community service, the Long-Termers also perform typing for the blind community, using equipment provided by the Helen Keller Foundation. In addition, Long-Termers are eligible to participate in the master's program sponsored by Mercy College and are encouraged to develop academic interests.

In contrast, for males, the Lifer's group at Auburn Correctional Facility is an advocacy group that focuses on issues relevant to inmates serving life sentences. The Lifer's group focuses its energies on lobbying for good-time off the minimum sentence and issues related to the lifetime inmate's condition of civil death.

For example, one issue that lifers have been extremely interested in is the reinstatement of their right to marry, a right taken away as a function of the civil death imposed upon them when sentenced to life imprisonment. Last year, the Lifer's group succeeded in their efforts to have the right to marry restored.

Each of the groups described above, and the activities in which they engage, represent strategies designed to give meaning and direction to the time the inmate spends in confinement. However, these are not the only strategies utilized by long-term inmates to cope with long-term confinement.

The Industries Program is one of the most important programs the department offers as a coping strategy for long-term inmates. It provides the inmates with a long-term activity in an environment that approximates, as much as possible, the work environment of the outside world.

Industries participation also provides the inmate with the status of a good paying job (by prison standards) and enough self-esteem to comfortably deal with the day-to-day reality of long-term confinement. In fact, for some inmates, industry participation affords sufficient financial and psychological rewards that they actually choose to work two shifts instead of one when the work is available.

Long-term inmates may, therefore, experience some problems directly related to the length of their confinement. However, existing department resources appear to be adequately addressing these problems. When programming or services are not the issues, inmates appear to be motivated and resourceful enough to develop their own strategies.

CONCLUSION

In the final analysis, I would argue that long-term inmates do have the potential for adjustment and coping with problems that are qualitatively different from those experienced by short-term inmates. However, an individual inmate's ability to adjust and cope with confinement cannot be predicted by an arbitrary classification into long-term versus short-term groups.

The reality is that individuals vary in their ability to adjust to and cope with their environment. In New York State, we provide a variety of programming options for all inmates, regardless of sentence length, such as the education and art programs.

The diversity of the programs offered in New York State tacitly acknowledges the individual differences among inmates and allows inmates to develop their own coping strategies. When programming is not the only issue, the emergence of inmate organizations such as the Long-Term Committee at the Bedford Hills Correctional Facility and the Lifer's Group at the Auburn Correctional Facility are examples of inmates coming together to develop their own coping strategies.

In sum, the New York State Department of Correctional Services does not provide special counseling or programming specifically designed for long-term inmates. When problems do arise for individual inmates, these problems appear to be adequately addressed within the framework of existing services provided by the department.

Managing Long-Term Inmates in the Federal Prison System

Strategies to Accommodate Inmate Population Shifts

J. Michael Quinlan

In the past, it was believed that long-term inmates served as a calming and stabilizing influence in correctional institutions. Although this bit of conventional wisdom was never, to my knowledge, "proven" via social science research, it has indeed seemed that inmates who expected to be spending a significant portion of their life in prison had a vested interest in perpetuating a nonvolatile, stable living environment because the facility was, in a sense, to be their "home."

Conversely, it was felt that shorter-term inmates lacked this incentive, because they could view their term in prison as more of a temporary visit that did not require them to settle in for the long run. Furthermore, long-termers of the past often were serving sentences for types of crimes very different from shorter-term inmates—crimes that did not necessarily indicate a propensity to disruptiveness.

Today, however, as a result of the implementation of the U.S. Federal Sentencing Guidelines and antidrug legislation, as well as other public policy shifts and demographic changes in society, the federal inmate population is changing. The sentencing guidelines, developed by the U.S. Sentencing Commission as required by the 1984 Comprehensive Crime Control Act, establish a range of sentences for all categories of federal offenses and defendants, according to specific, detailed factors. Also under the guidelines, parole is abolished and good-time provisions are significantly reduced.

These guidelines and other sentencing laws are expected to cause an increase in both the size of the federal inmate population and the lengths of stay of individual inmates. In addition, because of the changing nature of the crimes for which people are receiving lengthy sentences (e.g., drug-related crimes) and the overall aging of the U.S. population, a shift in the demographic and criminal history characteristics of long-term offenders is a possibility for which we must be prepared.

Although it is still too soon to gauge the full impact of the guidelines on the inmate population, certain trends—whatever their cause may be—are already evident. In 1980, the number of prisoners with sentences of more than 1 year was 139 per 100,000. For 1988, it was 237 per 100,000. As of June 30, 1989, the figure was 260. With regard to offense category, at the beginning of 1980, 22.7% of the Bureau's population were drug offenders; now that figure is 47.8%. In addition, the Administrative Office of the U.S. Courts reported a

229% increase in drug-related criminal cases in the past decade. As for the "graying" of the inmate population, at the end of 1979, 35% of the population was older than 35; now 50% is in that category.

These changes, particularly in conjunction with the steadily growing inmate population, pose a considerable challenge for the federal prison system, which strives to provide confinement services appropriate to the varying custody needs of its population. Ideally, the strategies for managing long-term inmates will differ somewhat from those used with shorter-term inmates. For example, with regard to long-termers, it is our intent to minimize the potential for monotony, hopelessness, and fear of deterioration that can occur among individuals serving long sentences. Conversely, the bureau seeks to ensure that long-termers occupy their time productively and that they learn skills that will be useful to themselves and, if possible, to the prison and eventually society. It seems reasonable to expect that by providing long-term inmates with opportunities to maintain and improve their sense of self-worth, through employment, education, recreation, and so on, there will be less need on the part of these individuals to assert or prove themselves through disruptiveness and violence.

The bureau anticipates that changes of this type in the federal offender population will have a significant impact on its inmate classification system. This system provides staff with a well-developed structure for weighing and applying information about sentence length and various background factors, such as history of violence, escape, drug use, and other factors. This system has been continually refined throughout its use. However, additional changes may be necessary over time to ensure that the system adequately takes into account additional differences in this changing long-term population.

Although the need to prepare and provide for this growing segment of the federal inmate population is well established, there are a number of questions that need to be investigated as we develop and enhance the programs available for long-term inmates. One fundamental issue is, what constitutes a long-term sentence? We suspect that if we look at the 5% to 10% of the population serving the longest sentences today, as compared with that proportion of the population 10 years ago,

the sentences of those today will be much longer. If this is true, within the social ecology of the prison the meaning of long-term may be changing. We will need to exercise caution in projecting what cutoff point will best serve as a definition of long-term. There is also the question of how much in resources to invest in long-termers when it is the shorter term inmates who need more immediate preparation for their forthcoming release.

Other questions include:

Are the typical long-term inmates sentenced today significantly different from those sentenced in the past?

Are long-term inmates still seen as a stabilizing force in prisons?

Will strategies that worked in the past for managing this segment of the inmate population still work today?

Is there a substantial change in the way that long-termers serve time?

Do inmates pass through various psychological stages of adjustment to a long-term sentence, and if so, can the bureau anticipate inmates' needs during these periods?

Should long-termers be mainstreamed with the general population or housed separately?

What motivates long-termers to behave responsibly in prison?

Does the typical long-term inmate tend to be older than in the past?

Does age affect adjustment?

What are long-termers' educational, vocational, and prison employment goals, and how can the bureau help them to achieve these goals?

What services and opportunities can be provided to long-termers without angering the public and raising objections about the way in which tax dollars are spent?

The bureau's Office of Research and Evaluation has begun a project to investigate these and other questions concerning long-termers. Existing research indicates a possible need for the development of "career planning" programs to help long-term inmates map out their prison career. Such a plan might offer inmates an individually tailored, structured program path to follow during their incarceration to achieve a certain series of goals, prepare for their eventual release, and, possibly, earn a sense of accomplishment for their time in prison. Institutions may also benefit from such a program, because inmates who receive certain types of training might be able to "repay" the institution by training others in turn, or by serving productively in positions that require extensive training as a prerequisite.

Currently, most prison program opportunities are for relatively short spans of time, with the aim of keeping inmates busy and preparing them for release in the not-too-distant future. We intend to examine whether, through planning and focused program evaluations, the incarceration of long-term inmates can be made more beneficial for them and more productive for the institution and society.

This idea of a prison-career planning program is one option the bureau will consider in determining the optimum strategies for managing the growing number of longer term inmates in its custody. A necessary first step is our inquiry into the issues and questions raised above concerning the role that long-termers play in the federal system, their characteristics, and their program and service goals and needs. With such information, we can ensure that our strategies for managing this growing segment of the federal prison population are appropriate responses that will satisfy the bureau's mandate to provide custody and programs, based on the individual needs of offenders, our aim to provide these services in the most humane and professional manner, and the public's interest in accountability for the way its tax dollars are spent.

Life and Death in Prison

Richard L. Dugger

The problems associated with long-term incarceration have always existed and are currently becoming more significant. The increase in Florida's long-term offender population will require changes in existing policy, and research should be initiated to examine the full spectrum of implications of this population build-up. Administrative structure, techniques, practice, and functions may need to be revised. Programs need expansion to overcome the challenges associated with long-term, and thus aging, populations.

Events in several areas of criminal justice administration have shaped the long-term population in Florida:

1. In 1972, the Florida Legislature began to increase the length of incarceration for certain crimes. The death penalty was reinstituted in that year, and a 25-year minimum time to serve was mandated before capital felons under life sentence could be paroled. Minimum mandatory sentences, ranging from 3 to 25 years, were enacted for drug trafficking in 1979.

2. Sentencing guidelines were established in 1983 and parole abolished except for capital felonies, that is, death or life with a 25-year minimum mandatory. However, the exception did not extend to other life sentences, which thus became actual with no chance of parole.

3. The Habitual Offender Statutes, revised in 1989 to add a Habitual Violent Offender category, increased both sentence length and the proportion of the sentence that is actually served.

4. On January 1, 1990, the Law Enforcement Protection Act became effective and established minimum mandatory terms for a number of offenses involving law enforcement personnel.

As a result of these and other changes, in years time, Florida will house nearly three times as many long-term inmates as today.

PROFILE OF LONG-TERM INMATES

Out of Florida's status population of 40,078 on February 28, 1990, 8,111 were serving sentences of 25 years or longer. Included are 291 under sentence of death. Males numbered 7,918, females 193, whites 3,849, and blacks 4,131. Main primary offenses were murder (3,648), sexual offenses (1,713), robbery (1,566), and burglary (508). Half of these inmates are serving sentences of life or death.

The Minnesota Multiphasic Personality Inventory and certain other tests are administered to all inmates on admission. Prisoners with long sentences are considered escape risks and are generally designated close custody and assigned to one of the more secure institutions. Classification is reviewed at 6-month intervals. If the prisoner's behavior demonstrates adjustment, he or she may be moved to other institutions, and after several years of good behavior, the custody level may be reduced. The disciplinary record of inmates with life sentences is better than that of the general population, 92% disciplinary free to 88%.

Programmatically, the long-term population is of five kinds: younger offenders admitted with long sentences; the middle-aged offender, often a career criminal who will not be released until very old; elderly offenders who have grown old in prison; and offenders who were elderly on admission. Long-term female offenders are a distinct subgroup with their own program needs (MacKenzie, Robinson, & Campbell, 1989).

THE PROBLEM OF
LONG-TERM INMATES

In responding to the distinct needs of long-term inmates, the system must overcome several challenges:

1. Large offender populations that, in many facilities, have meant less program opportunities for work, and more time "locked up."
2. Proliferation of special programs that require integration with the total system, and with each other.
3. The conflicting requirements of security and program treatment.
4. The escalating costs of health care.

These problems are primarily due to the unprecedented strain on the system and the demands placed upon it. Also, in part, they are structural. We must learn to apply the various programs available in each institution so that they can be integrated in a plan that is relevant to the needs of a particular inmate during his incarceration, also one that will meet the needs of the institution, and of society on his release. Most prisoners will be released eventually. The long-term prisoners, in particular, are susceptible to "future shock" and frequently succumb to alcoholism and homelessness following release. Preparation for release should be a continuing program through the period of incarceration. Ideally, it should start with substance abuse treatment and education in life skills, to overcome as far as possible the in-

mate's tendency to manipulate the system for drugs, sex, money, or other gratifications; continue as a life plan with vocational education integrated with industrial or institutional work programs; and be followed after release with some form of support service. The scenario is in place, but some research is needed to see if it is happening.

AGING AND
THE LONG-TERM INMATE

The concern with long-term prisoners is associated with, but distinct from, the problems of aging prisoners. As the build-up in the long-term population increases, the numbers of inmates over 60 will rise and affect all services, especially health care. Health costs tend to increase as prisoners age, and the maintenance cost of an elderly prisoner may be three times that of a younger prisoner (Turley, 1989). Florida has not yet designated a specific geriatric care unit, though the numbers indicate that such a unit will eventually be required to provide special medical attention, nutrition, exercise, and health education.

In its report dated January 1, 1990, the Crime Prevention and Law Enforcement Study Commission, established by Governor Robert Martinez and the Florida Legislature, recommended that the department and the legislature consider the problems of elderly inmates. This support is welcome.

For some problems, study is needed; for others, money. The lives of prison inmates should have some meaning (Flanagan, 1982). The best program for long-term and aging inmates may be to provide avenues whereby those that will, can feel useful. There is skill and knowledge among the elderly that might be tapped, perhaps to provide problem-solving capabilities to assist local government and private enterprise. Many long-term inmates adjust to prison and might be involved in projects, which, though still within the perimeter, would benefit the local community and bring them visitors whose input could be integrated into their continuing life plan and prerelease program.

The increasing numbers of long-term and aging inmates present an urgent challenge that demands well-researched, well-planned, and, in some areas, innovative action. As correc-

tional administrators, we must meet these demanding problems decisively.

REFERENCES

Flanagan, T. J. (1982). Lifers and long-termers: Doing
big time. In R. Johnson & H. Toch (Eds.), *Pains
of imprisonment* (pp. 115-128). Newbury Park,
CA: Sage.

MacKenzie, D. L., Robinson, J. W., & Campbell,
C. S. (1989, June). Long-term incarceration of
female offenders: Prison adjustment and coping. *Criminal Justice and Behavior, 16*(2), 223-
238.

Turley, J. (1989, October 9). *The New York Times.*

Programming for Long-Term Inmates

Kenneth L. McGinnis

Currently in Illinois, 5,701 or 22% of the inmates are serving 7 years or more in prison. They will spend an average of 17 years in prison. Their average age is 33. Some will die of old age in prison, but the majority will walk out the doors. These inmates face two problems. The first is serving their sentence in a meaningful and productive manner. The second is being released into an unfamiliar world. Correctional programming, with the assistance of volunteers, may make a difference in how they deal with these problems.

Seventeen to 20 years is a significant portion of anyone's life. Time served by long-term inmates needs to be viewed as a total life experience and not just a small interruption in life. Most correctional programs, policies, and approaches are geared to the 80% of the population. We must, however, begin to realize that a growing proportion of our population will spend more time at a prison than most staff.

Correctional programming for long-term inmates should assist in making the time spent in prison meaningful. This begins at admission. The early period of incarceration appears to be particularly stressful for long-term offenders as they make the transition from the outside world to institutional life. With more time served, long-termers appear to develop strategies for coping with prison. This suggests that special supportive services be provided to long-termers shortly after admission to assist in the adjustment process.

We need to use citizen volunteers in programs for long-term inmates. One of the biggest problems that long-termers report is the eventual loss of family and friends. These are the contacts that anchor the long-termer to outside reality. Volunteers who visit and work with these inmates will help maintain a sense of connection and importance. This will benefit the long-term inmate but also begin to educate the public about these forgotten inmates. As the long-termer reaches his release date, a volunteer can act as a local sponsor and help him adapt to the new world.

A special "career track" for long-term inmates should be developed that would tie together educational, vocational, and industry programs. For example, industry programs that require special skills could be tied to the vocational programs that develop that skill. Long-termers could be recruited for the vocational programs, then move into industry and possibly up to crew chief. Thus, early in incarceration the long-termer would be presented with options to make the best of his time.

All the institutional programming will do little if community reintegration is ignored. Here lies the biggest challenge for both the long-termer and corrections. Illinois has a successful community correctional center program, where an inmate spends up to the last 2 years of his sentence. While in the program, the inmate must be employed, going to school, or involved in public work. The emphasis is on learning life skills and putting them into practice. As in other states, the longer-termer, by the nature of the offense, is not eligible for this program. Yet it is the long-termer who needs this type of programming the most.

A specialized deinstitutionalization program needs to be developed for long-termers. Just think back over the changes in the past 25 years and you will understand why this is necessary.

In the aftermath of Willie Horton, correctional officials are even more reluctant to take the risk of putting an inmate with a violent history into community-based programs. Almost all long-term offenders are in on a serious violent crime. Many of us know that the murderer who went into prison at the age of 25 is different from the one coming out at the age of 50. Nonetheless, the public and media sees a murderer regardless of age or life changes.

I believe that as a greater proportion of our inmate population become long-termers, the above options will become more necessary. The decision to put any inmate in a community program must be based on a risk assessment. Such a risk assessment cannot, however, rest solely on the offense but must take into the account the offender. By involving citizens in these programs, we can begin to build a support group for the inmates, the programs, and the tough decisions that must be made.

18

Management of Life Sentence Prisoners in England and Wales

Barry Mitchell

At present there are about 3,000 convicted offenders serving indefinite terms of imprisonment;[1] that is, they were sentenced to life imprisonment,[2] or ordered to be detained "during Her Majesty's pleasure,"[3] or sentenced to "custody for life."[4] The population of lifers is steadily increasing; in 1968 there were about 500, in 1975 about 1,200, and in 1985 slightly more than 2,000. Moreover, the average length of time served in custody by lifers has also been increasing. In the early 1970s it was in the region of 8 to 9 years, whereas a decade later the figure was roughly 10½ years. For those released between 1989 and 1992, the average is 12 to 13 years. In response to this trend, the Prison Department developed a management policy for life sentence prisoners founded on the "Revised Strategy," the modern version of which dates from about 1980. In recent years adjustments have been made to this, and the current arrangements and procedures were set out in Home Office Circular Instruction 2/1989.

THE STUDY: THEORY AND PRACTICE

As part of a larger project,[5] I sought to examine the extent to which the Prison De-partment's management policy for lifers is put into practice. The data were collected from three sources. First, I interviewed[6] a random sample of 82 convicted murderers[7] who had all received a provisional release date.[8] The principal objective was to talk about what had happened to the prisoner since the date of sentence: how many prisons the lifer had served in, the jobs he had done, how he had spent his recreation time, his relationships with other prisoners and with staff, how he had coped with the prospect of an indefinite sentence, and how he was preparing for release on license. Second, I was able to look at the prison file for each lifer, to examine staff reports on the prisoner's "progress." Third, I talked to a variety of staff governor grades, uniform officers, psychologists, and probation officers who had dealt with lifers at different stages in the sentence. The idea here was simply to invite each person to describe his or her own experience and to express personal opinions about potential improvements to the system.

On the assumption that they were all re-leased on the day provisionally given, the lif-ers in the sample would have served 11.35 years (11 years 4 months) on average since the date of sentence. The shortest period of deten-

NOTE: This is a revised version of an article that was originally published in *The Prison Journal*, Vol. 80, No. 1, Spring/Summer 1990, pp. 96-108. Copyright 1990 by Sage Publications, Inc.

tion was 6 years 6 months, and the longest was 24 years 10 months. It is worth bearing in mind that the Prison Department takes the view that it is undesirable to keep prisoners in the same establishment for too long. This is in order to prevent them from becoming so accustomed to the routine that they have no need to make decisions for themselves and thus give no indication about how they would behave if given their freedom. Obviously, those serving longer sentences are likely to be detained in a larger number of establishments. Sixty-five of the 82 (just less than 80%) were kept in no more than seven prisons, and a further 9 served time in eight institutions before being released on license.[9]

Although the department's policy is that prisoners should be detained in gradually less secure conditions, provided it is safe to do so, 37 lifers in the sample (45.1%) were transferred at some stage to a prison of equivalent security categorization. More important, 8 lifers had at some stage been moved back to conditions of higher security. One lifer was thought to have been transferred to a more liberal environment too quickly and was said to be unable to cope with the sudden increase in personal freedom and responsibility. Others were moved back because they were regarded as having taken unfair advantage of the more relaxed regime and had broken prison regulations.

MANAGEMENT POLICY

It is Home Office policy that a lifer's first allocation should be to a main center.[10] There the vital process of reviewing each prisoner begins: Staff can draft reports, and what were previously called lifers' career plans (now "life sentence plans") may then be prepared. In my study the average time waiting for this first allocation was 4.2 months, the shortest period was 3 days, and the longest was 12 months. Life sentence plans are particularly important because, as the policy circular acknowledges, they "should try to reflect the kind of progression" to conditions of lower security. According to current practice, they are drafted by civil servants in the Prison Department in the light of the reports made in the main centers. Some prison staff felt that more use should be made

of their opinions, on the ground that they are much closer to and have more contact with lifers and are thus in a better position to assess their needs. It is understood that the Department intends that although civil servants should continue to draft the plans, greater efforts should be made to take account of staff comments.

The Home Secretary is ultimately responsible for determining if and when a life-sentenced prisoner is to be released on license. Recent changes in the law have meant that a distinction is made between mandatory and discretionary lifers. In the case of mandatory lifers,[11] the Home Secretary can order release only if recommended to do so by the Parole Board, and after consulting the Lord Chief Justice and the trial judge for their views on the tariff period (i.e., the length of time to be served to meet the requirements of retribution and deterrence). The Home Secretary is not bound to accept the Parole Board's recommendation for release, nor need he accept the judiciary's view on tariff. In the case of discretionary lifers,[12] the Parole Board can direct release once the prisoner has served part of his sentence specified by the sentencing court as appropriate punishment, and provided the Board is satisfied there is an acceptable risk to the public. Before the Criminal Justice Act of 1991, the first formal consideration of release was when the Local Review Committee (LRC) met to make its recommendations to the Parole Board. Since October 1, 1994, LRCs have been replaced by new local review arrangements. The current procedure for setting the first formal review date stems from an announcement by the then Home Secretary, Leon Brittan.[13] It is fixed by the Home Secretary after he has consulted the judiciary on the question of tariff, and is set at 3 years before the tariff date. Some lifers will serve very long periods in custody, 20 years or more.[14] The Home Secretary announced in 1985 that no life sentence prisoner would be detained for longer than 17 years without his case being reviewed by the Parole Board machinery. Thus, where the tariff is 20 years or more, the first formal review is set at the 17-year stage. It should also be acknowledged that since this study was carried out, a greater degree of openness has been introduced in relation to release procedures. All lifers must be informed by the Parole Board of its decision and the reasons for it.[15]

FEATURES OF
LIFE SENTENCE PLANS

Life sentence plans can only be confidently prepared after the tariff date has been determined. Those concerned with plotting a lifer's progression through the sentence need to have some idea of the length of detention. There are three principal features of these plans. First, they contain a projected path, suggesting the prisons in which the lifer should be accommodated. In the "classic" case, the prisoner will move from a main center to a Category B establishment, then to a semiopen, and again to an open prison, and finally to a hostel on the Pre-Release Employment Scheme (PRES),[16] from where he will be released on license. Second, the plans identify the perceived "areas of concern"—whether the lifer has an alcohol or drug problem, whether he is unable to cope with pressure or stress, whether he has difficulties in relating to particular groups of people, and so on. Third, they set out what are thought to be the lifer's individual training and treatment needs—he may require some sort of medical or psychiatric help, or educational/vocational training, or assistance with basic social skills.

Formerly, the Department sought to make life sentence plans available by the time prisoners had served about 3 years since the date of sentence. One of the main criticisms staff constantly voiced was that in practice 4 or even 5 years elapsed before the plans materialized. In other words, lifers were well into or occasionally more than halfway through their detention before vital information became known to those who were most closely monitoring their progress and writing reports on them. In 1987 the Divisional Court was heavily critical of such delays,[17] as a result of which the present Home Secretary announced various adjustments, to be in effect from October 1 of that year, in an attempt to provide the relevant details more readily. As for those sentenced before October 1, 1987, the Prison Department undertook a catching-up exercise, and the judiciary's thoughts on tariff have been obtained and first review dates have been set.

The case of each lifer should be reviewed regularly, and at various points staff are asked to submit reports to the Department, the first set of which precede the drafting of life sentence plans. It is envisioned by the Department that after a copy has been forwarded to the prison, a member of staff should convey the essential features of the plan to the lifer concerned. Some uniform staff expressed confusion about the confidentiality of the plans, although the accompanying guidelines indicate the need for communication and explanation. Prison staff universally accepted that life sentence plans are useful management aids, but they stressed the need for them to be regularly revised and updated in light of developments that might only become apparent at a relatively late stage in the sentence.

TRANSFER POLICY
AND RISK ASSESSMENT

It is the policy of the Life Sentence Section in the Home Office that prisoners should be transferred to a semiopen establishment[18] as soon as it is practicable and safe to do so. Although the tariff is determined by the requirements of retribution and deterrence, prison staff and the Department concentrate on the other major factor in considering whether and when to release a lifer, namely, the risk that is posed to the public. This is not something that can be assessed in a wholly scientific or foolproof way. Testing suitability for release can best be carried out in semiopen or open conditions, where the regime is more informal and relaxed, and prisoners are more able to be responsible for their own conduct. Nonetheless, in recent years, psychologists have also begun to work with lifers who are still in closed conditions on risk testing.

In the present survey, only 48 of the 82 lifers (58.5%) spent time in both Category C and D prisons, 2 were never transferred to an open establishment, 28 (34.1%) went directly from a Category B to a Category D prison, and 4 served no time in either type of institution.[19] It is worth noting that those who were never moved to semiopen conditions tended to have been sentenced more recently; that is, from 1977 onwards. Furthermore, the average aggregate time spent in Category C and D prisons was barely more than 3 years 1 month, the longest period was 6 years 10 months, and the shortest was 4 months. During my discussions with staff, particularly those in Category C and D prisons, the opinion was frequently expressed that lifers should spend longer periods in these conditions so that the assessment of risk might be improved. However, it is only right to acknowledge that the Department claims that the situation has since changed. About 1,000 lifers are currently held in semi-open conditions, and more establishments—especially Category C prisons—now accommodate life-sentence prisoners.

Transfer to a semiopen prison may be seen as a "step in the right direction," but it also signals a diminution in what are generally known as perks and privileges. The lifers I spoke to on this issue unanimously denounced it as an example of sheer bloody-mindedness. Why should they suddenly have to give up wearing their own shoes, or having their own bedspread, or keeping a budgerigar in their room? Staff generally agreed, although one governor in a semiopen prison argued that perks were necessary in the early and middle stages of the sentence to appease prisoners and keep them happy, but this no longer applied by the time they reached Category C environments. It is understood that the Department is aware of the disquiet among the lifer population, but it takes the view that this is a matter for the prison governor's discretion.

One of the principal objectives of the Department's policy is to encourage lifers to take a constructive approach to the time they spend in detention. Given that the vast majority of them will not remain in custody for the rest of their natural lives, the desire is to maximize the chances of successful reestablishment in the community. The Department seeks to use the period of imprisonment to identify and remedy any problems or deficiencies that might prejudice this. Understandably, however, anyone facing an indeterminate sentence may find it difficult to contemplate a future outside prison. Common sense suggests that this will be most acute in the early and middle stages, either when the lifer has not been told how long he is likely to serve in prison or when his earliest possible release date is still some way off.[20] Of the 82 lifers interviewed, 20 (24.4%) said they could begin to look ahead to release while in a main center, and 17 (20.7%) were in a Category B prison. For 10 (12.2%) it was only when transferred to a Category C establishment that they were able to do so. A further 5 (6.1%) could only think about release when moved to open conditions. But for 29 (35.4%), thoughts of the future were precipitated when they received their provisional date. The other lifer said he made no plans at all until he was at a prison hostel on the PRES.

Each of the 29 who made up the largest single group felt that regardless of what had been indicated to them by staff and/or other prisoners, and regardless of the implications of being transferred to lower security-establishments, their situation had always been so uncertain that they could not or dare not think about release. Many had learned from bitter personal experience that they could not rely on encouraging remarks or statements about their projected progress. Many had been shocked and dismayed at what happened to other lifers who were ultimately detained for longer than expected.

It was extremely difficult to identify any characteristics of lifers that would indicate whether they were likely to be able to consider release at a particular stage in their sentence.[21] The one possible exception was previous experience of custody. It is dangerous to attach any real weight to the figures because some of them are very small, but it is worth noting that 50% of those who could think about life outside prison in the first 3 years of their sentence had previously served a custodial sentence. (In other cases, the proportion with such a background was usually much lower.)

In addition to the indeterminacy of their sentence, lifers are subjected to regular review of their progress. Without exception, those in the sample were always aware of the fact that they were constantly being watched and their behavior analyzed. Of course, they knew it was being done with the ultimate aim of assessing their potential safety to the public, but it also added to the list of stresses they had to endure and further distinguished them from fixed-term prisoners.

TRAINING AND EDUCATION PROGRAMS

One of the obvious ways in which lifers can make use of their imprisonment is by undertaking educational and/or vocational training courses. Some require assistance at a very basic level, either in reading and writing and so on, or in social skills. Others need something more advanced. All but 14 of the lifers in the study pursued courses of some sort; 43 (52.4% of the total sample) did them in an effort to enhance their prospects of obtaining employment when released, but 25 (30.5%) simply wanted to help pass the time. However, a number of reservations were expressed, especially by lifers, but also some staff, about the provision of courses. First, many prisons offered only a limited variety so that there was nothing of interest to the lifer. Second, transfers or impending moves to other prisons could also be very unhelpful. A lifer who is in the middle of a course may be transferred to another establishment, where his course is unavailable. Alternatively, a lifer may wish to embark on a particular course but will be dissuaded from doing so because he expects to be moved in the near future and is not sure he will be able to complete it. Staff accepted these criticisms and added the point that more care needs to be taken with the timing of these courses. All too often, a lifer had undertaken a course to improve his employment prospects some years before being released, so that by the time he is actually doing the job, he has probably lost some of the benefit of the course. In such instances, some sort of refresher course seems to be the obvious answer.

PRISONER PERCEPTIONS

The likelihood of a prisoner adopting a constructive approach toward his detention raises a number of issues, including his feelings about the justification of his conviction[22] and sentence. Clearly, a sense of injustice is likely to have an unsettling effect and produce a negative attitude to the system. Seven lifers denied any responsibility for the victim's death, though 4 of these accepted they were peripherally involved in the incident. Another 52 (63.4%) admitted responsibility for killing, either alone or with others, but maintained they ought to have been convicted of manslaughter rather than murder. (Thirty-five denied acting with malice aforethought, and the remainder claimed they had been provoked to kill.) Only 22 (26.8%) agreed with the conviction for murder.

Prisoners' thoughts about the justification of the sentence ought not to be dismissed simply because of their subjectivity. There is an obvious danger that the lifer may reach the point where he feels he has been imprisoned for too long, so that he becomes unsettled and loses motivation. Taking into account their view of the heinousness of the crime and the progress they felt they had made, nearly two thirds of the lifers in the sample—perhaps not surprisingly—felt they had been detained more than necessary, usually by a matter of 2 to 4 years. In some cases their comments were supported by those of prison staff. Naturally, all of them prefaced their remarks by acknowledging the difficulty of measuring the loss of liberty against the loss of life, but only 9 were unable to offer any answer. Eighteen thought they had been punished correctly, and one man felt he ought to have served a longer sentence.

In their written reports some staff expressed concern that lifers were in danger of being detained in custody for too long. The writers clearly felt that there is an optimum time at which a prisoner should be released, so as to maximize his chances of successful reestablishment in the community. These views were confirmed in talks with staff, especially those who work in open prisons, and it was stressed that not only might the prospects for successful release be threatened, but also the task of staff in those prisons in motivating and encouraging lifers becomes distinctly more difficult.

The current policy is to release lifers through the Pre-Release Employment Scheme, which means that they will spend the final months, usually the last 6 or 9, at a prison hostel. This is the period that most closely approximates life outside, for the lifer has to obtain a job in the community, although he will have his morning and evening meals and he will sleep in the hostel. The idea is that he can get back into the routine of an ordinary working lifestyle, hopefully resume some sort of social life outside the prison environment, and perhaps save a little money. When the lifers in the sample were interviewed, only 22 (26.8%) had had any direct personal experience of PRES, although they all understood its rationale and how it worked; 46 (56.1%) felt it would serve a useful purpose to them personally for the reasons given above. But 32 (39.0%) thought that although they would not personally derive any benefit from it, the scheme might help those who had no support from family or friends and were thus approaching release largely by themselves. Four felt that PRES could be of no value to anyone. For them, life in any form of penal institution, regardless of the nature of the regime, is unreal and cannot hope to offer any lessons for what will happen when they are released.

PRISON CONDUCT

As a general rule, the tariff date represents the earliest point at which a lifer may be released on license. Yet it is, at least theoretically, possible for the release date to be brought forward in instances where the Home Secretary is satisfied that exceptional progress has been made during imprisonment. The provision for such exceptions is important. Some of the wider implications of the apparent dominance of the tariff have already been identified by Maguire, Pinter, and Collis (1984).[23] It was therefore interesting to note that more than three quarters (63 out of 82) of the lifers interviewed always felt that good conduct and a positive attitude to the sentence could never hasten the timing of their release. Bad behavior could, on the other hand, delay it. An additional 12 said that conduct in prison was simply irrelevant: Shortly after conviction a period of imprisonment is determined and that can never be altered unless something quite extraordinary occurs. For them the single relevant factor is the gravity of the offense as perceived by the Prison Department and the Home Secretary. Only 7 lifers showed any optimism about the matter, and they tended to express their feelings as hopes rather than expectations. No one felt confident that good conduct would be of any benefit.

Their comments about the insignificance of good behavior in prison was typical of a general distrust that lifers had in the penal system, and in some respects the staff sympathized with the prisoners. Expectations generated by encouraging comments from staff proved to be unfounded, there was an apparent inconsistency in the way in which lifers were treated, and (predictably) the system was inefficient— the classic example of which was the delay in getting the results of parole applications. Very few of the lifers interviewed expressed any confidence in what they had been told by staff. Most said that a few staff seemed to mislead them quite deliberately (regarding this as part of their just deserts), and many were simply out of touch with the views of the Department and the Home Secretary.

Because one of the basic objectives of the Department's policy is to remedy prisoners' training or treatment needs, I felt it would be interesting to elicit the lifers' own views on the impact of their incarceration. Criminologists have been and still are very concerned about the possibility of damaging effects of long-term imprisonment,[24] and the comments of both lifers and staff showed a keen awareness of this. Many prisoners stressed the measures they had taken to maintain a strong sense of what was happening in the outside world. When transferred to more liberal institutions, they almost invariably denied experiencing any problems of adjustment. In contrast, staff felt that many lifers did show signs of having difficulty in coping with more freedom and being left to make decisions for themselves. More than three quarters of the lifers said that their sentence had had no apparent effect on them. Quite a few felt they had mellowed as the years passed but attributed this simply to the natural process of aging; 18 suggested that imprisonment had helped them to mature. They had met people who had had to overcome greater problems than their own. They had learned to be more tolerant and how to deal with difficult or stressful situations. One young man, though, could not say whether, on balance, he had benefited from his imprisonment. He had matured and learned to understand and control his emotions, but he had also become rather devious through having to find ways of dealing with what he saw as the pettiness of prison regulations.[25]

CONCENTRATION OR DISPERSAL?

At a more general level, there is the important question of whether lifers should be detained separately from other prisoners, or whether the Department's current policy of integration should be continued. The Revised Strategy accepts that lifers have "special needs, because of the indeterminate sentence and the psychological and practical problems created by that" (Circular 2/1989, para 9(i)), but does not generally accommodate them in separate prisons. In practice there seems to be some variation in that sometimes all lifers are accommodated on one wing (often with other long-term prisoners), whereas in other prisons, they are spread throughout the institution. On the whole, staff regard lifers as a settled group and thus find it very tempting to disperse them throughout the prison, so that they might have a stabilizing influence on other prisoners. Kingston Prison is perhaps an exception insofar as its inmate population are all serving indefinite (or, in one or two instances, lengthy determinate) sentences. Some staff complain that the more professional offenders sometimes had an adverse, "contaminating" effect on the other, less sophisticated ("domestic") lifers. The governor, however, indicated that as soon as such dangers appeared, the offending professional criminal transferred to another establishment.

Since indeterminacy is a characteristic of their sentence that distinguishes them from fixed-term prisoners, it may be thought that lifers tend to associate only with those in the same predicament as themselves. It was found that 27 (nearly one third of the sample) mixed only with the lifers, one mixed only with short-term prisoners, and 47 (57.3%) associated with all sorts of inmates, regardless of the length of sentence. Two main reasons were given for keeping out of the way of short-term prisoners in particular. Many of the latter were high-spirited young men who quite frequently broke prison regulations, so any apparent involvement with them could be extremely damaging to lifers. Being associated with the antics of such "young tearaways" could delay a lifer's release by a matter of years. Second, it was said that short-term prisoners were in the habit of talking constantly about their impending release and their personal problems, which some lifers, especially those for whom there seemed to be no sign of release, found very stressful. Conversely, comments were also made that mixing with short-term prisoners was beneficial because by talking about what was happening in the world outside, they helped lifers to retain a sense of reality—what life was like beyond the prison walls and the sort of problems lifers would have to face when finally released. This was one way that some lifers thought they might stave off institutionalization.

IMPLICATIONS FOR THE FUTURE

The growing numbers of life-sentence prisoners and the apparent increase in the time spent in custody may indicate that more accommodations must be found for them within the penal system. Paragraph 9(iii) of Circular 2/1989 states that "A wider variety of prisons should accommodate lifers" and adds that "further locations will be added as overall numbers increase." Since 1990, lifer accommodations have been made available at 21 more prisons.

It is clear that some lifers do not follow a simple path leading to a gradual diminution of personal restrictions. Whether as the result of being transferred too quickly to liberal conditions, or on the manifestation of a previously latent area of concern, a few prisoners will at some stage be moved to a more closed environment. This obviously reinforces the need for flexibility and for the constant reviewing and updating of life sentence plans.

EARLY PLANNING

If life sentence plans are to be an effective managerial tool in establishing a sense of purpose and direction, they should be available at a relatively early stage in the sentence. In addition, the success of these plans in generating a constructive attitude toward detention appears to be seriously undermined in the light of lifers' views about their ability to quicken their release. If the tariff assumes unqualified dominance, then in the early and middle stages in particular, lifers will be disinclined to use their imprisonment positively, and correspondingly staff will find it very difficult to motivate prisoners and are likely to regard their reports as being of only limited value. In addition, there is the danger that lifers who are detained beyond the optimum release time will incur greater problems adjusting to life in the community. Thus, the extent to which the Home Secretary exercises his power to bring forward the tariff date is crucial.[26] There is a very efficient grapevine within the prison population, and the way in which the Home Secretary uses him prerogative in this respect will be very closely monitored by lifers.

ROLE OF STAFF

The Department's stated intention to make greater use of the time spent with lifers by prison staff is naturally to be welcomed. However, one of the most striking features of many of the reports on lifers, especially those written by uniformed officers, was that they were both extremely brief (sometimes no more than four or five lines) and of a purely descriptive nature. It is therefore necessary, as those interviewed universally recognized, for staff to be properly trained in appropriate aspects of human behavior and psychology and in report writing.[27] Those who have regular contact with lifers must have the necessary skills to analyze and assess prisoners' progress, and to communicate this to their colleagues and to the Department.

Both in absolute terms and as a proportion of the overall period of detention, lifers spend relatively little time in the more liberal conditions that prevail in semiopen and open prisons. The task of prison staff in assessing the question of risk to the public is extremely difficult and requires adequate time if it is to be attempted with any real degree of seriousness and confidence. There is evidence that the staff themselves had genuine doubts about the current situation, and it is to be hoped that the Department's stated intention of transferring lifers to Category C establishments as soon as it is safe to do so is carried out. Certainly, the results of this study suggest that the process should be hastened so that lifers are given more opportunity to show how they behave when given greater personal responsibility.

Notwithstanding the view of one governor in a Category C prison that there is no need for the same level of perks and privileges as there is at earlier stages of the sentence, lifers themselves clearly resent the idea. More significantly, many of them complained that the benefits to be derived from what is essentially a step nearer to release are effectively nullified by what is seen as an example of the pettiness and bloody-mindedness of the Department. The obvious solution is to bring the perks and privileges in semiopen and open prisons into line with those in closed institutions. This ought not to be seen as a major concession to prisoners, but merely as a matter of managerial common sense.

One of the unsurprising implications of this study is that there is a very real need for more resources in the lifer system, especially those of a financial nature. Reference has already been made to the requirement of a thorough program of staff training. A likely cause of further expenditure is the expansion and improved organization of the provision of educational and vocational training courses for lifers. The additional drain this would be on the Treasury's resources may not be as great as might initially be imagined, for the difficulties highlighted in the study may be at least partially remedied by better planning of prisoners' future needs. Moreover, the point made by one prison officer that lifers should, just before they are released, receive training that is relevant to their subsequent employment, is obviously sound.

Although the Department's stated policy is to integrate lifers with other prisoners, there seems to be some evidence of de facto separation. The claim made by the governor at Kingston Prison that professional criminals are quickly transferred if they are thought to have a contaminating effect on their less sophisticated counterparts is a clear illustration. To a lesser degree, separation is achieved in those establishments where lifers (and other long-term prisoners) are accommodated in different wings from those serving shorter sentences.

From a management perspective, there are two distinct potential advantages of integration. First, lifers can be used as a stabilizing influence on other prisoners. The vast majority of lifers want to get through their sentence quietly and as quickly as possible, and thus have a vested interest in avoiding any disruption. Second, staff appreciate that integration with short-term prisoners is a common cause of stress and they use this as an aid in their assessment of risk to the public which lifers would pose if released. Coping with pressure and dealing with difficult situations are regarded as important indicators of a lifer's progress.

On the other hand, many lifers argued that although they fully accepted the need for them to be tested, the problems caused by integration were unrealistic and thus a false means of determining their suitability for release. For them, the simplest and usually most effective way of avoiding trouble is to walk away from it, yet integration largely denies them the opportunity to do so. This is particularly true when they are accommodated in dormitories where prisoners are serving a variety of sentences. Even where lifers are assigned to single rooms, they will not be able to avoid short-term prisoners entirely during recreation or while at work or at meal times.

It may be argued that separation is undesirable because it is likely to encourage lifers to think they are unique, and that integration is necessary both to dispel this belief and to demonstrate their ability to deal with difficult situations. But as the Revised Strategy acknowledged, lifers do have special needs by virtue of the indeterminacy of their sentence, and this study has provided evidence that many of them regard integration as another example of bloody-mindedness on the part of the Home Office. Rather than working with the prison system in an attempt to resolve their personal problems and inadequacies, lifers often feel they are simply being made to "jump through hoops." In other words, insistence on a policy of integration appears to undermine the achievement of the Department's major objective of maximizing the chances of successful reestablishment in the community.

NOTES

1. Home Office (1994) Prison Statistics, England and Wales, 1992, Cm 2581, Chapter 8. London: HMSO.

2. Such a sentence is mandatory where an offender is convicted of murder and who was at least 21 years of age at the time of the offense—see Section 1(1) Murder (Abolition of Death Penalty) Act 1965—although the sentencing judge may recommend to the Home Secretary that a minimum period of imprisonment should be served before release on life license. Life imprisonment is also the maximum sentence for other serious crimes such as manslaughter, robbery, rape, aggravated burglary, and arson.

3. By virtue of section 53(1) Children and Young Persons Act 1933, a person convicted of murder, and who was under 18 years of age at the time of the offense, will be sentenced to be detained "during Her Majesty's pleasure." This is very similar to life imprisonment, though the offender is detained "in such a place and under such circumstances as the Secretary of State may direct." Under section 53(2), those under 17 years of age when they commit offenses other than murder, for which a life sentence may be imposed on an adult, may be ordered to be detained for life. This is effectively the same as detention during Her Majesty's pleasure.

4. A person who commits murder when under the age of 21 years should, according to section 8(1) Criminal Justice Act 1982, be sentenced to "custody for life," unless he is liable to be detained during Her Majesty's pleasure. If the court thinks it is appropriate to do so, it may impose a similar sentence on a person aged at least 17 but under 21 years who commits any other offense for which a life sentence may be passed on an adult (see section 8(2)). "Custody for life" is similar to life imprisonment, except that "the Secretary of State may from time to time direct that an offender . . . who is female, or who is male and under 22 years of age, is to be detained in a youth custody center (now known as a young offender institution in the light of the Criminal Justice Act 1988) instead of a prison" (see section 12(7)).

5. The Home Office provided a grant to fund a two-part project. The first part examined the nature of 250 cases of people convicted of murder between 1978 and 1982 inclusively. The fieldwork for the research on lifers was carried out in 1986 and early 1987. A fuller account of the whole study was published in Murder and Penal Policy (Mitchell, 1990).

6. In every case the interview took place in a room where there was just the lifer and myself. With one real exception, the lifers were detained at the time in an open prison or in a prison hostel. One young man, however, was in a nondispersal Category B prison (and was soon to be transferred to a hostel). He was an epileptic and it was felt inappropriate for him to serve time in a Category C or D establishment because of the possible physical danger to himself. (Another younger man was being detained at a youth custody center, but in conditions very similar to those in a hostel.)

7. Convicted murderers constitute about 79% of the total population of life-sentence prisoners. (A further 8% have been convicted of manslaughter.)

8. There were two reasons for this qualification. The interviews sought to elicit information about what had happened during imprisonment. I was also keen to assure potential interviewees that their participation in the project would have no bearing on the timing of their release.

9. These figures do not include instances where only a very short time was spent in a prison, for example, while en route from one establishment to another or while having accumulated visits. But they do include time spent in hostels.

10. There are three main center prisons—Wakefield, Wormwood Scrubs, and Gartree. For females, Durham (H-wing) and Bulwood Hall fulfill this function.

11. Criminal Justice Act 1991.

12. Criminal Justice Act 1991. This change in the law was prompted by judgments of the European Court of Human Rights in the cases of Weeks (1987) 10 EHRR 293, and Thynne, Wilson and Gunnell (1990) 13 EHRR 666.

13. Previously, a Joint Committee, originally set up in 1973 and consisting of the Chairman and Vice-Chairman of the Parole Board, a psychiatrist from the Board, and two senior officials from the Life-Sentence Sections of the Prison Department, recommended to the Home Secretary when the first parole review by the LRC should be held. This consultation between the Joint Committee and the Home Secretary usually occurred when the lifer had served about 3 years. The new procedure was first announced in a speech at the Conservative Party Conference at Blackpool on October 11, and was then amplified in a statement to the House of Commons— see House of Commons Debates, Vol. 49, Written Answers to Questions, November 30, 1983, col 514.

14. The then Home Secretary, in 1983, identified four broad categories of cases where such a term

could normally be expected, vis-à-vis murders of police and prison officers, terrorist murders, sexual or sadistic murders of children, and murders by firearm in the course of robbery. He added that other types of case might also attract similar or even longer periods of detention.

15. In the case of discretionary lifers, this follows from the European Court of Human Rights decisions; and in the case of mandatory lifers, the then Home Secretary announced the new procedures in Parliament (see House of Commons Debates, Vol. 216, Written Answers to Questions, December 16, 1992, Vols. 218, 219).

16. This is discussed more fully below.

17. See *R v Secretary of State for the Home Department, ex parte Handscomb and others (1988) 86 Cr App R 59-84.*

18. There are no semiopen prisons as such that accommodate female prisoners. P4 Division, which is responsible for female lifers, argues that it is the nature of the regime within the institution rather than the physical manifestations of security that are important, so that female lifers who would otherwise be transferred to a semiopen prison are accommodated in closed prisons and then moved to an open establishment.

19. One was a young man suffering from epilepsy, mentioned in Note 6. Another, also referred to in Note 6, was only 14 years of age at the time of the offense. He had made substantial progress, and there was no suitable semiopen or open prison available for him. It was possible to simulate hostel conditions at the youth custody center where he had been detained, and the Department felt able to adopt a rather experimental approach in his case. The third lifer had been detained for a considerable time in closed conditions and was in danger of becoming so institutionalized that his reestablishment in the community would be markedly prejudiced. He was well supported by his family and spent the last 9 months of this detention in a hostel. Finally, a lifer had been recalled to prison on four occasions after his first release on license in 1977. There was never any doubt about his ability to look after himself, so that semiopen and open conditions were regarded as unnecessary.

20. Interviews showed that right from the start some lifers had an idea what a life sentence might mean—they knew what the average length of detention was. But many had little or no idea of the implications of being a lifer, and most expressed no confidence in the intimations they received from lawyers, prison staff, or fellow prisoners.

21. A feature of the study was that it was very difficult to identify any general trends or patterns. Neither the personal details of the lifers nor the nature of their offenses tended to indicate their likely attitude toward the sentence.

22. Although staff stress the need for prisoners to accept responsibility for their offenses and come to terms with what they did, it is only right to acknowledge that there was no absolute insistence that each and every lifer must satisfy staff that he genuinely admitted liability for the crime of which he was convicted. In a few instances, staff may accept or sympathize with the lifer's account of what happened even though that differed from the view adopted by the court.

23. See Maguire, Pinter, and Collis (1984). The authors point out, for example, that the judiciary are given a central role in determining the minimum lengths of detention by making confidential recommendations to the Home Secretary, whereas the sentencing function ought to be carried out in open court. Furthermore, the Home Secretary's policy of categories that attract minimum periods of 20 years' detention effectively enables him to usurp the role of the judiciary (especially the Lord Chief Justice) in assessing the penalty that is necessary in the interests of justice.

24. See, for example, Cohen and Taylor (1981) and Coker and Martin (1985).

25. One of his hobbies was long-distance running, which effectively meant that he needed more food than was normally permitted. His official request for extra food was rejected, so that he had to obtain it "unofficially," a practice of which staff were fully aware.

26. I was unable to find any instances of lifers "beating the tariff."

27. I am told that staff working with lifers now have a 1-week training course that includes guidance on report-writing.

REFERENCES

Children and Young Persons Act, 1933.

Cohen, S., & Taylor, L. (1981). *Psychological survival: The experience of long-term imprisonment.* Harmondsworth, UK: Penguin.

Coker, J. B., & Martin, J. P. (1985). *Licensed to live.* Oxford, UK: Basil Blackwell.

Criminal Justice Act (1982).

Criminal Justice Act (1988).

Criminal Justice Act (1991).

Home Office. (1994). *Prison statistics England and Wales, 1992;* Cm 2581. London: HMSO.

House of Commons Debates. (1983). *Written answers to questions 49.*

House of Commons Debates. (1987). *Written answers to questions 120.*

House of Commons Debates. (1992). *Written answers to questions 216.*

Maguire, M., Pinter, F., & Collis, C. (1984). Dangerousness and the tariff. *British Journal of Criminology, 24,* 250.

Mitchell, B. J. (1990). *Murder and penal policy.* London: Macmillan.

19

Situational and Social Approaches to the Prevention of Disorder in Long-Term Prisons

Anthony E. Bottoms

William Hay

J. Richard Sparks

This chapter arises from research conducted in two prisons for adult men serving long sentences in England. The research was commissioned by the Home Office as part of a wider program of research studies focusing in various ways on issues of control and order in long-term prisons in England, and on the management of long-term prisoners deemed to be "control problems" (for a fuller understanding of this policy background, see Bottoms & Light, 1987; Home Office, 1984, 1987).

Our research was designed as a sociological study, in which a central concern was to understand how "control problems" in long-term prisons were related to the everyday life of the prison, including the nature of its regime. The research was carried out in Albany Prison on the Isle of Wight (inmate population about 350) and Long Lartin Prison in the southwest of England (inmate population about 400). Both prisons are specifically designated as maximum security institutions for men serving long terms of imprisonment, and both are part of the so-called "dispersal system" in England.[1]

These two prisons have similar origins but significantly different subsequent histories and current regimes. Both were originally built in the 1960s, and were at that time designed for low-security inmates; the first governors of both prisons were renowned in the English prison service for their liberal policies. Long Lartin has largely retained this liberal ethos and has deliberately tried to keep, as far as possible, some of the features of its original regime, despite the early upgrading of the prison to a maximum security institution and the influx of a markedly different population (see Jenkins, 1987). At the time of our research, it had had no riot or other major control incident in its 20-year history. Albany, on the other hand, had been less fortunate and had suffered major disturbances in 1972, 1983, and 1985.[2] Following the 1985 incident, a "restrictive regime" was put in place to enable

AUTHORS' NOTE: The research in Albany and Long Lartin prisons that is drawn upon in this paper was carried out in the Institute of Criminology, University of Cambridge, under a research contract with the Home Office.

staff to regain and retain effective day-to-day control of the prison. A key feature of this regime is that it places more pronounced restrictions on the freedom of movement of prisoners, to reduce the total number of prisoners out of cell at any one time, and hence to reduce opportunities for disorder.

At the time of our research, the regimes of these two prisons therefore differed in a number of respects, despite the essential similarities of the two institutions in security status, formal privilege lists, and so on. In practice, the main regime differences were:

1. Each prisoner at Albany was allowed out of his cell for "evening association" for only 2 nights out of every 3; at Long Lartin, "evening association" was available to all inmates every night.[3] At other times of the day, numbers of inmates out of cell at any one time (for receiving meals, showering, etc.) were also more tightly controlled at Albany than at Long Lartin.

2. Prisoners' movements outside the wing were more stringently regulated and supervised at Albany than at Long Lartin.

3. "Cell association" (two or more prisoners mixing informally in an inmate's cell) was permitted at Long Lartin, but not (or at any rate, not officially) at Albany.

4. There was no access to night sanitation at Albany, by contrast with Long Lartin.

5. Prisoners at Long Lartin had more access to gymnasium and sports facilities (linked to the more liberal rules of association). Albany, on the other hand, delivered more time in formal regime activities, including work.

6. At Long Lartin, prisoners were paid in cash, using ordinary coin of the realm, and they were able to use cash for canteen purchases and the like; at Albany, there was officially no cash in the prison, and payments and purchases were handled on a credit basis.

Reflecting on these regime differences, it occurred to us that in many ways the different emphases of these two prisons resembled two styles of contemporary approaches to crime prevention in the outside community, namely the *situational* and the *social* (see Bottoms,

1990; Rosenbaum, 1988). Although very frequently employed in the wider crime prevention literature, this terminology has not, to our knowledge, been previously applied to custodial institutions; nor, more generally, have analogies between control problems in prisons and other varieties of offending been sufficiently well explored.

Situational crime prevention has been helpfully defined in the following way:

1. measures directed at highly specific forms of crime;

2. which involve the management, design or manipulation of the immediate environment in which these crimes occur;

3. in as systematic and permanent [a] way as possible;

4. so as to reduce the opportunities for these crimes. (Hough, Clarke, & Mayhew, 1980, p. 1)

Opportunity-reduction and *manipulation of the immediate environment* are, therefore, the key concepts in this kind of crime prevention. Social crime prevention measures, by contrast, rely on more general changes in social relationships or socialization to achieve their intended crime-preventive effects—perhaps, for example, through community action or changes in the social climate of a school. The contrast between the two styles of crime prevention can be effectively illustrated with a simple example from domestic life: Some parents may lock cupboards and drawers to prevent their young children from stealing loose cash or chocolates from around the home (situational prevention); others will prefer, from as early an age as is possible, to socialize their children so that they will not take cash even if it is left lying around in the home (social prevention).

The regimes of Albany and Long Lartin are not polar examples of social and situational approaches to the prevention of disorder in the prison context. Both, in fact, employ elements of both styles, with, for example, both placing the usual restrictions on the availability of knives and sharp tools (situational prevention), and a strong emphasis in both prisons on fostering good relationships between uniformed staff and inmates (social prevention). Nevertheless, there is no doubt that the two prisons do differ in emphasis on the situational/social aspects of the preservation of order in their respective institutions. Long Lartin, proud of its riot-free history and liberal traditions, emphasizes the so-called "Long Lartin ethos," in which as much freedom as is thought possible is allowed to the inmates; close staff-inmate relationships are encouraged; and there is an explicit recognition that the regime may entail a degree of negotiation and the creation of informal contracts (see Jenkins, 1987). Albany, on the other hand, believes that in its situation and for its population,[4] a more liberal regime would carry an unacceptable level of risk not only for staff but also for other inmates, and that to maintain adequate order a significant degree of opportunity restriction is important and necessary. As one member of the senior management team in the prison put it:

> If you run a relaxed regime in a penal institution then you need to be eagle-eyed about what is really going on . . . and I have no confidence in the ability of the Prison Service to run a regime in the long term which is relaxed and unoppressive and all those things, [and] at the same time to control it so that [some] inmates are not abused. I think it would be a wonderful trick if one could do it, but I have no confidence in our ability to do it.

The full results of the Albany-Long Lartin study will be published elsewhere. In this short chapter, we want to elaborate more fully, and more generally, the concepts of social and situational prevention which that study drew to our attention, and to discuss their relevance in the prison setting. We do so because we believe that a careful analysis of the contrasts between these two concepts offers much of value both to the prison theorist and to the prison manager. Before tackling this task, however, it is important to interject a brief note on our general theoretical approach.

STRUCTURATION THEORY AND THE PRISON

In a series of important publications in recent years, Anthony Giddens has developed a general sociological approach known as the *theory of structuration* (see especially Giddens, 1984). It is impossible within the space of this chapter to provide a full summary of this approach, but among its features are:

1. An emphasis on human subjects as knowledgeable agents, though this knowledgeability is bounded on the one hand by the unconscious, and on the other hand by unacknowledged conditions and/or unintended consequences of actions.

2. The need for sociologists to acknowledge the significance of "practical consciousness" in everyday life,[5] since if one restricts what agents "know" to what they can say about what they know, a wide area of knowledgeability is excluded.

3. "Routine" is a predominant form of agents' day-to-day activity: Most daily practices are not directly motivated, and routinized practices are a prime expression of the "duality of structure" in respect of the continuity of daily life.[6]

4. Structuration theory seeks to escape from the traditional dualism in sociological theory between *objectivism* on the one hand and *subjectivism* on the other. Thus, structuration theory accepts concepts of *structure* and *constraint* (associated with objective sociology) but insists that they be understood only through the actions of knowledgeable agents; on the other hand (see above) it believes that subjectivist sociologists have overemphasized the degree to which everyday action is directly motivated.

5. The theory argues that there are not and will not be any universal laws in the social sciences, because "the causal conditions involved in generalizations about human social conduct are inherently unstable in respect of the very knowledge (or beliefs) that actors have about the circumstances of their own actions" (Giddens, 1984, p. xxxii).

6. For similar reasons, the theory is skeptical about general sociological theories of social change, believing that such theories are mistaken about the types of account of social change that are possible.

It should be evident from this brief resume that structuration theory has relevance for the study of prisons. The emphases on knowledgeable subjects, practical consciousness, and routines must surely strike chords with anyone who has ever spent time observing prison life, or who has talked at length with prison staff and inmates, especially long-term inmates. We would argue that Giddens's understanding of routines and routinization is particularly salient in relation to prisons. As we discuss more fully below, structuration theory regards routine activity as crucial both to the reproduction of social life and to the fending away of personal anxiety and insecurity. On a more academic note, the attempt to overcome the objectivist/subjectivist division in sociology is also of considerable importance to the prison sociologist, given the early theoretical dominance of the field by objectivist structural-functional writers (see, e.g., Sykes, 1958), subsequent attempts at subjectivist approaches (e.g., Cohen & Taylor, 1972), and the relative absence of recent innovative theorizing in the field.

It is from a perspective grounded in the theory of structuration that we propose to elaborate the importance of social and situational approaches to the avoidance of disorder in prisons. Among other things, this implies that we do not claim any element of universal social law about the generalizations that follow; but, equally, adoption of structuration theory does not imply relinquishing all general concepts in social analysis (Giddens, 1984).

SITUATIONAL APPROACHES TO THE PREVENTION OF DISORDER IN PRISONS

Hough et al. (1980, pp. 5-10) have provided a helpful typology of various difficult kinds of situational measures that might be attempted in the general field of crime prevention. We will use an adapted version of this typology to consider possible situational approaches to disorder in prisons.

Target Hardening

In the crime prevention field, this familiar concept refers to programs such as the strengthening of doors and windows in houses and apartments, or the toughening of cash boxes in public telephone booths. Most day-to-day

prison disorder (or at least, the disorder of most concern to prison officials) is of an interpersonal kind, and therefore this kind of situational approach is of less relevance in the prison setting than outside. However, some target hardening measures may still be possible in the prison context. For example, a favorite tactic for prisoners during disturbances in British prisons in the past few years has been to climb onto the prison roof and then use tiles and bricks from roofs and chimneys as weapons with which to repel attempted invasions.[7] Target hardening situational measures making it more difficult to gain access to the roof could therefore potentially make an important contribution to the limitation of disorder.

Target Removal

An interesting British example of target removal in the general crime prevention field has been the removal of domestic cash prepayment meters for fuel consumption (i.e., household electricity and gas) and their replacement by token-operated meters. This measure has been successful in reducing property crime, including burglaries (see Forrester, Chatterton, & Pease, 1988; Home Office, 1988).

In prisons the abolition of an official cash economy might also be a form of target removal, though the main benefits of such a strategy would probably be of a somewhat different kind (see further below). Another kind of target removal practiced in many prison systems is the isolation of prisoners vulnerable to attack (e.g., sex offenders or prisoners who are in debt to fellow inmates). This example, however, also illustrates a potential difficulty with the target removal approach: Should one, morally, accede to prisoners' threats by deliberately isolating targeted offenders? This dilemma is especially acute if the isolation accommodation offered is of a substandard nature (see, generally, H. M. Chief Inspector of Prisons, 1986; Home Office, 1989; Priestley, 1980).

Removing the Means to Crime

A standard example of this kind of situational crime prevention is the screening of baggage by airlines to try to prevent guns and other weapons being taken aboard. Similar weapon-removal examples are routinely applied in the prison context and require no elaboration here.

Restriction on the Movements of Potential Offenders

This kind of situational crime prevention is not usually mentioned in general crime prevention discussions, though it clearly fits the definition of situational crime prevention (see above), involving as it does a manipulation of the immediate environment resulting in opportunity reduction. Despite the absence of comment in the crime prevention literature, however, practical examples of this kind of measure in the general community are not unknown, for example, in electronic tagging schemes.

In the prison context, restriction of offenders' movements can be a powerful tool for preventing disorder, because an inmate alone in a cell obviously has restricted scope for causing trouble; hence, the standard resort to a "lockdown" (locking all inmates in cells) when it looks like a threatening situation is developing. However, there may also be other and more indirect intended benefits from the restriction of offenders' movements. We have already seen that, at Albany Prison, two of the main features of the restricted regime were (1) the restriction of evening association to two thirds of the population at any one time and (2) the restriction of inmates' general movements in the wing and around the prison. The main purpose of these restrictions was not so much to deliberately restrict offenders' movements as to restrict the number of inmates in the open at any one time, so that (given fixed staffing resources) more effective surveillance could be effected upon those inmates who were allowed out of cells. The extreme end point of this kind of restriction on movement is perhaps to be found at Marion Penitentiary in Illinois, where, under "lockdown" conditions, prisoners are allowed out of cells only when in handcuffs and leg irons and accompanied by guards (Ward, 1987; Ward and Breed, 1985).

At this point we may return to structuration theory. The standard general literature on situational crime prevention tends to be associated with a theoretical standpoint in rational choice theory (see, e.g., Cornish & Clarke, 1986); that is to say, it assumes that situational

crime prevention works because, for example, the potential offender rationally realizes that the house is now too heavily defended to enter easily, or that (given ZIP-coding of property) the payoff from the crime will be reduced, and so on.[8] Yet there has not always been much close empirical investigation of the offender's views in the context of discussions on situational crime prevention (but see Bennett, 1986); in other words, rational choice is sometimes assumed rather than investigated. In the prison context, it is vital to consider how prisoners, *as real human subjects and as knowledgeable agents*, react to situational restrictions on movement, and what the unintended consequences of their reactions are to the prison. Suppose, for example (as seems not unlikely), that prisoners resent a regime that significantly restricts their movements: This could increase their frustration and make them more likely to commit assaults when they are out of their cells, or, under certain conditions, it could cause their relationships with uniformed staff to deteriorate markedly, again with unintended consequences for the state of order in the prison.

Surveillance

Human and electronic surveillance are also forms of situational crime prevention, because by altering the immediate environment, such surveillance can reduce offenders' perceived effective opportunities to offend. It is clear from the general crime prevention literature that measures of this kind can have a crime reducing effect, for example, as seen in experiments that have increased the number of supervisory personnel on public transport (Van Andel, 1989).

In the prison context, surveillance is closely associated with architectural issues: It is well known, for example, that some architectural designs provide better "sight lines" (and hence natural surveillance) than others. In contexts where natural surveillance is difficult, it can be boosted by such things as television cameras in prison corridors, or uniformed staff patrolling into areas of the prison that are not visible from standard staff vantage points. But again, although tactics such as these might indeed reduce the perceived opportunities to offend, they might also enhance resentment and/or alienation among prisoners, with possible unintended effects. For example, prisoners could very easily be irritated by what they would probably regard as unreasonably frequent staff intrusions into the "semiprivate" space of a wing television room. Part of the apparent advantage of so-called "new generation architecture" (see Home Office, 1985) is precisely that it provides surveillance *unobtrusively*, though that is not to say that it is a magic solution in the prevention of prison disorder (see Rutherford, 1985).

Environmental Management

The final kind of situational crime prevention to be discussed here is that of "environmental management," which, as Hough et al. (1980, p. 9) point out, has "some but not all the characteristics of the situational approach," in particular because measures of this kind are "opportunity reducing only in an extended sense." An example given by these authors is the organization of soccer matches in England:

> Good liaison between the police, the two football clubs and supporters' clubs can reduce the opportunities and temptations for vandalism and violence; arrival and departure of supporters can be better managed so as to avoid long periods of delay; within the grounds routes of access to stands and occupation of stands can be co-ordinated so as to minimize contact between rival supporters . . . (p. 10)

In the prison context, the single most important example of environmental management that we have encountered is the existence or not of a cash economy. It is not so much that cash economies provide targets for theft (see above); the issue is the *indirect* impact of a cash economy. It is much easier for prisoners to run various kinds of rackets if a cash economy exists, not least because in a cash prison economy the money supply can be fairly easily increased (illegitimately) by the smuggling in of additional cash. In a noncash economy, cash in the prison is immediately suspect to the staff; and, although other currencies will inevitably develop (tobacco, chocolate bars, etc.), there are limits to the extent to which most prisoners wish to acquire goods of this sort. A cash economy, in short, indirectly encourages racketeering, and its abolition

should reduce the scale of racketeering. That in turn could make an important contribution to the reduction of violence and disorder in the prison, because there is clear evidence that interpersonal violence and threats in long-term prisons are not infrequently associated with conflicts generated by racketeering activities.

SOCIAL APPROACHES TO THE PREVENTION OF DISORDER IN PRISONS

Just as there are different kinds of situational approaches to the prevention of disorder, so too there are different kinds of social approaches. Let us take just two examples.

The Barlinnie Special Unit is a small special unit for long-term male prisoners who have proved disruptive in the mainstream Scottish prison system.[9] It was originally designed on therapeutic community lines, to which it no longer adheres in full; nevertheless, the notion of "the community" within the unit (embracing both inmates and staff) remains an important one, and "community meetings" are regularly held (see Whatmore, 1987, for a description of the unit, and Boyle, 1984, for an inmate's account). Another extremely important feature of life in the unit is its high level of privileges, which are significantly greater than those available to most long-term inmates.[10] Special unit privileges include virtually unlimited visiting facilities for families and friends, the right not to work if one does not wish to do so, the opportunity to cook and eat nonprison food, and access to in-cell television. Of these, it is quite clear that the visiting privilege is particularly valued by prisoners, not least because (1) visits may, for most inmates, be taken in cells, and (2) the prison is situated in the heart of Glasgow, the city in which most of the inmates' families live.

Cooke (1989) has shown that the level of assaults and other serious incidents committed by prisoners in the Special Unit is very much less than for the same inmates in the years in prison before their unit experience; his analysis also indicates that post-unit behavior, though worse than behavior in the unit, is a considerable improvement on pre-unit behavior. Cooke postulates that the reason for the immediate drop in the level of incidents on entering the unit is largely a *situational* one (p. 139): Living conditions in the unit are radically different from those in "the mainstream," and this change, it is suggested, affects prisoners' behavior. Cooke argues that a main situational factor in operation is that of greater autonomy for the prisoner; that is, prisoners have much more say in their choice of daily activities in the unit than in mainstream prisons, and more say also about the way that the unit is run. A further situational mechanism he suggested (p. 141), which others might regard as more important than the autonomy factor, is the level of privileges; that is, prisoners greatly prefer the special unit environment (especially the visits), and they are aware that a serious incident in the unit will result in immediate expulsion, which they are very anxious to avoid. (The unit has a strict rule disallowing physical violence.)

Cooke's use of the term *situational* is broader than the definition of "situational crime prevention" offered by Hough et al. (1980) (see above), because, of course, the special unit is not opportunity-restricting, but rather the reverse. The suggestion that a radical change in situation has nevertheless produced a marked and immediate change in inmate behavior is however of great interest, not least because the mechanisms postulated for the effect produced emphasize the importance of *the prisoners' reaction to the altered environment*—an emphasis very similar to our own (see above).

Cooke goes on to argue (although not using these terms) that the apparent long-term effect of the unit on prisoners' behavior is largely the product of social processes rather than the changed situational context (which, of course, no longer exists once inmates have left the special unit). He suggests three main possibilities for this long-term effect, though these are not themselves empirically investigated in his study:

First, that prisoners living in the unit over a number of years learn new (nonaggressive or at least nonphysical) ways of coping with frustration and anger. Cooke notes in particular that the verbal fluency of many inmates has improved as a result of regular attendance at community meetings.

Second, that some prisoners have been able to develop from the unit a new and noncriminal social network (the unit is regularly visited by a range of noncriminal contacts), and thus to absorb different values.

Third, that certain prisoners have been able to develop talents (especially artistic talents: see Carrell & Laing, 1982), which have provided them with new skills and interests of positive value to them after leaving the unit.

Although this interpretation is not wholly uncontroversial,[11] most observers would probably agree that, on the limited available evidence, at least some of these "social" processes postulated by Cooke have occurred at Barlinnie. In that sense, the unit can be regarded as a genuinely successful example of "social crime prevention" in the prison context. More generally, the study illustrates the interesting possibilities that may arise from the interaction between changed situational features (not necessarily of an opportunity-reducing kind) and changed social relationships (community meetings, a different relationship between inmates and staff, greater contact with noncriminal outsiders, etc.).

But the special unit is a very unusual kind of prison setting, and it caters to a very small number of inmates. Can one also see scope for "social crime prevention" in a more general and more normal prison context?

An important recent policy committee on long-term imprisonment in England, the Control Review Committee, certainly thought so. Set up to improve conditions of order in English long-term prisons, the committee went out of its way to make the following remarks:

our package of specific proposals is only part of the story. At the end of the day, nothing else that we can say will be as important as the general proposition that relations between staff and prisoners are at the heart of the whole prison system and that control and security flow from getting that relationship right. Prisons cannot be run by coercion: they depend on staff having a firm, confident and humane approach that enables them to maintain close contact with inmates without abrasive confrontation. Nothing can be allowed to qualify the need for staff to be in control at all times, but we are sure that the very great majority will agree with us that this is best achieved by the unobtrusive use of their professional skill at involvement with prisoners. (Home Office, 1984, para. 16)

The majority of prison managers and staff at both the prisons we studied agreed in subscribing to this viewpoint. The viewpoint was, however, particularly strongly held by staff at Long Lartin, reflecting the more relaxed regime that had been developed there.

In discussions of crime prevention (or analogous measures in prison) it is always important to specify the relevant preventive *mechanisms*—that is, exactly *how* is this or that particular measure supposed to reduce crime or contribute to social order? We have already examined this question in the context of situational crime prevention (various kinds of opportunity reduction) and of the Barlinnie Special Unit (Cooke's various suggestions, discussed above). But how might the Control Review Committee's approach be expected to work?

To answer this question, we think it is best to return to structuration theory. Giddens (1984, p. 60) emphasizes the great importance of *routines* in everyday life. At the level of the ontological security of individual actors, he points out, through a discussion of Bettelheim's (1960) description and analysis of life in the concentration camps of Dachau and Buchenwald, the need that most individuals have for a level of predictability in daily encounters: It was precisely the unpredictability of life in the concentration camps that produced radical personal insecurity. Equally, at the level of societal analysis, it is vital to recognize that "the institutions of society *are* such only through their continued reproduction" by knowledgeable actors (Giddens, 1984, p. 60); that is, social structures themselves depend upon routines, continually reenacted by social actors. Hence:

An examination of routinization . . . provides us with a master key to explicating the characteristic forms of relation between the basic security system [of individuals] on the one hand, and the reflexively constituted processes inherent in the episodic character of [social] encounters on the other. (p. 60)

What are the implications of this, translated into the prison context? First, prisoners are (at least potentially) in a deprived and dependent state, suffering "the pains of imprisonment" (Sykes, 1958, Ch. 4) and to an extent dependent on the staff to at least alleviate those pains (Mathiesen, 1965). The existence of some routines and predictability in prison life operates to reduce personal insecurity. However, that is only half the story, because obviously routines that prisoners regard as reasonable and acceptable are more likely to achieve a reduction in insecurity than are routines regarded as merely tolerable, or downright dreadful.

So what kind of routines do prisoners find reasonable and acceptable? Individual prisoners obviously differ in this respect, but as a broad generalization, something like the following list would perhaps be regarded as important by most prisoners:

1. Delivery of an acceptable level of provision for the basic necessities of life, together with the retention of links with significant others outside the prison (i.e., reasonable food, reasonable clothing, reasonable arrangements for family visits, etc.).

2. Being treated as an autonomous person, with an element of staff respect for privacy, personal feelings, and the like, and a certain freedom to choose what activities to pursue within the inevitable confines that the prison environment creates.

3. Elements of fair treatment from day to day, so that today's rule-enforcement will be more or less the same as yesterday's, unless reasons for a change are clearly explained.

4. Fair treatment vis-à-vis other inmates.

If a regime is delivered that prisoners regard as reasonable in all its circumstances, they are (in general) likely to perceive themselves as deriving some benefit from it.[12] This in turn means that such a regime will be more likely to receive a level of endorsement, or in sociological terms *legitimation*, from the prisoners.

This line of reasoning, we would suggest, implicitly lies behind the important and now common concept of *dynamic security* (that is, the delivery of security and order in the prison through relationship-based and activity-based regimes: see Dunbar, 1985); though in our view that concept is incomplete because it pays insufficient attention to perceived *fairness* in regime delivery (see, especially, Mathiesen, 1965). The reasoning adopted also clearly suggests that attention to the services offered to prisoners, the way they are personally treated in the institution, accountability systems, grievance procedures, and the like, are all important not simply as a matter of humaneness or of inmates' rights, but also in the reproduction of social order in the prison (see also Davies, 1982).

There are, however, also some risks in taking this approach. If one delivers good services and runs a relaxed and fair regime, the legitimation accorded to the prison and the prison staff will probably be greater; but there are potential difficulties, because the very liberalism of the regime will in all likelihood allow greater opportunities for some inmates to commit unacceptable acts such as assaulting other inmates. A simple example of this point can be seen in the practice of cell association. This privilege, where available, is greatly appreciated by most long-term prisoners because it allows them to invite their friends in to their cell (the nearest equivalent to home in prison) and to hold private discussions there. On the other hand, in most prisons activities in cells are notoriously difficult to monitor,[13] given the simple facts of sight lines and standard staff patrolling tactics. Since long-term prisons, by definition, contain a proportion of inmates who are not angels, it is obvious that cell association does increase the level of opportunity for some preplanned assaults to take place in private.[14]

CONCLUSION

In Molière's *Le Bourgeois Gentilhomme*, M. Jourdain asks his mentor whether, when he says "Nicole, bring me my slippers and give me my nightcap," that is prose. On receiving an affirmative reply, he exclaims: "By my faith! I've been talking prose for the last forty years, and I've never known it!"

We realize that, in a way, this chapter has some similarities with M. Jourdain's discovery. Prisons everywhere, it can certainly be

said, have for many years been practicing both situational and social control without using that terminology—so is there any point in introducing the terminology? We believe that there is. The use of explicit terminology, we would suggest, helps one to conceptually disentangle exactly what is being attempted in a given prison; and the emphasis on the precise explication of mechanisms when discussing crime prevention measures forces one to be explicit about exactly how, say, "improving relationships between staff and prisoners" is supposed to reduce disorder in the prison.

Is it possible to offer any broad conclusion to this essay? We think it is, and this can be encapsulated in four main propositions.

First, unless one is prepared to run a regime based on virtually total inmate confinement, as in the Victorian "separate system" (Ignatieff, 1978) or in the modern special context of Marion (Ward, 1987), then *some measure of social crime prevention in long-term prisons is essential.* That in turn means that serious attention has to be paid to the issue of *legitimation*, which itself requires attention to the daily routines of the prison, the level of services offered to prisoners, accountability and grievance procedures, and so on. These concerns are, in our view, inescapably entailed in a serious focus upon social crime prevention.

Second, in most prison settings *social crime prevention has its costs* (see above), *notably in increased opportunities.* Close attention therefore needs to be paid to situational methods of reducing opportunities for disorder while maintaining the maximum commitment to social crime prevention and its emphasis on legitimation.

Third, it must be recognized that *situational measures are reacted to by sentient and knowledgeable actors.* These actors will vary in their reaction to different situational measures: In general, measures that directly restrict the daily life of the prisoner will be regarded more negatively than less personally restrictive measures. (For example, abolition of a cash economy is likely to be less unpopular than increased time locked up in a cell; more liberal situational changes, such as the enhanced visits and other privileges at Barlinnie, are likely to be particularly popular.)

Fourth, therefore, it follows that in trying to use opportunity-reducing situational measures to restrict the possibilities for offending, which social crime prevention otherwise tends to create, *there are advantages in employing (wherever possible) less personally restrictive rather than more personally restrictive situational measures, because the former will threaten legitimation less than the latter.*

These conclusions are supported by our empirical study of Albany and Long Lartin prisons, which will be published at a later date. But that study also suggests, as do the principles of the theory of structuration, that every prison has its own unique features, linked inter alia to its history, its architecture, the composition of the prisoner population, and the prior experiences and memories of staff and inmates as knowledgeable agents. Every prison, therefore, can only properly be understood in its own context. Hence, anyone interested in applying the principles we have suggested in this conclusion to a particular prison setting should do so only in the context of a thorough understanding of the specific features of that setting.

NOTES

1. The "dispersal system" refers to the main prisons within which long-term Category A (maximum security) men may be held. The system is so called because within each dispersal prison there is only a small proportion of Category A prisoners (usually about 15%); hence the Category As are "dispersed" among Category B men.

2. For a detailed study of Albany in its early years, including the 1972 disturbances, see King and Elliott (1977); for a brief summary of the 1983 incident, see Home Office (1984, p. 67).

3. "Evening association" means informal mixing of prisoners in their residential unit: They may talk together, watch television, play games, cook additional food, and so on.

4. As compared with Long Lartin, Albany has a higher proportion of younger prisoners under 25, more serving determinate sentences of less than 10 years, and more with previous convictions for robbery and firearms offenses.

5. "Practical consciousness" is defined by Giddens (1984, p. 375) as "what actors know (believe) about social conditions, especially the conditions of their own action, but cannot express discursively; no bar of repression, however, protects practical consciousness as is the case with the unconscious."

6. "Duality of structure" means "structure as the medium and outcome of the conduct it recursively organizes; the structural properties of social systems do not exist outside of action but are chronically implicated in its production and reproduction" (Giddens, 1984, p. 374).

7. Occupation of the roof is also strategically and symbolically useful to rioting prisoners because from the roof they can convey messages to television crews and other observers outside the prison.

8. "Reducing payoff" is another distinct form of situational crime prevention discussed by Hough et al. (1980, p. 7), of which property marking schemes are a prime example. We have not discussed it separately here because of its limited applicability in the prison context.

9. It should be noted that Scotland has a separate legal jurisdiction within the United Kingdom, and the Scottish prison system is completely distinct and separate from that of England and Wales.

10. Given this fact, there have been suggestions that inmates may misbehave elsewhere in order to qualify for the special unit. However, this is unlikely because of (1) the substantial amounts of extra prison time for misbehavior usually acquired before an inmate is admitted to the unit and (2) the very small size of the unit, and the long average stay of each inmate, which together mean that vacancies are infrequent and difficult to predict.

11. Given the long average stay in the unit, aging/maturation processes might be at least partly relevant in explaining the post-special unit diminution of violence, as also might proximity to the end of the sentence (on which, see Cooke, 1989, p. 140).

12. One difficult point here is that to an extent it may be comparative regime features (is this prison better than a nearby one?) rather than absolute features that are regarded as important by inmates; the full implications of this point cannot be explored here.

13. Especially in England, where cells have doors, not open grilles.

14. The Barlinnie Special Unit, where cell association is freely allowed, could be regarded as an exception to this rule, but note that (1) there are no targeted prisoners, such as sex offenders, in the unit; (2) the prisoners have a degree of say about who is allocated to the unit; and (3) violence results in immediate expulsion to the much less agreeable conditions of the mainstream prison system.

REFERENCES

Bennett, T. H. (1986). Situational crime prevention from the offenders' perspective. In K. Heal & G. Laycock (Eds.), *Situational crime prevention: From theory into practice.* London: HMSO.

Bettelheim, B. (1960). *The informed heart.* Glencoe, IL: Free Press.

Bottoms, A. E. (1990). Crime prevention facing the 1990s. *Policing and Society, 1.*

Bottoms, A. E., & Light, R. (1987). *Problems of long-term imprisonment.* Aldershot: Gower.

Boyle, J. (1984). *The pain of confinement*. London: Canongate.

Carrell, C., & Laing, J. (Eds.). (1982). *The special unit, Barlinnie prison: Its evolution through its art.* Glasgow: Third Eye Centre.

Cohen, S., & Taylor, L. (1972). *Psychological survival*. Harmondsworth, UK: Penguin.

Cooke, D. J. (1989). Containing violent prisoners: An analysis of the Barlinnie special unit. *British Journal of Criminology, 29,* 129-143.

Cornish, D. B., & Clarke, R. V. (1986). Situational prevention, displacement of crime and rational choice theory. In K. Heal & G. Laycock (Eds.), *Situational crime prevention: From theory into practice*. London: HMSO.

Davies, W. (1982). Violence in prison. In M. P. Feldman (Ed.), *Developments in the study of criminal behaviour: Vol. 2. Violence.* Chichester: John Wiley.

Dunbar, I. (1985.) *A sense of direction*. London: Home Office.

Forrester, D., Chatterton, M., & Pease, K. (1988). *The Kirkholt burglary prevention project, Rochdale* (Crime Prevention Unit Paper No. 13). London: Home Office.

Giddens, A. (1984). *The constitution of society*. Cambridge, UK: Polity Press.

H. M. Chief Inspector of Prisons. (1986). *A review of the segregation of prisoners under rule 43*. London: Home Office.

Home Office. (1984). *Managing the long-term prison system: The report of the control review committee*. London: HMSO.

Home Office. (1985). *New directions in prison design: Report of a Home Office working party on American new generation prisons*. London: HMSO.

Home Office. (1987). *Special units for long-term prisoners: Regimes, management and research*. London: HMSO.

Home Office. (1988). *Report of the working group on the costs of crime*. London: Home Office.

Home Office. (1989). *The management of vulnerable perspectives: Report of a prison department working group*. London: Home Office.

Hough, J. M., Clarke, R. V., & Mayhew, P. (1980). Introduction. In R.V.G. Clarke & P. Mayhew (Eds.), *Designing out crime*. London: HMSO.

Ignatieff, M. (1978). *A just measure of pain*. London: Macmillan.

Jenkins, M. (1987). Control problems in dispersals. In A. E. Bottoms & R. Light (Eds.), *Problems of long-term imprisonment*. Aldershot: Gower.

King, R. D., & Elliott, K. W. (1977). *Albany: Birth of a prison, end of an era?* London: Routledge & Kegan Paul.

Mathiesen, T. (1965). *The defences of the weak*. London: Tavistock.

Priestley, P. (1980). *Community of scapegoats: The segregation of sex offenders and informers in prisons*. Oxford: Pergamon.

Rosenbaum, D. P. (1988). Community crime prevention: A review and synthesis of the literature. *Justice Quarterly, 5,* 323-395.

Rutherford, A. (1985, September 20). The new generation of prisons. *New Society*, pp. 408-410.

Sykes, G. M. (1958). *The society of captives*. Princeton, NJ: Princeton University Press.

Van Andel, H. (1989). Crime prevention that works: The care of public transport in The Netherlands. *British Journal of Criminology, 29,* 47-56.

Ward, D. A. (1987). Control strategies for problem prisoners in American penal systems. In A. E. Bottoms & R. Light (Eds.), *Problems of long-term imprisonment*. Aldershot: Gower.

Ward, D. A., & Breed, A. F. (1985). *The United States penitentiary, Marion, Illinois: Consultants' report submitted to the Committee on the Judiciary, U.S. House of Representatives*. Washington, DC: Government Printing Office.

Whatmore, P. B. (1987). Barlinnie special unit: An insider's view. In A. E. Bottoms & R. Light (Eds.), *Problems of long-term imprisonment*. Aldershot: Gower.

20

Using Multiple Perspectives to Develop Strategies for Managing Long-Term Inmates

Michael J. Sabath

Ernest L. Cowles

Growth in the long-term inmate population continues to be a major concern for correctional managers throughout the United States. This concern is fueled by speculation about the gravity of problems and consequences resulting from increasing numbers of inmates being sentenced to prison for long periods of time. Among the most disturbing scenarios envisioned by experts is the emergence of a large, disgruntled, and potentially violent group of inmates with special management needs that cannot be met by correctional systems (Flanagan, 1985; Unger & Buchanan, 1985; Williamson, 1985).

Indeed, there is a large and expanding body of information about the problems associated with long-term incarceration and growth in the long-term offender (LTO) population. Researchers have identified numerous effects that are likely to arise including inmate boredom and monotony, lack of meaningful work opportunities, breaks in family and community ties, loss of privacy, geriatric-related health care needs, and verbal and physical friction among inmates and guards (Flanagan, 1982; Walker, 1983). They have also recommended a variety of programs and approaches for responding to these problems, some of which involve creating long-term prison career opportunities, redesigning physical plants, and sentence planning for the long-termer (Flanagan, 1985; Palmer, 1984, 1985).

Although this information is useful for understanding LTO confinement problems, more is needed to support the development of productive strategies for managing long-termers. In particular, there is a need for more concrete data pertaining to how key stakeholders in the correctional environment perceive the problems of long-term confinement. There is also a need for more planning technology that helps correctional administrators organize thinking and information about LTO problems in ways that facilitate the development of practical LTO management strategies. As noted by management scientists, the term *technology* has

AUTHORS' NOTE: This chapter is based on research supported by grant 84-IJ-CX-0043 from the National Institute of Justice. Opinions expressed are those of the authors and do not necessarily represent the official position or policies of the National Institute of Justice or the U.S. Department of Justice.
NOTE: This is a revised version of an article that was originally published in *The Prison Journal*, Vol. 80, No. 1, Spring/Summer 1990, pp. 58-72. Copyright 1990 by Sage Publications, Inc.

such strong engineering connotations that it should be redefined when used in the context of policy planning and analysis (Mitroff, Barabba, & Kilmann, 1977). By planning technology we mean a set of methods, procedures, or exercises that helps correctional administrators to identify problematic situations related to long-term confinement, examine assumptions held by stakeholders about these problematic situations, and then design interventions that are responsive to them.

In this chapter we argue that information on the perceptions and values held by correctional stakeholders, such as long-termers and corrections officers, can be put to practical use when designing operational strategies for improving the management of long-termers. The argument is presented by means of example, drawing on the authors' experiences with a project to design and implement programs for handling long-term offenders in Missouri's correctional system. The project, hereafter known as *The Missouri Project*, began in the fall of 1985 and ended in the spring of 1989. Although much of the project involved implementing exploratory programs for managing LTOs, this chapter focuses on the problem structuring methodology that guided the project and led to the selection of the exploratory programs. The exploratory programs that were eventually implemented in Missouri's correctional system are the subject of the companion chapter that follows this one.

THE APPLICATION OF PROBLEM STRUCTURING TECHNOLOGY IN THE MISSOURI PROJECT

The major purpose of the Missouri Project was to explore different approaches to managing long-termers in the Missouri corrections system and to assess their demonstration value for other correctional systems. From the beginning of the project there were no preconceived notions about which particular long-term confinement problems should be given attention or which policies and programs should be implemented. However, after we reviewed materials pertaining to long-term confinement and interviewed several key actors in Missouri's correctional system, four conclusions came to shape our thinking about LTO problems and guided our approach to the project. Briefly, these conclusions are:

1. The growth of the LTO population and attendant consequences represents an ill-structured problem that is interpreted in markedly different ways by correctional stakeholders, that is, those persons in the correctional environment who affect or are affected by LTO problems;

2. There are actually many problematic situations associated with long-term confinement and LTO growth. Not all of these problems fall within correctional administrators' spheres of influence;

3. For LTO management strategies and programs to be maximally effective, they should be responsive to stakeholder problem interpretations and be seen as workable by all stakeholders; and

4. Problems associated with LTO confinement may vary in scope and severity across correctional institutions.

LTO Growth and Confinement: An Ill-Structured Problem

Early in our interviews and discussions it became apparent that LTO growth and confinement is a highly complex and multidimensional problem area that can be interpreted in substantially different ways by stakeholder groups in the corrections system. It is what is called an "ill-structured problem" (Dunn, 1994). By their nature, ill-structured problems are highly subjective. Key decision makers or groups define them according to their values, which are often unknown or conflicting and impossible to rank. Typically, appropriate policy interventions for addressing the problem and intervention outcomes are unknown as well. The task with ill-structured problems becomes not to uncover known deterministic relations, or to calculate risk and uncertainty attached to policy and program alternatives, but to define the nature of the problem itself. In contrast, well-structured problems involve only a few decision makers whose values are known and can be ranked. The range of appropriate problem interventions is limited, and outcomes are known with certainty or a high degree of probability. Because of these differences, the approaches required to solve ill-structured problems are different from those required to solve well-structured problems (Dunn, 1994; Mitroff & Blankenship, 1973).

Because correctional stakeholders represent different sets of values and concerns that can govern the way LTO confinement problems and solutions are defined, we thought it was crucial to the project's success to try to include as many of them as possible in the problem identification and structuring process. This is not to imply there is vast disagreement among correctional stakeholders about what constitutes an LTO confinement problem. Very few stakeholders would quarrel that boredom, unproductive time, or the lack of meaningful work opportunities are not problems for long-termers. Yet, correctional stakeholders often see these problems in different ways. For example, prison psychologists may perceive such problems in terms of social and psychological functioning, whereas correctional officers see them in terms of security. Economy and efficiency may dominate the views of correctional administrators. It is these sorts of differences in orientation and values that contribute to disagreements about the nature and causes of LTO problems, and to disagreements about appropriate policies and programs for responding to them. Ultimately, it is these disagreements we wished to uncover in the course of structuring LTO confinement problems and developing programs for long-termers in Missouri.

Using Multiple Perspectives to Structure Long-Term Confinement Problems

Given this context, we adopted a *multiple perspectives* approach for identifying problematic situations associated with long-term incarceration and designing LTO programs. The approach involved soliciting viewpoints on long-term confinement from many key actors and participants in the correctional system, including superintendents, caseworkers, psychologists, correctional officers, and inmates. We assumed that gathering input from different vantage points on problems associated with long-term imprisonment would improve the likelihood of developing workable policies and programs for managing long-term inmates compared with pursuing more conventional approaches to problem structuring and problem solving. By workable policies and programs we mean those seen by most stakeholder groups as viable and meaningful responses to long-term confinement problems.

Although the multiple perspectives approach seems to be common sense, it is not frequently used in corrections to support decision making or to develop inmate management strategies or programming. This is particularly true with respect to including inmate viewpoints in the structuring of problems and solutions (Juliani, 1981; McNeece & Lusk, 1979). We implemented the multiple perspectives approach in three phases.

Phase One: Identifying Problematic Situations Associated With Long-Term Incarceration

The first phase of the multiple perspectives approach involved generating an inventory of problematic situations related to long-term imprisonment. Roundtable discussions were conducted with groups of correctional administrators, correctional officers, treatment professionals, and long-term prisoners to identify the range of concerns associated with long-term confinement. Prison environmental assessment instruments used by Toch (1977) and the Federal Bureau of Prisons were reviewed with these groups to stimulate discussion about problems of long-term confinement. These activities resulted in a rather lengthy inventory of long-term confinement problems and issues that, through further review and discussion, was pared down to 32 problems. Generally, these fell into one of six categories:

- inmate-staff relationships/communications
- physical environment
- programs and activities
- family/community relationships
- institutional careers
- institutional services

The 32 problems included concerns about the quality of prison medical care, inmate privacy, noise in housing units, the lack of meaningful treatment programs, food quality, and verbal abuse from staff. This inventory was then used to design a questionnaire for surveying correctional stakeholders' opinions about these problems.

TABLE 20.1 Response to the Surveys of Stakeholders

Questionnaires	Long-Term Inmates	Short-Term Inmates	Women Inmates	Correctional Officers	Treatment Professionals
Sent	256	300	356	340	300
Returned	162	209	196	171	195
Response Rate	63%	70%	55%	50%	65%

Phase Two: Surveying Stakeholder Perspectives on LTO Problems

In the second phase, the mail surveys were administered to five stakeholder groups: long-term offenders (LTOs), short-term offenders (STOs), female offenders, corrections officers, and treatment professionals (e.g., caseworkers, teachers, psychologists). These surveys comprise the backbone of what we dubbed the multiple perspectives approach. The surveys were designed around the inventory of 32 problems and asked respondents to review and rate the problems in terms of their severity. The primary purposes of the review and rating were to find out how stakeholder groups saw the severity of problems associated with long-term incarceration and to assess the consistency in their severity ratings. Consistency in the views of the different groups on the existence of a problem and its severity was seen as a target of opportunity for developing long-termer management strategies. Management strategies for such problems would be easier to develop and implement, and would likely be more effective in dealing with long-term offenders. In contrast, inconsistency in the views of stakeholder groups would point to areas where problem dimensions were not well understood or agreed upon, and workable management strategies or programs would be more difficult to identify. Though sorely needed, it was felt that interventions formulated in response to these problems would be less likely to gain serious or lasting support from both staff and inmates.

The Survey and Subjects

During 1986, the questionnaire was sent to 1,552 long-term inmates, short-term inmates, women inmates, corrections officers, and treatment professionals in the Missouri correctional system. Long-term inmates were operationally defined as those who had served, or would serve, a minimum of 6 years' confine-

ment. Short-termers were defined as those inmates who would serve less than 6 years prior to release. Corrections officers varied from inexperienced new officers to veterans in mid-level management positions with years of experience. Treatment professionals included psychologists, caseworkers, counselors, teachers, and medical personnel. With the exception of the 356 women inmates included in the survey, subjects were randomly selected from their respective populations. All women inmates were surveyed because of concern that their perceptions of long-term confinement would not be represented in data from a random sample of Missouri's inmate population. Short-term inmates were surveyed to discern whether there are substantial differences in their views of confinement and long-termers' views of confinement.

In the questionnaire, subjects were asked to review the 32 problem areas associated with long-term incarceration and to indicate whether each was perceived as a severe problem, a moderate problem, a minor problem, or not a problem at all. An "unsure" response option was provided. Additionally, open-ended questions were used to ask respondents what they thought were the three most serious problems associated with long-term imprisonment and to solicit qualitative comments about the problems they were rating. A brief demographic section was also included in the instrument to obtain background information on respondents. The questionnaires administered to the five groups were essentially identical. Table 20.1 summarizes the response rates to the survey for the various stakeholder groups.

Slightly more than 60% of those surveyed returned usable questionnaires. Response rates for stakeholder groups were quite good, ranging from 50% for correctional officers to 70% for short-term inmates. The low, but nonetheless respectable, response rate for corrections officers was attributed to skepticism about the use of the results and the confidentiality of responses. This skepticism was reflected in comments received, such as "the administration doesn't really want to hear about problems" and "nobody's going to do anything about it anyway."

The survey data were analyzed in several ways. First, problem severity ratings and rankings were examined to identify the most severe problems associated with long-term incarceration from the perspective of each stakeholder group. Second, the ratings and rankings were analyzed across groups to assess the consistency in perceptions of LTO problems. This was accomplished (1) by correlating the problem rankings of the five groups and (2) by creating a bivariate display of LTO problems by their severity rankings for two groups: corrections staff (combining corrections officers and treatment professionals) and long-term inmates. Table 20.2 shows a mock-up of this display and how LTO problems that fall into each cell are evaluated in terms of promise for developing LTO management strategies and programs.

As can be seen in the table, the better candidates for problem structuring and program development are those LTO problems in the four cells in the upper left-hand portion of the table. There is moderate to strong agreement among stakeholders about the severity of these problems; in addition, they are seen as moderate to high priority problems by both of the stakeholder groups. This contrasts with four other LTO problem groupings that are characterized by disagreement among stakeholders on the severity of problems and low priority rankings by at least one stakeholder group. Problems in these cells may be poor candidates for program development. Similarly, problems falling into the remaining cell, in the lower right-hand corner, may also be poor candidates for program development, especially if they are seen as relatively inconsequential problems by most stakeholders.

Phase Three: Examining Assumptions Underlying Stakeholder Perspectives

The survey also gathered qualitative information in the form of written comments about LTO problems. Whereas the problem identification efforts of the first two phases were designed to provide information about the existence and severity of LTO problems and the consistency in stakeholder views, the third

phase was intended to obtain a more in-depth elaboration of the problems that surfaced during the earlier phases. A central objective of phase three was to explore the similarities and differences in problem characterizations and to make the assumptions underlying them explicit. This was to be accomplished through the use of qualitative commentary obtained from the surveys of stakeholder groups and through face-to-face interactive sessions with representatives of the same groups. In this fashion we planned to engage in an assumptional dialogue that would likely result in high-quality suggestions for strategies and programs for managing long-term incarceration. For example, prison teachers and inmates alike may concur a problem exists with vocational programming for LTOs in the institutions. Both point to low enrollments in programs when identifying the problem but offer markedly different explanations or assumptions for the situation. Although prison teachers may attribute low enrollments to a lack of interest and motivation on the part of LTOs, inmates may counter that low enrollments are due to poor quality instruction, obsolete programming (e.g., typewriter repair program), and participation restrictions (e.g., life without parole inmates being barred from enrolling). If strategies for dealing with the problem are grounded exclusively in the assumptions of prison teachers, then motivational policies that tie class attendance and program completion to good-time credits may be seen as potentially successful interventions. Only when we consider the validity of the inmates' assumptions do the potentially dysfunctional consequences of such policies become apparent.

Thus, even though correctional stakeholders may agree on the existence and severity of problematic situations, they can still interpret them in substantially different ways that lead to different conclusions about what should be done to ameliorate them.

SURVEY RESULTS

Analysis of the survey data is presented below in three sections. The first section focuses on stakeholder ratings of LTO problem severity and rater agreement among stakeholder groups. This is followed by an analysis of LTO problems, as outlined in Table 20.2, to

TABLE 20.2 Agreement Between Key Stakeholders on the Severity of Problems Associated With Long-Term Confinement: Candidates for Problem Structuring and Developing Management Strategies

| | | Long-Term Inmate Perceptions of Problems | | |
		Most Severe	Somewhat Severe	Least Severe
	Most Severe	Strong agreement about the severity of problems. Problems of high priority. Good candidates for problem structuring and strategies.	Moderate agreement about the severity of problems. Good candidates for problem structuring and strategies.	Strong disagreement about the severity of problems. Likely to be poor candidates for problem structuring and strategies.
Correctional Staff Perceptions of Problems	Somewhat Severe	Moderate agreement about the severity of problems. Good candidates for problem structuring and strategies.	Strong agreement about the severity of problems. Problems of moderate priority. Good candidates for problem structuring and strategies.	Disagreement about the severity of problems. Likely to be poor candidates for problem structuring and strategies.
	Least Severe	Strong disagreement about the severity of problems. Likely to be poor candidates for problem structuring and strategies.	Disagreement about the severity of problems. Likely to be poor candidates for problem structuring and strategies.	Strong agreement about the severity of problems. Problems of low priority. May be poor candidates for problem structuring and strategies.

identify promising targets for developing LTO management strategies and programs. Finally, assumptional information pertaining to prison medical care is presented to demonstrate how such qualitative data can improve our understanding of long-term confinement problems and contribute to more effective correctional policies and programs.

Stakeholder Perspectives on 32 Problems

Table 20.3 summarizes the responses to the survey for the five stakeholder groups. It presents the percentage of each group that rated the problem areas as severe or moderate and shows the group rankings of the 32 problems based on these percentage responses. The problem descriptions in the table are shortened because of space limitations. Results reveal that long-termers' views of confinement problems are reasonably consistent with the views of other inmate groups, particularly with regard to the 10 problems ranked as severe by the largest proportions of LTOs. Notable ex-

ceptions include proportionately fewer female inmates seeing crowding in the institution and housing units as severe problems, and proportionately more females ranking frequency of visitation as a severe problem. It is likely these differences reflect real-world differences between conditions at the facility where women are incarcerated in Missouri and conditions at the facilities where male inmates are incarcerated.

The 10 problems that are the most widely perceived as severe by LTOs are related to inmate-staff relations (staff ignoring inmate suggestions and complaints), institutional services (counseling, medical care), physical environment (noise, crowding, privacy), and family relationships (travel distance). More than 75% of LTO's saw staff ignoring inmate suggestions and complaints, the quality and availability of medical care in prison, and travel barriers to family visitation as being the most serious problems associated with long-term incarceration. Problems seen by most LTOs as minor, or not problems at all, included the

TABLE 20.3 Multiple Perspectives on 32 Problems Associated With Long-Term Confinement

	Citing as Severe or Moderate Problem										
	Long-term Inmates (n = 162)		Short-term Inmates (n = 209)		Women Inmates (n = 196)		Correctional Officers (n = 171)		Treatment Professionals (n = 195)		Mean Ranking
Problem Area	Percent	Rank	Percent	Rank	Percent	Rank	Percent	Rank	Percent	Rank	
Staff Ignoring Inmate Complaints and Suggestions	77	2.5	69	4.0	62	3.5	27	22.5	35	25.0	11.5
Quality of Medical Care	77	2.5	65	7.0	66	2.0	38	16.0	47	19.0	9.3
Availability of Medical Care	77	2.5	63	10.0	62	3.5	39	12.5	51	16.0	9.0
Travel Distance for Family and Friends to Visit	77	2.5	75	2.0	68	1.0	49	7.5	77	6.0	3.8
Noise Level in Housing Unit	73	5.0	76	1.0	59	5.0	66	4.0	90	2.5	3.5
Crowding in Housing Unit	69	6.0	73	3.0	42	17.5	75	2.0	85	4.0	6.5
Crowding in Institution	68	7.0	63	10.0	37	19.0	49	7.5	54	13.0	11.3
Food Quality	67	8.0	63	10.0	48	10.5	39	12.5	37	24.0	15.5
Privacy in Housing Unit	66	9.0	68	5.0	48	10.5	45	9.5	80	5.0	7.8
Counselor Availability	63	10.0	58	13.0	46	13.5	39	12.5	50	18.0	13.4
Privacy During Visitation	62	11.0	63	10.0	56	6.0	30	20.5	52	14.5	12.4
Attitude of Staff Toward Inmates	60	12.0	56	14.0	51	8.0	24	25.0	39	22.5	16.3
Vocational Programs	59	13.0	53	15.0	48	10.5	52	6.0	64	9.5	10.8
Caseworker Availability	55	14.0	52	16.0	48	15.0	37	18.0	42	21.0	16.8
Unproductive Time	53	15.5	67	6.0	46	13.5	85	1.0	92	1.0	7.4
Safety of Personal Property	53	15.5	63	10.0	31	22.0	39	12.5	66	8.0	13.6
Frequency of Visits	52	17.0	40	20.0	54	7.0	30	20.5	64	9.5	14.8
Condition of Recreation Facilities	51	18.0	49	17.0	42	17.5	15	26.0	25	26.5	21.0
Planning Education Programs	49	19.0	43	18.0	48	10.5	38	16.0	57	11.5	15.0
Verbal Abuse from Staff	40	20.5	31	23.0	29	23.5	6	20.5	25	26.5	24.8
Academic Programs	40	20.5	38	21.0	28	25.0	38	16.0	44	20.0	20.5

Continued

TABLE 20.3 Continued

Problem Area	Long-term Inmates (n = 162)		Short-term Inmates (n = 209)		Women Inmates (n = 196)		Correctional Officers (n = 171)		Treatment Professionals (n = 195)		Mean Ranking
	Percent	*Rank*	*Percent*	*Rank*	*Percent*	*Rank*	*Percent*	*Rank*	*Percent*	*Rank*	
Access to Recreation Facilities	39	22.0	31	23.0	36	20.0	11	28.0	19	29.0	23.6
Access to Library Materials	37	23.0	28	24.0	27	26.0	8	29.0	23	28.0	26.0
Availability of Treatment Programs	34	24.0	25	26.0	43	16.0	25	24.0	52	14.5	20.9
No Room in Treatment Programs	31	25.0	15	28.0	23	27.0	27	22.5	39	22.5	25.0
Availability of Religious Programs and Services	26	26.0	13	29.5	20	28.0	6	30.5	7	31.0	29.0
Noise Level During Visitation	24	27.0	33	27.5	29	23.5	31	19.0	51	16.5	21.6
Assaults by Other Inmates	23	28.0	27	25.0	12	30.0	59	5.0	67	7.0	19.0
Opportunity to Visit Other Inmates	22	29.0	22	27.0	32	21.0	13	19.0	11	30.0	26.8
Assaults by Staff	14	30.0	9	31.5	7	32.0	4	32.0	4	32.0	31.5
Understanding Information Presented in Class	10	31.0	9	31.5	15	29.0	45	9.5	57	11.5	22.5
Reading and Writing Skills	9	32.0	13	29.5	8	31.0	67	3.0	90	2.5	19.6

Citing as Severe or Moderate Problem

TABLE 20.4 Spearman Correlation Coefficients for Group Rankings of 32 Problem Areas

Stakeholder Groups	1	2	3	4	5
1. Long-Term Inmates	1.00	.93	.86	.38	.23
2. Short-Term Inmates		1.00	.80	.51	.37
3. Women Inmates			1.00	.23	.27
4. Corrections Officers				1.00	.81
5. Treatment Professionals					1.00

availability of religious programs and services, assaults by staff, assaults by other inmates, and the availability of treatment programs. LTOs concern about literacy, reading and writing skills, ranked dead last.

Overall, the severity ratings and rankings for short-term inmates and women inmates do not seem to differ greatly from those for LTOs. However, this is not true for correctional staff and LTO responses. In several instances, corrections officers or treatment professionals do not share the same perceptions of problem severity held by LTOs. This is especially noticeable in those problem areas associated with services provided by staff (for example, educational programming and health care) and problem areas related to interactions between staff and inmates (for example, staff ignoring inmate complaints and suggestions, attitudes of staff persons toward inmates). On the other hand, according to the survey rankings, LTOs and staff share similar views of many problems in the institutional environment such as noise levels, crowding, and lack of privacy in inmate housing units. The relative agreement on problem perceptions among all five groups is shown in the correlation matrix in Table 20.4.

Correlations between inmate groups reflect strong agreement (.80 to .93) in perceptions of LTO problems among short-term men, women, and long-term inmates. Similarly, agreement between the problem perceptions of corrections officers and treatment personnel is strong (.81). However, the strong associations within inmate groups and within staff groups stand in marked contrast to the weak (.23) to moderate (.51) associations between the perspectives of staff groups and inmate groups. These latter associations suggest substantial discord in the ways staff persons and inmates see confinement problems.

Targets for Developing LTO Management Strategies and Programs

One of the major functions of the multiple perspectives approach as a problem identification and structuring method is to help correctional managers see where consensus and differences exist in the views of various stakeholder groups and to make this information useful in LTO program development. Table 20.5 organizes the survey data pertaining to staff and LTO stakeholder perceptions of problems associated with long-term confinement.

Table 20.5 mirrors Table 20.2 and presents the 32 LTO problems according to how widespread the perceptions of problem severity are among staff and LTO groups. As in the earlier table, problems listed in the four cells in the upper left-hand portion of the table represent good candidates for strategy development because there is reasonably good agreement among stakeholders on problem severity and stakeholder perceptions are fairly widespread (i.e., no fewer than 40% of either group of stakeholders see these as moderate or severe problems). According to the table, strategy or program development will be most responsive to LTO concerns if directed to problems related to institutions' environments (e.g., crowding, noise, and privacy) and barriers to maintaining family and community ties. LTO management strategies may be more difficult to identify and develop for problems related to staff interaction with inmates (e.g., staff ignoring inmate suggestions, verbal abuse from staff) because of disagreement about the severity of these problems between stakeholder groups. Finally, the table points to several problem areas that are not considered severe by the majority of LTOs or the majority of correctional staff, including assaults by staff and access to library and recreational facilities.

TABLE 20.5 Stakeholder Perceptions of Problems Associated With Long-Term Confinement

		Long-Term Inmate Group Perceptions of Problems		
		Most Widespread (top 10 problems; rated moderate or severe by 63% to 77%)	Moderately Widespread (middle 11 problems; rated moderate or severe by 40% to 62%)	Least Widespread (bottom 11 problems; rated moderate to severe by 22% to 39%)
Correctional Staff Group Perceptions of Problems	Most Widespread (top 10 problems; rated moderate to severe by 63% to 77%)	travel distance for family visitation noise in housing units crowding in housing units privacy in housing units	vocational programming providing useful skills unproductive time safety of personal property frequency of visits	assaults by other inmates reading and writing skills
	Moderately Widespread (middle 11 problems; rated moderate to severe by 42% to 57%)	quality of medical care availability of medical care crowding in institution counselor availability	privacy during visitation caseworker availability planning education to fit needs academic programs providing useful knowledge or skills	availability of treatment programs that are needed noise level during visitation understanding information presented in class
	Least Widespread (bottom 11 problems; rated moderate or severe by 4% to 41%)	staff ignoring inmate complaints and suggestions quality of food	attitude of staff toward inmates condition of recreation facilities verbal abuse from staff	access to recreational facilities access to library materials no room in treatment programs you need availability of religious programming opportunities to visit other inmates assaults by staff

Analysis of Stakeholder Assumptions

Although the survey rating and ranking data are useful in establishing the existence of LTO problems and provide some indication of the extent to which various stakeholder groups share perceptions of severity, they do not reflect the assumptions held by stakeholders about LTO problems. Assumptional information is valuable in formulating effective LTO management strategies and programs because it offers explanations as to why stakeholders hold differing views of problems and offers clues as to how to address these problems.

TABLE 20.6 Stakeholder Perceptions of Medical Care

LONG-TERM INMATES	CORRECTIONAL OFFICERS
A man laid up here in bed 2 months with severe pain, could hardly walk, and sometimes couldn't. His body was starting to deform. They would not give him anything to stop the pain. He lost weight because he couldn't walk to the kitchen to eat. Maybe they didn't do anything because of too much red tape. I don't know. After 4 months of suffering they finally took him to the city hospital and operated. Would you suffer for 4 months severely?	No inmate is constantly ill day after day; yet, on every sick call the same names appear. Some inmates make several hospital trips a day. For what?
	TREATMENT PROFESSIONALS
The prison hospital is in bad shape, a man could die up there before they got anything done.	The staff is highly motivated and very dedicated to providing quality health care, but our resources are predicated on an inmate population of 636, and we have more than 1,800 inmates. We provide a very high quality care, given limitations of staff and budget, and the lack of resources, that is, inability to refer inmates to specialist physicians when their medical needs are outside our ability to handle. Our segregation sick call and doctor's appointment procedure is the result of a court ordered consent decree and was made without consulting medical staff. There are elements which are inconsistent with standards of medical practice, and others which are physically impossible given the ratio of inmates to medical staff.
I've had trouble getting help on this subject. My kidney has been giving me hell. The only thing that has ever been done for me is a urine test. I'm not a doctor, but I know pain. I've got to watch what I drink. At night it's really bad.	
I feel that if our supervisors would work with us, this could be a safe prison both for staff and inmates. I think it's a goddamn shame that one can get cable TV and can't even get a bad tooth pulled or get any pain medication. I for one have been lying in my cell with a toothache for weeks so you know what kind of burning hate that brings on.	
	I am very concerned about the medical care available. Inmate fears of what goes on at the Department of Corrections hospital is not rumor based. Treatment for potentially critical problems is too slow. Why there are no more lawsuits than there are is beyond me.
Long-termers have to take what they can get. They can't shop around for doctors and hospitals.	

In The Missouri Project we planned on using two methods for generating assumptional information: (1) compiling and indexing qualitative commentary on LTO problems from the surveys and (2) holding interactive sessions with representatives from each of the stakeholder groups. In the end, it wasn't possible to hold interactive sessions with groups of stakeholders because of limited project resources. However, qualitative data from the multiple perspectives survey were compiled and indexed. Some of these data related to stakeholder perceptions of medical care problems are presented in the table below.

Juxtaposed in the table are selected comments from long-termers, corrections officers, and treatment professionals concerning views on prison medical care. Although the data do not directly suggest strategies for improving

the management of LTO medical needs, they do point to assumptions about medical care problems that need to be addressed when designing strategies for improving the quality and availability of medical care in prison. For example, both long-term inmates and treatment professionals single out the slow and generally inefficient state of service delivery in the prison medical care system as a major reason for their concerns about medical care. Long-termers go on to identify some of the personal consequences resulting from inadequate service delivery, including hatred, pain, and frustration with the system. Treatment personnel further point to causes for poor medical care service delivery, such as limited staff and budget, existing policies and procedures, and legal constraints over which they have no control. Finally, custody personnel express skepticism about the causes of medical care problems and suggest that inmates may actually abuse medical care services.

Although these stakeholder perceptions and assumptions do not immediately suggest solutions for dealing with LTO medical care problems, they can help correctional administrators judge the adequacy of interpretations of the problem area and provide a useful basis for designing strategies that are responsive to concerns about the availability and quality of medical care. Such an approach proved useful in The Missouri Project. The selection and design of interventions and programs, such as the Missouri State Penitentiary software development program described in the article that follows, were influenced greatly by the problem structuring activities of The Missouri Project.

DISCUSSION

In this chapter we described planning technology used in The Missouri Project to structure information about long-term offender confinement problems in ways that contribute to the development of strategies and programs for improving the management of LTOs and LTO problems. A central feature of this technology was the use of a multiple perspectives approach to gather data on the nature and severity of LTO confinement problems from various stakeholder groups in the prison system. These data were used to identify LTO problems of concern to stakeholders in Missouri's system and to outline some of the assumptions underlying perceptions of the severity of these problems.

When analyzing the data we found that many of the problems widely perceived as severe by long-term inmates were linked to conditions in prison environments such as noise levels, privacy, and crowding. The availability and quality of medical care, staff-inmate relations, and family visitation barriers were also perceived by the vast majority of LTOs to be severe problems resulting from confinement.

Results of the survey further suggest that long-termers generally experience the same confinement-related problems experienced by other inmate groups. However, this result may be clouded by the way LTOs were defined in the research (i.e., those who have served or are likely to serve 6 years or more). Future re-

search should examine perceptions of long-term confinement problems for groups defined in terms of time served rather than time sentenced. This could be done using inmates facing exceptionally long sentences, such as life without parole, to maximize the variance between long-term and short-term inmate groups.

Although the survey data show a great deal of agreement within inmate groups on the perceived severity of LTO problems, they indicate that corrections officers and treatment professionals hold perceptions of the severity of LTO confinement problems much different from long-termers in areas related to staff-inmate interactions and treatment services provided by staff. The survey data suggest it is likely that LTO program development will be less productive if it attempts to address LTO problems related to staff-inmate relations; and it will be more productive if directed toward problems such as noise levels, privacy, and crowding, as well as unproductive time and poor vocational programming options. Perceptions of the severity of these latter problems are shared widely by corrections staff and LTOs alike.

Finally, much of the value of using multiple perspectives as a planning technology to develop strategies for managing long-term inmates rests not in the specific strategies or programs that may result from the effort, but in the improved understanding of boundaries and dimensions of problems related to confinement. As a practical matter, the multiple perspectives approach can help correctional managers organize their thinking about confinement problems in ways that enable them to gauge which programs are likely to be implemented successfully in their prison setting and which ones are not.

REFERENCES

Dunn, W. (1994). *Public policy analysis: An introduction.* Englewood Cliffs, NJ: Prentice Hall.

Flanagan, T. (1982, January). Correctional policy and the long-term prisoner. *Crime and Delinquency,* 82-95.

Flanagan, T. (1985). Sentence planning for long-term inmates. *Federal Probation,* 23-28.

Juliani, T. J. (1981). The prisoner's perspective: A needed view in policy formulation. *International Journal of Comparative and Applied Criminal Justice, 5*(1), 119-124.

McNeece, C., & Lusk, M. (1979). A consumer's view of correctional policies. Inmate attitudes regarding determinate sentencing. *Criminal Justice and Behavior, 6*(4).

Mitroff, I., Barabba, V., & Kilmann, R. (1977). The application of behavioral and philosophical technologies to strategic planning: A case study of a large federal agency. *Management Science, 24*(1), 44-58.

Mitroff, I., & Blankenship, L. V. (1973). On the methodology of the holistic experiment: An approach to the conceptualization of large scale social experiments. *Technological Forecasting and Social Change, 4*, 339-353.

Palmer, W. (1984). *Programs for long-term inmates.* Pilot proposal for Workworth Institution, Correctional Service of Canada, Cambellford, Ontario.

Palmer, W. (1985). *Maintaining community ties for long-term inmates.* Transcripts of a program presented by the LifeServers of Workworth Institution, Cambellford, Ontario.

Toch, H. (1977). *Living in prison.* New York: Free Press.

Unger, C., & Buchanan, R. (1985). *Managing long-term inmates: A guide for the correctional administrator.* Washington, DC: National Institute of Corrections, U.S. Department of Justice.

Walker, N. (1983). Side-effects of incarceration. *British Journal of Criminology, 23*(1), 61-71.

Williamson, H. (1985, April). Rule violation: Will lifers play by the rules? *Corrections Today,* 138-140.

21

Addressing the Program
Needs of Long-Term Inmates

Ernest L. Cowles

Michael J. Sabath

For the convicted offender sentenced to spend a major portion, if not the entire remainder, of his or her adult life in a prison, the mechanisms of "doing time" become part of a permanent lifestyle. The imprisonment becomes a total life experience rather than simply an interruption in the offender's life, or as Unger and Buchanan (1985) succinctly put it, "The essence of this position is that long-term inmates are not tourists in prison; that is, they are not 'just passing through'" (p. 9). This notion requires an examination of the suitability of traditional correctional management strategies and programs for this long-term inmate population. More than a decade and a half ago, Toch (1977) pointed out that programs offered for short-term inmates facing only a few years of confinement before their return to society were not appropriate for those facing decades of imprisonment. More recently, Flanagan (1985) argued in a similar vein that long-term inmates need more than just prison "program planning," they need "sentence planning." Our research on problem

identification by long-termers reported in our companion chapter (Chapter 2) in this book revealed that as a group these individuals are more concerned with quality-of-life issues, including the quality and availability of medical care, noise and crowding, food quality, and staff-inmate communication, than with more traditional treatment program issues. These results echo the need to address the totality of extended prison existence for long-termers through integrated approaches, rather than simply plugging them into traditional correctional programs.

The exploratory programs discussed in this chapter were developed as part of a larger project on "Handling Long-term Offenders" in Missouri (hereafter referred to as The Missouri Project: Cowles, Sabath, Pickett-Putnam, Stecker, Crumes, & Riley, 1989). The Missouri Project began with an exercise aimed at identifying problematic situations associated with long-term correctional incarceration, using a multiple perspectives approach (see the accompanying chapter in this book for a detailed

AUTHORS' NOTE: This chapter is based on research supported by grant 84-IJ-CX-0043 from the National Institute of Justice. Opinions expressed are those of the authors and do not necessarily represent the official positions or policies of the National Institute of Justice or the U.S. Department of Justice.
NOTE: This is a revised version of an article that was originally published in *The Prison Journal*, Vol. 80, No. 1, Spring/Summer 1990, pp. 73-82. Copyright 1990 by Sage Publications, Inc.

review of the methodology and results). This work resulted in the identification of 32 problems that were then collapsed into six general areas:

- inmate-staff relationships/communication
- institutional careers
- institutional services
- programs and activities
- physical environment
- family/community relationships

In considering potential program approaches, we attempted to address problems highlighted in our problem identification study within the context described above. The following discussion focuses on three long-term inmate programs designed and developed to address three identified problem areas: institutional careers, institutional services, and inmate-staff relationships/communications. The first exploratory approach deals with the concept of institutional work careers that provide the long-term inmates with a meaningful occupation while simultaneously benefiting the correctional agency. The second describes a similar endeavor to provide long-termer career opportunities while enhancing institutional services. The third presents an attempt to deal with the issue of communications/relationships between staff and long-termers. This is an area in which the two groups appear to hold very different perceptions. These particular programs are reviewed because they illustrate the strategies that were employed during The Missouri Project within an existing facility. Another group of integrated programs intended to address some of the other problem areas was prepared during the project for the department's new maximum security institution, which was under construction during most of the project (Cowles et al., 1989). Table 21.1 presents a summary overview of these programs.

DEVELOPING LONG-TERMER PROGRAMS

Philosophically, we believed that three key elements—security, control, and quality of life—needed to be considered when developing programs directed toward long-term inmates.

The first two elements, security and control, are traditionally identified with the mission and operation of prisons. The first of these, security, refers to the prevention of the offender's escaping the confines of the institution. The second, control, identifies the processes and mechanisms employed to establish internal order within the facility. Unfortunately, the distinction between the two frequently becomes clouded, promoting the development of very high security institutions with extremely restrictive internal environments into which all "security" problems are dumped. The third element encompasses an area perhaps a bit more difficult to define, involving the humane treatment, the allowance for basic human dignity, and preservation of hope for the future for a long-term inmate.[1] In order for a long-term inmate program to be successful, we assumed that it must simultaneously address all three key elements' areas. This is based on the belief that key actor or stakeholder groups, whose participation is vital to the successful operation of the program, have different concerns regarding these key areas. For example, a program that improves the quality of life for long-term inmates but ignores security concerns might be acceptable to the long-termers but not to the correctional officers. Therefore, a critical aspect of this program design strategy was to identify the perceptions held by the different groups as reported in the companion chapter included in this book.

Institutional Environment

The programs included in this discussion were conceptualized as part of the larger Missouri Project. Although four of the state's 10 closed-custody correctional institutions existing at the time of the project held some long-termers, the vast majority, and in particular those serving very long determinant sentences, were housed in the state's single maximum security facility, the Missouri State Penitentiary.[2] At the time of the project, this institution held about 1,900 inmates. Of this population, approximately 55% were expected to serve at least 6 years of actual imprisonment before their release, and about 11% were very long-termers, that is, those who had no parole or other release possibilities for at least 30 years. Because the Missouri State Penitentiary was located close to the Department's Central

TABLE 21.1 Summary of Program Activity in the Missouri Project

Programs	Problem Categories Addressed	#LTOs Involved	Consensus Level	Expected Outcomes	Results
Software Development	Institutional careers	6-40	moderate/high	Meaningful LTO work	No inmate dropouts/dismissals
	Programs & activities			Better LTO management	Improved inmate behavior
				Manpower resources for Department applications with measurable cost savings to department	Production of 4 major software
Jefftown Productions	Institutional careers	6-12 (benefits for entire pop.)	moderate	Meaningful LTO work	Wired entire prison with cable
	Institutional services			Improve Department media capabilities	Production of 4 videos at substantial cost savings
				Better access to information/education /vocational training	Supplied information on topics such as AIDS education for LTOs
Inmate Forums	Inmate-staff communi-cation/ relationships	6	low	Establish communication linkages between project staff & LTOs	Used successfully during project
				Provide informal avenue for communication between LTOs & administration	

Office, which housed the project staff, and because this facility did hold the majority of the state's very long-term inmate population, much of the project's program effort was located at this site.

The Missouri State Penitentiary, which is the oldest prison west of the Mississippi River, suffered most of the ailments that trouble many of this nation's old, maximum security prisons. It was a mosaic of old and new construction and required extensive ongoing maintenance and repair just to remain operational. Because it lacked most of the sophisticated technology found in modern prisons, its operations were very staff-intensive, particularly regarding security. The inmate population had grown far beyond the institution's original capacity in terms of both living space and support facilities, including the recreational and dining areas. Complicating the overcrowding problem was the fact that as the state's only male maximum security prison, it not only held those with very long terms but also housed the state's death row population and a "super max," or prison-within-a-prison, facility for those creating severe disciplinary problems throughout the correctional system. Additionally, because it also was the site of the system's prison hospital, most of the inmates with serious medical problems were also held there. This hospital facility was more than 50 years old and had been chronically under-funded in terms of both equipment and medical staff. It had reached the point where it could in no way meet acceptable medical accreditation standards and was the subject of many inmate complaints.

In terms of education and vocational programs, the prison did house a sizable prison industry complex; however, it was concentrated in metal working and furniture manufacturing. Consequently, most of the long-termers were ineligible to work there because of their security status. Although the institution did have a fairly new school, it was difficult to provide education programs in the traditional classroom style because many of the inmates were in some type of "restricted" movement status. With the exception of the prison industry, vocational programs were virtually nonexistent, and for a period of time during the project, the vocational-technical building had to be converted to an inmate dormitory. This compounding lack of space and meaningful activities to fill the inmates' time created problems for both inmates and staff.

The problems relating to the daily living environment of long-term inmates highlighted above are not intended to provide a complete picture of the prison; rather, they represent areas perceived as problematic by a large percentage of the long-termers (see the companion chapter) and are likely encountered by long-termers in similar facilities throughout the country.

Meaningful Institutional Careers

One of the major philosophical differences in program planning identified between short-term and long-term inmates is in the skill/vocational training and institutional work assignment areas. For individuals who will be spending decades, and perhaps the remainder of their lives, in a correctional institution, many of the traditional job preparation programs, particularly in rapidly changing technological skill areas, have little meaning relative to their long sentences. Long-termers frequently feel frustrated that although they complete training courses, they achieve no recognition for their efforts and are provided little opportunity to utilize these skills productively in a prison career. The comments

provided by a long-term inmate responding to one of the surveys conducted in our research exemplifies this feeling:

> 181: I have 18 hours of college credit and have been certified for being a G.E.D. facilitator. I also have taken Typing I, II, and III and I have just completed the paralegal course. I have also been through the two food preparation courses which the institution used to offer . . . so can anyone tell me why I've been assigned to work in the laundry?

The problematic nature of unproductive time seems to be a perception shared by staff (85% of the correctional officers and 95% of the treatment staff saw this as a moderate or severe problem) as well as long-termers (53% saw this as a moderate or severe problem). Similarly, more than half of both staff (52% of correctional officers and 64% of treatment personnel) and long-termers (59%) saw "vocational programs providing useful skills" as a moderate or severe problem. There is a tremendous potential resource in the time long-term inmates are mandated to serve. For example, an institution containing 500 long-termers working only 6 hours per day, 5 days per week, 52 weeks per year for 20 years would generate more than 15,600,000 hours. This time could applied to activities worthwhile to both the inmates and the administration. The following discussion briefly describes the two experimental approaches to managing these long-term incarceration problems that illustrate the benefits of moving long-termers away from traditional institutional "jobs" toward institutional "careers" within an existing facility structure.

The Software Development Program

The Software Development Program module was conceived as an experimental effort that would enable us to learn more about the possibilities for meaningful job programming in prisons and the effects on long-termers. This type of program is particularly suited for long-term inmates because the acquisition of programming skills requires extended study and involvement. Additionally, the career is one that offers a continuing challenge and progression to higher skill levels.

The basic assumption underlying the Software Development Program (hereafter referred to as SDP) was that improvements in the quality and nature of work for long-termers would improve their behavior and likewise the correctional personnel's ability to influence and manage it.

Therefore, based on this assumption, the most important goal of this effort was to increase the ability of correctional personnel to manage the long-term segment of the prison population by influencing their attitudes and behaviors. This was achieved by reducing some of the debilitating effects of extended incarceration (e.g., the boredom arising from monotonous make-work jobs) that can lead to unrest and disorder, by instead offering incentives such as better than average inmate pay and the opportunity to spend time pursuing a meaningful productive career within the institutional confines.

Inmates selected for the SDP were trained to work with software packages commonly used in government and private industry. They were also taught programming knowledge and skills that enabled them to develop operational software applications, such as accounting and inventory systems. Emphasis was placed on having the program resemble, as closely as possible, an organization in the civilian population by maintaining set work hours, lines of authority, standards for work quality, performance evaluation, and procedures for managing work flow. Inmate workers were also given an opportunity to have input into operations and provide training to new workers, thus giving them a feeling of ownership.

The SDP was initiated by enlisting the support of key department administrators, long-termers, security personnel, educators, and information systems staff who would be interacting with the program and its participants. In this way, issues concerning security (of workers, equipment, and computer transactions), physical location of the program, training of the workers, supervision of work, and other concerns could be dealt with in a manner acceptable to all.

The actual operation of the SDP started with the employment of six long-termers and the purchase of six stand-alone personal computers. Common software packages were also acquired as well as emulation software. This was to prevent the inmates from having any direct connection to computer networks outside the prison but enabled them to produce programs usable by systems outside "the walls." Participation in the program was made very attractive to the inmates because the lead workers were paid $100 per month, and those in training received $30 per month. These amounts were far above the typical prison wages at that time of $7.50 to $12 per month. Additionally, they had relatively pleasant surroundings, including an air-conditioned workplace, which was a rare privilege within this prison. Although the SDP was highly structured in terms of both work and behavioral expectations for the inmates, it quickly became evident the inmates had assumed a professional orientation toward their work and were maintaining a self-disciplined control over their behavior. This was quite surprising to many in the institution.

Within the year and a half remaining in which The Missouri Project existed, the experimental SDP demonstrated that such a program could operate effectively in a prison environment and have a positive impact on the participating inmates. During this time, there was no damage or destruction to any of the equipment. In terms of misconduct reports, none of the program participants received such reports on the job, and only four minor violations occurred off the job (a violation rate significantly below that of the general population). These offenders not only received financial incentives for working but also seemed to derive a great deal of personal satisfaction from their work. This was exemplified by most of the workers preferring to stay and continue working after the official workday had ended. Many even spent much of their leisure time reading computer magazines and working on programs. The following comments offered by one long-term inmate programmer mirror statements made by the long-termers regarding their work situation in the SDP program: ". . . After being treated like nothing . . . to work with someone (i.e., civilian staff) that ask (sic) your opinion . . . and utilize it . . . makes you feel good."

Within the first year of its operation, the program produced three major software systems for the department, including the information system for the Long-term Offender Project, an inmate education tracking system, and a maintenance management system. Bolstered by these early successes, the SDP was integrated into the department's information system section, and the State Legislature authorized a spending appropriation of $260,473 to expand the SDP's personnel and equipment. The inmate staff was increased to 12, and a new stand-alone mainframe was purchased in order to allow the SDP to take work on larger applications.

At the completion of The Missouri Project, the SDP not only served as a viable production unit of the department's computer section but did so at approximately a 27:1 cost-saving ratio over hiring comparable civilian staff. Additionally, the program began contracting with several other state agencies to provide programming services. The information systems director estimated that the program would be generating about $1 million in revenue within 3 years of its inception and planned to increase the long-termer staff to 40 inmates.

Jefftown Productions

This experimental program was also envisioned as an alternative to traditional prison occupations, which are generally characterized by low-skilled, repetitive work, or to those prison occupations that are not available to long-termers because of their potential security risks. The primary goal of this approach was to provide a viable institutional career for long-term inmates by exploring the feasibility of developing a video production studio inside a maximum security prison. It was hoped that if such a career would interest long-term inmates, they could develop the necessary expertise to operate an institutional cable system and allow the department a practical way to operate its own video production facility. This would give the department the ability to produce and edit educational and informational programs, thereby increasing the availability of these services to the entire inmate population.

Similar to the Software Development Program, incentives for the Jefftown Productions program included a higher inmate wage, pleasant working conditions, and involving work that supplied considerable status within the prison because of its technical and professional nature. Again, as was the case with the SDP, the idea was that a positive work environment would provide incentives for constructive behavior both on and off the job.

The Jefftown Productions approach differed from the Software Development Program in that it grew from an existing operation rather than being implemented as a totally new program. The Missouri State Penitentiary had a cable TV system designed to provide educational, religious, and entertainment programming to the inmate population. This existing system was known as Jefftown Cable Network and was manned by five long-term inmates. During The Missouri Project, the Jefftown station was relocated to the prison's school building. Providing Jefftown with more space within the school permitted the development of an inmate vocational training program while continuing cable TV services to the institution. The institutional administration was particularly interested in the possibilities of using a cable network to provide educational services to the prison's lockdown population areas, such as death row and certain segregation units where the inmates were not permitted to mix with the general population and therefore could not attend traditional classes in the prison school.

Again, in keeping with a belief in the need to involve the group of key actors who would impact or be impacted by the activities of the Jefftown project, a committee reflecting the various group perspectives was formed to provide the project with direction. A video media instructor was hired and the training of the long-termers begun. With the support of the institution's administration, the department's education section, and the inmate canteen, equipment was slowly acquired to provide the Jefftown project with true video production capabilities. As the long-termer crew developed skills, they began to experiment with video production, taping various institution events and messages from the administration. After several short productions were completed, including one on the Long-term Offender Project that was taken to an American Correctional Association meeting, production requests from throughout the department and beyond began to flood the project. It was decided that the scope of the activities for the Jefftown Project should be broadened to include the needs of the entire department. The oversight committee was transformed to include representatives from throughout the department and was given the task of establishing guidelines for productions.

In the year of operation before the completion of The Missouri Project, the Jefftown Productions unit successfully completed several production efforts. Among these efforts was a video production that focused on AIDS issues and prevention. This video was disseminated as part of an AIDS education/training package provided to inmates and staff of the correctional system. Additional projects were a staff training video on proper security search procedures, a public awareness video produced for a nonprofit organization that operated an inmate parent and child visitation program for incarcerated mothers, and a video on the system's death row operations that was produced for use by the general television news media. All of these efforts were completed at a fraction of the cost that would have been incurred had the Jefftown Productions project not existed, allowing the department to provide services not otherwise possible. Regrettably, no other evaluation of the Jefftown project was initiated, although the same type of intensity and professional orientation was seen in the work of the long-termers in this program as had been observed by those participating in the Software Development Program.

Inmate-Staff Relationships/Communication

The area of inmate-staff relationships/communication is inherently problematic due to the fundamental nature of incarceration and the roles of the keepers and the kept. Problem identification efforts revealed a considerable difference in perceptions between long-termers and staff regarding this area. There was a very widespread perception (77%) among the long-termers that "staff ignoring inmate complaints and suggestions" was a moderate or severe problem, whereas less than one third (27% of the correctional officers, 35% of the treatment personnel) of the staff held the view that this was a moderate or severe problem. Similarly, 60% of the long-termers held the perception that the "attitude of the staff" posed a moderate or severe problem, but staff perceptions differed markedly in that only 24% of the correctional officers and 39% of the treatment staff held the view that this was a moderate or severe problem. Since the relationships and communication between staff and inmates form the cornerstone for building other problem-

solving efforts, it was believed that this area was worthy of special attention. The information presented below briefly reviews the attempt made at improving the flow of information and communication linkages between the two groups.

Inmate Forum

The Inmate Forum was designed as a mechanism to ensure that the perspectives of a primary group of stakeholders, namely the long-term inmates, were included in the activities of The Missouri Project. It was believed that by establishing a relationship with influential long-termers, the project stood a better chance of gaining acceptance by the inmate population, and that forum members would serve to represent the larger population in providing feedback on various aspects of the project. It was also hoped that if the forum gained acceptance, it might continue to provide an ongoing communication link between the long-termers and staff.

Much of the communication effort within the correctional bureaucracy has become so formalized, to the point of ritual, that the medium of the communication frequently becomes the primary emphasis, rather than the content of the message. Statements such as "If you want to get their (the administration's) attention, you file a lawsuit!" or "We always provide a written response to an inmate's grievance within 15 working days" reflect this orientation. For this reason, it was decided that the atmosphere of the Inmate Forum should be kept as informal as possible, that is, to provide an atmosphere where all the participants would feel at ease and constraints would not be placed upon the level or direction of discussion.

The forum was initiated by asking the institution's administrative staff to identify long-term inmates whom they believed would interact in such a program and could articulate the long-termers' position. In general, the project staff was interested in having forum members who were knowledgeable about the institution and long-term inmates' concerns; could articulate the viewpoints, opinions, and concerns of the larger population; and who reflected the diversity within the long-term population. Long-termers initially identified by the administrators as potential candidates

for membership on the forum were interviewed by the project staff to determine their
interest in participating. All those selected for
the forum through this process accepted the
invitation to become members. While The
Missouri Project was operating, the project
staff was responsible for coordinating the activities of the forum, including establishing
meeting times and arranging for space, maintaining contact with forum members, and con-
tacting staff members who were asked to attend particular meetings to address issues.
Some meetings focused on a particular topic
or aspect of the project; others were simply
unstructured discussions, that is, bull sessions, on various topics related to prison life
and inmate concerns.

Because the forum was originally intended
as a mechanism to help the project develop
programs, rather than to stand as a demonstration model itself, formal evaluation was neither planned nor conducted on it. However, it
did prove to be very helpful in establishing a
relationship between project staff and the long-
term inmates. The forum members became a
sounding board for ideas, a way to get feedback from the long-termer population on issues and programs, and a means of establishing linkages to the long-term population.
The assistance of the forum members was also
invaluable in collecting information, providing suggestions on content areas addressed in
the project's inmate surveys, and improving
survey response rates. Further, over the length
of the project, the forum concept appeared to
have gained acceptance by administration,
line staff, and inmates. Perhaps the most significant reflection of this is that the institutional administration at the department's new
long-termer facility, under construction during the project, planned to import the forum
concept from the Missouri State Penitentiary
at the point when the inmates were transferred
to the new facility.

The Programs Five Years Later

The "what ever happened to . . ." question
always leads to interesting and often informative discussions regarding the promise of new
correctional programs, their growth and evolution, and in many cases, their demise. Six
years have now passed since the NIJ funded
project discussed in the first part of this chap-

ter ended. It seemed appropriate, therefore, to
include in this discussion a brief review as to
the current state of these programs.

The Missouri State Penitentiary has undergone a name change to the Jefferson City Correctional Center. With the opening of the state's
new state-of-the-art super maximum security
prison, the role of the Jefferson City institution
changed. No longer is it the "big house," the
institution housing the worst of the worst.
Gone are the death row population, the 50-
year, no-parole inmate population, and the
system's inmate troublemakers. What remains
is an antiquated, overcrowded facility requiring costly maintenance and intensive staffing,
still housing a high-security inmate population with long sentences. Thus, long-termer
programs remain an important operational
component in this prison.

The Inmate Forum, conceived as a mechanism to facilitate communication between staff
and inmates, appears to have disappeared.
According to an institutional official, the forum
hasn't been functional since it was used to
facilitate discussion between the inmates and
staff during the planning and start-up of the
new maximum security prison.

The Jefftown Video Production Unit has
undergone changes, although its basic purpose and activities have remained essentially
unchanged. For a period of time after The
Missouri Project ended, the Jefftown Unit was
administratively housed in the department's
Central Office public affairs unit, though its
physical operations remained within the penitentiary. With this organizational structure,
the role of Jefftown Productions was viewed as
an arm of the department's public information
efforts, rather than as an institutional service
provider. As a result of personnel changes and
administrative decisions, however, administrative oversight of the program was returned
to the institutional administration, where it
remains at the current time. The Jefftown program has remained fairly static in terms of its
size—about eight inmates are involved—but
has continued to improve its equipment and
production expertise. The Jefftown Unit remains actively engaged in video production
for other state agencies and has even produced
materials for the governor's office. Within the
Jefferson City Correctional Institution it continues to offer educational, informational, and
entertainment programming and has been fea-

tured in the national media as a unique training program for inmates. The deputy superintendent who oversees its operation views it as an important information link between the administration and the inmate population. Further, it is viewed as an inmate project—a program run by inmates for the benefit of inmates (personal communication with D. Cline, September 30, 1994). Perhaps the best indicator of this orientation is the fact that the main source of funding for Jefftown Productions comes through funds generated by the inmate canteen operations.

The third project developed as part of the Missouri Long Term Offender's Project, the Software Development Project, is probably the best example of the potential that exists when programs are designed that simultaneously meet the needs of both the inmates and the agency. Like the Jefftown Productions efforts, the Software Development Project has experienced changes through both administrative restructuring and natural maturation. After the National Institute of Justice project ended, the SDP was placed under the administrative direction of the Correctional Industries unit, where it remained for about 3 years. During this time, the SDP was viewed as a revenue-generating activity as the production of software for other state agencies was promoted. In the past year and a half, the SDP has returned to the administrative control of the department's information systems section. This administrative change has also resulted in a change in production orientation to one totally focused on software development for the corrections department. These changes notwithstanding, the SDP has continued to grow and mature as a viable long-term inmate program and service provider to the department.

The SDP has now grown to 24 male inmate workers, and further expansion is currently planned. According to the director of the information systems section, the only thing that has prevented the program from previous growth has been a limitation on physical space available to the program. The expansion of the SDP is now possible because the program has been able to secure additional space, allowing for 10 to 15 additional inmate programmers. Perhaps even more intriguing is the current plan to expand the SDP to another correctional facility, which houses long-term female inmates. These plans call for 10 to 15 female inmates to be trained in software develop-

ment. Once this unit is operational, trained female inmate programmers will work with six civilian staff members on the department's personnel and fiscal management software applications (D. Ingle, personal communication, September 29, 1994).

As might be surmised from the above, one of the unique features of the SDP is the relationship between inmate and civilian workers in this project. In present operations, more than half (eight) of the civilian information systems staff work inside the prison alongside inmate workers. Project teams consist of both inmate and civilian staff, and although inmates are not placed in direct supervisory roles, senior inmate programmers frequently are involved in the training of junior inmate and civilian staff. In this regard, the information systems unit views the inmate and civilian staff members as part of a singular work force.

Integrating long-term inmates into this work force continues to provide benefits in two major areas. First, there is the resource advantage. The director of the department's information systems unit indicates that it costs about $3,000 in equipment to set up a work station for either a civilian or inmate worker. However, civilian programmers are paid, on average, around $32,000 per year, and it additionally costs about 30% of their salary base to cover the costs of their fringe benefits. The most experienced and highest paid inmate workers make about $3,000 a year. The overall cost saving ratio for the department for its software application development activities is approximately 18:1. The director estimates that the SDP saves the department hundreds of thousands of dollars each year in applications development costs. Further, several inmate programmers who have been with the SDP since its inception have now both the familiarity and the expertise to work in systems development. A statement made by the director, indicating that "he couldn't buy that talent on the street," reflects the value he places on the abilities of the long-term inmates working for the SDP (D. Ingle, personal communication, September 29, 1994).

The second area of benefit seems to be the continued positive influence that working for the SDP has on the attitudes and behavior of the inmate workers. The director notes that, in the program's 6 years of operations, there have been no inmate grievances or lawsuits arising from conflicts, complaints, or problems within the SDP. Further, during the same period of time, there has only been one violation of institutional rules by an inmate worker at the SDP workplace. This involved an inmate worker having a jar of fruit in his desk that he was fermenting to make "hootch" (the institutionally prohibited homemade alcoholic beverage). This inmate was terminated from the program for this violation as per the basic rules established at the program's inception. Thus, the relatively high inmate wage scale, pleasant working conditions, and opportunity to be involved in a satisfying institutional career appear to have had the desired long-term individual and system impacts described earlier. Asked to sum up his feeling about the success of the Software Development Program over the past 6 years, he replied simply, "It has worked stupendously" (D. Ingle, personal communication, September 29, 1994).

INTEGRATED LONG-TERM INMATE STRATEGIES

At best, the experimental approaches reviewed in this discussion represent very modest attempts to move away from more traditional prison programs toward ways to better address the needs observed in the long-term inmate population, and were provided primarily to illustrate the techniques that were employed in The Missouri Project. A more central concept in the process of addressing the needs and problems of long-term sentences is the development of a methodology to identify these needs and problems within the context of the prison environment in which they must be faced. This process must involve the key actors or stakeholders who affect or are affected by both the problems and the potential solutions. For this reason, we stress a utilization of the problem identification techniques we employed, rather than a simple adaptation of the program approaches.

Another aspect that should be considered in the development of long-termer programs is the totality of extended incarceration. The creation of singular program approaches will likely not improve the management of long-

term sentences unless these approaches are integrated into the various facets of the offender's long-term prison career. By concentrating long-term offenders within specialized and, hopefully, specifically designed institutions, the most promising opportunity for such an integrated system arises.[3] This approach allows for the concentration of resources for specialized programs and services designed to satisfy the needs of this inmate population rather than attempting to force fit these offenders into existing programs and services targeted at relatively short-term confinement.

NOTES

1. For an excellent discussion of these elements see Bottoms and Light (1987).

2. A separate women's prison housed all security classifications of female inmates including the long-termers. Although the women were included in the project, the assessment and programs involving these individuals is not reported in this piece.

3. For a more in-depth discussion of these ideas, see our discussion of the Potosi Plan in the Final Handling Long-term Offenders Report (Cowles et al., 1989).

REFERENCES

Bottoms, A., & Light, R. (1987). Introduction: Problems of long-term imprisonment. In A. Bottoms & R. Light (Eds.), *Problems of long-term incarceration.* Brookfield, VT: Gower.

Cowles, E. L., Sabath, M. J., Pickett-Putnam, S., Stecker, A., Crumes, K. R., & Riley, D. (1989). *Handling long-term offenders: The Missouri project* (Final Report on National Institute of Justice Grant 84-IJ-CX-0043). Washington, DC: National Institute of Justice.

Flanagan, T. (1985, January). Correctional policy and the long-term prisoner. *Crime and Delinquency,* 82-95.

Toch, H. (1977). The long-term prisoner as a long-term problem. In S. Rizkalla, R. Levy, & R. Zauberman (Eds.), *Long-term imprisonment: An international seminar.* Montreal: University of Montreal.

Unger, C., & Buchanan, R. (1985). *Managing long-term inmates: A guide for the correctional administrator.* Washington, DC: National Institute of Justice.

22

Programming for Long-Term Inmates

A New Perspective

William R. T. Palmer

It is a paradox that the best adjusted residents of our penitentiaries are often those serving the longest terms, whose instant offenses are the most heinous, who are perceived by citizens as presenting the greatest risk, and for whom public approval for leniency is least available (Alper, 1974; Flanagan, 1982; Zink, 1958; Zubrycki, 1983). Further, prison programs are typically designed for inmates spending one to three years incarcerated; thus, those least problematical seem also to be least rewarded with relevant programs. The present paper reports an alternative, a group program called *LifeServers* which has operated since 1976 at Warkworth Institution particularly for long-term inmates. Also discussed will be some of the practices and procedures which the institution's case management teams have evolved in relation to members of this group. Finally, there will be comments offered in regard to a number of long-term inmate issues which reflect our experience over the years with the program's participants.

Much that follows is based upon the beliefs that prison sentences generally, and long-term sentences in particular, are likely to remain features of the Canadian justice system, and that the appropriate role of corrections must involve attempts to deal effectively within the framework of the existing law. Acceptance of these premises does not necessarily represent endorsement of the policy of long-term incarceration; it does, however, lead to a call for action on behalf of the affected prisoners.

Since 1976 Warkworth has housed approximately 170 individuals serving life or indefinite terms who have been eligible for group membership. Thirty-one were involved initially and are the primary subject of this report. As of June 1, 1983, all but three of the original members had been transferred or paroled. We currently house 66 such individuals, approximately three-quarters of whom have some involvement in the program.

To put the penitentiary in context, Warkworth is a medium security "living unit" institution. Within the constraints of a secure setting, the organizational model attempts to encourage inmates to learn social skills, to develop responsibility and to accept social

AUTHOR'S NOTE: The author has been a psychologist on staff at Warkworth Institution since February, 1975. He has been the staff member involved with the *LifeServers* group since its inception in mid-1976. The opinions expressed in this chapter are his own. They do not necessarily reflect the views or policies of the Ministry of the Solicitor General of Canada.

restrictions. Staff are deployed and administered on an integrated team basis with each group working consistently with a constant group of inmates. In comparison to other penitentiaries in Ontario, Warkworth has historically been a relatively program-oriented institution, especially so during the formative years of the program described here. Programs and security continue, as in the past, to coexist with minimal friction. The institution is located in rural eastern Ontario, midway between Toronto and Kingston. The inmates number slightly under 600. We have a staff complement of approximately 290.

THE ORIGINAL
PROGRAM PARTICIPANTS

As mentioned above there were 31 charter members of the *LifeServers* group. Their average age was slightly over 31 years, ranging from 20 to 58. An interesting subgroup of six had received their life sentences prior to their 18th birthdays. Each of these young inmates had gone directly from the social role of "dependent adolescent," living within his own family, to the role of "inmate" without any intervening status or period of independence. Approximately two-thirds of the original group (20), including all of the young inmates, were first-time offenders. The remaining 11 had criminal convictions and/or incarcerations prior to the sentences which they were serving in 1976. All had begun their sentences in other institutions, having then transferred to Warkworth prior to this project's initiation. On average, they had served just under three years within Warkworth, two months being the minimum and ranging up to seven years and three months. Nine of the initial 31 had been admitted to the institution within the 12 months previous.

Of the 31, two were serving life-minimum commuted capital sentences. Twenty-five were serving life-minimum sentences for noncapital murder. The other four were serving life as a maximum punishment; two for importing narcotics, one for rape and one for kidnapping. Those whose life sentences were automatic, i.e., life as a minimum punishment, were required by law to serve at least 10 years before being eligible for parole. The four whose life sentences represented maximum punishment were eligible for parole after seven years. Three

years prior to their eligibility for parole, all were eligible for day parole which is a form of conditional release requiring nightly residence in either a penitentiary or a community correctional centre. At the time the program was initiated 23 of the 31 men were already eligible for short, unescorted, pass-type releases from close confinement. This privilege had been granted only to five of the eligible 23.

It is noteworthy that one-third of the charter members (10) were housed on one range with a capacity of 17. The remaining 21 were distributed throughout the remaining 23 ranges of the institution. The range which housed those 10 long-term inmates had the reputation of being the "best" in the prison in the sense that it was quiet and trouble free. The inmates reputedly granted more respect to the rights of other inmates than was typical on other units. The residents of that range also tended to be more supportive of each other than was general throughout the prison.

CURRENT STATUS OF
ORIGINAL PROGRAM PARTICIPANTS

As of June 1st, 1983, 27 of the original 31 inmates had been released into the community for periods ranging from three months to six and one-half years. The majority had been on parole for more than two years. Of the four not then released, three were on pre-release programs, two of these within Warkworth and one while housed in a minimum security institution. The single remaining inmate continued to serve time at Warkworth, not having been granted any type of pre-release program despite having been eligible for such privileges for several years.

Figure 22.1 illustrates the four different program routes utilized by the 28 individuals discharged. One individual transferred as a result of security concerns was still serving his sentence. Thus, 27 of the original group had been released into the community. Twenty-five of these were maintaining acceptable adjustments. Two had been reincarcerated; the first as a result of a drug-related charge after four years on parole, the second as a result of a conviction for theft after two years on parole.

During the past 10 years there have been 308 individuals granted parole while serving life sentences in Canada and their average length of time to first release has been 11.96

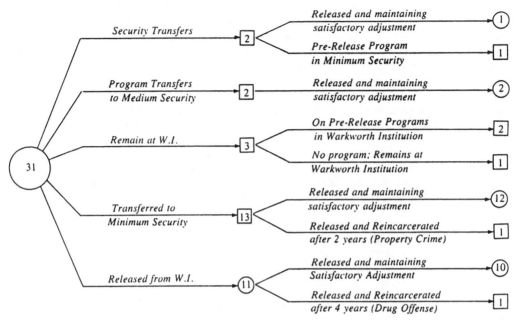

Figure 22.1. Program Routes and Disposition of Thirty-One Original Members of *LifeServers*

years (National Parole Board Statistical Liaison Officer, 1983). The modal time served by those in the *LifeServers* program has been nine years. An "eyeball" comparison of the data strongly suggests that the success rate of those released in nine years versus those released in 12 years is virtually identical. The national revocation rate for new offenses—no subsequent murders—was 6.5% (National Parole Board Statistical Liaison Officer, 1983). The Warkworth revocation rate for new offenses—obviously also without subsequent murders—was 7.7%. Given the size of our sample it is impossible to more closely approximate the national statistic.

THE LIFESERVERS PROGRAM

Formal Program Elements

The *LifeServers* group operates under a constitution approved by the institutional administration which states, in part, that,

> It shall be the goal of the *LifeServers* to initiate, develop and maintain community programs or projects which will serve to contribute to the mutual benefit

of the *LifeServers*, our own community and the community at large. Membership is open to all residents of the population serving life sentences. The group meets twice monthly for general meetings. There is an executive committee. Additionally, all group programs or functions will be administered by subcommittees of members who have special interests in those projects.

The reader will note the similarities of the group's goals, purposes and organization to those generally found in community service clubs. The purpose is not overtly therapeutic, though such is clearly legitimized for any subgroup which chooses to pursue goals of personal development. Generally, the group is best construed as providing a framework within which individual members can find assistance in achieving the legitimate goals which they establish for themselves. Such goals include personal growth, service to others and service to the group membership.

Some *LifeServers'* projects happen on a regular, ongoing basis with the group providing organizational support to ensure that they remain continuous. Other projects tend to rely on the presence of given individuals with specific interests. Such latter projects tend to be organized and/or funded by the *LifeServers* throughout the duration of a key individual's participation, ending when that individual is transferred or paroled. For example, for several years the *LifeServers* organized and funded a "jogging" program in conjunction with the institution's recreation department. Interested inmates were provided with assistance and advice on training routines, diet, shoe choice, etc. Five successively longer distance runs were organized on weekends throughout the spring and summer months. The group organized the events, publicized them, provided lap scoring and timing and rewarded all runners with trophies or prizes. Despite being a successful program involving literally scores of inmates over a span of several years, the program was returned to the recreation department when the key individual in *LifeServers* was paroled. In some sense, then, the *LifeServers* were providing support to one of their own. That specific individual made meaning of his sentence by encouraging fitness in others. The group's commitment was to his attempt to derive value from his sentence rather than to jogging per se.

In terms of continuous programs, the *LifeServers* run quarterly sales of confections as a way of raising revenue. They also sell candy and soft drinks at the weekly movies though the profits from these sales are committed entirely to the support of international foster children. The group organizes and provides trophies and prizes for an annual baseball tournament. Similar services are provided on an occasional basis for such activities as billiards, bridge and volleyball. The group also organizes and funds an annual inmates' children's Christmas party which provides an opportunity for those inmates who are fathers to be with their children in a party atmosphere and for a traditional supper each year during the holiday season. Financial support is provided to other inmate groups including, for example, the purchase and donation of an electric typewriter to the institution's inmate operated "Community Information Service." Also, for the past two years the group has organized bimonthly seminars which are open for all interested inmates to attend.

Additionally, at times in the past, the group has worked for the Rotary's Easter Seal campaign, has hand sewn colours for a local troup of cub scouts and organized a "media day" on which local print, radio and TV journalists toured the institution escorted by *LifeServers*. Collectively, the members produced the paper "Sentenced to Life! To Find It or To Endure It?" (Lifers in Warkworth Institution, 1976). A day long seminar was organized three years ago on "Vocational Programs for Long-Term Inmates"; another was held last year on "Maintaining Community Ties for Long-Term Inmates" (Palmer, 1984a). The group also maintains a dialogue with the National Parole Board and meetings are held at least yearly with NPB members in order to clarify issues of special concern to long-term inmates.

Finally, there are always members of the *LifeServers* who have interests in personal growth and many have been active in programs with therapeutic emphases. The Psychology Department coordinates the group, thus tending to create a special connection between treatment services and those serving life sentences. *LifeServers* members have been especially active in our relaxation training and biofeedback programs, both as clients and as inmate technicians. The psychology department has run a number of time-limited group therapy programs over the years and *LifeServers* have typically been over-represented in those groups. At one point several years ago, the institution found its treatment services severely curtailed as a result of fiscal restraints and staff illness. During that period the *LifeServers* organized and partially funded a service contract with a part-time gestalt therapist. Three hours of group gestalt training were provided weekly for 12 inmates over several months funded equally by the institution, the *LifeServers* group and the participants themselves. Finally, it is hoped a *Toastmasters* subprogram can be added in the future to assist those members who experience some difficulty in speaking spontaneously. Such skills are highly valued, especially since each member sees his eventual release as being partially dependent upon his ability to "sell" himself to the parole board during a series of interviews.

Informal Program Elements

Additionally, a full appreciation of the *LifeServers* group is not possible without an understanding of the informal impact of the group upon its members, particularly insofar as they share common problems. It was mentioned earlier that a substantial percentage of the *LifeServers* are first-time offenders; in prison argot, they tend to be "square johns." The difficulty of being a square peg in a rounder's hole is a problem which can find expression in the context of the group. To illustrate, the long-termer's tendency to refer to his cell as his "house" versus the more typical use of the term "drum" implies strongly contrasting cognitions about prison life. Such differences hardly escape the notice of long-term inmates. Generally, they recognize that they have different interests than other inmates; consequently, they tend to be appreciative of a forum in which their interests and concerns are recognized, shared and legitimized.

Over the years, through discussion, the group has achieved a fairly sophisticated view of the emotional pressures and changes experienced by men convicted of violent crimes and sentenced to long periods in prison. One of the important informal functions of the group is the transmission of such insights and/or coping strategies both across individuals and across time. The collective experience is shared widely. Similarly, the group encompasses a good deal of what might be called peer-counseling. When needed, this service may extend as far as supportive Big-Brother-type relationships established informally. The insight and support of the group often proves useful to specific individuals experiencing emotional difficulties at some particular point in their sentence.

As a start in illustrating the type of belief systems developed by the group, one might suggest that everyone achieves his own perspective. A lawyer friend of mine refers to the *LifeServers* as "failed defenses to murder." The police, media and/or public views tend to portray them as violent and maniacal threats to public safety. Correctional officers often see them as stabilizing influences within prisons. In my role as psychologist, I have a tendency to see within the group a high proportion of individuals who are struggling with feelings of guilt and depression. Not surprisingly, then, the *LifeServers* tend also to have their own self view, likewise developed as a function of their unique perspective and circumstances. Most frequently, they tend to see themselves as individuals who committed manslaughter and who were subsequently misunderstood in court and convicted in error of murder. A majority appear to have entered prison expecting that

the appellate courts would rectify the error and properly sentence them for the lesser offense. This view appears a function both of self-protective mechanisms and our adversarial criminal justice system.

To continue, in the cases of most men who are involved in a homicide, immediately after the event there occurs a need to create a *meaning* out of what has happened; further, it appears highly desirable that this *meaning* permits the maintenance of some sense of self esteem. To fail in this regard is to absolutely define oneself in the most heinous of terms based solely on what was undoubtedly the *worst* moment in one's life. In most instances the facts of the offense are evident. The interpretation offered by the police and crown attorney may well represent the worst of what the confused offender is afraid to believe about himself. At this time in this frame of mind, the offender is introduced to the justice system's white knight, the defense attorney, the man whose role it is within our adversarial system to create the most charitable possible interpretation from the known facts. Given his role, it is predictable that counsel's interpretation will include understanding of, and compassion for, the offender himself. Given the offender's psychological needs, it is hardly surprising that he tends to endorse the view espoused by his counsel, then to forge a strong emotional commitment to the justice system's *benevolent* explanation of his acts. Subsequently, when the defense fails, he feels both misunderstood and the object of a miscarriage of justice. From a therapeutic point of view, his conceptualization of the offense is likely to include both rationalizations and some denial of moral responsibility.

Nonetheless, especially for the first-time offender, there is some advantage in feeling the victim of a judicial error. It provides an honest form of hopefulness; that is, that the error will be corrected by the appeal. Thus, when the man enters prison to begin his sentence, he does not really believe that the sentence is for *life*. He hopes he is simply there temporarily. He trusts that ultimately the justice system will rectify the error. Life doesn't become LIFE until two or three years later when the appeal fails. By this time he knows from experience that he can survive in prison. A period of mourning for his lost hope and freedom invariably follows. Ideally and ultimately, he does come to terms with the full impact of his offense, conviction and incarceration. This process, however, is likely to involve surrendering beliefs and defenses which have protected him thus far in his journey through the justice system.

In regard to adaptation to prison, the *Life-Servers* have developed an understanding of the process in terms of Kubler-Ross's (1969) stages of dying. Those who have been through the process understand what the new lifer experienced and endures. They tend not to confront, but rather to be supportive as he experiences his anger and self-pity. Similarly, as he "bargains" by focusing his hopefulness on the appeal, no one tells him that the majority of appeals are unsuccessful. When the appeal has failed and the man needs support through his mourning, his peers are there to offer it. At the point of acceptance, however, reality is reimposed. Those who have been through the process earlier discuss it fully with him and, with their support, he begins to accept his situation. By this time he is three years or more into the sentence, which itself has begun to appear at least manageable; more manageable certainly than it ever could have appeared on the day that prison gates first closed behind him. To quote the *LifeServers* themselves (Lifers in Warkworth Institution, 1976):

> That only a lifer can know and help his fellow may soon become as acceptable as "It takes a thief to catch one." That we may be the only ones capable of empathy must become our calling and an asset to the Canadian Penitentiary Service. We as lifers may indeed be the only ones who can show that to hope and to search is not only possible, but can lead to fulfillment of our potentialities: the finding of freedom—not to be just enduring life, but finding it.

The Development of Inmate/Institution Cooperative Case Management

In illustrating the coping strategies developed and transmitted by the *LifeServers*, it will be useful to understand the "time-framing" of sentences. As the belief developed that it took three to four years to come to terms with the offense, conviction and sentence, the group also developed a concomitant belief that planning for one's future should begin as soon as one had resolved the issues of the past. Prior to 1976, most case management officers at Warkworth believed that "with a lifer, there was no need to be concerned about him until a year prior to his parole eligibility date." The group, assisted by one particular classification officer, was successful in substantially moderating that viewpoint. Clearly, the staff were prepared to adopt an alternative conception. With their concurrence, the *LifeServers* were able to get themselves reconstrued as *having* program needs throughout their sentences. The staff's goals became redefined in such a way that success was now measured in terms of having each man ready to accept responsibility at the earliest point in his sentence that he was eligible for some privilege which would let him demonstrate that responsibility. The goal became one of using the system to fully prepare the inmates for parole at the earliest possible date. Sentence time-framing became the norm. The initial three to four years were seen as a time for supportive counseling, the development of insight, educational preparation for vocational training, and an emotional acceptance of the offense, conviction and sentence. Satisfactory progress was typically rewarded with the beginning of a series of infrequent, brief, escorted passes into the local community. Successful completion of these, along with continued acceptable behaviour and progress toward mutually agreed upon personal, social and/or vocational goals typically led, within one to two years, to a program of unescorted temporary absences, generally for up to 72 hours per calendar quarter. The receipt of the privilege of unescorted temporary absences seemed to provide some psychological moderation of the sentence for the inmates. In addition to being tangible evidence of progression towards eventual release, the unescorted passes provided something in the immediate future to look forward to. In some psychological sense, the recipients were now serving a series of three month "bits" rather than *life*.

Additionally, there appears to be an element of "affirmation" experienced by the inmates at this stage in their progress. In effect, the society which ostracized them was perceived as once again acknowledging their humanness and their right to at least limited freedom. The psychological effect of this reaffirmation appears to be one of the factors con-

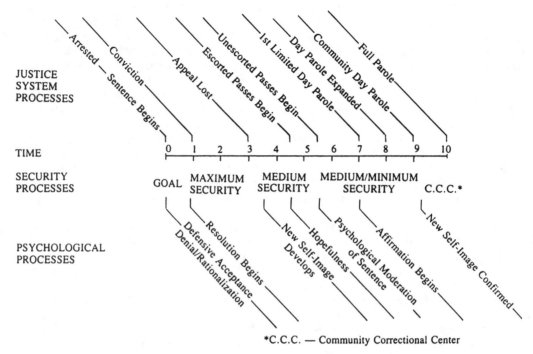

Figure 22.2. Sentence Time-Framing

tributing to the virtual 100% success rate of this particular program element.

Assuming 10 years to parole eligibility, by the time a man had received two or three unescorted temporary absences he was typically well onto the downhill side of his sentence. Programs were highly individualized from this point on depending upon the needs and goals of the individual inmates. One can, however, generalize about these individual programs simply by conveying the idea of gradually increasing privileges/responsibilities.

The major features of "Time-Framed Sentences" are outlined in Figure 22.2. The steps generally combined into what came to be called "pre-release programs" included fence clearance, escorted and then unescorted temporary absenses, transfer to minimum security, penitentiary based day paroles and community correctional centre based day paroles, all leading toward full release. Such releases were only granted for *purpose;* that is, purposefulness was required in addition to having met each of the other program requirements. *Purpose* typically included such things as family life, personal development programs, education, vocational training, paid employment, and volunteer involvement in social, religious

or recreational programs. Illustrating the latter, we have had *LifeServers* on day-parole actively involved with Alcoholics Anonymous, Canada JayCees, minors sports organizations as umpires and referees, anti-delinquency and anti-drug counseling for community adolescents, Correctional Services of Canada public relations, music programs, little theatre and puppetry for children.

It can be argued that time-framing permits the maintenance of hopefulness. It encourages the inmate to sustain his motivation, his striving for release. It also provides him with tangible feedback. Making a sentence "marker" confirms he is on schedule. Missing a sentence "marker" provides early warning that something is considered to be amiss. In our system, at least, this *striving* is one of the primary features which appears to distinguish those lifers who serve "minimum" time from those who serve substantially more. The payoffs are obvious, both for the offender and to taxpayers. When handled well, the risk is minimal. The problems of the process are somewhat more subtle.

Problematically, time-framing is generally contradictory to the values of the traditional inmate subculture. Conventional inmate belief systems argue a sentence is best served "one day at a time." Also, negotiating with "the man" is traditionally not a highly esteemed behaviour. In the case of a time-framed sentence the inmate behaves in nontraditional fashion, committing himself to some mutually agreed upon course of action based upon *the belief* that his effort will ultimately be rewarded. The process requires a level of communication and trust between inmates and staff which is neither easily achieved nor easily maintained. A system which encourages positive inmate/staff relationships obviously makes the process easier. Further, there is an advantage to having an established lifers organization since those inmates who are significantly involved with staff members are likely to be the object of some mistrust on the part of their more conventional peers. The group provides both social support and legitimacy for the action of its members; additionally, it provides an informal means of communication and confirmation of the fact that many members *are* progressing toward release.

Though staff may refer to the process as time-framing, there is a tendency on the part of inmates to label it a "head game." There exists a tendency on their part to withdraw from the process. From their point of view, such withdrawal amounts to avoiding the "head game" and resolving to serve "one day at a time."

THE DEVELOPMENT AND MAINTENANCE OF MEANING, PURPOSE AND HOPE

Selznick (1968) has said, in relation to inmates and the world in which they live, that:

Men live out their lives in specific settings, and it is there, in the crucible of interaction, that potentialities are sealed off or released. The micro-world is the world of the here-and-now; if an inmate's future is to be affected, that future should have a dynamic, existential connection with the experienced present.

In this context, the time-framing of long prison terms can be seen to have two distinct objectives; first, it attempts to assist inmates to develop meaningfulness in their present; second, it attempts to use this meaning as a

bridge to the future, encouraging purposefulness and the maintenance of hope. These concepts are closely related to what Toch (1977) and Flanagan (1982) have termed the "prison career" of the long-term inmate.

In describing their needs the *LifeServers* typically talk about a search for individuality, dignity, worth, happiness and peace of mind. They emphasize the need to find personal satisfaction and they generally agree that a man *must* remain active, at the same time maintaining a clear recognition that the interests and activities he develops are *for himself*; that is, that what each man engages in, he does because it is intrinsically interesting and satisfying to him. In discussion, they are able to present a logical case for the opportunity for long-term inmates to earn their way into some relatively "naturalized" environment, one which permits both sources of personal satisfaction and avoidance of the characteristic frustrations of traditional prisons. They see the opportunities to earn, to have personal possessions, to be relatively free from petty rules and regulations and to be permitted ways of expressing their individuality as being the factors which, without compromising the social purpose of the sentence could nonetheless make prison both more humane and tolerable. From the *LifeServers'* point of view, a man will be open to his life as long as he can find a valid reason for being so; when irritants and dissatisfiers become overwhelming then he will either fight back or withdraw. Either response leads to his ultimate dehumanization.

PROGRAMS FOR LONG-TERM INMATES

As suggested earlier, most prison programs are designed for inmates who spend one to three years incarcerated. The term "time-framed sentences" implies planning much longer periods. The "prison career" of the long-term inmate described by Toch (1977) and Flanagan (1982) is a similar concept. A number of Warkworth *LifeServers* have illustrated the development of useful and rewarding "prison careers," having worked as peer counsellors, psychotechnicians, program coordinators and tutors (Palmer, 1980). In some sense, time-framing may be the curricula of prison careers. Our programs have featured such curricula since 1976 and, in our opinion, they have proven both useful and successful.

The list of potential "prison careers" need not be limited. Long-term inmates should be encouraged to qualify for and fill positions as clerks, accountants, vocational counsellors, health care assistants, life-skills coaches and lead hands in industrial shops. One might create positions in which inmates would act as institutional research assistants: for example, monitoring the environment of the prison and aiding the administration and inmate committee to identify needs, plan programs, resolve grievances and advantageously allocate resources. Such a role might help generally in the reduction of tension within prisons.

Essentially, the process described above involves encouraging useful elements of adaptation to institutional living while simultaneously supporting the specific forms of meaning, purpose and hopefulness which assist inmates to minimize or avoid both institutionalization and prisonization. Based upon our experience, one would conclude that an environment can be created which will facilitate men's adaptation to prison. The required communication and trust between inmates and staff *can* be achieved given reasonable initial selection from both groups. Experience leads us further to conclude that, once established, peer pressure operates to maintain such an environment. When most inmates on a unit have had pro-social values, the occasional "solid con" could be introduced and it would tend to be the individual rather than the group who changed. Thus, in developing such programs careful selection is crucial in the short term; long term, it simply becomes desirable.

MINIMIZING INSTITUTIONALIZATION

As mentioned, 20% (6) of the charter members of the *LifeServers* began their sentences prior to their 18th birthdays. This proportion of young inmates has remained relatively constant across the total of lifers which the institution has housed since 1976. These individuals are of special interest. Their lack of alternative life experiences to prison, their "dependent" status immediately prior to incarceration, and their coming-of-age in a penitentiary environment would all appear to make

them particularly vulnerable to institutionalization. Their number is small. We have no *hard* data demonstrating that differences were not due to pre-existing individual differences. Nonetheless, some clinical observations *may be* of special significance in relation to the issues of institutionalization and prisonization.

Three of the six young inmates were sentenced in the mid-1960s and served substantial initial proportions of their sentences in traditional penitentiaries. The remaining three, sentenced in the early 1970s, were transferred to Warkworth after only a short reception period in maximum security. The former served 1.78-times their minimum period to parole eligibility; the latter, 0.83-times their minimum period before being placed in the community. Their remaining time was (or is being) served in community correctional centres. In addition to the "saving" of virtually the entire period to parole-eligibility, the latter group also served substantially more of their total time in relatively low cost minimum security (20% versus 2.5%). Apart from humanistic objectives, based upon these small groups one might conclude that a good case exists for economic arguments favouring program-oriented long-term incarceration.

The foregoing suggests that the three young inmates who were provided program-oriented incarceration suffered less institutionalization than the three subjected to substantial periods in traditional penitentiaries. This accords well with clinical judgement. There were no obvious differences in intellect. None of the six would be described as a "trouble-maker" by prison standards. Though the former group might sometimes have been considered impulsive, essentially they worked consistently toward release. Two of the three completed high school. All acquired trade certificates and skills saleable in the community. Conversely, the latter group seemed less impulsive and more predictable. They were also easier to deal with in the sense that they made fewer demands on staff. They might best be described as emotionally isolated, apathetic and difficult to motivate. None acquired trade skills while incarcerated, though one substantially improved skills he possessed prior to incarceration and would probably be considered an artisan. One of the individuals who failed and was reincarcerated was a member of this group. In fact, the other individual who also failed missed being included only by a few months on the age criterion. Each of the former could be adequately represented as having played the "head game." Each of the latter could be as well described as having served "one day at a time" waiting for release. In my judgement a large measure of the difference between these two small groups can be ascribed to the members of the latter having learned "passivity" as a coping strategy in traditional settings. This "learned passiveness" did not facilitate their return to normal society. In terms both of time served and human values, they paid dearly for their acquired behaviours and beliefs; in relative dollars, so did the society which segregated them.

The majority (67%) of long-termers are first-time federal inmates (Zubrycki, 1983) who have no previous experience with penitentiaries, their practices or with the parole process. They are admitted with little knowledge of what to anticipate or expect. A number have commented that when they were sentenced to spend "the rest of your natural life in penitentiary," they thought that the judgement meant *precisely* that. At the time of their admission they "just wanted to shut everything out—do their time—escape if they can" (Palmer, 1984a). Currently, these naive newcomers are again being housed in the most restrictive institutions where they are having minimal contact with staff while getting their primary orientation from the worst of the system's failures. The development of their initial attitudes toward prison is highly predictable, as are the behaviours and coping strategies they are likely to be introduced to. Clearly, if there is an advantage having long-term inmates learn "how to do time" *productively*, the process should begin early before contradictory attitudes and behaviours become ingrained and habitual. In providing role models, it would make better sense to utilize successful inmates than chronic failures. In this regard, those housed in maximum security by virtue of "sentence alone" should be separated from those so classified by virtue of attitude and behaviour.

THE ISSUE OF DISCRETE UNITS FOR LONG-TERM INMATES

It has been noted that one-third of the charter *LifeServers* members were housed on one

range and that psychosocial advantages accrued as a consequence of that arrangement. Notwithstanding, the majority of the prison's staff were not enthusiastic about long-term inmate units. Though some dissented, most felt that the long-termers provided a stabilizing influence and they preferred this influence distributed rather than concentrated on single ranges. Further, it was acknowledged that when long-term inmates were housed together their cooperativeness and behaviour justified privileges which were not generally available. There was some difficulty in *rationally* insisting upon the enforcement of unnecessary rules or the denial of deserved privileges for this group. Alternatively, there was concern about the precedent of moderating rules or privileges for a single range.

A number of authors have considered how best to house long-term inmates. Each has concluded the most desirable arrangement would seem to involve housing them together in discrete units within existing prisons (Corves, 1977; Flanagan, 1982; Hale, 1984; Radzinowicz, 1968). Also, this appears to be the solution most favoured by inmates (Lifers in Warkworth Institution, 1976; Sakowski, 1983). It avoids the ghetto institutions implied by the designation of entire prisons to serve this population; nonetheless, it still permits the long-termers to avoid the frustrations of milieus created for and dominated by short-term inmates. It further allows the special programs, the utilization of specially trained staff and the evolution of a distinctive pro-social perspective toward the serving of time. Housed in this fashion, the long-termers would be free to form the types of relationships and support groups desirable when serving long time while still retaining access to the diversified general prison environment. There should be no loss to the prison as a whole. The institutions should continue to benefit from the long-termers' contributions to both prison stability and prison programs. Further in this regard, it would be argued that if contributions to stability are legitimately the role of long-term inmates then these should be established in program-mode and not simply handled informally within cell-blocks.

The idea of discrete units may challenge the premise that all inmates within a single institution must be treated exactly alike; however, this assertion appears oversimplified. For example, within our P4W we have, for years, operated with the inmates classified individually by security level but all housed within the same penitentiary. Similarly, the U.S. Bureau of Prisons has successfully experimented with "Functional Units" in which residential groups have been formed on the basis of treatment needs and, in fact, treated differently according to those needs. There is no immediately obvious reason why a similar model should not perform satisfactorily in this instance.

The use of discrete units as a means of encouraging the development of mutual support networks among long-term inmates deserves further comment. Generally, support groups are an issue about which the prisoners themselves are apprehensive, but which they find to be advantageous when they overcome their misgivings. The traditional inmate belief system produces loneliness, a sparsity of friendly and caring relationships, the alienation of inmates, one from another, and demands to constantly play a "cool," detached and noncaring role. Our quasi-experiments both with long-term ranges and the *LifeServers* group clearly suggest that, first, this element of the inmate code can be rather easily broken down and, second, that there are advantages to long-term inmates when this is accomplished. Our more comprehensive efforts have produced quiet and trouble-free units on which the inmates have respected each other's rights while simultaneously offering each other both understanding and support. Isolation and alienation have been relatively unknown. Friendships have carried through the sentences to the time of release. Those paroled earliest have helped their later-released peers financially, vocationally and with general moral support. One group of six, for example, have met four times in the past three years to celebrate one of their numbers' marriage. A fifth "reunion" for one of the remaining bachelors is now planned. As a group, they take pride in having "helped each other through."

Previously it was noted that a high proportion of long-term inmates are well adjusted in prison and cause few problems. Typically, they are not considered for minimum security due to the absence of separation between those institutions and their surrounding communities. In other respects, however, many appear to be good candidates for the better housing conditions, the increased responsibility and the reduced level of supervision associated

with minimum settings. Given the above, and recognizing the recommendation that long-term inmates be housed in "discrete units" within existing prisons, one would infer that these discrete units might well mirror the conditions found in minimum security. Security would be maintained at the perimeter. Neither the outside community nor the purpose of the sentence would be compromised. The possibility of earning one's admission into such a "naturalized" environment, however, may be seen as *one* of the incentives needed for the ever-increasing population of long-term inmates.

Reflect upon living in the same undecorated, 7-foot × 10-foot space for 10, 15, 20 or even 25 years with simply a small, hard cot, a poor quality desk, a sink, and a seatless, lidless toilet. Quickly, it becomes obvious that "segregation from society" is not the *sole* punishment. For long-term inmates especially, a humanistic case can be made for cells sufficiently spacious to be furnished and arranged as comfortable bed-sitting rooms. The environment within these discrete units should be "naturalized"; that is, it should provide the nearest normal living conditions which are consistent with *tangible* security concerns.

The architectural style envisioned would be similar to that used for housing children in residential treatment. Using such cottages, the cost of additional cells would approximate $11,000, one-fifth the cost of traditional cells. Given the major cell shortage anticipated in Canada's prisons in the immediate future, the possibility seems one that should be actively investigated. More than economical to build and operate, such units would also facilitate rather than frustrate the serving of long sentences.

"NATURALIZING" THE PRISON ENVIRONMENT

In order to "naturalize" the prison environment for long-term inmates one would start by developing the "time-framed sentence" or "prison career" concept so as to initially provide the inmates with access to sources of personal satisfaction, self esteem and status through academic development and employment. One would then attempt to reinforce acceptable behaviour and career achievement by providing access to better living quarters.

Such quarters would look like contemporary houses; they would provide adequate personal space, both private and individualized; and they would make provision for communal space which encourages, if not a family lifestyle, at least a friendly boarding-house lifestyle. To the largest degree possible such units would be inmate self-governed. Those decisions which can be made by residence committees should be; consultation should be developed relative to the decisions which authorities reserve to themselves. Also, to the maximum extent feasible, "moral suasion" should be made the primary administrative technique, replacing threats and coerciveness. Our experience with staff at Warkworth leads us to conclude that we have no shortage of correctional officers capable of supervising inmates in mutually respectful fashion under such conditions. Staff members should be selected for these units on the basis of both interest and the ability to work effectively in such a milieu.

Such items as furniture. personal clothing, aquaria, plants and gardens should be approved in order to increase the opportunities for the expression of individuality. One might also consider the approval of such personal pets as birds in order to permit the inmates some long-term interests other than themselves upon which to focus. Pets are being successfully used with long termers in a number of U.S. forensic psychiatric facilities. They are reported to be beneficial in combatting depression and providing the inmates with renewed interest in their surroundings (personal communication, Dave Lee, Lima State Prison Hospital, Lima, Ohio).

Granting the privilege of ownership as a means of encouraging the expression of individuality implies there should also be some mechanism for transfer of ownership. Such is a logical extension of the concept of "naturalizing" the environment. Further, residents should be enabled to order personal items and snacks from some outside supplier, allowing them the same variety and choice available to free citizens. As other citizens, they would be obliged to be financially responsible for their choices.

The separation from family and friends is reported by the *LifeServers* to be a never ending concern. Similarly, both British and American long-term inmates have reported that "missing family" (Richards, 1978) and "loss of social life" (Flanagan, 1980) are among the major problems experienced in prison. It has been suggested that our prisons should be designed to " . . . 'contain' the offender without further weakening his ties with the community" (Waller, 1974). In this regard, residents of such units should have access to pay telephones under minimal supervision. Weekend visits should be permitted in the unit dayroom, or in nice weather, visitors should be permitted to bring in picnic lunches and there should be no restrictions governing the "sharing" of visits. One advantage of this for long-term inmates is that men who have few remaining community contacts are often included in visits by their more fortunate peers. This process should be encouraged.

Finally, with provisions in the design for both laundry and general purpose space, the care and maintenance of personal issue or possessions should become entirely an individual matter. In this jail, laundry, hygiene, appearance and the maintenance of quarters at lower than suitable standards would be essentially group or casework issues, not subject to resolution by rule.

CONCLUSIONS

Long-term incarceration is a growth industry in Canada. It is expected that by the turn of the century one inmate in five in federal correctional institutions will be serving a life sentence (Vantour, 1983). Moreover, of the increasing number of long-term inmates, a substantial proportion appear to result from what may be an unintended(?) secondary effect of the legislation. Previously, plea-bargaining invariably produced manslaughter verdicts; now, it often results in a guilty plea to second degree murder, implying a 5-times longer period of incarceration (Palmer, 1984a). To a penitentiary psychologist, it seems that the law which Parliament intended should deal with the most heinous of our homicides, premeditated murder, has in practice ended up dealing relatively more harshly with the less shocking end of the homicide spectrum. Some cases, despite having bargained to plead guilty to second degree murder, appear very similar to cases we saw previously as "drunken and/or domestic manslaughters."

The increased use of life terms, together with their increased length, implies an increasing financial burden on taxpayers and ever-increasing human costs in our penitentiaries. Given the trends, it would appear incumbent upon policy makers to actively investigate both programs and institutional alternatives designed to deal with these inmates economically, humanely, and, of course, in a fashion which assures their continued custody. It is argued elsewhere (Palmer, 1984b) that a process-oriented approach to selected long-term inmates can provide appropriate security, is more humane, and costs *very substantially less* than does the security oriented alternative. The process should begin virtually at the time of admission. The scheduling of the elements in the process should be consistent with what is known about the adaptation of long-term inmates to prison (see Figure 22.2). More research, better classification practices, appropriate programs early in the process, time-framed prison careers, mutual support groups amongst the inmates themselves and "naturalized" prison environments are the keystone of such a process. Though maximum security may be the only answer for *some* long-term inmates, it is clear that it is not required for all, nor even for most. Given the successful experiences which we have had in programming lifers; given also the knowledge "that very little can be observed to set . . . [the group of first-degree murderers] . . . apart from others, particularly from previous lifers with shorter periods of parole ineligibility" (Zubrycki, 1983); then, it appears that the techniques for managing all of these cases are available. They should be refined, further developed and implemented more widely.

The foregoing is based largely upon experience with men serving 10-year minimum life; it appears equally relevant, however, to those with longer periods of parole ineligibility. Recent experience tells us that these individuals are not without hope. Most appear to have spontaneously re-focused their sights on their 15th year judicial reviews. In effect, they have modified their time perspective into a realm close to one with which we do have both familiarity and expertise. One of the primary challenges for corrections will be to use that experience to assist these inmates to maintain their hopes and their legitimate goals.

REFERENCES

Alper, B. S. (1974). *Prisons inside-out: Alternatives in correctional reform*. Cambridge, MA: Ballinger.

Corves, E. (1977). Adverse results of long prison terms and the possibilities of counteracting them. In R. Levy, S. Rizkalla, & R. Zauberman (Eds.), *Long-term imprisonment: An international seminar*. Montreal: University of Montreal.

Flanagan, T. J. (1980). The pains of long-term imprisonment: A comparison of British and American perspectives. *British Journal of Criminology*, *20*(2), 148-156.

Flanagan, T. J. (1982, January). Correctional policy and the long-term prisoner. *Crime and Delinquency*, 82-85.

Hale, M. (1984, January). *Long-term imprisonment: Policy considerations and program options*. Ottawa: The Correctional Service of Canada, Offender Programs Branch.

Kubler-Ross, E. (1969). *On death and dying*. New York: Macmillan.

Lifers in Warkworth Institution. (1976, November). *Programs for long-term offenders: Sentenced to life! To endure it or to find it?* Warkworth Institution: Author.

National Parole Board Statistical Liaison Officer. (1983, December). *Re: Capital and non-capital murderers*. Ottawa: The Correctional Service of Canada.

Palmer, W. R. (1980, February). *Inmate-assisted programs at Warkworth Institution*. Paper presented to the annual meeting of the Ontario Psychological Association, Toronto.

Palmer, W. R. (1984a). *Maintaining community ties for long-term inmates: A "day of awareness" for families*. Warkworth Institution.

Palmer, W. R. (1984b, April). *Programs for long-term inmates: A process-oriented approach for the Ontario region and a "pilot" proposal for Warkworth Institution*. Ottawa: The Correctional Service of Canada, Offender Programs Branch.

Radzinowicz, L. (1968). The regime for long-term prisoners in conditions of maximum security. *Report of the advisory council on the penal system*. London: HMSO.

Richards, B. (1978). The experience of long-term imprisonment. *British Journal of Criminology*, *18*(2), 162-169.

Sakowski, M. H. (1983). *Preliminary report on long-term offenders*. Correctional Services of Canada, R.H.Q. (Prairies).

Selznick, P. (1968). Foreword. In E. Studt, S. L. Messinger, & T. P. Wilson, *C-unit: Search for community in prison*. New York: Russell Sage.

Toch, H. (1977). The long-term prisoner as a long-term problem. In R. Levy, S. Rizkalla, & R. Zauberman (Eds.), *Long-term imprisonment: An international seminar*. Montreal: University of Montreal.

Vantour, J. (1983, April 30). Long-term inmates on the increase. *Let's Talk*.

Waller, I. (1974). *Men released from prison*. Toronto: University of Toronto Press.

West, D. J. (1967). *Murder followed by suicide*. Cambridge, MA: Harvard University Press.

Zink, T. M. (1958). Are prison troublemakers different? *Journal of Criminal Law, Criminology and Police Science, 48*(4), 433-434.

Zubrycki, R. M. (1983, August). *Long-term incarceration in Canada*. Paper presented at the Second World Congress on Prison Health Care, Ottawa.

23

Sentence Planning for Long-Term Inmates

Timothy J. Flanagan

Long-term incarceration is a "growth industry" in America. In fact, long-term prisoners may be the fastest growing segment of the United States prisoner population during this decade. This growth can be attributed to: (1) public demand for longer prison terms for serious offenders; (2) enhanced law enforcement and prosecution efforts focused on career criminals; (3) changing judicial attitudes in sentencing; and (4) legislative revision of sentencing codes to require longer, more determinate, and in some cases mandatory terms.

For example, mandatory sentencing legislation has reduced or eliminated judicial discretion over the "in/out" decision for a variety of offenses. The Bureau of Justice Statistics reported that as of January 1983, 43 states had mandatory imprisonment legislation for specific violent categories. Mandatory prison terms for "habitual offenders" (variously defined) were in place in 30 states. Twenty-nine states and the District of Columbia had enacted mandatory imprisonment laws for drug law violators, and 37 jurisdictions had enacted firearms laws that incorporate mandatory imprisonment provisions for certain offenses (U.S. Department of Justice, 1983). In addition, in several jurisdictions where determinate sentencing structure has been adopted, provisions that explicitly recognize aggravating factors such as an extensive criminal record or weapon use during the commission of the crime increase sentence lengths when these factors are present.

Sophisticated projection models are not necessary to suggest that the "downstream effects" of much of this legislation will be an increase in the number and proportion of long-term inmates in the American prisoner population. Not only is the absolute and proportional *size* of the long-term prisoner population likely to increase, but the *composition* of the long-term group may change as well. In the past, for example, the lifer population in most state prisons included a large proportion of homicide offenders, many of whom had few prior contacts with the correctional system. Today, however, and increasingly in the future, the long-term inmate group is more diverse on a number of important characteristics, including offense, prior record, criminal sophistication, age, and others. Correctional administrators perceive this new cohort of long-term inmates to be younger, more violent and more volatile in prison than their predecessors (Correctional Services Group, 1985).

EDITOR'S NOTE: This article is based on a paper presented at the 47th Annual Meeting of the Middle Atlantic States Correctional Association, Farmington, Connecticut, May 7, 1985.
NOTE: Reprinted from *Federal Probation*, Vol. 69, No. 3, September 1985, pp. 23-28.

MANAGING LONG-TERM PRISONER POPULATIONS

Are correctional agencies prepared to manage inmate populations that include an increasing share of long-term inmates? The answer to this question appears to be negative on several counts. First, the correctional "experience" in most state prison systems was designed with rapid turnover of short-term inmates in mind. For example, vocational and educational programs in prisons are designed to cycle inmates through in periods of 12 to 36 months. Except for sequential secondary and postsecondary educational programs, few efforts are planned to involve inmates in a sustained effort of learning and growth over many years. Hypothetically, a long-term inmate could select from these training programs cafeteria-style, and emerge from the sentence an odd sort of "Renaissance Man" with certificates in plumbing, computer programming, small engine repairs, and an A.S. degree in sociology.

In addition to the historical legacy of correctional programming, administrators face several contemporary obstacles to designing relevant programs for long-termers. First, the present body of knowledge about institutional experience of long-term prisoners provides little insight into which programs are relevant for this group, or how a lengthy but meaningful prison career can be organized. Second, pressure to reap the greatest possible return on agency efforts argues for focusing program resources on short-term inmates. Short-termers present the most immediate need (and also the most immediate danger of appearing in the recidivism statistics by which many agencies are judged). Third, long-term inmates' serious crimes and/or extensive prior records make them the least inviting group in which to invest resources and attempt innovative efforts (Flanagan, 1982). Fourth, the immediate demands of managing crowded prisons may paralyze official thinking and relegate program development for long-term inmates and other "special category prisoners" to the back burner.

The combined influence of these obstacles helps to explain why little has been attempted in terms of innovative programs for long-term offenders, but the increasing size of this inmate group suggests that the problem cannot be ignored much longer.[1] To shape a prison system that is responsive and relevant to the *needs* of long-term inmates (in the context of security levels that are appropriate to the *risk* presented by these offenders) will require administrators to begin thinking, planning and testing new approaches, ideas and programs.

A NEW PERSPECTIVE

This planning and development must proceed on three interdependent levels. First, correctional administrators must adopt a rational *perspective* toward long-term prisoners, one which simultaneously recognizes the *differences* between the experience of long-term incarceration and shorter term incarceration, but which is also cognizant of the *diversity* of the long-term inmate group (Flanagan, 1982). This perspective requires administrators to consider that long-term confinement may entail problems and needs that are different from those presented by shorter-term incarceration (see Correctional Services Group, 1983; Flanagan, 1980; Richards, 1978). Thus, the potential and consequences of new policies, programs, construction plans, and other developments must be assessed for long-term inmates and others *independently*. Efforts that appear to be relevant and appropriate for shorter-term prisoners may be inappropriate or even dysfunctional for the management of long-term inmates.

This statement does not imply, however, that there are singular prescriptions for managing the "long-term inmate group." The second element of the perspective requires that the diversity within the long-term group also be considered. An example of correctional thinking that ignores this element of the perspective is the continuing debate over *concentration* of long-term prisoners in single facilities versus *dispersal* of this group throughout a multi-facility correctional system (Home Office, 1984; Home Office Advisory Council on the Penal System, 1968). It is clear that the concentration model would have merit for *some* long-term prisoners (depending on the nature of the facility) but that it would be contraindicated for others. Toch's research, for example, suggested that socioenvironmental features favored by long-term prisoners are distinguishable from those which are prized by shorter-term inmates (Toch, 1977a). To ignore these differences is analogous to prescribing a single therapeutic regimen to all patients, regardless of symptoms.

Another feature of a reasonable perspective toward management of long-term inmates is the concept of *time-bounding*. For short-term prisoners, the correctional experience can be conceived as a series of discrete programs which provide the inmate with skills, experience and learning directed toward release. Sound correctional practice in the case of short-term inmates focuses on the relevance and utility of "release preparation" programs, and sentence planning for these inmates essentially consists of "release planning." For long-term inmates, however, this model may be largely irrelevant. The notion that a job training program in which the prisoner enrolls during the second year of a 25-year minimum sentence will be relevant to the job market a quarter-century in the future is obviously questionable. The concept of "release planning" at this point in the term may be similarly questionable. The Council of Europe's Committee on Crime Problems has observed that:

A term of five, ten or more years of imprisonment cannot reasonably be planned from the outset *only* as a transition to future life in freedom. There must also be provision of more immediate aims which the prisoner can achieve, involving some adjustment to the inevitable conditions of prison life and meaningful use of the prisoner's abilities. (Council of Europe, Committee on Crime Problems, 1977, p. 14)

Similarly, Toch has observed that:

Freedom for the long-term inmate is decades away and is thus not a meaningful behavioral goal, and life without goals is an exercise in eventlessness and monotony. The challenge is that of building highlights into imprisonment, things to aim for and achieve and to take pride in when achieved. (Toch, 1984)

Sentence planning for long-term inmates must emphasize *prison-relevance* of work, training and educational experiences offered to these inmates, at least during the majority of the prisoner's confinement. This does not mean that release preparation should not be considered, and a release focus will obviously

become more relevant as release nears. However, to focus on release preparation during the early period of the term is tantamount to preaching retirement planning to students in high school.

GUIDING PRINCIPLES

The second stage of the planning process involves the formulation of *principles* to guide the development of *programs* for long-term prisoners. Overarching goals for the management of long-term inmates must be defined, and objectives to guide program development must be articulated. I have suggested elsewhere that since removal from society is the principal sanction that falls most heavily on long-term prisoners, reduction of the "secondary sanctions" inherent in imprisonment should be the superordinate goal in managing long-term offender populations.[2] This approach has been characterized by Cohen and Taylor as the pursuit of "humane containment" under conditions of maximum security (Cohen & Taylor, 1981). This may sound like a "minimal" goal for the management of long-term offender populations, but a great investment on the part of correctional officials will be required if the goal is to be more than a convenient slogan.

Several objectives in pursuit of this goal have been offered. The Home Office Advisory Council on the Penal System considered the objectives to be sought in designing a "regime" for long-term prisoners. These objectives included maintenance of self-respect, preservation of opportunities for choice and variety in the environment, a degree of movement and the ability to change environmental stimuli, and opportunities for the inmate "to *earn* for himself improvements in the conditions of his existence" (1984, p. 28). Similar principles were embodied in the report of the Council of Europe's Committee on Crime Problems, *Treatment of Long-term Prisoners* (1977). Bennett contends that the principal objective of programming for long-term prisoners should be to foster *involvement* in constructive endeavors, and to develop *commitment* among long-term prisoners to prosocial activities and relationships (Bennett, 1977). Toch has argued that programming for long-term inmates should focus on four objectives: accurate and beneficial placement of inmates (in facilities and programs that help such prisoners to cope); making the prison permeable so that positive extra-prison relationships can be maintained and nurtured; helping the inmate's ego fashion successful coping strategies; and providing options which enable long-term inmates to build effective prison careers (Toch, 1977b). I have argued that a relevant management *strategy* for long-term inmates, including its programs and policies, should be guided by three basic objectives. First, *maximization of choice* is important to foster not only the "illusion of control" (which is a basic human need) but also to allow real opportunities for inmates to design their futures and chart their development. This objective must, of course, be read in the context of resource availability and the security constraints which inhere to these offenders, but these constraints should be regarded as outside boundaries rather than as excuses for inaction. Second, the concept of a *meaningful life* in prison should guide program development for long-term inmates. "Meaning" refers to the opportunity to contribute positively to one's environment and to others, to make linear progress toward realistic and important goals, and to engage in activities that foster a sense of personal worth. The third objective of program development for long-termers is to sustain a measure of *permeability* of prison walls. That is, efforts must be made to reduce the social isolation of long-term inmates from family and friends as well as other positive role models in the free community (to the extent that this is possible within the constraints of security).

A BRIEF CATALOG OF ATTEMPTS

It is difficult to move from pious principles about the management of long-term prisoners to concrete examples that illustrate those principles. First, as noted earlier, little in the way of innovative or imaginative programming has been attempted with long-term inmates, so tailor-made examples of generalizable programs are hard to find. Second, suggesting ways to build meaningful careers for persons who will spend most of their adult lives behind bars spawns feelings of impotence in even the most dedicated reformer (Williams, 1977). Nevertheless, we can learn from the few attempts that have been made.

Bennett observed that the oldest prison programs for long-term inmates are the "Lifer's Clubs" and similar organizations that have existed in many prisons for years. "These groups or organizations attempt to serve a variety of functions all related to ameliorating the debilitating effects of long-term deprivation of normal social stimulation" (Bennett, 1977, p. 416). The scope, impact and importance of these groups has varied widely, and has depended on the composition of the membership, the support of key staff, and the nature of the activities in which the organizations engage.

Related to these organizations are the "prison preventers" groups, often involving long-term inmates, whose goals are to communicate to persons outside the walls (usually youth) the risks and costs of criminality. Bennett notes that maintenance of both of these types of organizations requires openness and flexibility on the part of staff.

Some long-term prisoners groups have adopted a broader "community service" orientation. The "community" may be either the institutional population or the broader community outside of prison. Palmer described the work of the *LifeServers* organization operating at the Warkworth Institution in Canada since 1976. The group's constitution describes the focus of the organization: "It shall be the goal of the *LifeServers* to initiate, develop and maintain community programs or projects which will serve to contribute to the mutual benefit of the *LifeServers*, our own community and the community at large" (Palmer, 1984, p. 441). This community service orientation is also part of the charter of the Long-Termers Program at the Utah State Prison (n.d.). A strong public service focus also characterizes a number of programs in which long-termers are engaged within the Connecticut Department of Corrections.

Beyond involvement in these specialized activities, it is imperative that programs for long-term prisoners be developed within the "mainstream" of institutional life. It is in this context that many observers have seen real opportunities for long-term prisoners to engage in sustained, growth-potential involvement. For example, the "prison career" model of education programs described by Toch, Flanagan, and Palmer goes far beyond the inmate-as-student conception of these programs. Instead, this model views education as a long-term *process* in which considerable resources are invested in the education of prisoners, but where these investments are returned to the correctional agency through the involvement of inmates as tutors, teacher's aides, and eventually as instructional staff. The involvement of long-term offenders in prison industry can also be structured so well-trained and experienced inmate-trainees graduate to positions of responsibility, share their experience and training with other inmates, and provide a valuable service to the prison. Bennett had provided examples of more imaginative roles that long-term inmates can assume, and many of his examples share the community service focus that characterizes much of the thinking in this area.

The catalog of previous efforts is not long, and much of the writing on programming for long-term inmates is suggestive rather than descriptive of successful efforts. This is both a strength and a limitation. For while the anxious administrator may desire a catalog of proven programs from which to choose, and such a catalog might provide a useful reference point for program development, the dearth of "proven remedies" in this area encourages exactly the sort of experimental, imaginative thinking that this problem requires.

RESPONSIBILITY AND AUTHORITY FOR SENTENCE PLANNING

Planning constructive prison terms for long-term inmates involves developing an answer (or group of answers) to what Williams calls "the most basic question": "What should these people be doing for these long periods of time?" (Williams, 1977, p. 441). To provide the broadest possible set of alternatives to address this question, the correctional agency must consider *where* to locate responsibility and authority for this task. In multifacility correctional systems, program opportunities and housing alternatives for long-term inmates will span more than one facility. Therefore, should responsibility for sentence planning for long-term prisoners be located within the central office of the agency, or should this task be distributed to program officials in specific institutions? A task force within the British penal system recently considered this issue.

The Control Review Committee described sentence planning in these terms:

> We propose that an individual career plan should be drawn up for each prisoner at the start of his sentence. The plan would be discussed with the prisoner and would take account of his personal circumstances and needs; it would suggest the likely shape of his sentence including when he might be expected to be re-classified, the sort of establishments he should be transferred to at different stages of his sentence and for how long, and kinds of vocational training, education or other programs from which he might benefit. In time it might be possible to draw up more detailed career plans than this. But the important point is that a plan of any sort, however basic, would be preferable to the present arbitrary and unintelligible prison experience. . . .
> (Home Office, 1984, p. 11)

Since the decision about appropriate facility placement constrains subsequent program, security and work assignment decisions, the British task force concluded that rational sentence planning for long-term offenders could only be achieved if administrative responsibility for planning was centralized. The task force noted that "We do not think that sentence planning could sensibly go ahead on any other basis" (Home Office, 1984, p. 13). This approach calls for the establishment of "Sentencing Planning Units" within reception facilities. The role of these units is much broader than the current view of reception units. Operating in conjunction with central office staff, the Sentence Planning Units would serve as the coordinative link between the long-term inmate and the resources of the *entire* correctional system. If a long-term prisoner presented serious control problems that made him unacceptable in a particular prison or program, the Control Review Committee's proposal would send the inmate back to the Sentence Planning Unit for reassessment:

> In some cases the reassessment period may reveal that prisoner's disruptive behavior was a response to a particular problem; after receiving help in the sentence planning units such prisoners

might well be transferred back to the same or another long-term prison. In other cases, however, a prisoner may be identified as presenting control problems which cannot be dealt with in normal prison conditions and we propose that a number of small units should be established to cater for prisoners in this group. (Home Office, 1984, p. 16)

The concept of a coordinative link between the long-term prisoner and the entire correctional system was also endorsed in a recent report of the Long-term Offender Task Force of the Arizona Department of Corrections. The Arizona task force suggested the creation of staff positions titled "long-term offender program manager" to serve as a focal point for sentence planning and programming for long-term prisoners. This proposal envisions the formulation of contracts between the long-term inmate and the agency. These contracts would specify short and long-range goals, and would contractually bind the agency to rewards (including reduced custody status, participation in prerelease programs, and others) for achievement of these goals (Arizona Department of Corrections, n.d.).

Centralization of decisionmaking authority will be resisted by many correctional administrators. Objections will range from perceptions of unwarranted central office intrusion in the daily management of facilities, to the position that staff who are "closest" to the prisoner at any point in the sentence are best equipped to judge the inmate's progress and needs. These objections may have merit, but the fact remains that in correctional systems where inmates move from facility to facility during the course of the term, rational sentence planning for long-term inmates requires coordination of the inmate's progress throughout the term. Moreover, these Sentence Planning Units represent a resource not only for inmates, but also for the institutional officials in the prisons where long-termers will be housed.

PROBLEMS AND PROSPECTS

Planning and executing constructive sentences for long-term prisoners will tax the resources and imagination of the entire correc-

tional agency. Centralized coordination of planning may introduce conflict between facility staff and personnel of the Sentence Planning Units. Other prisoner subgroups, including violence-prone prisoners, the mentally and physically handicapped, the drug-dependent, the retarded, and others demand specialized attention as well. Why should an agency with this menu of problems and demands focus resources and staff talent on long-term prisoners? This question is particularly ironic given the perception among correctional staff that long-term inmates tend to be among the most quiescent and least troublesome of inmates (Wardlaw, 1980). Shouldn't squeakier wheels be greased before an agency makes a commitment to long-termers?

The answer to this dilemma lies in appreciation of the unique circumstances of the long-term prisoner. These are the inmates who have the most time to fill, the least hope, and who are most in need of credible incentives in order to cope. The direction of public policy in terms of recent sentencing legislation is toward the reduction of hope. Natural life terms and minimum sentences of 25, 30 or more years illustrate this direction.

It is correctional staff, however, who must live with the consequences of these policies. These consequences can be profoundly negative, not only for inmates but also for prison staff and the correctional agency. Thus while it may *seem* cheaper to operate prisons "in which inmates unobtrusively and very gradually waste away" (Toch, 1977b) the true costs of this nonstrategy may be enormous. Conversely, when long-term prisoners are viewed not only as an economic drain but as a potential resource, the marginal costs of imaginative and sustained programming for these inmates decline. As the Arizona Department of Corrections' Long-term Offender Task Force recently observed: "The use of long-term offenders in the institution is a logical and reasonable step in providing benefits for both the institution and the offender" (Arizona Department of Corrections, p. 80). The subsequent improvement in institutional climate, inmate-staff relations, and other less easily measured dimensions cannot be discounted. As Toch has observed, "prisons must promote constructive change *especially* in long-term inmates because prisons benefit from such impact themselves" (1984, p. 513).

POSTSCRIPT:
A NOTE ON PROGRAM ELEMENTS

As noted earlier, garnering support from correctional administrators, budget personnel, legislators and the public for innovative programming for long-term inmates is a difficult task. While the needs of these inmates for such programs can be easily documented, the label of "least deserving" also characterizes these serious offenders. Several elements found in a number of operating programs may help to generate support (or at least temper opposition) to the development of programs for long-term inmates.

First, a *public service focus* may be critical to engendering public and political support for program efforts for long-term inmates. Involvement of long-term inmates in nonprofit, nonpartisan "worthy" causes will highlight the contributory nature of these efforts.

Second, the presence of an *external advisory board* or group serves several important purposes. First, it helps to legitimize the program in the eyes of prison staff, administrators, and others. Second, these groups may have important benefits for inmate participants, in terms of permeability of the prison walls, new stimuli, and contact with real-world role models, issues, and problems.

Third, innovative programming efforts require staff linkages that are sympathetic/supportive in nature. Staff members selected to work with long-term inmates in specialized programs should be recruited on a voluntary basis, and should indicate a clear interest in working with long-term inmates. In many such programs the supportive role of the staff member is apparent, but it is also clear that staff do not *direct* program activities in authoritarian ways. This approach enhances the inmates' sense of ownership of the effort, particularly in the case of inmate-initiated community service projects. However, the unobtrusive but supportive staff posture may be difficult to maintain in the face of constantly changing staff. Given this issue, a degree of permanence of staff assignment to long-term inmate programs is important.

Fourth, many innovative long-term inmate programs involve a *small, self-selected group of inmates*. There are a number of benefits to keeping such programs small and to allowing member selectivity. These include fostering of group cohesion (both within the group and between the group and staff members), reducing the problems associated with large inmate groups, and continuity of program participants over time.

Fifth, programs for long-term inmates will have a better chance to succeed if they present *minimal costs* to the state. Minimization of costs can be achieved through cost recovery (if products or services are sold), or if the program's efforts are very labor-intensive. Costs can also be contained by donations of time and/or materials from extraprison resources. In any event, modest investments by the agency can be balanced by the "experimental" or innovative nature of the program, and by the public service element.

Sixth, it is critical that programs for long-term inmates not be competitive with the private sector. Given the undesirable nature of these offenders in the public eye, and the abuses of profitable inmate enterprises that periodically come to light, this is likely to be an important and highly sensitive aspect of programming for long-term offenders.

Seventh, institution-based programs often benefit in many concrete ways from a regular liaison person with the outside, either in the form of a volunteer or paid staff member. These people help mobilize community involvement and support, help cut red tape, and provide opportunities to solve "little" problems that are endemic to the institution such as purchasing materials, mailing correspondence, conducting library research, gathering information, and others.

Finally, many small, selective programs for long-term prisoners provide what Toch calls a "sanctuary" for long-term prisoners. Program activities take place in an environment that provides a definable "place" for inmates to go each day. This environment is important as it allows lower social density than other areas of the prison, promotes group identity, allows closer and more natural interaction with staff members, and represents a respite from "general population." This aspect of programming for long-term inmates may be difficult to achieve in crowded prisons, but flexibility and a time-sharing approach to these "sanctuary" areas may alleviate these space problems.

NOTES

1. See Bennett (1977) Also, a recently completed survey by Correctional Services Group (1985) found few programs for long-term inmates in U.S. state correctional systems.

2. "Secondary sanctions" refers to conditions of confinement that are usually associated with life in prison. These features of the prison, which Sykes (1957) referred to as the "pains of imprisonment," are generally regarded as a necessary element of imprisonment. As suggested here, they need not be.

REFERENCES

Arizona Department of Corrections. (n.d.). *Long-term offender task force report.* Phoenix: Arizona Department of Corrections.

Bennett, L. (1977). Some suggested programs for long-term inmates. In S. Rizkalla, R. Levy, & R. Zauberman (Eds.), *Long-term imprisonment: An international seminar* (pp. 413-434). Montreal: University of Montreal.

Cohen, S., & Taylor, L. (1981). *Psychological survival: The experience of long-term imprisonment* (2nd ed.). New York: Penguin.

Correctional Services Group, Inc. (1983). *Long-term offenders in the Pennsylvania correctional system: Findings and recommendation.* Kansas City, MO: Author.

Correctional Services Group, Inc. (1985). *The long-term inmate phenomenon: A national perspective* (Draft final report). Kansas City, MO: Author.

Council of Europe, Committee on Crime Problems. (1977). *Treatment of long-term prisoners.* Strasbourg: Council of Europe.

Flanagan, T. (1980, April). The pains of long-term imprisonment: A comparison of British and American perspectives. *British Journal of Criminology,* 148-156.

Flanagan, T. (1982, January). Correctional policy and the long-term prisoner. *Crime and Delinquency,* 82-95.

Home Office, Advisory Council on the Penal System. (1968). *The regime for long-term prisoners under conditions of maximum security.* London: HMSO.

Home Office. (1984). *Managing the long-term prison system: Report of the control review committee.* London: HMSO.

Palmer, W. R. T. (1984, October). Programming for long-term inmates: A new perspective. *Canadian Journal of Criminology,* 441.

Richards, B. (1978, April). The experience of long-term imprisonment. *British Journal of Criminology,* 162-169.

Sykes, G. (1957). *Society of captives.* Princeton, NJ: Princeton University Press.

Toch, H. (1977a). *Living in prison: The ecology of survival.* New York: Free Press.

Toch, H. (1977b). The long-term inmate as a long-term problem. In S. Rizkalla, R. Levy, & R. Zauberman (Eds.), *Long-term imprisonment: An international seminar* (pp. 283-292). Montreal: University of Montreal.

Toch, H. (1984, October). Quo Vadis? *Canadian Journal of Criminology,* 514.

U.S. Department of Justice, Bureau of Justice Statistics. (1983, August). *Setting prison terms.* Washington, DC: Government Printing Office.

Utah State Prison. (n.d.). *Longtermers* (pamphlet). Draper, UT: Utah State Prison.

Wardlaw, G. (1980). Are long-term prisoners a management problem in Australian prisons? *Australian and New Zealand Journal of Criminology,* 6-10.

Williams, M. (1977). Commentary. In S. Rizkalla, R. Levy, & R. Zauberman (Eds.), *Long-term imprisonment: An international seminar* (pp. 435-442). Montreal: University of Montreal.

■ Afterwords

24

The Long-Term Inmate as a Long-Term Problem

Hans Toch

Prisons are comparable to other large, complex institutional environments in that they contain stressful features, which affect some people (inmates, students, patients, or workers) more or less than they do others. In fact, just as patients have to be thrown out of hospitals and some of us never leave school, so some inmates are comfortably prisonized. And whereas institutional assimilation may leave an inmate a healthy person, it may also make him or her less competent in the short run. At minimum, prison adaptation makes the average prisonized inmate somewhat different from the way he acts on the street— meaning he looks more socialized or healthy in some ways and less so in others. The same point holds for the least "adjusted" inmates, who may range from appearing unhappy or acting obnoxious to being mildly or diagnosably disturbed.

None of this means that it is possible to separate the impact of prison on an inmate from the personality the inmate brings to prison. We sometimes think we notice the effects of a person's being in prison when we see behavior that the same inmate manifested in nursery school. In other instances, we assume we see a twisted ego where we see a trapped man or woman.

SELF-ISOLATION OF LONG-TERM INMATES

Rasch (1977) sensed that there was some "emotional withdrawal" in lifers, and it stands to reason that a person who spends much time in prison is likely to increase his sense of solitude and his concern for being left uninvaded. A lifer is well advised to select his companions with increasing care, for one of several reasons: (1) he has things on his mind, and any overstimulation when one is preoccupied is upsetting; (2) he wishes to serve unimpeded time, which in part means not getting in trouble; (3) he has little in common with short-term inmates; their concerns with self-amusement seem flippant, and their "outside world" interests can be disequilibrating. To someone who serves consequential time, short-termers are bearers of irritating stimuli and conveyers of frustrations. The same point holds for staff members, who come in from a good breakfast and ostentatiously go home at night.

With this sort of adaptive reaction, it is difficult to separate the chicken from the egg. For example, older inmates tend to be more concerned about privacy than younger inmates, who as a group are more gregarious and active. But when we have a long-term inmate

NOTE: This is an extensive revision of a paper originally presented at Long-Term Imprisonment: An International Seminar (University of Montreal, October 1977).

who is also older than the average inmate, and who is surrounded by young inmates playing loud music and talking about their impending return to romance on the streets, it is hardly surprising that the lifer becomes withdrawn. It becomes even less surprising if the inmate feels remorseful about a bloody murder or is experiencing a touch of psychosis or an episode of severe depression.

DISPOSITIONS THAT EVOLVE OVER TIME

I have noted (Chapter 16, this volume) that some old-time inmates have grown up in prisons that are not as progressive as ours, and such inmates can be nostalgic in the same way as veteran prison guards can be nostalgic. More important, the inmate may forget that his or her concerns have changed over time. He does not realize that he no longer resonates to an erstwhile concern about autonomy and freedom, which means resentment of staff. He is not conscious of the fact that, now that he is older, he feels a strong need for structure. As long as age is correlated with length of incarceration, the issue of rebelliousness and conformity is entangled with prison adjustment processes and with preprison personality issues.

Another theme that necessarily changes connotations over time is one we call *emotional feedback* (Toch, 1992), which means the importance that is assigned by the inmate to personal ties. Older inmates tend to rank high on this theme, in part because many such inmates arrive in prison with established links to the community. But although older inmates as a rule do not voluntarily disassociate themselves from the outside to cope with imprisonment, some attrition is bound to occur as families give up on prisoners with the passage of time.

DOING TIME

Whatever else prisons do, they present time to be filled. One way in which this challenge can be met by prisoners is to keep busy as an end in itself, and we see many inmates to whom activity is important. For example, anyone who has been around prisons has seen inmates who spend years working on transpar-

ently fruitless appeals, which has the combined virtue of keeping busy and nurturing hope. But most inmates are not just concerned with *filling* time, but with *using* time to advance themselves. They want to make sure that prison is not simply a sterile interlude, but provides an opportunity to gain tangible improvements in skills and a better chance to negotiate life following release. Glaser (1964), in an early comprehensive study of prisons, noted that self-advancement ranked highest among the concerns of inmates. Irwin (1970) also reported that many inmates in the prisons he studied were obsessed with self-improvement.

Self-improvement needs of inmates are motives that lead the inmates to participate in educational, vocational, and other programs that promise remediation of deficits, personal growth, and material advancement. It is with respect to such self-advancement motives that we encounter acute challenges. The facts are these: (1) The motives that lead to program participation are strongest among the young, which is as it should be. The young, after all, have more to learn and a longer life to apply learning to. Older inmates may have too much of life lived and may see themselves as finished products. (2) By contrast, though, young inmates are often disposed in ways that make sustained learning hard, and their rambunctiousness makes life harder for other program participants who must learn in surroundings tainted by playfulness and noise.

Although older inmates are usually equipped for work and study, they have few incentives to work and study. The lifers, and the long-term inmates generally, are the extremes. They have too much time to fill, too remote a future, and too little hope. How many correspondence courses can a man take, how many vocational programs can he complete? And what is the point of it all, when the time for learning is indefinite, and the time to apply learning is limited? And to bring us back to our starting point, how can one learn among noisy young inmates playfully filling in a few painless days in a brief interlude of captivity? The social climate, the lack of incentive, and the pointlessness make most prison programs irrelevant to the lifer and convert most programs into demonstrations of the fact that prisons are designed for the short-term inmates, that they have nothing of consequence to offer to those persons who need support the most.

BENIGN NEGLECT BY DEFAULT

With this statement, I come back to the title of this comment. Long-term inmates are "long-term problems" because they quietly and undramatically suffer and silently permit us to ignore them. I have noted elsewhere that:

Short-term inmates can get more help than long-term inmates because there are so many of them; if we did not address their illiteracy or their lack of vocational skills our computers would complain loudly or would flash red lights. If we did not keep short-termers occupied, hundreds of them would noisily mill around prison yards looking unhappy. We have no choice, either, about helping our more visible minorities, the most vociferous psychotics, the helplessly and blatantly feeble-minded, the persistently and severely disruptive. Such persons earn the benefit or brunt of special programs so that we can go on about our business elsewhere. We cannot run prisons in which men need help getting dressed, proclaim themselves kings, or attack fellow-inmates. But we can run prisons in which inmates unobtrusively and very gradually waste away. (Toch, 1977)

Long-term inmates are also forgotten because we don't have salient concerns about reintegrating them into society. During most of his stay, the long-term inmate is in cold storage, but the conditions for the inmate's storage are inappropriate because they are unstable. Most other inmates are coming and going, engaging in short-term adjustment, and doing things that prepare them for release. Only in a few select, end-of-the-road prisons, in traditional institutions for old-timers, was their life quiescent and relatively bearable. In such prisons it was the short-termer who suffered, because these prisons were high on structure and privacy but short on programs.

End-of-the-road prisons were stable prisons, with little spectacular violence and with an inbred, routine-oriented parochial climate. Such prisons maximized the inmates' psychological survival, but by the same token they offered little more. They were "closed" in the same sense as long-term hospital wards (Goffman, 1961) and other settings removed from the outside world. There was also, in

such prisons, little meaningful activity. In such prisons for long-termers prisonization, or adaptive coping, took its classic forms, with the creation of artificial worlds into which inmates (and staff) could retreat. Such worlds were testimonials to human resilience and institutional inflexibility. They were also a monumental waste of human resources.

EVOLVING AN AFFIRMATIVE STRATEGY

What can we do to serve our permanent resident population now that institutions for long-termers no longer exist? On the mental health front, a task we can set ourselves is to help the inmate work out some sort of strategy for coping with long-term incarceration, rather than have him or her fall back on defensive adjustment modes, such as fantasy and withdrawal. Problem solving can be fostered or encouraged in groups in which long-term inmates can share the dilemma of doing time over an extended period, and work on it as a problem with programmatic implications. In such groups, mutual support networks can be created and prison staff can be presented with requests for relevant institutional supports.

For its part, staff must consider and devise realistic options for sustained long-term programming. This could include educational and vocational *careers* where we now offer short-time assignments. A career implies progression and advancement. It also implies a mission, a function, and chances to be of use. A kitchen worker can become a head cook or prison chef. The inmate obsessed with his legal appeal can become a law clerk, an informal legal consultant to other inmates, or a qualified paralegal professional. Most prison service needs can be filled with experienced inmates, who can be trained to perfect specialized skills in careers ranging from pharmacy and paramedical services to accounting and plumbing. Long-term inmates in such positions can afford a luxury that few outsiders can afford, such as reading trade journals and exploring recent techniques of their chosen fields, relying on correspondence courses, outside consultants, and so forth.

Long-term prison careers must be planned. The type of planning involved is career planning, which has some essential attributes. One such attribute is sequencing. Sequencing involves progression from higher- to lower-security settings, with increments of freedom and amenities. For prisoners who are eligible for parole, sequencing means movement toward a light at the end of a long tunnel. One problem the prisoner has is to adjust to the length of the tunnel. Later, the inmate must adapt to the light, with help from prerelease programs.

Career planning must also be *contingency* planning. We can be certain of the first steps we take but must be tentative about the forks in the road that lie ahead. Experience with one program or milieu can affect our assessment of the profitability of the next step. More important, the prisoner's experience at one stage of the process can change his or her perspective about the next stage. If possible, prisoners must be afforded choices, not only about their initial placements but also about subsequent assignments. A career must be a series of choice points at which preliminary plans are ratified or modified through consultation between inmates and staff.

A career must also be contingent on what the prisoner does, in the sense that improvements must be attained as a result of achievements. Increments of status must be rewards the inmate has earned by making valued contributions (Toch, 1988). A meaningful career *in the prison* has the virtue of capitalizing on the long-term inmate's only real world—that of institutions—and giving him or her a useful and meaningful role. Such a role can yield rewards and status as well as being intrinsically interesting to the inmate. It can be a role that is *needed* by fellow inmates and by staff, and that offers opportunities for real teamwork with staff members.

The long-termer as a prison careerist can not only have a legitimate mission, but can also improve the delivery of all kinds of services in prisons. If the inmate is willing, he or she can be sent to other prisons to improve service delivery in his or her area of specialty. The inmate can help set up a pharmacy or infirmary at a youth camp, install a heating plant at a new institution, or set up a computerized information system at a reception center. Such rotation makes the inmate a participant in corrections, which will be his or her only world for a good many years. Active participation of this kind can yield self-esteem, provide self-respect, and restore life to men and women who are now vegetating and are sadly useless to themselves and to the rest of us.

REFERENCES

Glaser, D. (1964). *The effectiveness of a prison and parole system.* Indianapolis: Bobbs-Merrill.

Goffman, E. (1961). *Asylums: Essays on the social situation of mental patients and other inmates.* New York: Anchor.

Irwin, J. (1970). *The felon.* Englewood Cliffs, NJ: Prentice Hall.

Rasch, W. (1977, June). *The development of the mental and physical state of persons sentenced to life imprisonment.* Paper presented at Seminar on Long-Term Incarceration and Programs for Long-Term Inmates, Montreal.

Toch, H. (1977). The long-term inmate as a long-term problem. In S. Rizkalla, R. Levy, & R. Zauberman (Eds.), *Long-term imprisonment: An international seminar.* Montreal: University of Montreal.

Toch, H. (1988, June). Rewarding convicted offenders. *Federal Probation, 52*, 42-48.

Toch, H. (1992). *Living in prison: The ecology of survival.* Washington, DC: American Psychological Association.

25

Correctional Policy and the Long-Term Prisoner

Timothy J. Flanagan

Long-term prisoners present correctional policymakers with formidable problems. These problems are rooted in the varied membership of the population of long-term prisoners and in the seriousness of crimes for which these offenders are imprisoned. A new perspective for the administration of prison systems containing such inmates is offered. In terms of the loss associated with imprisonment, it is assumed that removal from society is perceived by most prisoners as the principal punishment inherent in incarceration. Since this punishment bears most heavily on long-term prisoners, special efforts must be made to ameliorate the secondary sanctions that accompany imprisonment.

The proposals offered for improving the treatment of long-term inmates include the creation of subdivisions within the prison according to the unique circumstances of prisoner subgroups and the adoption of a long-range perspective in programming for long-term inmates. The proposals call for the development of an eclectic program which long-term prisoners can use to build meaningful careers.

THE DILEMMA CREATED BY THE LONG-TERM PRISONER

Prisoners incarcerated for long periods present correctional policymakers and administrators with several formidable problems. These problems stem from two principal characteristics of this prisoner population: (1) its diversity and (2) the serious offenses that eventuated in the inmates' long prison sentences. Taken together, these factors create a dilemma that makes it extremely difficult for correctional reformers to devise realistic and useful programs specifically for long-term prisoners.

Available data on the criminal histories of long-term prisoners indicate that diversity is a hallmark of this group (Flanagan, 1979). It includes career criminal robbers, in whose lives before imprisonment crime was a daily activity and who adapt to incarceration by continuing careers of deceit and violence. In contrast, other long-term prisoners are essentially noncriminal individuals, whose act of

AUTHOR'S NOTE: Support for this project was provided, in part, by grant No. 76-SS-99-6038, awarded to the Criminal Justice Research Center by the Bureau of Justice Statistics, United States Department of Justice. Points of view or opinions expressed herein are those of the author and do not necessarily represent the official position or policies of the Department of Justice.
NOTE: Reprinted from *Crime and Delinquency*, Vol. 28, No. 1, January 1982, pp. 82-95. Copyright 1982 by Sage Publications, Inc.

violence was unprecedented and is unlikely to be repeated, and whose interests and perspectives within the prison coincide more closely with those of officers than with those of fellow inmates. Although murderers make up a large percentage of long-term prisoners, the motives, justifications, and behaviors that are incorporated under the "homicide" label are themselves of broad scope (see Wolfgang, 1958).

This diversity has important implications for those proposing policy changes and initiatives relating to long-term prisoners. In short, it clouds the issue, makes determination of proper policy woefully complex, and requires that difficult choices be made when resources are limited. Failure to recognize the variation among members of the long-term inmate group leads to proposals that are uniquely suited to the needs of some members of the group but are inappropriate and possibly harmful for others. For example, some observers have suggested that because of the unique nature of their situation and the distinctive lifestyle they adopt while in the prison, all long-term prisoners would benefit if they were concentrated in special facilities designed to suit their special circumstances. Although such a proposal would be welcomed by a proportion of the long-term population, there are other prisoners in this group for whom the special programming would not be appropriate (see Home Office Advisory Council on the Penal System, 1968).

Despite the difficulties that are a concomitant of this diversity, correctional policymakers should not be paralyzed into indecision in regard to these prisoners. Rather, it should be kept in mind that diversity requires choice; because single solutions to the special problems presented by long-term prisoners will not be successful, a measure of flexibility and experimentation in program and policy development will be required.

Unfortunately, the second aspect of the dilemma presented by long-term prisoners— that they are incarcerated for committing heinous crimes—serves to undermine the drive for a varied approach. The problem is this: In the development of correctional policy, public approval of policy changes may be least likely when the offenders affected are long-term prisoners, especially if the changes are perceived by citizens either as presenting a greater risk to society of repeated victimization by these offenders or as representing leniency

toward this group. The public does not support practices that are perceived (or defined) as "coddling criminals" (Flanagan, Hindelang, & Gottfredson, 1980). Moreover, because of the serious offenses committed, the long-term prisoner group is likely to be the target of the most vociferous public demands for strict custody, control, and punishment.

In summary, the dilemma facing correctional administrators responsible for long-term inmates is twofold: The inmates who will most tax the imagination and resources of the correctional system, and who are in greatest need of a variety of programs, are the inmates least desirable, in terms of political and public acceptance, as candidates for new programs. A further irony is that although the instant offenses of long-term prisoners suggest that they may present a serious risk to society if alternative approaches are attempted, the institutional behavior of this group tends to be better (as assessed both qualitatively and quantitatively) than that of short-term prisoners. A practical example of this dilemma follows.

Assume that a correctional administrator has at his disposal a highly regarded trade training program that is located within a minimum security or community-based facility. Demand for the program is high, so the number of inmates who can take advantage of it is limited. Among the many applicants for the program are several long-term inmates, serving terms of various lengths for serious offenses against other persons. The institutional adjustment records of the long-term inmates suggest that they are well suited to the minimum security custody level; moreover, the nature of their prior training indicates that the inmates could profit from involvement with this program. Given only these considerations, the decision might be to accept the applications of these prisoners for placement in the program. However, at least two additional factors—neither related to the appropriateness of these inmates for this program—will undoubtedly enter into the decision making. These are (1) whether it is appropriate, especially given the limited openings available, to accept an inmate who will not be released for many years, and thus will not be able to apply the training in the larger society; and (2) the potential for criticism if the press, legislature, or general public discovers that an inmate who was sentenced to a long prison term for a serious personal crime has been transferred to minimum security before he has reached the final stages of his sentence. The *principle of least eligibility*, which holds that the persons convicted of violations of the law should be least eligible to be beneficiaries of the fruits of participation in society, applies to long-term prisoners in a manner that defines these inmates as the least eligible members of the least eligible class. The potential for reform, then, is dependent upon the willingness of correctional policymakers to adopt a new perspective in regard to long-term inmates.

THE NATURE OF REFORM

The specific proposals for changes in policy and practice that follow rest on the assumption that, at least in the foreseeable future, imprisonment generally and long-term prison sentences in particular are likely to remain features of the American justice system (see Irwin, 1980). Acceptance of this premise does not represent endorsement of the practice, nor does it exclude the possibility of changes in penal policy that would render the long prison sentence obsolete. It does, however, suggest the worth of immediate changes that could make prisons less destructive of inmates and prison workers, and therefore less destructive of society. As Hawkins has stated:

The origins of imprisonment are lost in antiquity. It has proved to be the most perdurable of all penal methods, despite all the premature obituary notices. It is quite possible that eventually the maximum-security prison as we know it will be replaced by . . . "small non-punitive custodial centers, psychiatrically and/or sociologically based, and adapted to individual needs." But it is surely both a perverse denial of experience and totally irresponsible to abjure attempts to deal with present problems because of the prospect of an imagined futurity.[1]

The principal punishment inflicted on the majority of offenders receiving the sanction of incarceration is deprivation of liberty, autonomy, and relationships with persons in the larger society. In several recent studies, data derived from interviews with long-term prisoners have shown that these types of deprivation, which are inherent in the sanction of removal and confinement, are perceived by the inmates as its most serious consequences (Flanagan, 1980; Richards, 1978). Secondary punishments inflicted on the offender—including denial of certain political rights, lack of meaningful work opportunities, restricted personal space, loss of privacy, substandard medical care, economic dependency, regimentation, verbal and physical harassment by fellow inmates and guards, a milieu of tension and violence—pale in comparison with the primary sanction of removal from society.[2] Geis (1979) has written in this regard that:

. . . the worst part of imprisonment is the loss of autonomy and the concomitant deprivation of so many things that allow a human being to esteem himself. In an important observation Sykes notes that for men the loss in prison of the opportunity for heterosexual contacts does not produce sexual frustration in any important sense; rather it is especially painful because it removes from the prisoners' world a token of worth and self-value. (p. 203)

Of course, the "pains of imprisonment" are not uniform. The degree to which inmates suffer deprivation through confinement will vary considerably. However, in the case of the long-term prisoner, because incarceration (and the primary deprivations inherent in incarceration) will be prolonged, special efforts should be made to minimize secondary punishments. The proposals that follow are based on the general principle that the longer an offender will remain in prison, the greater must be the steps taken to ameliorate the secondary punishments associated with incarceration.

The overall goal of the reform proposals is conservative. I do not suggest that ameliorating the secondary sanctions of imprisonment will be followed by "rehabilitation" of the prisoner, however that is defined. Rather, I assume that if we are unsure of how best to help offenders, the correctional system is obliged to take steps to counteract the potential for deterioration that is inherent in imprisonment (see McKay, Jayewardene, & Reedie, 1979).

Although humanization of the prison is needed for all offenders, the need is greatest among the prisoners who will serve long terms.

In summary, the proposals to minimize the potentially deleterious consequences of confinement are advanced not because of an assumption that humanizing prisons will make them any more effective in rehabilitating or reintegrating offenders; rather, prisons need not be onerous places in which to live and work in order to accomplish the tasks assigned them by society—protecting the public and punishing offenders.

IMPLICATIONS
OF THE PRINCIPLE

Creating Discrete
Units in the Institution

The recent work of Toch and his colleagues highlights the importance of matching people with the environments appropriate for them (Toch, 1977a). The environmental features prized by long-term inmates appear to be distinguishable from those of short-term prisoners. Therefore, a first step that could be taken to reduce the secondary sanctions of confinement for long-term inmates would be to create separate units within the prison that are designed to serve the needs of these inmates. Although this proposal is similar to the previously mentioned recommendation that long-term inmates be concentrated in a single facility, there are important differences. A separate prison is not being proposed, obviating the realistic concern of many inmates that the correctional system would respond by building maxi-maximum security prisons with repressive regimes for the custody of long-term prisoners. Moreover, dividing existing facilities into units may result in economic savings to the correctional system.

In a large institution encompassing a number of buildings, the inmate population may be subdivided on the basis of many relevant criteria. These criteria have customarily included age, sex, sentence length, and recidivist versus first-timer status. Recently, the Federal Bureau of Prisons experimented with *functional unit programming*, in which residential groups were formed in terms of treatment needs. Correctional administrators should investigate the feasibility of creating discrete subdivisions in the prison on the basis of prisoners' lifestyles or views toward serving time—extending the subclassification beyond

the long-term group. Although classification of this kind would be difficult initially, it is likely that after a time each of the subdivisions of the prison would develop a "reputation" for a particular environment—as do college dormitories, for example, or prisons themselves—and assignments could be made on the basis of these characteristics. Toch's Prison Preference Inventory could be used to determine the characteristics of the subdivisions and as an aid in placing inmates.

Recent research suggests that over time many long-term inmates develop a distinguishable "perspective" toward serving time in prison (Flanagan, 1981). Despite the numerous other differences among long-term prisoners, inmates who hold this perspective share common views on many issues and tend to adopt similar lifestyles within the prison. Voluntary congregation of these prisoners in a unit within the prison could solve many of their perceived problems.

Another advantage to this approach is that correctional officers could be assigned to the unit they preferred, to the extent possible given the need to maintain regular schedules within the prison, uphold union contracts and agreements, and similar constraints. Many officers would prefer to work exclusively with older men serving long sentences, and others might prefer association with younger, first-term inmates.

Within the units proposed in this plan, the mode of living, including styles of rule enforcement, could be adapted to the particular needs of the members. Of course, all inmates must be subject to general rules of behavior; but within the smaller units, various practices might be accepted by inmates and guards alike as being within the bounds of permissible behavior. This proposal is not without precedent. Variations in styles of rule enforcement and institutional climate already characterize correctional systems encompassing more than one prison, and these differences are well known to both inmates and staff.

Because many prisons are quite large, a degree of centralization would necessarily remain, despite the division of the inmate population. For example, at least in the immediate future it seems inevitable that meals will continue to be served in the large prison mess halls. Yet even here the different subdivisions could be permitted some autonomy. For instance, if members of the long-term prisoner unit were bothered at mealtimes by loud noise made by younger short-termers, arrangements could be made to serve different units at different times. Although annoyances such as this might seem trivial to a person on the outside, it should be understood that over the course of a long sentence of confinement such factors contribute to the secondary punishments imposed on the inmate.

This proposal may appear in one sense quite radical, although in practical terms it would demand merely a moderate shift in organizational design. Historically, a premise that has been central to the operation of prisons is that all inmates within a single institution are to be treated exactly alike. The excesses of the trusty system—in which some inmates are elevated to guard status over their colleagues—have been seen as evidence of the problems of departing from the "all are equal" position. However, a theme that emerges from the research on this population is that long-term inmates are, in many ways, different from short-term inmates. Those differences should be addressed by correctional administrators. Viewed simply as an organization, the hospital provides a useful analogue. It is not presumed that all hospital patients require the same kind or level of care, even though they are all housed under a single roof. The organization is subdivided into units according to patients' needs and the level of care necessary. Staff members are recruited and assigned to functional units on the basis of experience and interest, and the units enjoy some autonomy within the larger organization. The central administration manages such divisions as the pharmacy, food service, and laundry, which provide services to all units.

Changes such as these require considerable work on the part of prison staff, particularly first-line correctional officers. Mattick (see Hawkins, 1976, p. 168) has contended that the primary impediment to change in correction is "custodial convenience"—the fact that it is easier to continue the way "it has always been done" than to introduce what may well be needed change, because new programs and organizational change require a great investment of effort. Hawkins (1976) reminds us that:

[I]t is important to note that Mattick does not attribute this phenomenon to the character of the custodial staff. He says

explicitly: "It is not a matter of mere laziness or that prison staffs do not do any work." It is rather, he maintains, "the characteristic mode of adjustment" to program innovation of understaffed and underfinanced institutions. Resistance to change is a function of the institutional situation rather than of an ideological commitment on the part of the guard force.

To counteract this inertia, subdivision of the prison environment could present the prospect of better working conditions for correctional staff, as well as better living conditions for inmates, without weakening prison security. Dealing with smaller groups of inmates on a more personal level would appeal to many officers who desire to function as more than turnkeys.

The Prison Career of the Long-Term Inmate

A second general policy change recommended here was first proposed by Toch, in a paper titled "The Long-Term Prisoner as a Long-Term Problem" (Toch, 1977b). In short, a new perspective toward the inmate who comes to prison facing a sentence of 10, 15, 20, or more years is needed. Such an inmate must be viewed as a person who will spend a significant proportion of his adult life within the prison. It is grossly inappropriate to treat him as we would an offender facing 3 years. The approach to correction that is taken with the latter typically revolves around programs that run 12 to 24 months and focus on the development of specific skills.

On its face, such a piecemeal approach is not useful with an offender who enters prison at age 18 and may not be released until he is nearly 40. Most of this person's adult and working life will be spent in prison. Given this situation, it is incumbent on the correctional system to work with the offender to plan a worthwhile career, one that not only will be beneficial to both the offender and others but also will be transferable and capable of supporting the offender upon his eventual release. Moreover, there is no reason why, during their long imprisonment, many long-term inmates cannot make a substantial contribution to society through help provided to fellow inmates.

An example illustrates this career approach to planning programs for the long-term prisoner. An inmate is received in the prison who has a high school education and a desire to enter teaching. The prisoner faces a minimum sentence of 20 years. If the prisoner embarked on a planned course of study leading to undergraduate and graduate degrees, he could become a certified teacher in 4 to 10 years, depending on his pace of advancement and such other commitments as prison work assignments. The prisoner could then become a prison instructor, and his talents would therefore be reinvested in the program for the period remaining before release. A similar progression can be envisioned for the inmate inclined toward trade training: from student to teacher, with other inmates reaping the benefits of the prisoner's experience. The essential difference between the career approach to program planning and the current piecemeal approach is that the goals of the former are long-term. And, as Toch comments:

> A meaningful career *in the prison* has the virtue of capitalizing on the long-term inmate's only "real world" and giving him a useful and meaningful role. Such a role can yield rewards and status, as well as being intrinsically rewarding to the inmate. It can be a role that is *needed* by fellow inmates and by staff, and that offers opportunities for *real teamwork* with staff members. (Toch, 1977b, p. 290)

The prison career approach to programming for long-term inmates requires correctional administrators to break away from the old notion of the 12- or 24-month program that results in a certificate and little else for the prisoner. Instead, correctional officials and the inmate must jointly develop a plan oriented to accomplish long-range goals, and then ensure that the learned skills are put to use. Toch notes that long-term prisoners could eventually provide many of the services needed in prison, through their skills as pharmacists, paramedics, accountants, teachers, master plumbers, and so on.

It should be noted that the essential components of the plan are already part of many prison programs, in the form of college courses, trade training, and other programs. Moreover, because the prison career model reinvests the inmate's talent in the program, overall costs to the taxpayer may be reduced. Although this program will not ensure that the prisoner is released to a receptive community with appropriate job opportunities, it at least places him in a more competitive position in the marketplace. Finally, rather than serving to force people to waste half their adult lives regressing within a restricted, nonproductive world, the prison would release to the community persons who have made at least some contribution while incarcerated, and who are better equipped to cope with life on the outside.

Equal Career Opportunities

In line with both the proposal regarding the prison environment and the proposal pertaining to career planning, it is critical that long-term inmates enjoy equal access to programs and work assignments within the prison. Today, they are often denied access to certain programs because of their status as lifers or long-term inmates. This "cold-storage" model is a source of discontent, stimulating complaints of discrimination among long-term prisoners.

In the state of Indiana, for example, prisoners are considered for certain rehabilitative programs only when they become eligible to apply for clemency. In a recent court decision, a challenge to this policy was denied. The court did not find the policy unreasonable, "as a matter of practicality," given prisoners' relative chances of release.[3] State administrative regulations also serve to exclude long-term inmates from programs. For example, the New York statute that authorizes temporary release programs (work, education, and furlough programs) defines an eligible inmate as a prisoner within one year of parole eligibility.[4] The use of temporary release to ease reentry into the community, and its consequent restriction to prisoners nearing the end of their sentences, is common in the United States. New York's Department of Correctional Services has issued regulations for temporary release programs, including a list of categories of inmates "who shall not normally be granted furloughs or leaves of absence." Included on this list are "those with very long sentences."[5]

In addition to their exclusion from program opportunities on the grounds of statute or administrative regulations, long-term prisoners are often left out of programs because the economics of scarcity demand that they be last in line for these services. Because correctional resources are limited, it does not seem unreasonable to postpone the long-term prisoner's participation in a specific program if demand is high and an inmate with a short sentence could also profit from participation. However, such postponements should not amount to cold-storage for the long-term inmate until shortly before release. To continue current practice is to conduct decision making based on labels rather than needs.

Preserving the Family

Given the strained conditions under which prisoners make contact with their families, it should not be surprising that many long-term prisoners have difficulty maintaining effective communication with family members over the course of a long prison term. That marriages and other relationships survive the experience of lengthy imprisonment of one party is surprising. Yet family members and friends are perceived by the long-term inmate as a source of strength. The importance of maintaining relationships with family and other external supports is underscored by the results of a recent study of the postrelease adjustment of West German lifers, in which the investigators identified two factors that "vitally determine the extent of effects from [long-term] imprisonment" (Albrecht, 1978, p. 153). These factors were the offender's postinstitutional position in the social structure and the attitude of the released prisoner's family toward him. Moreover, the data support earlier analyses which suggest that "the longer the prison term, the worse the relationships with parents, siblings, wife, and children become. . . ." (Albrecht, p. 156).

Of course the preservation of family relationships is an objective that raises substantial questions for the correctional policymaker. First, what should social policy be regarding family ties in the case of long-term inmates? Should the state encourage a prisoner who will serve 15 years to keep the marriage intact? And what are the implications of this policy for the nature of family life? In addition, the correctional administrator knows that, with respect to the orderly operation of the prison, family ties create many problems. Visits increase the problem of security and contra-

band, disrupt work schedules, and can cause conflicts if the inmate leaves the visit with personal problems.

Despite these problems, data from recent research suggest that knowing there are persons who care "out there" is a source of strength and hope to many long-term prisoners that can moderate the negative effects of imprisonment (see Flanagan, 1979). Ellis, Grasmick, and Gilman (1974) have reported that frequency of visitation is inversely related to inmates' aggressive behavior within prisons. Given the importance of family and other personal relationships, especially for long-term inmates, and the special need to ameliorate secondary punishments in the case of long-term prisoners, several steps could be taken by correctional officials to help maintain close family ties. Conjugal visitation programs have been part of prison services in the country for years, but they have operated in only a very few prisons and have permitted only infrequent contact between family members. Home furloughs are generally recognized as a better strategy for maintaining family relationships, but isolated incidents involving furlough participants, resulting in public criticism that the system is too lenient with criminals, have made correctional officials wary of furlough programs and promoted rules and statutes that tighten up the criteria governing candidacy for home furlough programs.

Much can be done within the prison to foster family ties. Family counseling programs can be organized to help families work out problems in communication. Family-centered visits can be planned so that larger groups of family members can arrange to visit an inmate and stay in comfortable surroundings for several days. Finally, security, program considerations, and other factors permitting, inmates who prefer to be close to their families should be located as close as possible to their home communities. The maintenance of family ties should also play a major part in the selection of sites for prisons in which inmates will be held over long periods.

Preparation for Release[6]

It is obvious that the release of a person who has spent a significant portion of his adult life behind prison walls presents problems that are different from those presented by the

short-term prison inmate. In this regard, four suggestions are offered for the parole release of long-term inmates.

First, inmates incarcerated for long periods should be seen by the parole board annually, even though they may not be eligible for release for a decade or more. The rationale for this proposal is twofold. First, annual contacts with the parole board will allow board members an opportunity to review the inmate's career plan within the prison, chart his progress toward goals, and revise the plans, if necessary. Prison officials, parole officials, and the inmate could use this meeting to assess the prisoner's unmet needs and evaluate his progress toward established goals. If poor institutional conduct or other problems are apparent, these issues can be discussed. This proposal coincides with the prison career approach to programs for long-term prisoners.

Second, from the inmate's perspective, these annual meetings can serve to reduce the apparent arbitrariness of parole board reviews. Many prisoners complain that parole release decisions, made following only a brief meeting yet encompassing many years of an offender's life in prison, do not reflect a true understanding of the person. It is not difficult to see how this perception could arise under a system in which an offender served many years without seeing the parole board. In contrast, annual meetings with the release authority would ensure that the inmate's case was reviewed several times before the release hearing, could warn the inmate if necessary of the possible consequences of his troublesome behavior before the single "denial" decision, and help to alleviate this perception of arbitrariness.

Also related to parole release is predischarge preparation. Although long-termers are not completely isolated from the outside world during their confinement, subtle changes may have taken place in society for which the inmates are unprepared. In this regard, a period to prepare for release would seem essential for many such prisoners. The program should go beyond the recitation of parole rules and regulations, and ample opportunities for contact with people from the outside should be offered. Former offenders who have made the adjustment could be used as resources for this training, and professional personnel who are aware of the potential for stress and anxiety among long-term inmates before and immediately after release should also be available.

Finally, the parole rules imposed on inmates released after long terms of confinement should recognize that these persons have spent a significant proportion of their lives in a prison environment. For example, prohibitions against association with former prisoners should be reconsidered in light of the fact that these may be the only people the parolee knows. The former long-termer may encounter other difficulties in adjustment that are directly related to his extended period of imprisonment. The parole officer must be aware of the potential problems and special needs.

CONCLUSION

Traditionally, the young first offender has been the primary target of correctional reform, which has typically taken the shape of (1) diversion of the offender from the formal correctional system or (2) provision of services and programs whose objective is rehabilitation. The offenders who are seen as requiring close custody for extended periods because of the heinous nature of their instant offenses or their propensity for future dangerousness (or both) have been largely ignored by correctional reformers.

Toch observes that this view of long-term prisoners has several sources:

> Short-term inmates can get more help than long-term inmates because there are so many of them; if we did not address their illiteracy or their lack of vocational skills our computers would complain loudly or would flash red lights. If we did not keep short-termers occupied, hundreds of them would noisily mill around prison yards looking unhappy. We have no choice, either, about helping our more visible minorities, the most vociferous psychotics, the helplessly and blatantly feebleminded, the persistently and severely disruptive. . . . We cannot run prisons in which men need help getting dressed, proclaim themselves kings, or attack fellow-inmates. But we can run prisons in which inmates unobtrusively and very gradually waste away. (Toch, 1977b, p. 288)

Cohen has also warned of the tendency of correctional administrators to reduce the considerable managerial problems posed by long-term prisoners by waving the "magic wand of classification." By this he refers to the most common approach to the management of long-term prisoners: concentrating them in a single maximum security prison (Cohen, 1974). Cohen contends that the continued segregation of long-term prisoners from the balance of the prison population creates environments aptly termed "human warehouses."

The proposals advanced in this chapter seek to create an awareness among correctional decision makers of the unique pains of long-term imprisonment and offer direction for ways to deal with these problems. As noted earlier, what is needed at the outset is a new perspective toward long-term prisoners, one rejecting the old notion that long-term inmates can be ignored until they are close to release and also recognizing the diversity within the long-term group. This subgroup of the prison population, which poses a special challenge to the resources and imaginations of correctional officials, will be most usefully served by an eclectic program of alternatives suited to the unique needs of—and among—long-term prisoners.

NOTES

1. See Hawkins (1976, p. 44). The reference is to Sington and Playfair (1965, p. 336).

2. Secondary punishments refer to aspects of the conditions of confinement that are customarily associated with life in prison. These features of the prison, which Sykes (1957) refers to as the "pains of imprisonment," are generally conceived as a necessary part of imprisonment. As suggested here, they need not be.

3. *Jennings v. State*; Ind. Sup. Ct. 5/17/79; cited in 25 CrL 2278, 6-20-79.

4. *New York State Correction Law*, sec. 851.2 (McKinney Supp. 1973).

5. "Although technically applicable only to furlough and leaves of absence, the categories have also been a consideration in decisions regarding work release," quoted in "Temporary Release in New York State Correctional Facilities," *Albany Law Review*, Summer 1974, p. 691, citing New York State Department of Correctional Services, *Administrative Bulletin No. 63* (June 22, 1972).

6. This discussion assumes the continuation of discretionary release, however circumscribed the decision maker's discretion may eventually be.

REFERENCES

Albrecht, P. A. (1978). The effects of imprisonment on the self-image of "lifers." *International Summaries* (Vol. 2, National Criminal Justice Reference Service). Washington, DC: Law Enforcement Assistance Administration.

Cohen, S. (1974, November). Human warehouses: The future of our prisons? *New Society*, 407-411.

Ellis, D., Grasmick, H., & Gilman, B. (1974). Violence in prisons: A sociological analysis. *American Journal of Sociology*, 16-43.

Flanagan, T. (1979). *Long-term prisoners: A study of the characteristics, institutional experience and perspectives of long-term inmates in state correctional facilities*. Doctoral dissertation, State University of New York at Albany.

Flanagan, T. (1980, April). The pains of long-term imprisonment: A comparison of British and American perspectives. *British Journal of Criminology*, 148-156.

Flanagan, T. (1981, June). Dealing with long-term confinement: Adaptive strategies and perspectives among long-term prisoners. *Criminal Justice and Behavior*, 201-222.

Flanagan, T., Hindelang, M., & Gottfredson, M. (Eds.). (1980). *Sourcebook of criminal justice statistics—1979*. Washington, DC: Government Printing Office.

Geis, G. (1979). Epilogue: On imprisonment. In M. E. Wolfgang (Ed.), *Prisons: Present and possible* (p. 203). Lexington, MA: Lexington Books.

Hawkins, G. (1976). *The prison: Policy and practice*. Chicago: University of Chicago Press.

Home Office Advisory Council on the Penal System. (1968). *The regime for long-term prisoners under conditions of maximum security*. London: HMSO.

Irwin, J. (1980). *Prisons in turmoil*. Boston: Little, Brown.

McKay, H. B., Jayewardene, C. H. S., & Reedie, P. B. (1979). *The effects of long-term incarceration and a proposed strategy for future research*. Ottawa: Ministry of Supply and Services.

Richards, B. (1978, April). The experience of long-term imprisonment: An exploratory investigation. *British Journal of Criminology*, 162-169.

Sington, D., & Playfair, G. (1965). *Crime, punishment and care*. London: Secker & Warburg.

Sykes, G. (1957). *Society of captives*. Princeton, NJ: Princeton University Press.

Toch, H. (1977a). *Living in prison: The ecology of survival*. New York: Free Press.

Toch, H. (1977b). The long-term prisoner as a long-term problem. In S. Rizkalla, R. Levy, & R. Zauberman (Eds.), *Long-term imprisonment: An international seminar* (pp. 283-291). Montreal: University of Montreal.

Wolfgang, M. (1958). *Patterns in criminal homicide*. Philadelphia: University of Pennsylvania.

About the Editor

Timothy J. Flanagan, Ph.D., is professor of Criminal Justice and dean of the College of Criminal Justice at Sam Houston State University in Huntsville, Texas, where he also serves as director of the university's Criminal Justice Center. Previously, he was associate professor and associate dean of the School of Criminal Justice at the University at Albany, State University of New York. He directed the project that produced the *Sourcebook of Criminal Justice Statistics* on behalf of the U.S. Department of Justice from 1977 to 1991, and was executive director of the Hindelang Criminal Justice Research Center. He has published scores of journal articles, reviews, edited books, and research reports. He teaches courses in criminal justice administration, corrections, and research; his research focuses on the effectiveness of correctional programs, criminal justice statistics, public opinion on justice issues, and criminal justice higher education. He has served as a consultant to numerous state and federal justice agencies and commissions and is a Distinguished Alumnus of the Rockefeller College of Public Affairs and Policy of the University at Albany, a Fellow of the Academy of Criminal Justice Sciences, and a Fellow of the American Council of Education.

About the Contributors

James Bonta is Chief of Corrections Research for the Ministry Secretariat Solicitor General of Canada and an adjunct research professor at Carleton University. He received a Ph.D. in psychology from the University of Ottawa. He has authored or coauthored more than 25 articles on psychological and corrections issues and has served as a manuscript reviewer for both Canadian and American journals. He has presented papers for the Canadian Psychological Association, the International Association of Residential and Community Alternatives, and the American Corrections Congress, among other organizations.

Anthony E. Bottoms is Wolfson Professor of Criminology, University of Cambridge. His research has focused on a wide range of topics in criminology and penology. Among his many publications, he is coeditor of *Problems of Long-Term Imprisonment* (Cambridge Studies in Criminology LVIII, 1987).

Carol S. Campbell is an assistant professor at McNeese State University, where she teaches sociology, social work, and criminal justice. She holds a master's degree in sociology, social work, and criminal justice, and a Ph.D. in sociology from Louisiana State University. She has published in several journals.

Thomas A. Coughlin III is the former commissioner of the Department of Correctional Services of New York. He entered state service with the New York State Police in 1962 and served as deputy commissioner for Mental Retardation in the Department of Mental Hygiene and as commissioner of the Office of Mental Retardation and Developmental Disabilities. A graduate of Goddard College in Vermont, he also attended Syracuse University law school.

Ernest L. Cowles is the director of the Legal Studies Center and an associate professor of criminal justice at Sangamon State University. In addition to a longstanding research interest in long-term incarceration, he has recently been involved in correctional policy research focusing on alternative sanctions. He is also presently engaged in a study of the impact of drug enforcement groups. Dr. Cowles received his Ph.D. in criminology from Florida State University in 1981.

Richard L. Dugger is a second-generation corrections administrator. He has a bachelor's degree in criminal justice and 30 years' service with the Florida Department of Corrections. He began his career as a correctional officer and was promoted through the ranks to positions in classification, administration, and the Parole Commission, and then to Prison Superintendent. In 1987 he was appointed Secretary of the Florida Department of Corrections and continued in that capacity until 1991. He is currently Superintendent of the Putnam Correctional Institution.

Laura T. Fishman is an associate professor of sociology at the University of Vermont. She holds an M.A. in sociology from the University of Chicago and a Ph.D. in sociology from McGill University. Her major research and teaching interests include crime, corrections, women and crime, domestic violence, and families of prisoners. She is the author of *Women at the Wall: A Study of Prisoners' Wives Doing Time on the Outside*. Currently she is engaged in field research for her project, "Reactions of African-American and Hispanic Prisoners with HIV/AIDS and Their Significant Women to Imprisonment."

Burk Foster is an associate professor of criminal justice at the University of Southwestern Louisiana in Lafayette. A native of Oklahoma, he is a former police officer and Air Force officer. Most of his current research concerns jail and prison operations, long-term imprisonment, crime rates, and the death penalty.

Elaine Genders is a lecturer in laws at University College, London. She holds the Master of Philosophy in Criminology from Cambridge University and was previously a research fellow in criminology at the Center for Criminological Research, University of Oxford. Her research interests include various aspects of prisons, sentencing, and violent crime; her publications include *Race Relations in Prisons* and *Grendon: A Study of a Therapeutic Prison*, both coauthored with Elaine Player.

Paul Gendreau is a professor of psychology and director of the graduate program at the University of New Brunswick. He received his Ph.D. in psychology from Queen's University, Ontario, in 1968. He began working in criminal justice settings in 1961, and for 15 years was an administrator of clinical services in the Ontario corrections system. He has published extensively on correctional program effectiveness, prediction of criminal behavior, the effects of prison life, and the development of assessment tools for evaluating the quality of offender programs.

Lynne Goodstein is a professor of administration of justice and women's studies and Director of the Women's Studies Program at Pennsylvania State University. She has published extensively on inmate adjustment to prison and sentencing, including *Determinate Sentencing and Imprisonment: A Failure of Reform* and *The American Prison: Issues in Research and Policy*. Her current interests include feminist criminology and the status of women's studies in the academy.

William Hay is a lecturer in social work at the University of Plymouth. He was previously at the Institute of Criminology and conducted research at the University of Hall. His research focuses on court welfare work involving decision making when parents separate and there are disputes over children.

Carl Kummerlowe has served 25 years of a life sentence in the Arizona Department of Corrections. He has studied long-term confinement for more than 20 years and has written several publications on the subject. Due to his interest in and knowledge of long-term imprisonment, he was selected to participate in a study of long-term imprisonment conducted by the Arizona Department of Corrections.

Doris Layton MacKenzie is an associate professor in the Department of Criminal Justice and Criminology at the University of Maryland. She has edited three books—*The American Prison, Measuring Crime*, and *Drugs and Crime*—and has published more than 30 articles on corrections and inmate adjustment and behavior. She directed the National Institute of Justice-sponsored multisite study of boot camp prisons, which investigated the effectiveness of boot camp programs in eight states. She has consulted with state and local jurisdictions and has testified before U.S. Senate and House committees.

Kenneth L. McGinnis has served as the director of the Michigan Department of Corrections since 1991. He holds a bachelor's degree in administration of justice and a master's degree in rehabilitation administration, both from Southern Illinois University. He began his career in corrections as a correctional counselor at Menard Correctional Center in Illinois prior to being named its director and has also held a variety of other positions with the Illinois Department of Corrections.

Barry Mitchell is a reader in criminal justice at Coventry University, England. For the past 10 years he has been researching and writing on various aspect of the homicide laws and the policies and practices relating to life imprisonment in England and Wales.

William R. T. Palmer was trained in both clinical and forensic psychology. He has worked in corrections since 1965, initially with institutionalized young offenders, both male and female. For the past 20 years he has been a psychologist with the Correctional Services of Canada at Warkworth Institution in rural Eastern Ontario.

Elaine Player is a lecturer in the law school, King's College, London. She has coauthored (with Elaine Genders) *Race Relations in Prisons* and *Grendon: A Therapeutic Prison*, and coedited (with Michael Jenkins) *Prisons After Woolf: Reform Through Riot.*

J. Michael Quinlan served as director of the Federal Bureau of Prisons from 1987 to 1992 and was responsible for more that 80,000 inmates in 75 correctional facilities across the United States. He holds a law degree from Fordham University and a master's degree in law from George Washington University. He currently works as director of strategic planning for Corrections Corporation of America and publishes *Corrections Alert*, a biweekly newsletter.

James W. Robinson is an associate professor at Louisiana State University, Eunice, where he currently teaches sociology, psychology, and criminal justice. He holds master's degrees in criminal justice and sociology, and a Ph.D. in sociology with minors in psychology and experimental statistics. He has published articles in several journals.

Michael J. Sabath is an associate professor of public administration and urban affairs at San Diego State University—Imperial Valley Campus, and director of the Justice Research Institute. Before joining the faculty at San Diego State University, he was director of the Center for Criminal Justice Research and Information of the Indiana Criminal Justice Institute. He has been a faculty member or adjunct faculty at the University of Missouri, Indiana University, Indiana State University, and the University of Indianapolis and has taught courses in criminal justice administration, public policy, and drug crime control. His current research interests include a study of factors affecting criminal justice research capacity in state government.

Michael G. Santos is a prisoner confined at the federal correctional institution at McKean, Pennsylvania. He is in his eighth year of a 45-year prison sentence. He has been working on a master of arts program at Hofstra University. His area of concentration is the federal correctional system and his work includes research on prison management, prisoner adjustment to incarceration, educational opportunities for federal prisoners, and an ethnography of prisoners confined at the U.S. Penitentiary in Atlanta.

J. Richard Sparks teaches criminology at Keele University, having previously worked for The Open University and the University of Cambridge. He is the coeditor (with John Muncie) of *Imprisonment: European Perspectives* and (with A. E. Bottoms and W. T. Hay) of *Prisons and the Problem of Order.*

Hans Toch is Distinguished Professor of Criminal Justice at the University at Albany, State University of New York. Among his latest books are *Police as Problem Solvers* and *Mosaic of Despair*, and revised editions of *Living in Prison, Violent Men,* and *The Disturbed Violent Offender* (with Kenneth Adams).

Nigel Walker, C.B.E., D.Litt., Hon.L.L.D., was professor of criminology, director of the Institute of Criminology, and a Fellow of King's College at Cambridge. He is an Hon. Fellow of the Royal College of Psychiatrists and has worked in or visited prisons in several countries. Most of his books concern the theory and practice of sentencing (e.g., *Why Punish?*).

John R. Weekes received his doctorate in psychology from Ohio University. He is a research manager with the Correctional Service of Canada and an adjunct professor of psychology at Carleton University in Ottawa. His research interests include offender substance abuse assessment and treatment, cognitive-behavioral interventions with offenders, long-term offenders, and forensic psychology.

Ronald Wikberg, a convicted armed robber and murderer, spent 23 years in prison in Louisiana. He became associate editor of *The Angolite*, the prison magazine of the Louisiana State Penitentiary, and coauthor of two corrections books. Released on parole in 1992, he died at his home in Maryland in October, 1994.

J. Stephen Wormith received his Ph.D. in psychology in 1977 from the University of Ottawa. He is Psychologist-in-Chief for the Ontario Ministry of the Solicitor General and Correctional Services, an adjunct professor at Carleton University, and a clinical professor at the University of Ottawa. His current research focuses on young offenders, sexual offenders, and mentally disordered offenders.

Edward Zamble was educated at the University of Pennsylvania and Yale University. He has contributed frequently to the literature on criminal offenders and imprisonment, including *Coping, Behavior, and Adaptation in Prison Inmates*. A professor of psychology at Queen's University at Kingston (Canada), he is currently completing a monograph on the recidivism process.